Blackstone's Police Manual

Crime

Blackstone's Police Manual

Volume 1

Crime

2016

Paul Connor

Cert Ed (FE), PG Cert Ed (ODE), LLB

Consultant Editor: Paul Connor

OXFORD

UNIVERSITY PRESS

OXFORD
UNIVERSITY PRESS

Great Clarendon Street, Oxford, OX2 6DP,
United Kingdom

Oxford University Press is a department of the University of Oxford.
It furthers the University's objective of excellence in research, scholarship,
and education by publishing worldwide. Oxford is a registered trade mark of
Oxford University Press in the UK and in certain other countries

First Edition published in 1998
Eighteenth Edition published in 2015

Impression: 1

Published in the United States of America by Oxford University Press
198 Madison Avenue, New York, NY 10016, United States of America

British Library Cataloguing in Publication Data

Data available

ISBN 978–0–19–874342–2

Printed in Italy by
L.E.G.O. S.p.A.

Foreword for 2016 Blackstone's Police Manuals

The police service currently faces a series of challenges; from the changes that police forces must make to deliver savings and reduce crime to the increasing complexity of the threats to national security, public safety and public order. Underpinning the ability of officers to deal effectively with these challenges is the knowledge and understanding of relevant law and procedure and the ability to apply this on a daily basis. This understanding is the cornerstone in providing a professional policing service.

The College of Policing plays a vital role in the development of police officers and staff, helping them to obtain and retain the skills and knowledge they need to fight crime and protect the public. The College has a remit to develop, maintain and test standards to ensure suitability for promotion. Part of this responsibility requires the College to ensure a comprehensive and relevant syllabus is produced. As such, the College works alongside Oxford University Press to ensure these Manuals are an accurate and up-to-date source of information and that they reflect what is required by people working across policing.

The *Blackstone's Police Manuals 2016* are the definitive reference source and official study guide for the national legal examination which all candidates must successfully pass in order to be promoted to sergeant or inspector. Their content is derived from evidence gathered from operational sergeants and inspectors alongside input from the wider police service. Whilst they are primarily designed to support officers seeking to progress their careers in preparing for their promotion examinations, they also provide a reference point for officers and staff seeking to continue their professional development and maintain their knowledge as a professional in policing. If you are using these Manuals to prepare for your promotion examinations I would like to take this opportunity to wish you the very best of luck in your studies, and I hope these books will assist you in progressing your career within the police service.

Alex Marshall
Chief Executive Officer
of the College of Policing

Preface

Many readers of the Blackstone's Police Manuals are studying for promotion examinations, either to the rank of sergeant or inspector. To assist in this process the Manuals not only provide the reader with the law in statute form but also numerous examples of the law in action, offering pragmatic explanations to sometimes complex legal issues (particularly in the 'Keynote' sections). This enables practically minded individuals to make the connection between the law on the streets and the law as it is applied and interpreted by the courts.

All the Manuals include explanatory keynotes and case law examples, providing clear and incisive analysis of important areas. As well as covering basic law and procedure they take full account of the PACE Codes of Practice and Human Rights implications. They can also be used as a training resource for police probationers, special constables and PCSOs, or as an invaluable reference tool for police staff of all ranks and positions.

Oxford University Press are always happy to receive any useful written feedback from any reader on the content and style of the Manual, especially from those involved in or with the criminal justice system. Please email this address with any comments or queries: police.uk@oup.com.

The law is stated as at 1 June 2015.

Acknowledgements

Blackstone's Police Manuals have become a firmly established 'household name' in the context of police law, particularly to candidates studying for the police promotion examinations.

The production of the Manuals could not be accomplished without the professional participation of a great many people in a variety of capacities.

Many thanks to the production, editorial and marketing team at Oxford University Press, particularly Peter Daniell, Lucy Alexander, Pam Birkby, Matthew Humphrys and Stuart Johnson.

Thanks must also go to the team of legal checkers and the staff of the College of Policing for their work in reviewing the 2016 editions.

And last but by no means least I thank my wife, whose continued whole-hearted support and understanding for me and my work has been, and continues to be, the primary reason you are reading these words.

Paul Connor

Contents

Table of Cases

Table of Statutes

Table of Secondary Legislation

Table of Codes of Practice

Table of European Law

Table of Home Office Circulars

Table of International Treaties and Conventions

How to use this Manual

Volume numbers for the Manuals

The 2016 Blackstone's Police Manuals each have a volume number as follows:

Volume 1: *Crime*
Volume 2: *Evidence and Procedure*
Volume 3: *Road Policing*
Volume 4: *General Police Duties*

The first digit of each paragraph number in the text of the Manuals denotes the Manual number. For example, paragraph 2.3 is chapter 3 of the *Evidence and Procedure* Manual and 4.3 is chapter 3 of the *General Police Duties* Manual.

All index entries and references in the Tables of Legislation and the Table of Cases, etc. refer to paragraph numbers instead of page numbers, making information easier to find.

Material outside the scope of the police promotion examinations syllabus—blacklining

These Manuals contain some information which is outside the scope of the police promotion examinations. A full black line down the margin indicates that the text beside it is excluded from Inspectors' examinations.

PACE Code Chapters

The PACE Codes of Practice have been taken out of the appendices and are now incorporated within chapters in the main body of the *Blackstone's Police Manuals*. A thick grey line down the margin is used to denote text that is an extract of the PACE Code itself (i.e. the actual wording of the legislation) and does not form part of the general commentary of the chapter.

The PACE Codes of Practice form an important part of the police promotion examinations syllabus and are examinable for both Sergeants and Inspectors. They are not to be confused with 'blacklined' content that is excluded from the syllabus for Inspectors' examinations (see 'Material outside the scope of the police promotion examinations syllabus—blacklining').

Length of sentence for an offence

Where a length of sentence for an offence is stated in this Manual, please note that the number of months or years stated is the maximum number and will not be exceeded.

Any feedback regarding content or other editorial matters in the Manuals can be emailed to police.uk@oup.com.

Police Promotion Examinations Rules and Syllabus Information

The rules and syllabus for the police promotion examinations system are defined within the Rules & Syllabus document published by College of Policing Selection and Assessment on behalf of the Police Promotion Examinations Board (PPEB). The Rules & Syllabus document is published annually each September, and applies to all police promotion assessments scheduled for the calendar year following its publication. For example, the September 2015 Rules & Syllabus document would apply to all police promotion assessments held during 2016.

The document provides details of the law and procedure to be tested within the National Police Promotion Framework Step 2 Legal Examination, and also outlines the rules underpinning the police promotion examination system.

All candidates who are taking a police promotion examination are strongly encouraged to familiarise themselves with the Rules & Syllabus document during their preparation. The police promotion examination rules apply to candidates undertaking the National Police Promotion Framework.

The document can be downloaded from the Development Section of the College of Policing website, which can be found at <http://www.college.police.uk>. Electronic versions are also supplied to all force examination officers.

If you have any problems obtaining the Rules & Syllabus document from the above source, please contact the Candidate Administration Team via the 'Contact us' section of the College of Policing website (see above).

Usually, no further updates to the Rules & Syllabus document will be issued during its year-long lifespan. However, in exceptional circumstances, the College of Policing (on behalf of the PPEB) reserves the right to issue an amended syllabus prior to the next scheduled annual publication date.

For example, a major change to a key area of legislation or procedure (e.g. the Codes of Practice) during the lifespan of the current Rules & Syllabus document would render a significant part of the current syllabus content obsolete. In such circumstances, it may be necessary for an update to the syllabus to be issued, which would provide guidance to candidates on any additional material which would be examinable within their police promotion examinations.

In such circumstances, an update to the Rules & Syllabus document would be made available through the College of Policing website, and would be distributed to all force examination contacts. The College of Policing will ensure that any syllabus update is distributed well in advance of the examination date, to ensure that candidates have sufficient time to familiarise themselves with any additional examinable material. Where possible, any additional study materials would be provided to candidates free of charge.

Please note that syllabus updates will only be made in *exceptional* circumstances; an update will not be made for every change to legislation included within the syllabus. For further guidance on this issue, candidates are advised to check regularly the College of Policing website, or consult their force examination officer, during their preparation period.

1.1 State of Mind

1.1.1 Introduction

Any analysis of law begins with an examination of *mens rea* (state of mind) and *actus reus* (criminal conduct). These concepts are fundamental to understanding all offences and the idea of criminal liability generally.

Mens rea alone will not amount to an offence; thinking about committing a crime is not committing a crime. In fact, the default position is that the application of the mind is essential for liability to exist as acts (or omissions) alone cannot amount to a crime unless they are accompanied by '*mens rea*' at the time of the act (or omission).

It is therefore vital to consider, among others, what is meant by terms such as 'intent' and 'recklessness'.

1.1.2 Offences of 'Specific' and 'Basic' Intent

Crimes of 'specific' intent are only committed where the defendant is shown to have had a particular intention to bring about a specific consequence at the time of the criminal act. Murder is such a crime as is burglary with intent (Theft Act 1968, s. 9(1)(a)). The common feature with these offences is that the *intention of the offender* is critical—without that intent, the offence does not exist.

Other criminal offences require no further proof of anything other than the 'basic' intention to bring about the given circumstances. For example, burglary under s. 9(1)(b) simply requires proof that the person entered the building/part of a building as a trespasser and that he/she went on to commit one of the prohibited acts (steal/attempt to steal; inflicting/attempting to inflict grievous bodily harm). Another example would be the offence of maliciously wounding or inflicting grievous bodily harm (Offences Against the Person Act 1861, s. 20).

The important difference between offences of specific and basic intent is that, in the case of the latter, *recklessness* will often be enough to satisfy the mental element.

1.1.3 Intent

'Intent' is a word often used in relation to consequences. If a defendant intends something to happen, he/she wishes to bring about a consequence. In some offences, say burglary under s. 9(1)(a) of the Theft Act 1968, the defendant's *intention* may be very clear; he/she may enter a house as a trespasser *intending* to steal property inside.

However, there will often be consequences following a defendant's actions that he/she did not *intend* to happen. What if, in the above burglary, the householder came across the burglar and suffered a heart attack? It might be reasonable to suggest that it was the defendant's behaviour that had brought about the situation (**see chapter 1.2**). The defendant, however, may argue that, although he/she intended to break in and steal, there had never been any *intention* of harming the occupant. At this point you might say that the defendant should have thought about that before breaking into someone else's house. This brings in the concept of *foresight*, a concept that has caused the courts some difficulty over the years—for several reasons.

First, there is the Criminal Justice Act 1967 which says (under s. 8) that a court/jury, in determining whether a person has committed an offence:

(a) shall not be bound in law to infer that he intended or foresaw a result of his actions by reason only of its being a natural and probable consequence of those actions; but

(b) shall decide whether he did intend or foresee that result by reference to all the evidence, drawing such inferences from the evidence as appear proper in the circumstances.

Secondly, there is the body of case law which has developed around the area of 'probability', culminating in two cases in the House of Lords (*R* v *Moloney* [1985] AC 905 and *R* v *Hancock* [1986] AC 455). Following those cases it is settled that foresight of the probability of a consequence *does not amount to an intention to bring that consequence about, but may be evidence of it.*

So you cannot claim that a defendant *intended* a consequence of his/her behaviour simply because it was virtually certain to occur. What you can do is to put evidence of the defendant's foresight of that probability before a court, which may infer an intention from it. Such an argument would go like this:

- at the time of the criminal act there was a *probability* of a consequence;
- the greater the probability, the more likely it is that the defendant *foresaw* that consequence;
- if the defendant foresaw that consequence, the more likely it is that the defendant *intended* it to happen.

Whether or not a defendant intended a particular consequence will be a question of fact left to the jury (or magistrate(s) where appropriate). In murder cases (**see chapter 1.5**), where death or serious bodily harm was a *virtual certainty* from the defendant's actions and he/she had appreciated that to be the case, the jury *may* infer that the defendant intended to bring about such consequences (*R* v *Nedrick* [1986] 1 WLR 1025). Therefore, where the defendant threw a three-month-old baby down onto a hard surface in a fit of rage, the jury *might* have inferred both that death/serious bodily harm was a virtual certainty from the defendant's actions and that he must have appreciated that to be the case; they should therefore have been directed by the trial judge accordingly (*R* v *Woollin* [1999] 1 AC 82).

Finally, the relevant intent may have been formed, not of the defendant's own volition, but influenced in some way by other external factors. An example is where the defendant's thinking is affected by duress (as to which **see para. 1.4.6**).

1.1.4 Recklessness

Following the case of *R* v *G and R* [2003] UKHL 50, the approach taken to the interpretation of the word 'reckless' is that it will be 'subjective'.

The requirements of subjective recklessness can be found in the case of *R* v *Cunningham* [1957] 2 QB 396 and are satisfied in situations where the defendant foresees the consequences of his/her actions as being probable or even possible. In cases requiring subjective recklessness, the fact that the consequences *ought to have been foreseen* by the defendant will not be enough.

An example of 'subjective recklessness' in action can be seen in *D* v *DPP* [2005] EWHC 967. In that case a police officer arrested a man in order to prevent a breach of the peace. During a subsequent struggle the defendant bit the officer on the hand. The magistrates' court convicted the defendant of assaulting the officer in the execution of his duty (**see para. 1.9.8.2**) on the basis that the biting of the officer had been 'reckless'. The defendant appealed, arguing that a bite could not be reckless; either it was deliberate or it was accidental. The Divisional Court dismissed the appeal and held that the test of recklessness involved the defendant having *foreseen the risk* that the victim would be subjected to unlawful force and *having gone on to take the risk*.

1.1.5 Malice

The term 'malice' is particularly relevant to ss. 18, 20, 23 and 24 of the Offences Against the Person Act 1861 (offences relating to grievous bodily harm/wounding and poisoning). It *should not* be considered as one relating to ill will, spite or wickedness. 'Malice' requires either the actual intention to cause the relevant harm or at least foresight of the risk of causing *some harm* (though not the extent of the harm) to a person.

....

EXAMPLE

D throws a coin at V thinking that this will result in a small cut to V's forehead (so D has foresight that *some harm*, albeit minor, will befall V as a result of D's actions). The coin actually strikes V in the eye, causing V serious injury and the loss of sight in the eye.

It does not matter that the harm that D foresaw was minor compared to the resultant harm caused to V. D has committed a s. 20 grievous bodily harm offence because D has behaved 'maliciously'—D saw the risk of some harm befalling V but went on to take the risk anyway.

....

1.1.6 Wilfully

'Wilfully' is mentioned in offences such as child cruelty (s. 1 of the Children and Young Persons Act 1933). Like the term 'maliciously' (**see para. 1.1.5**) the term 'wilfully' should not be understood in a literal sense as meaning 'deliberate' or 'voluntary'. It is taken to mean intentionally or recklessly (subjective) (*Attorney-General's Reference (No. 3 of 2003)* [2005] QB 73).

1.1.7 Dishonestly

The concept of 'dishonesty' is of importance to a number of offences, including theft and fraud. This expression is defined for certain purposes in s. 2 of the Theft Act 1968. However, it has also been extended by common law decisions of the courts (*R v Ghosh* [1982] QB 1053) and it is critical, in dealing with offences requiring proof of dishonesty, that you identify the nature of the state of mind required and the ways in which it can be proved/disproved. For a full discussion of this concept, **see chapter 1.14**.

1.1.8 Knowing

The term 'knowing' is relevant to several offences such as s. 22 of the Theft Act 1968 (handling stolen goods). One *knows* something if one is absolutely sure that it is so. Since it is difficult to be absolutely sure of anything, it has to be accepted that a person who feels 'virtually certain' about something can equally be regarded as 'knowing' it (*R v Dunne* (1998) 162 JP 399).

1.1.9 Belief

The degree of certainty required to be experienced by an accused to create a 'belief' would appear to be the same for 'knowing'—the difference is that knowing something implies correctness of belief whereas a 'belief' could turn out to be mistaken. This is how 'belief' has been interpreted by the courts for the purposes of handling stolen goods (s. 22 of the Theft Act 1968) where it has been stressed that there is a need to distinguish belief from recklessness or suspicion and that it is not sufficient that an accused believed it to be more probable than not that the goods were stolen.

1.1.10 Negligence

Negligence is generally concerned with the defendant's compliance with the standards of reasonableness of ordinary people. The concept of negligence focuses on the consequences of the defendant's conduct rather than demanding proof of a particular state of mind at the time and ascribes some notion of 'fault' or 'blame' to the defendant who must be shown to have acted in a way that runs contrary to the expectations of the reasonable person.

The most important criminal offence that can be committed by negligence is manslaughter (manslaughter by gross negligence), which is also one of the only offences to include specific reference—at common law—to the word 'negligence'. Other offences that can be committed by negligence do not usually contain the word itself but attract that test in relation to the mental element. Good examples are offences involving the standard of driving.

1.1.11 Strict Liability

Some offences are said to be offences of 'strict liability'. This expression generally means that there is little to prove beyond the act itself, however in most cases it is more accurate to say that there is no need to prove *mens rea* in relation to one particular aspect of the behaviour. There have been isolated instances in which the courts have held that an offence does not require any *mens rea* to be proved. For example, in *DPP* v *H* [1997] 1 WLR 1406 it was stated that the offence of driving with excess alcohol, contrary to the Road Traffic Act 1988, s. 5 (see *Road Policing*, **chapter 3.5**) did not to require proof of any *mens rea*.

In rarer cases absolute liability is imposed, reducing even further the burden on the prosecution.

Situations where strict or absolute liability is imposed are usually to enforce statutory regulation (e.g. road traffic offences), particularly where there is some social danger or concern presented by the proscribed behaviour.

Some other offences such as public nuisance at common law require only strict liability in relation to some elements of the criminal conduct (see *General Police Duties*, **chapter 4.8**).

As a general rule, however, there is a presumption that *mens rea* is required for a criminal offence unless parliament clearly indicates otherwise (*B (A Minor)* v *DPP* [2000] 2 AC 428). This rule should be borne in mind, not only when approaching the rest of the material in this Manual, but also when considering criminal law in general.

1.1.12 Transferred *Mens Rea*

The state of mind required for one offence can, on occasions, be 'transferred' from the original target or victim to another. *This only operates if the crime remains the same*. In other words, a defendant cannot be convicted if he/she acted with the mens rea for one offence but commits the *actus reus* of another offence. For example, in *R* v *Latimer* (1886) 17 QBD 359 the defendant lashed out with his belt at one person but missed, striking a third party instead. As it was proved that the defendant had the required *mens rea* when he swung the belt, the court held that the same *mens rea* could support a charge of wounding against any other victim injured by the same act. If the *nature of the offence* changes, then this approach will not operate. Therefore if a defendant is shown to have thrown a rock at a crowd of people intending to injure one of them, the *mens rea* required for that offence cannot be 'transferred' to an offence of criminal damage if the rock misses that person and breaks a window instead (*R* v *Pembliton* (1874) LR 2 CCR 119).

The issue of transferred *mens rea* can be important in relation to the liability of accessories (as to which, **see chapter 1.2**). If the principal's intentions are to be extended to an accessory, it must be shown that those intentions were either contemplated and accepted by that person at the time of the offence, or that they were 'transferred'.

··

EXAMPLE

A person (X) encourages another (Y) to assault Z. Y decides to attack a different person instead. X will not be liable for that assault because it was not contemplated or agreed by X. If, however, in trying to assault Z, Y happens to injure a third person inadvertently, then 'transferred *mens rea*' may result in X being liable for those injuries even though X had no wish for that person to be so injured.

··

1.2.1 Introduction

Having considered state of mind, the next key element is that of the criminal conduct. Many statutory offences describe the sort of behaviour that will attract liability, but there are some important general rules that also need to be considered.

For a person to be found guilty of a criminal offence you must show that he/she:

- acted in a particular way
- failed to act in a particular way (omissions) or
- brought about a state of affairs.

This is the *actus reus* of an offence, i.e. the behavioural element of an offence.

When proving the required *actus reus* you must show:

- that the defendant's conduct was voluntary, and
- that it occurred while the defendant still had the requisite *mens rea*.

1.2.2 Voluntary Act

You must show that a defendant acted or omitted to act 'voluntarily', that is, by the operation of free will.

If a person is shoved into a shop window, he/she cannot be said to be guilty of criminal damage even though he/she was the immediate physical cause of the damage. Similarly, if a person was standing in front of a window waiting to break it and someone came up and pushed that person into the window, the presence of the requisite *mens rea* would still not be enough to attract criminal liability for the damage. In each case, the person being pushed could not be said to be acting of his/her own volition in breaking the window and therefore could not perform the required *actus reus*.

This aspect of voluntariness is also important when defendants have lost control of their own physical actions. Reflexive actions are generally not classed as being willed or voluntary, hence the (limited) availability of the 'defence' of automatism (**see chapter 1.4**).

Likewise, the *unexpected* onset of a sudden physical impairment (such as severe cramp when driving; actions when sleepwalking) can also render any linked actions 'involuntary'. If the onset of the impairment could reasonably have been foreseen (e.g. where someone is prone to blackouts) the defendant's actions may be said to have been willed in that he/she could have prevented the loss of control or at least avoided the situation (e.g. driving) which allowed the consequences to occur.

1.2.3 Coincidence with *Mens Rea*

It must be shown that the defendant had the requisite *mens rea* at the time of carrying out the *actus reus*. However, there is no need for that 'state of mind' to remain unchanged throughout the entire commission of the offence. If a person (X) poisons another (Y) intending to kill Y at the time, it will not alter X's criminal liability if X changes his mind immediately after giving the poison or even if X does everything he can to halt its effects (*R v Jakeman* (1983) 76 Cr App R 223).

Conversely, if the *actus reus* is a continuing act, as 'appropriation' is (**see chapter 1.14**), it may begin without any particular *mens rea* but the required 'state of mind' may come later while the *actus reus* is still continuing. If this happens, whereby the *mens rea* 'catches up' with the *actus reus*, the offence is complete at the first moment that the two elements (*actus reus* and *mens rea*) unite.

For example, in a case where a motorist was directed to pull his car over to the kerb by a police officer and drove it onto the officer's foot, there was no proof that he did so deliberately. However. it was clear that he deliberately left it there after the officer told him what he had done. His conviction for assaulting the officer was upheld by the Divisional Court on the basis that there was an ongoing act, which became a criminal assault once the motorist became aware of it (*Fagan* v *Metropolitan Police Commissioner* [1969] 1 QB 439).

1.2.4 Omissions

Criminal conduct is most often associated with *actions* but occasionally liability is brought about by a failure to act.

Most of the occasions where failure or omission will attract liability are where a **DUTY** *to act* has been created. Such a **DUTY** can arise from a number of circumstances, the main ones being:

D Dangerous situation created by the defendant. For example, in *R v Miller* [1983] 2 AC 161 the defendant accidentally started a fire in a house (a fact that he became aware of), but instead of putting the fire out, he moved to another room taking no action to counteract the danger he had created, resulting in the house being damaged by fire.

U Under statute, contract or a person's public 'office'. Examples would include:
  - Statute—a driver who is involved in a damage or injury accident fails to stop at the scene of the accident (s. 170 of the Road Traffic Act 1988).
  - Contract—a crossing keeper omitted to close the gates (a job that was part of his contractual obligations) at a level crossing and a person was subsequently killed by a passing train (*R v Pittwood* (1902) 19 TLR 37).
  - Public office—a police officer failed to intervene to prevent an assault (*R v Dytham* [1979] QB 722).

T Taken it upon him/herself—the defendant decides to carry out a duty and then fails to do so. For example, in *R v Stone* [1977] QB 354 the defendant accepted a duty to care for her partner's mentally ill sister who subsequently died from neglect.

Y Young person—in circumstances where the defendant is in a parental relationship with a child or a young person, i.e. an obligation exists for the parent to look after the health and welfare of the child and he/she does not do so.

Whether or not there is a sufficient proximity between the defendant and the victim brought about by a duty to act will be a question of law (*R v Singh* [1999] Crim LR 582 and *R v Khan* [1998] Crim LR 830).

Having established such a duty, you must also show that the defendant has *voluntarily* omitted to act as required or that he/she has not done enough to discharge that duty. If a defendant is unable to act (e.g. because someone else has stopped him/her) or is incapable of doing more because of his/her own personal limitations (e.g. an inability to swim), the *actus reus* will *not* have been made out (*R v Reid* [1992] 1 WLR 793).

Some statutory offences are specifically worded to remove any doubt as to whether they can be committed by omission as well as by a positive act (e.g. torture under the Criminal Justice Act 1988, s. 134, **see para. 1.10.2**). Other offences have been held by the courts to be capable of commission by both positive acts and by omission (e.g. false accounting under the Theft Act 1968, s. 17, **see chapter 1.15**).

1.2.5 Causal Link or Chain of Causation

Once the *actus reus* has been proved, you must then show a *causal link* between it and the relevant consequences. That is, you must prove that the consequences would not have happened 'but for' the defendant's act or omission.

In a case of simple criminal damage it may be relatively straightforward to prove this causal link: a defendant throws a brick at a window; the window would not have broken 'but for' the defendant's conduct. Where the link becomes more difficult to prove is when the defendant's behaviour triggers other events or aggravates existing circumstances. For example, in *R v McKechnie* [1992] Crim LR 194 the defendant attacked the victim, who was already suffering from a serious ulcer, causing him brain damage. The brain damage (caused by the assault) prevented doctors from operating on the ulcer which eventually ruptured, killing the victim. The Court of Appeal, upholding the conviction for manslaughter, held that the defendant's criminal conduct (the assault) had made a significant contribution to the victim's death even though the untreated ulcer was the actual cause of death.

In some cases a significant delay can occur between the acts which put in train the criminal consequences. An example is where a defendant transported an accomplice to a place near to the victim's house some 13 hours before the accomplice shot and killed the victim. Despite the delay and despite the fact the accomplice had not fully made up his mind about the proposed shooting at the time he was dropped off by the defendant, there was no intervening event that diverted or hindered the planned murder—*R v Bryce* [2004] EWCA Crim 1231.

In a case which had similar facts to our 'simple damage' example above, the defendant entered a house after throwing a brick through a window. Although the defendant did not attack the occupant, an 87-year-old who died of a heart attack some hours later, the Court of Appeal accepted that there could have been a causal link between the defendant's behaviour and the death of the victim. If so, a charge of manslaughter would be appropriate (*R v Watson* [1989] 1 WLR 684).

1.2.6 Intervening Act

The causal link can be broken by a new intervening act provided that the 'new' act is 'free, deliberate and informed' (*R v Latif* [1996] 1 WLR 104).

If a drug dealer supplies drugs to another person who then kills him/herself by taking an overdose, the dealer cannot, without more, be said to have *caused* the death. Death would have been brought about by the deliberate exercise of free will by the user (*R v Kennedy* [2007] UKHL 38 (**see para. 1.5.4.1**)). The supplier is unlikely to be held liable for *causing* death in such a case unless he/she actually takes a more active part in the administering of the drug (*R v Dias* [2001] EWCA Crim 2986).

If the medical treatment which a victim is given results in their ultimate death, the treatment itself will not normally be regarded as a 'new' intervening act (*R v Smith* [1959] 2 QB 35). However, in *R v Jordan* (1956) 40 Cr App R 152, where the defendant had stabbed the deceased, it was held that death could not be attributed to the defendant. In this case the actual cause of death had been the administration of a drug (terramycin) after the deceased had shown he was intolerant to it (treatment described as 'palpably wrong' by the court) and when his original wound had nearly healed. *R v Jordan* has been described as a very particular case, depending on its exact facts. The basic rule is that an intervening act will not generally break the causal link/chain of causation.

There is also a rule which says defendants must 'take their victims as they find them'. This means that if victims have a particular characteristic, such as a very thin skull or a very nervous disposition, which makes the consequences of an act against them much more acute, that is the defendant's bad luck. A 'classic' eggshell skull case is *R* v *Harvey* [2010] EWCA Crim 1317 where, during a 'domestic tiff' the offender threw a television remote control at his wife, which hit her behind the ear. Unknown to anyone, she had an unusual weakness of the vertebral artery, which ruptured and caused her death. Save for the death, the offence charged would have been one of common assault. Such characteristics (e.g., where an assault victim died after refusing a blood transfusion on religious grounds (*R* v *Blaue* [1975] 1 WLR 1411) will not break the causal link.

Actions by the victim will sometimes be significant in the chain of causation such as where a victim of a sexual assault was injured when jumping from her assailant's car (*R* v *Roberts* (1971) 56 Cr App R 95). Where such actions take place, the victim's behaviour will not necessarily be regarded as introducing a new intervening act. If the victim's actions are those which might reasonably be anticipated from any victim in such a situation, there will be no new and intervening act and the defendant will be responsible for the consequences flowing from them. If, however, the victim's actions are done entirely of his/her own volition or where those actions are, in the words of Stuart-Smith LJ 'daft' (see *R* v *Williams* [1992] 1 WLR 380), they will amount to a new intervening act and the defendant cannot be held responsible for them.

1.2.7 Principals and Accessories

Once you have established the criminal conduct and the required state of mind, you must identify what degree of involvement the defendant had.

There are two ways of attracting criminal liability for an offence: either as a *principal* or an *accessory* (accessories can also be referred to as *secondary parties*).

A principal offender is one whose conduct has met all the requirements of the particular offence. An accessory is someone who helped in or brought about the commission of the offence. If an accessory 'aids, abets, counsels or procures' the commission of an offence, he/she will be treated by a court in the same way as a principal offender for an indictable offence (Accessories and Abettors Act 1861, s. 8) or for a summary offence (Magistrates' Courts Act 1980, s. 44). The expression 'aid, abet, counsel and procure' is generally used in its entirety when charging a defendant, without separating out the particular element that applies. Generally speaking, the expressions mean as follows:

- aiding = giving help, support or assistance
- abetting = inciting, instigating or encouraging.

Each of these would usually involve the presence of the secondary party at the scene (unless, for example, part of some pre-arranged plan):

- counselling = advising or instructing
- procuring = bringing about.

These last two activities would generally be expected to take place before the commission of the offence. These are purely guides by which to separate the elements of this concept and will not necessarily apply in all cases.

If an accessory is present at the scene of a crime when it is committed, his/her presence may amount to encouragement which would support a charge of aiding or abetting if he/she was there as part of an agreement in respect of the principal offence. This would not be the case if a person was simply passing by and watched the offence. It is not an offence to do so as the ordinary citizen is not under a duty to prevent an offence occurring and failing to do so will not create liability as an accomplice (*R v Coney* (1882) 8 QBD 534).

'Counselling' an offence requires no causal link (*R v Calhaem* [1985] QB 808). As long as the principal offender is aware of the 'counsellor's' advice or encouragement, the latter will be guilty as an accessory, even if the principal would have committed the offence anyway (*Attorney-General v Able* [1984] QB 795).

However, if you are trying to show that a defendant *procured* an offence you must show a causal link between his/her conduct and the offence (*Attorney-General's Reference (No. 1 of 1975)* [1975] QB 773).

1.2.7.1 State of Mind for Accessories

Generally, the state of mind (*mens rea*) which is needed to convict an accessory is: 'proof of intention to aid as well as of knowledge of the circumstances' (*National Coal Board v Gamble* [1959] 1 QB 11 at p. 20). Whether there was such an intention to aid the principal is a question of fact to be decided in the particular circumstances of each case. The requirement for proof of intention to aid means that the wider notions of recklessness and negligence are not enough to convict an accessory.

The *minimum* state of mind required of an accessory to an offence is set out in *Johnson v Youden* [1950] 1 KB 544. In that case the court held that, before anyone can be convicted of aiding and abetting an offence, he/she must at least know the essential matters that constitute that offence. Therefore the accessory to an offence of drink/driving (see **Road Policing**, **chapter 3.5**) must at least have been aware that the 'principal' (the driver) had been drinking (*Smith v Mellors and Soar* (1987) 84 Cr App R 279).

Occasionally statutes will make specific provision for the state of mind and/or the conduct of accessories and principals. An example can be found in s. 7 of the Protection from Harassment Act 1997 (see **General Police Duties**, **chapter 4.8**).

1.2.7.2 Joint Enterprise

A joint criminal enterprise exists where two (or more) people embark on the commission of an offence by one or both (or all) of them. It is a joint enterprise because all the parties have a common goal—that an offence will be committed.

KEYNOTE

As the parties to a joint enterprise share a combined purpose, each would be liable for the consequences of the actions of the other in the pursuit of their joint enterprise (but see below for such liability when the nature of the offence changes). This is the case even if the consequences of the joint enterprise are a result of a mistake. For example, two offenders (A and B) agree to carry out a burglary on a particular house. Offender A leads the way but makes an error and mistakenly breaks into the wrong house. This error by offender A will not prevent offender B being guilty as an accomplice to the burglary offence.

What happens when one party to the joint enterprise goes beyond that which was agreed or contemplated by the other?

....

EXAMPLE

Two men (A and B) agree to carry out an offence of theft. During the course of the offence, the owner of the property subject of the offence appears and tries to prevent the offence taking place. Offender A produces a flick-knife and stabs the victim, causing grievous bodily harm. Offender B had no idea that offender A had a flick-knife and had never contemplated the use of violence during the theft offence.

....

The actions of offender A are a departure from the nature and type of crime that was envisaged by offender B who did not know that A possessed a flick-knife; it is an act so fundamentally different from that originally contemplated by B that B is most unlikely to be liable for the injuries caused to the victim (*R v Anderson* [1966] 2 QB 110).

The situation would alter if offender B knew that offender A possessed the flick-knife. Here, offender B could be convicted of a wounding offence if he had contemplated as a real possibility that offender A might commit the wounding offence but nevertheless still took part in the theft.

An example of this approach can be seen in *R v Powell* [1999] 1 AC 1, where two defendants accompanied a third defendant to a drug dealer's house to buy drugs. When the drug dealer came to the door he was shot. It was unclear who had fired the fatal shot but the prosecution argued that, if the third defendant had done so, then the first two defendants were guilty of murder because they knew that the third defendant was armed with a gun. The first two defendants were convicted of murder. They appealed but the House of Lords dismissed the appeal holding that where one party (D) to a joint enterprise to commit an offence foresees as a real possibility that another party (E) may, in the course of it do an act, with the requisite *mens rea*, constituting another offence (and E does so), D is liable for that offence. This is the case even if D has not expressly or tacitly agreed to that offence, and even though he expressly forbids it.

The principle can be seen in a case relating to manslaughter by unlawful act where the victim of a burglary was run over and killed by a vehicle driven by escaping burglars. There was no evidence as to who was the driver or who was a passenger in either of the two vehicles which ran over and killed the victim but there was sufficient evidence against each appellant to implicate him in the burglary by being present at it and that the burglary was a joint enterprise. The Court of Appeal considered that the features of this particular burglary were capable of making it dangerous when coupled with the foresight of the risk intervention to prevent escape and that 'the jury could safely conclude that the team [of burglars], on being confronted by the victim, shared an immediate intention to get away, as planned, and carried that intention forward. It was open for the jury to conclude that each burglar intended vehicular escape, should it arise in the circumstances, that the escape should be achieved at speed and with determination, and if necessary with no respect for property or person that might get in the way.' The appeals against a conviction for manslaughter were dismissed (*R v Bristow (Terrence)* [2013] EWCA Crim 1540).

What of the situation where the accessory or secondary party is not present during the substantive offence? In such circumstances involved in the example above, the position can be summarised as follows:

Where the principal (P) relies on acts of the accessory (D) which assist in the preliminary stages of a crime later committed in D's absence, it is necessary to prove *intentional assistance by D* in acts which D knew were steps taken by P towards the commission of the crime. Therefore the prosecution must prove:

- an act done by D;
- which *in fact* assisted the later commission of the offence;
- that D did the act deliberately realising that it was capable of assisting the offence;
- that D, at the time of doing the act, contemplated the commission of the offence by P, (e.g. D foresaw it as a real or substantial risk or real possibility); and
- that when doing the act D intended to assist P.

(*R v Bryce* [2004] EWCA Crim 1231.)

If the principal cannot be traced or identified, the accessory may still be liable (*Hui Chiming v The Queen* [1992] 1 AC 34). Similarly, an accessory may be convicted of procuring an offence even though the principal is acquitted or has a defence for his/her actions. This is because the principal often supplies the *actus reus* for the accessory's offence. If the accessory also has the required *mens rea*, the offence will be complete and should not be affected by the fact that there is some circumstance or characteristic preventing the principal from being prosecuted.

Additionally, if the accessory had some responsibility and the actual ability to control the actions of the principal, his/her failure to do so may attract liability (e.g. a driving instructor who fails to prevent a learner driver from driving without due care and attention (*Rubie* v *Faulkner* [1940] 1 KB 571)).

It is possible for an accomplice to change his/her mind before the criminal act is carried out. However, the exact requirements of making an effective 'withdrawal' before any liability is incurred is unclear. Evidence such as how far the proposed plan had proceeded before the withdrawal and the amount/nature of any help or encouragement already given by the accessory will be relevant. Simply fleeing at the last moment because someone was approaching would generally not be enough. In the absence of some overwhelming supervening event, an accessory can only avoid liability for assistance rendered to the principal offender towards the commission of the crime by acting in a way that amounts to the *countermanding* of any earlier assistance such as a withdrawal from the common purpose. Repentance alone will not be enough (*R* v *Becerra* (1976) 62 Cr App R 212 and *R* v *Mitchell* (1999) 163 JP 75).

A person whom the law is intended to protect from certain types of offence cannot be an accessory to such offences committed against them. For example, a girl under 16 years of age is protected (by the Sexual Offences Act 2003 (**see chapter 1.11**)) from people having sexual intercourse with her. If a 15-year-old girl allows someone to have sexual intercourse with her she cannot be charged as an accessory to the offence (*R* v *Tyrrell* [1894] 1 QB 710).

1.2.8 Corporate Liability

Companies which are 'legally incorporated' have a legal personality of their own—they can own property, employ people and bring law suits—they can therefore commit offences. There are difficulties associated with proving and punishing criminal conduct by companies. However, companies have been prosecuted for offences of strict liability (*Alphacell Ltd* v *Woodward* [1972] AC 824); offences requiring *mens rea* (*Tesco Supermarkets Ltd* v *Nattrass* [1972] AC 153); and offences of being an 'accessory' (*R* v *Robert Millar (Contractors) Ltd* [1970] 2 QB 54—aiding and abetting the causing of death by reckless (now dangerous) driving). There are occasions where the courts will accept that the knowledge of certain employees will be extended to the company (*Tesco Stores Ltd* v *Brent London Borough Council* [1993] 1 WLR 1037).

Clearly there are some offences that would be conceptually impossible for a legal corporation to commit (e.g. some sexual offences) but, given that companies can be guilty as accessories (*Robert Millar*), they may well be capable of aiding and abetting such offences even though they could not commit the offence as a principal.

A company (OLL Ltd) has also been convicted, along with its Managing Director, of manslaughter (*R* v *Kite* [1996] 2 Cr App R (s) 295). Companies can be prosecuted for such offences under the terms of the Corporate Manslaughter and Corporate Homicide Act 2007 (**see chapter 1.5**).

1.2.9 Vicarious Liability

The general principle in criminal law is that liability is *personal*. There are, however, occasions where liability can be transmitted *vicariously* to another.

The most frequent occasions are cases where a statutory duty is breached by employees in the course of their employment (*National Rivers Authority* v *Alfred McAlpine Homes (East) Ltd*

[1994] 4 All ER 286), or where a duty is placed upon a particular individual such as a licensee who delegates some of his/her functions to another (see *General Police Duties*, chapter 4.8). The purpose behind this concept is generally to prevent individuals or organisations from evading liability by getting others to carry out unlawful activities on their behalf. A common law exception to the rule that liability at criminal law is personal can be found in the offence of public nuisance (as to which, see *General Police Duties*, chapter 4.8).

1.3 | Incomplete Offences and Police Investigations

1.3.1 Introduction

There are circumstances where defendants are interrupted or frustrated in their efforts to commit an offence, perhaps as a result of police intervention or as a result of things not going as the defendants had hoped. In these cases, the defendant's conduct may be dealt with using incomplete offences.

It should be noted that most incomplete offences *cannot* be mixed, and that most *cannot* be attempted. For instance, you *cannot* conspire to aid and abet, neither can you attempt to conspire. There are, as ever, limited exceptions to this rule.

1.3.2 Encouraging or Assisting Crime

The common law offence of inciting an offence was abolished by the Serious Crime Act 2007. Incitement was replaced by the offences under ss. 44, 45 and 46 of the Act.

> **KEYNOTE**
>
> Note that any references in existing legislation to the common law offence of incitement are to be read as references to the offences in ss. 44, 45 and 46, i.e. to be read as 'encouraging or assisting an offence'.

OFFENCE: **Intentionally Encouraging or Assisting an Offence—*Serious Crime Act 2007, s. 44***
  • Triable in the same way as the anticipated offence • Where the anticipated offence is murder the offence is punishable by life imprisonment • In any other case a person is liable to any penalty for which he/she would be liable on conviction of the anticipated offence

The Serious Crime Act 2007, s. 44 states:

(1) A person commits an offence if—
  (a) he does an act capable of encouraging or assisting in the commission of an offence; and
  (b) he intends to encourage or assist its commission
(2) But he is not to be taken to have intended to encourage or assist the commission of an offence merely because such encouragement or assistance was a foreseeable consequence of his act.

OFFENCE: **Encouraging or Assisting an Offence Believing it will be Committed—*Serious Crime Act 2007, s. 45***
  • Triable in the same way as the anticipated offence • Where the anticipated offence is murder the offence is punishable by life imprisonment • In any other case a person is liable to any penalty for which he/she would be liable on conviction of the anticipated offence

The Serious Crime Act 2007, s. 45 states:

A person commits an offence if—
  (a) he does an act capable of encouraging or assisting in the commission of an offence; and
  (b) he believes—
    (i) that the offence will be committed; and
    (ii) that his act will encourage or assist its commission.

OFFENCE: **Encouraging or Assisting Offences Believing One or More will be Committed—*Serious Crime Act 2007, s. 46***
  • Triable on Indictment • Where the reference offence is murder the offence is punishable with life imprisonment • In any other case a person is liable to any penalty for which he he/she would be liable on conviction of the reference offence

The Serious Crime Act 2007, s. 46 states:

(1) A person commits an offence if—
  (a) he does an act capable of encouraging or assisting the commission of one or more of a number of offences: and
  (b) he believes—
    (i) that one or more of those offences will be committed (but has no belief as to which); and
    (ii) that his act will encourage or assist the commission of one or more of them.
(2) It is immaterial for the purposes of subsection (1)(b)(ii) whether a person has any belief as to which offence will be encouraged or assisted.

KEYNOTE

Section 47 of the Serious Crime Act 2007 sets out what needs to be proved in order to establish guilt for each of the above offences.

Section 49(1) of the Act states that offences can be committed regardless of whether or not the encouragement or assistance has the effect which the defendant intended or believed it would have.

....

EXAMPLE

D, a surgeon, wishes to sexually assault his patients whilst they are unconscious under anaesthetic. To do so D will need the co-operation of his assistant, V. D puts his idea to V while they are having a drink in a pub, intending to encourage V to take part in the offences. V is outraged and wants nothing to do with D's plan. The fact that V is not remotely interested in D's plan and is not encouraged to take part in it will not alter the fact that D has committed an offence under s. 44 of the Act.

....

What of the situation where, rather than approaching others, an undercover police officer is approached to take part in a proposed offence?

In relation to this activity, s. 49(1) would still apply as there is no need for the person encouraged to have any intention of going on to commit the offence. In a case involving incitement (the predecessor of these offences) the Divisional Court held that there is no requirement for 'parity of *mens rea*' between the parties (*DPP v Armstrong* [2000] Crim LR 379). In that case the defendant had approached an undercover police officer asking him to supply child pornography. At his trial, the defendant argued that, as the officer in reality had no intention of supplying the pornography, there was no offence of incitement. On appeal by the prosecutor, the Divisional Court held that incitement, like conspiracies and attempts, was an auxiliary offence where criminal liability was attributed to the defendant where the full offence had not been committed. Consequently the intent of the person incited (in this case an undercover police officer) was irrelevant.

A person can be convicted of more than one of these offences (ss. 44, 45 or 46) in relation to the same act (s. 49(3)).

Section 50 of the Act sets out that it will be a defence to the offences under ss. 44, 45 and 46 if the person charged acted reasonably, that is in the circumstances he/she was aware of, or in the circumstances he/she reasonably believed existed, it was reasonable to act as he/she did.

Section 51 limits liability by setting out in statute the common law exception established in *R* v *Tyrrell* [1894] 1 QB 710. A person cannot be guilty of the offences in ss. 44, 45 and 46 if, in relation to an offence that is a 'protective' offence, the person who does the act capable of encouraging or assisting that offence falls within the category of persons that offence was designed to protect and would be considered as the victim.

....

EXAMPLE

D is a 12-year-old girl and encourages P, a 40-year-old man, to have sex with her. P is not interested and does not attempt to have sex with D. D cannot be liable of encouraging or assisting child rape despite the fact that it is her intent that P has sexual intercourse with a child under 13 (child rape) because she would be considered the 'victim' of that offence had it taken place, and the offence of child rape was enacted to protect children under the age of 13.

The offences under ss. 44, 45 and 46 do not apply to the offence of corporate manslaughter.

1.3.3   Conspiracy

Conspiracies can be divided into statutory and common law conspiracies.

1.3.3.1   Statutory Conspiracy

OFFENCE: **Statutory Conspiracy—*Criminal Law Act 1977, s. 1***
          • Triable on indictment • Where conspiracy is to commit murder, an offence punishable by life imprisonment or any indictable offence punishable with imprisonment where no maximum term is specified—life imprisonment • In other cases, sentence is the same as for completed offence

The Criminal Law Act 1977, s. 1 states:

(1) Subject to the following provisions of this Part of this Act, if a person agrees with any other person or persons that a course of conduct will be pursued which, if the agreement is carried out in accordance with their intentions, either—
   (a) will necessarily amount to or involve the commission of any offence or offences by one or more of the parties to the agreement; or
   (b) would do so but for the existence of facts which render the commission of the offence or any of the offences impossible,
he is guilty of conspiracy to commit the offence or offences in question.

KEYNOTE

A charge of conspiracy can be brought in respect of an agreement to commit indictable or summary offences. Conspiracy is triable only on indictment even if it relates to a summary offence (in which case the consent of the DPP will be required). Offences of conspiracy are committed at the time of the agreement; it is immaterial whether or not the substantive offence is ever carried out.

Agreeing with Another

For there to be a conspiracy there must be an agreement—a 'meeting of minds'. Therefore there must be at least two people (two minds) involved. Consequently, A cannot be guilty of a conspiracy with B (if B is the only other party to the agreement) if B intends to frustrate or sabotage it; there would not be a 'meeting of minds' in terms of an agreement to carry out an offence.

Each conspirator must be aware of the overall common purpose to which they all attach themselves. If one conspirator enters into *separate* agreements with different people, each agreement is a separate conspiracy (*R v Griffiths* [1966] 1 QB 589).

A person can be convicted of conspiracy even if the actual identity of the other conspirators is unknown (as to the affect of the acquittal of one party to a conspiracy on the other parties, see the Criminal Law Act 1977, s. 5(8)).

A defendant *cannot* be convicted of a statutory conspiracy if the only other party to the agreement is:

- his/her spouse or civil partner
- a person under 10 years of age
- the intended victim (Criminal Law Act 1977, s. 2(2)).

A husband and wife can both be convicted of a statutory conspiracy if they conspire with a third party (not falling into the above categories) (*R v Chrastny* [1991] 1 WLR 1381).

A person is not guilty of statutory conspiracy if the only other person with whom he agrees is his civil partner. A civil partnership is a same-sex partnership registered under the Civil Partnership Act 2004.

A corporation may be a party to a conspiracy (*R v ICR Haulage Ltd* [1944] KB 551), but a company and one of its directors cannot be the only parties to a conspiracy because there can be no 'meeting of minds' (*R v McDonnell* [1966] 1 QB 233).

The 'end product' of the agreement must be the commission of an offence by *one or more of the parties to the agreement*. Once agreed upon, any failure to bring about the end result or an abandoning of the agreement altogether will not prevent the statutory conspiracy being committed. An agreement to aid and abet an offence of conspiracy is not, in law, capable of constituting a statutory conspiracy under s. 1(1) of the Criminal Law Act 1977 (*R v Kenning* [2008] EWCA Crim 1534).

Note that if an agreement to commit a *summary offence which is not punishable by imprisonment* is made in contemplation or furtherance of a trade dispute, it must be disregarded (Trade Union and Labour Relations (Consolidation) Act 1992, s. 242).

What if a defendant enters into an agreement with another person to commit an offence but that other person is in fact a police officer? Under normal circumstances, forming an agreement with another person to carry out an offence is a conspiracy. If, however, one of only two conspirators is an undercover officer who has no intention of going through with the agreement, there is a strong argument that there can be no 'true' conspiracy as the only other person had no intention of going through with the plan (*Yip Chiu-Cheung* v *The Queen* [1995] 1 AC 111). In conspiracies, the intention of at least two parties *is* the basis of the whole offence. So, in cases where the only other 'conspirator' is a police officer, encouraging an offence may be a more appropriate charge.

1.3.3.2 Common Law Conspiracies

OFFENCE: **Conspiracy to Defraud—*Common Law***
- Triable on indictment • 10 years' imprisonment and/or a fine

Conspiracy to defraud involves:

> ...an agreement by two or more [persons] by dishonesty to deprive a person of something which is his or to which he is or would or might be entitled [or] an agreement by two or more by dishonesty to injure some proprietary right [of the victim]...

> (*Scott* v *Metropolitan Police Commissioner* [1975] AC 819).

This offence has been endorsed by senior judges as representing an effective means of dealing with multiple defendants engaged in a fraudulent course of conduct.

The common law offence of conspiracy to defraud can be divided into two main types. The first is contained in the case of *Scott*, the second involves a dishonest agreement to *deceive* another into acting in a way that is contrary to his/her duty (*Wai Yu-Tsang* v *The Queen* [1992] 1 AC 269).

Although the requirement for an agreement between at least two people is the same, this offence is broader than statutory conspiracy. There is no requirement to prove that the end result would amount to the commission of an *offence*, simply that it would result in depriving a person of something under the specified conditions or in injuring his/her proprietary right.

You must show *intent* to defraud a victim (*R v Hollinshead* [1985] AC 975).

You must also show that a defendant was dishonest as set out in *R v Ghosh* [1982] QB 1053 (**see para. 1.14.2.3**).

Clearly there will be circumstances where the defendant's behaviour will amount to both a statutory conspiracy and a conspiracy to defraud. The Criminal Justice Act 1987, s. 12 makes provision for such circumstances and allows the prosecution to choose which charge to prefer.

Examples of common law conspiracies to defraud include:

- Buffet car staff selling their own home-made sandwiches on British Rail trains thereby depriving the company of the opportunity to sell their own products (*R v Cooke* [1986] AC 909).
- Directors agreeing to conceal details of a bank's trading losses from its shareholders (*Wai Yu-Tsang*).
- Making unauthorised copies of commercial films for sale (*Scott*).
- Marketing devices to falsify gas or electric meters enabling customers (who were not party to the conspiracy) to defraud their gas and electric suppliers (*Hollinshead*).

A further example can be found in *R* v *Hussain* [2005] EWCA Crim 1866 where the defendant pleaded guilty to conspiracy to defraud after a widespread abuse of the postal voting system. In that case the defendant, an official Labour party candidate, collected uncompleted postal votes from households and completed them in his own favour.

1.3.4 Attempts

The Criminal Attempts Act 1981, s. 1 states:

(1) If, with intent to commit an offence to which this section applies, a person does an act which is more than merely preparatory to the commission of the offence, he is guilty of attempting to commit the offence.

...

(2) A person may be guilty of attempting to commit an offence to which this section applies even though the facts are such that the commission of the offence is impossible.

(3) In any case where—

   (a) apart from this subsection a person's intention would not be regarded as having amounted to an intent to commit an offence; but

   (b) if the facts of the case had been as he believed them to be, his intention would be so regarded,

then, for the purposes of subsection (1) above, he shall be regarded as having had an intent to commit that offence.

(4) This section applies to any offence which, if it were completed, would be triable in England and Wales as an indictable offence, other than—

   (a) conspiracy (at common law or under section 1 of the Criminal Law Act 1977 or any other enactment);

   (b) aiding, abetting, counselling, procuring or suborning the commission of an offence;

   (ba) an offence under section 2(1) of the Suicide Act 1961 (c 60) (encouraging or assisting suicide);

   (c) offences under section 4(1) (assisting offenders) or 5(1) (accepting or agreeing to accept consideration for not disclosing information about a relevant offence) of the Criminal Law Act 1967.

An Act which is More than Merely Preparatory

An attempt requires an act—an omission to act would not create liability for an attempt (e.g. a refusal to call an ambulance for a person who is gravely ill cannot amount to attempted murder).

A defendant's actions must be shown to have gone beyond mere preparation towards the commission of the substantive offence. Whether the defendant did or did not go beyond that point will be a question of fact for the jury/magistrate(s). There is no formula used by the courts in interpreting this requirement so it is useful to examine several cases where the courts have considered what this element of the offence means.

An example of where the defendant was held to have done no more than merely preparatory acts was *R* v *Campbell* [1991] Crim LR 268 where the appellant armed himself with an imitation gun, approached to within a yard of a post office which he intended to rob, but never drew his weapon; it was held that there was no evidence on which a jury could properly have concluded that his acts went beyond mere preparation. In *R* v *Bowles* [2004] EWCA Crim 1608 the defendant had been convicted of several offences involving dishonesty against an elderly neighbour. The neighbour's long-standing will left her estate to charity but, following his arrest, police officers searched the defendant's premises and found a new will, fully complete except for the signature. The defendant and his wife were named as the main beneficiaries and were to inherit the neighbour's house. Although the defendant's son was said to have been heard making reference to the fact that he was going to inherit the house, the 'new' will had been drafted over six months earlier and there was no evidence of any steps to have it executed, or any evidence of it being used. The Court of Appeal held that the making of the will was no more than merely preparatory and the defendant's conviction for attempting to make a false instrument (as to which **see para. 1.15.11.2**) was quashed.

In *R* v *Geddes* [1996] Crim LR 894, the defendant was found trespassing in the lavatory block of a school, armed with a knife, lengths of rope and tape. It appears he intended to kidnap a child; his conviction for attempted false imprisonment was quashed on appeal. Citing *Campbell* with approval, Lord Bingham CJ held that no jury could have concluded that the defendant's acts had gone beyond mere preparation. He may have equipped himself, and put himself in a position to commit the crime, but it could not be said that he had actually tried or started to commit it.

Courts have accepted an approach of questioning whether the defendant had 'embarked on the crime proper' (*R* v *Gullefer* [1990] 1 WLR 1063) but there is no requirement to have passed a point of no return leading to the commission of the substantive offence.

Mens Rea for Attempt

To prove an 'attempt' you must show an *intention* on the part of the defendant to commit the substantive offence.

This requirement means a higher level or degree of *mens rea* may be required to prove an attempt than for the substantive offence. For instance, the *mens rea* required to prove an offence of murder is the intention to kill *or* cause grievous bodily harm whereas the *mens rea* for attempted murder is nothing less than an *intent* to kill (*R* v *Whybrow* (1951) 35 Cr App R 141). In *R* v *Jones* [1990] 1 WLR 1057, the defendant was charged with attempted murder. He climbed into the car of the victim and drew a loaded gun with the intention of killing him, but was disarmed in a struggle that followed. The Court of Appeal held that it was open to a jury to regard this as attempted murder.

A defendant's intention may be *conditional*, that is, he/she may only intend to steal from a house if something worth stealing is later found inside. The conditional nature of this intention will not generally prevent the charge of attempt being brought and the defendant's intentions will, in accordance with s. 1(3), be judged *on the facts as he/she believed them to be*.

Although 'intent to commit' the offence is required under s. 1(1), there are occasions where a state of mind that falls short of such a precise intention may suffice. For instance, in cases of attempted rape (**see chapter 1.11**) the courts have accepted that recklessness as to whether the victim is consenting was (under the earlier sexual offences legislation) sufficient *mens rea* for attempted rape because it is sufficient for the substantive offence (*R* v *Khan* [1990] 1 WLR 813).

In proving an 'attempt' it is enough to show that defendants were in one of the states of mind required for the substantive offence and that they did their best, so far as they were able, to do what was necessary for the commission of the full offence (*Attorney-General's Reference (No. 3 of 1992)* [1994] 1 WLR 409).

1.3.5 Impossibility

Difficulties have arisen where, despite the efforts of the defendant, his/her ultimate intention has been impossible (such as trying to extract cocaine from a powder which is, unknown to the defendant, only talc). Impossibility is now far clearer following the Criminal Attempts Act 1981 and its interpretation through the courts. It differs however in some incomplete offences.

....

EXAMPLE

If a person tries to handle goods which are not in fact stolen, the following rules would apply:

- A defendant could *not* be guilty of encouraging another, nor of common law conspiracy to defraud in these circumstances. The *physical* impossibility (the goods are not actually stolen) of what the defendant sought to do would preclude such a charge.
- A defendant *could* be guilty of a statutory conspiracy with another to handle 'stolen' goods and also of attempting to handle 'stolen' goods under these circumstances. The physical impossibility would not prelude such charges as a result of the Criminal Attempts Act 1981 and the House of Lords' decision in *R* v *Shivpuri* [1987] AC 1 (you can conspire and/or attempt to commit the impossible). The only form of impossibility which would preclude liability under the Criminal Attempts Act 1981 or for a statutory conspiracy would be the *legal* impossibility.

....

1.3.6 Inter-relationship and Police Operations

The issues of involvement of a police officer in an incomplete offence are relevant to police officers particularly in the area of covert operations. Is it a conspiracy if one of the conspirators is an undercover police officer?

1.3.6.1 Undercover Operations

Defendants who are caught by undercover officers sometimes argue that they were induced or pressurised into committing the offence by the officers and, as a result, they should not be prosecuted or the evidence of the officer(s) should be excluded.

In *R* v *Loosely*; *Attorney-General's Reference (No. 3) of 2000* [2001] UKHL 53, the House of Lords set out the legal position in relation to these issues. Their lordships held that it is both unfair and an abuse of process if a person is incited (the predecessor of encouraging or assisting an offence) or pressurised by an undercover officer into committing a crime which the person would otherwise not have committed. If, however, the police officer(s) did no more than present a person with an 'unexceptional opportunity' to commit a criminal offence and the person took that opportunity, this would not amount to such an abuse of process.

1.3.6.2 Entrapment

In *Edwards* v *United Kingdom* (2005) 40 EHRR 24, the European Court of Human Rights re-stated the rights of defendants who are to be prosecuted on the basis of evidence obtained by undercover officers, and highlighted the tensions between protecting the sensitive sources of that evidence while affording the defendant a fair trial.

- It is not acceptable for the 'State' (police officers or other agents) to lure its citizens into committing acts that are against the law and then to prosecute those citizens for doing so; this amounts to entrapment, a misuse of power and abuse of the courts' process.
- If police officers acted only as 'detectives' and 'passive observers' of criminal activity that was to take place anyway, there would be no problem in drawing the line between what is allowable and what is not.
- However, some offences need a degree of active involvement by the police if those offences are to be successfully prosecuted. In such cases the police officers themselves become the reporters and witnesses of the offence as well as the investigators.
- The yardstick for judging the activities of the police in this regard is to ask whether the officers' conduct preceding the offence was no more than might have been expected from others in the circumstances. That is, did they do no more than give the defendant the 'unexceptional opportunity' to commit a crime as described above? If the answer is 'yes', the consequences below are not relevant. If the answer is 'no', there are several potential consequences for any subsequent trial.

The trial judge's task in such cases is to distinguish between legitimate crime detection and illegitimate crime creation (*R* v *Byrne* [2003] EWCA Crim 1073).

- The greater the inducement or persistence by the officers, the more readily the courts will conclude that they have overstepped the line.
- The greater the degree of intrusiveness into the 'target's' life, the closer the courts will scrutinise the 'proportionality' of the operation.
- The courts will also look at the defendant's personal circumstances including vulnerability and experience. What might be insignificant in terms of an inducement to one person may not be seen as so insignificant in relation to another.

The consequences are as follows:

- Courts have a general discretion to exclude evidence under the Police and Criminal Evidence Act 1984, s. 78 (see *Evidence and Procedure*, **chapter 2.7**).
- Courts also have a common law power to stay (discontinue) proceedings and order the release of a defendant where it becomes apparent that there has been a serious abuse of power by the State (*R v Horseferry Road Magistrates' Court, ex parte Bennett* [1994] 1 AC 42).
- Courts also have a general duty to consider the fairness of any defendant's trial under Article 6 of the European Convention on Human Rights (see *General Police Duties*, **chapter 4.4**). However, it should be noted that violations of Article 8 (right to privacy) will not by themselves usually give rise to exclusion of any evidence obtained as a result (*PG v United Kingdom* (2008) 46 EHRR 51).

What of the situation where, rather than approaching others, an undercover police officer is approached to take part in a proposed offence? In relation to this activity, there is no need for the person encouraged to have any intention of going on to commit the offence. The Divisional Court has held that there is no requirement for 'parity of *mens rea*' between the parties (*DPP v Armstrong* [2000] Crim LR 379). In that case the defendant had approached an undercover police officer asking him to supply child pornography. At his trial, the defendant argued that, as the officer in reality had no intention of supplying the pornography, there was no offence of incitement. On appeal by the prosecutor, the Divisional Court held that incitement, like conspiracies and attempts, was an auxiliary offence where criminal liability was attributed to the defendant where the full offence had not been committed. Consequently the intent of the person incited was irrelevant. The court also held that the issue of impossibility was irrelevant because it had been 'possible' for the officer to supply the material.

What if a defendant enters into an agreement with another person to commit an offence but that other person is in fact a police officer? Under normal circumstances, forming an agreement with another person to carry out an offence is a conspiracy. If, however, one of only two conspirators is an undercover officer who has no intention of going through with the agreement, there is a strong argument that there can be no 'true' conspiracy as the only other person had no intention of going through with the plan (*Yip Chiu-Cheung v The Queen* [1995] 1 AC 111). In conspiracies, the intention of at least two parties *is* the basis of the whole offence. In cases where the only other 'conspirator' is a police officer, encouraging an offence may be a more appropriate charge.

Making *an offer* which amounts *in itself* to a criminal offence (e.g. an offer to supply a controlled drug, **see chapter 1.6**) to an undercover officer may still amount to the offence and a defendant cannot claim that the offer was not 'real' because of the identity of the recipient (*R v Kray* [1998] EWCA Crim 3211).

1.4 General Defences

1.4.1 Introduction

'General defences' in criminal law are concerned with cases where the prosecution are unable to prove all elements beyond reasonable doubt because of some specific characteristics of the defendant or circumstances of a particular offence. This failure may come about at trial but will often be apparent at the evidence-gathering stage of an investigation.

Some offences have particular defences attached to them (e.g. criminal damage), others exist only in relation to murder. These defences are discussed in the relevant chapters.

1.4.2 Automatism

Strictly speaking, automatism is not a 'defence'; it is an absence of a fundamental requirement for any criminal offence, namely the 'criminal conduct' (*actus reus*). In **chapter 1.2** we considered the need for criminal conduct to be *voluntary* and *willed*. It follows that, if defendants have *total* loss of control over their actions, they cannot be held liable for those actions and there may be grounds to claim a defence of automatism. This view was confirmed in *R* v *Coley* [2013] EWCA Crim 223, where it was said that the question is not whether the accused is acting consciously or not but whether there is a 'complete destruction of voluntary control'. The best example of this defence is one where a swarm of bees flies into a car causing a reflex action by the driver resulting in an accident (an example given in *Hill* v *Baxter* [1958] 1 QB 277). As the driver's actions are involuntary and not sufficient to support a criminal charge, the defence of automatism would be available. Other examples might include a person inadvertently dropping and damaging property when suddenly seized by cramp or discharging a firearm as a result of an irresistible bout of sneezing.

If the loss of control is brought about by voluntary intoxication or by insanity, the defence becomes narrower.

1.4.3 Intoxication: Voluntary or Involuntary

There is no general defence of intoxication. If there were, a high proportion of criminal behaviour would clearly go unpunished. What intoxication does is potentially remove the necessary *mens rea* required for a defendant to commit an offence. There are some statutory offences where specific provision is made for drunkenness (e.g. the Public Order Act 1986, see *General Police Duties*, **chapter 4.11**).

Intoxication can be divided into two categories; voluntary intoxication (you got yourself in that condition) and involuntary intoxication (you are not responsible for getting in that condition). The distinction is important when considering whether the offence alleged is one of 'specific' or 'basic' intent (terms discussed at **para. 1.1.2**).

Where an offence is a specific intent offence, such as murder, defendants who were voluntarily intoxicated at the time the offence was committed may be able to show they were so intoxicated that they were incapable of forming the *mens rea* required for the offence. An individual who is voluntarily intoxicated *would not* be able to say this if accused of an offence of basic intent as the courts have accepted that a defendant is still capable of forming basic intent even when completely inebriated (*DPP* v *Majewski* [1977] AC 443).

Where the offence is a basic intent offence, such as s. 47 assault, defendants who were involuntarily intoxicated (perhaps because their drink had been spiked) at the time of the offence may be able to say that they lacked the *mens rea* for that basic intent offence.

KEYNOTE

Therefore, voluntary intoxication can be raised in answer to a charge of an offence of specific intent but not basic intent; involuntary intoxication can be raised in answer to a charge of both specific *and* basic intent.

If defendants simply misjudge the amount or strength of intoxicants which they take, this will not be regarded as involuntary intoxication (*R* v *Allen* [1988] Crim LR 698). Similarly, if defendants can be shown to have actually formed the required *mens rea* necessary for the offence, intoxication (voluntary or involuntary) will not be available as a drunken intent is still an 'intent' (*R* v *Kingston* [1995] 2 AC 355).

The source of the intoxication can be drink or drugs. In the latter case, however, the courts will consider the known effects of the drug in deciding whether or not defendants had formed the required degree of *mens rea*; the characteristics of the drugs will be relevant in determining whether defendants behaved recklessly in taking them.

Where the defendant forms a 'mistaken belief' based on the fact that he/she is intoxicated, that belief may sometimes be raised as a defence. In cases of criminal damage where a defendant has mistakenly believed that the property being damaged is his/her own property, and that mistaken belief has arisen from the defendant's intoxicated state, the courts have accepted the defence under s. 5 of the Criminal Damage Act 1971 (*Jaggard* v *Dickinson* [1981] QB 527) (**see chapter 1.16**). However, this appears to be confined to the wording of that particular statute and the courts have refused to accept similar defences of mistaken, drunken belief (e.g. in *R* v *O'Grady* [1987] QB 995 where a defendant charged with murder could not rely on a mistake induced by his own voluntary intoxication and claim 'self-defence'), or where the defendant mistakenly believed that the victim of a rape was consenting to sexual intercourse. The Court of Appeal has confirmed that the decision in *O'Grady* also applies to manslaughter (*R* v *Hatton* (2005) EWCA Crim 2951).

If defendants become intoxicated in order to gain false courage to go and commit a crime, they will not be able to claim a defence of intoxication *even if the crime is one of specific intent*. This is because they have already formed the intent required and the intoxication is merely a means of plucking up 'Dutch' courage to carry it out (*Attorney-General for Northern Ireland* v *Gallagher* [1963] AC 349).

1.4.4 Insanity

There is a rebuttable presumption in law that all people are sane. Where a person wishes to raise insanity as a defence, the burden of proof (on a balance of probabilities) rests with the defendant.

If a defendant claims to have been 'insane' at the time of the offence (to attract an acquittal in a summary trial or an order of the court when tried on indictment), that claim will be judged against the M'Naghten rules. The rules (*M'Naghten's Case* (1843) 10 Cl & F 200) state:

> . . . to establish a defence on the ground of insanity, it must be clearly proved that, at the time of the committing of the act, the party accused was labouring under such a defect of reason, from disease of the mind, as not to know the nature and quality of the act he was doing; or, if he did know it, that he did not know he was doing what was wrong.

The question of whether the defendant's attributes or condition amount to a 'disease of the mind' is a question of law and not a question of medical opinion (*R v Sullivan* [1984] AC 156).

An epileptic fit and a hypoglycaemic episode in a diabetic have both been deemed to be similar to insanity in respect of a defence to a criminal charge and therefore the M'Naghten rules should be applied (*Sullivan* and *R v Quick* [1973] QB 910).

A special verdict of 'not guilty by reason of insanity' is provided by the Trial of Lunatics Act 1883 if the defence is successful. Where a special verdict is returned under the Criminal Procedure (Insanity) Act 1965 (s. 5) the court has a range of orders from which to choose. These include an order for a hospital order (with or without a restriction order), a supervision order and even an absolute discharge.

1.4.5 Inadvertence and Mistake

There are occasions where a defendant makes a mistake about some circumstance or consequence, however, claims that a defendant 'made a mistake' or did something 'inadvertently' will only be an effective defence if they negate the *mens rea* for that offence. Therefore, if someone wanders out of a shop with something that has not yet been paid for, that mistake or inadvertence might negative any *mens rea* of 'dishonesty'. As the requirement for the *mens rea* in such a case is *subjective* then the defendant's mistake or inadvertence will be judged subjectively. The same will generally be true for offences requiring subjective recklessness. It does not matter whether the mistake was 'reasonable' (*DPP v Morgan* [1976] AC 182). The appropriate test is whether the defendant's mistaken belief was an honest and genuine one.

There are occasions where a genuine mistake on the part of the defendant may amount to a defence. In *R v Lee* [2001] 1 Cr App R 19, a case arising from an assault on two arresting police officers, the Court of Appeal reviewed the law in this area, reaffirming the following points:

- A genuine or honest mistake could provide a defence to many criminal offences requiring a particular state of mind, including assault with intent to resist arrest (*R v Brightling* [1991] Crim LR 364).
- A defence of mistake had to involve a mistake of fact, not a mistake of law (see below).
- People under arrest are not entitled to form their own view as to the lawfulness of that arrest. They have a duty to comply with the police and hear the details of the charge against them (*R v Bentley* (1850) 4 Cox CC 406).
- Belief in one's own innocence, however genuine or honestly held, cannot afford a defence to a charge of assault with intent to resist arrest under s. 38 of the Offences Against the Person Act 1861 (as to which, **see chapter 1.9**).

A defendant attempted to argue that his honest and reasonable mistake as to the *facts* of his arrest (as opposed to the law) after he was lawfully arrested for a public order offence was different from the decision in *Lee*. The Divisional Court did not agree with him (*Hewitt v DPP* [2002] EWHC 2801 (QB)).

Generally, it is no defence to claim a mistake as to the law because all people are presumed to know the law once it is made. With statutory instruments a defendant can show that the instrument in question was not in force at the time of the offence or that the behaviour that it sought to control was beyond the powers (*ultra vires*) of that instrument.

There is one particular example, however, where a mistaken belief in the legal position is specifically provided for in a criminal offence. This is where a person appropriates property in the belief that he/she has a legal right to deprive another person of it under s. 2 of the Theft Act 1968 (**see chapter 1.14**).

In relation to offences involving negligence, inadvertence would clearly not amount to a defence and any 'mistake' would generally need to be shown to be a reasonable one.

1.4.6 Duress

Where a person is threatened with death or serious physical injury unless he/she carries out a criminal act, he/she may have a defence of *duress* (*R v Graham* [1982] 1 WLR 294). The threat of serious physical injury does not appear to include serious *psychological* injury (*R v Baker* [1997] Crim LR 497). Where relevant intent is an ingredient of the offence, defendants might claim that they only formed that intent as a result of duress (e.g. an intent to supply controlled drugs—**see para. 1.6.4**). However, unless it is shown that the intent had or could have been formed *only* by reason of that duress (e.g. the duress was the only thing causing the defendant to form that intent), the defence will fail (*R v Fisher* [2004] EWCA Crim 1190).

It would seem that the threat need not be made solely to the person who goes on to commit the relevant offence; there are authorities to suggest that threats of death/serious harm to loved ones may allow a defence of duress.

> **KEYNOTE**
>
> The defence is not available in respect of an offence of murder (*R v Howe* [1987] AC 417) or attempted murder (*R v Gotts* [1992] 2 AC 412), as a principal or secondary offender. It is, however, available in other offences even in offences of strict liability (*Eden District Council v Braid* [1998] COD 259—taxi driver threatened and forced to carry excessive number of people in breach of his licensing conditions).

There are several key elements to this defence:

- the threat must have driven the defendant to commit the offence;
- the defendant must have acted as a sober and reasonable person sharing the defendant's characteristics would have done;
- the threatened death/injury must be anticipated at or near the time of the offence—not sometime in the distant future.

Duress is not available as a defence if it is proved that the defendant failed to take advantage of an opportunity to neutralise the effects of the threat (perhaps by escaping from it), which a reasonable person of a similar sort to the defendant would have taken in the same position. An example of this approach is the case of *R v Heath* [2000] Crim LR 109, where the defendant alleged that he had been pressurised into transporting drugs. Because the defendant had more than one safe avenue of escape (going to the police, which he did not do because he was scared and because he was a drug addict, and going to his parents in Scotland, which he did not do because he did not want them to know about the position he was in) the defence failed. Whether a defendant could be expected to take such an opportunity of rendering the threat ineffective, e.g. by seeking police protection, will be a matter for the jury. Therefore, a defendant who is ordered to steal from a shop in 24 hours' time or suffer a serious physical injury for failing to do so might be unable to utilise the defence as a jury may consider the defendant had ample opportunity to take evasive action and avoid the threat.

If defendants knowingly expose themselves to a risk of such a threat of death or serious physical injury, they cannot claim duress as a defence. So if a person joins a violent gang or an active terrorist organisation, he/she cannot claim duress as a defence to any crimes he/she may go on to commit under threat of death or serious injury from another member or rival of that organisation (*R v Sharp* [1987] QB 853). However, if the purpose of the organisation or gang is not predominantly violent or dangerous (e.g. a gang of shoplifters), the defence of duress *may* be available in relation to offences committed while under threat of death or serious physical injury from other gang members (*R* v *Shepherd* (1987) 86 Cr App R 47).

1.4.6.1 Marital Coercion

The defence of 'marital coercion' may be raised where a *wife*, charged with any offence other than treason or murder, maintains that she committed the offence in the presence and under the coercion of her husband (Criminal Justice Act 1925, s. 47 and *R* v *Shortland* [1996] 1 Cr App R 116). There is no need for threats of death or serious injury, it being sufficient that the wife acted because of the dominating influence of her husband, her will being 'overborne by the wishes of her husband' so that 'she was forced unwillingly to participate' (*Shortland*).

1.4.7 Duress of Circumstances

Although it was said for a long time that there was no defence of 'necessity' in the law of England and Wales, there is now authority for this defence, albeit in very narrow circumstances (*R* v *A* *(Children)* *(Conjoined Twins: Surgical Separation)* [2001] Fam 147). Effectively, the courts have recognised a defence of 'duress of circumstances' which achieves much the same result as what might be described as 'necessity'.

There may be times when circumstances leave the defendant no alternative but to commit an offence. If a doctor is suddenly called upon to use his/her car to get someone to hospital for emergency treatment, those circumstances may provide a defence for driving while disqualified (*R* v *Martin* [1989] 1 All ER 652). In such cases the court will consider the reasonableness of the defendant's behaviour in light of the prevailing circumstances. If the defendant commits a very serious offence in order to avoid very minor or trivial consequences, this defence is unlikely to be available.

This type of duress should be distinguished from that at **para. 1.4.6**. There the duress comes from a threat made to the defendant compelling him/her to commit an offence: a gun to the head type of situation where one person says to another '*Do this or else . . .*'. With duress of circumstances, there is no such threat being made. Rather there is a threatening situation or set of circumstances from which the defendant wishes to escape and, in so doing, feels impelled to commit an offence as the lesser of two present evils. Here the threat is 'situational' and the defendant feels '*If I don't do this, then I will suffer death or serious physical injury. . .*'.

This defence was examined by the Court of Appeal in a case where someone jumped onto the bonnet of the car that the appellant was driving. The appellant drove for some distance with the man on the bonnet of the car, braking after a short time to go over a speed ramp. The man fell from the bonnet and the appellant drove on, running the man over and causing him grievous bodily harm (as to which, **see chapter 1.9**). In determining whether or not the defence of 'duress of circumstances' was available, the court held that the jury must ask two questions in relation to the appellant:

- Was he (or might he have been) impelled to act as he did because, as a result of what he reasonably believed, he had good cause to fear he would suffer death or serious injury if he did not do so?
- If so, would a sober person of reasonable firmness and sharing the same characteristics, have responded to the situation in the way that he did?

If each question were answered with a 'yes', the defence would be made out (*R* v *Cairns* [1999] 2 Cr App R 137).

The important aspect to this defence then is that it will only avail defendants as long as they are acting under compulsion of the prevailing circumstances when committing the offence. It appears that defendants need only hold an *honest* belief that those circumstances exist without necessarily having *reasonable grounds* for that belief (*DPP v Rogers* [1998] Crim LR 202) and there is no need for the threat to be 'real'. There is certainly no need for the threat (perceived threat) to amount to a criminal offence and the Court of Appeal has accepted the possibility of a 'duress of circumstances' defence being applicable where a defendant acts in fear of the consequences of declaring war on Iraq (*R v Jones (Margaret)* [2004] EWCA Crim 1981). However, the defendant's actions in order to avoid that perceived threatening situation must be reasonable and proportionate to the threat presented. Therefore defendants in situations like *Willer* and *Cairns* would not be able to claim duress of circumstances if they drove at their victims repeatedly until all had been injured to a point whereby they no longer posed a threat.

An attempt to extend the defence was made in *R v Altham* [2006] EWCA Crim 7, where the defendant had been charged with possessing a controlled drug (cannabis). The defendant appealed against his conviction, arguing that he needed to smoke cannabis to ease the pain he suffered from injuries received in a car accident. It was argued that the defence of duress of circumstances should be open to the defendant on the basis that he was suffering serious physical harm. The prosecution countered that pain can never amount to serious physical harm. The appeal was dismissed and the court stated that the defence could not be available in this type of circumstance because it would allow unlawful activity to be undertaken and would conflict with the purpose and effect of the intention of the Misuse of Drugs Act 1971.

It seems that, apart from the offence of murder, attempted murder or treason, the defence is available against any other charge (including hijacking, *R v Abdul-Hussain* [1999] Crim LR 570).

1.4.8 Defence of Self, Others or Property

There are circumstances where the use of force against a person or property will be permissible. This aspect of criminal law is dealt with by s. 76 of the Criminal Justice and Immigration Act 2008. Section 76 provides a gloss on the common law of self-defence and the defences provided by s. 3(1) of the Criminal Law Act 1967, which relate to the use of force in the prevention of crime or making an arrest. Section 76 aims to improve understanding of the practical application of these areas of law using elements of case law to illustrate how the defence operates. It does not change the current test that allows the use of reasonable force.

KEYNOTE

The law can be formulated quite simply along the following lines:

A person may use such force as is reasonable in the circumstances as he believes them to be for the purpose of:

(a) self-defence; or
(b) defence of another; or
(c) defence of property; or
(d) prevention of crime; or
(e) lawful arrest.

1.4.8.1 The Use of Force

A defendant charged with an offence may seek to rely on the common law defence of self-defence or the defence provided by s. 3(1) of the Criminal Law Act 1967.

The Criminal Law Act 1967, s. 3(1) states:

> A person may use such force as is reasonable in the circumstances in the prevention of crime or in effecting or assisting in the lawful arrest of offenders or suspected offenders or of persons unlawfully at large.

It is to these potential defences that s. 76 of the Criminal Justice and Immigration Act 2008 applies, particularly to the question as to whether the degree of force used was reasonable in the circumstances. The 'degree of force' means the type and amount of force used. Section 76(10)(b) resolves the question as to whether reasonable force in self-defence would include acting in the defence of another person—it does.

The question whether the degree of force used by the defendant was reasonable in the circumstances is to be decided by reference to the circumstances *as the defendant believed them to be* (s. 76(3)). If the defendant claims to have held a particular belief as regards the existence of any circumstances, the reasonableness or otherwise of that belief is relevant to the question whether the defendant genuinely held it. If it is determined that the defendant did genuinely hold the belief the defendant is entitled to rely on it even if the belief was mistaken or, if it was mistaken, the mistake was a reasonable one to have made.

....

EXAMPLE

X has a long and violent history and has been convicted of several wounding offences involving the use of a knife. In an unprovoked attack, X attacks Y in a pub by punching Y in the face. Y is aware of X's violent past and after being punched, Y sees X's hand move towards the inside of his jacket. Y genuinely believes that X is going to stab him and so grabs hold of a chair and smashes it against X's arm, breaking X's arm in the process. X was not going to stab Y as he did not have a knife.

....

Y reacted to the circumstances as he believed them to be. The reasonableness of Y's belief is relevant in deciding whether or not Y actually held the belief. If the court accepted Y held the belief, the fact that X did not have a knife and was not going to stab Y (a mistake by Y) will not affect Y's ability to utilise the defence.

The situation would be different if Y had got himself drunk and, simply seeing X walk into the pub, mistakenly thought X was going to stab him. This is because s. 76(5) would not enable Y to rely on any mistaken belief due to intoxication that was voluntarily induced.

Section 76(6) adds that the degree of force used by the defendant is not to be regarded as reasonable in the circumstances as the defendant believed them to be if it was disproportionate in those circumstances.

In deciding whether or not the degree of force used was reasonable in the circumstances, s. 76(7) requires certain considerations to be taken into account:

- that a person acting for a legitimate purpose (the purposes of the defences to which s. 76 applies) may not be able to weigh to a nicety the exact measure of any necessary action; and
- that evidence of a person's having only done what the person honestly and instinctively thought was necessary for a legitimate purpose constitutes strong evidence that only reasonable action was taken by that person for that purpose.

This does not prevent other matters from being taken into account where they are relevant in deciding whether the degree of force used was reasonable in the circumstances.

KEYNOTE

Section 76 retains a single test for self-defence and the prevention of crime (or the making of an arrest). The law has been developed in line with case law regarding self-defence and the use of force, most notably *Palmer* v *The Queen* [1971] AC 814. The defence will be available if a person honestly believed it was necessary to use force and if the degree of force used was not disproportionate in the circumstances as he/she viewed them. The person who uses force is to be judged on the basis of the circumstances as he/she perceived them. In the heat of the moment he/she will not be expected to have judged exactly what action was called for, and a degree of latitude may be given to a person who only did what he/she honestly and instinctively thought was necessary. Defendants are entitled to have their actions judged on the basis of their view of the facts as they honestly believed them to be.

1.4.8.2 'Householder' Cases

Section 43 of the Crime and Courts Act 2013 amends s. 76 of the Criminal Justice and Immigration Act 2008 so that the use of *disproportionate* force can be regarded as reasonable in the circumstances as the accused believed them to be when householders are acting to protect themselves or others from trespassers in their homes (self-defence). The use of *grossly* disproportionate force would still not be permitted. The provisions also extend to people who live and work in the same premises and armed forces personnel who may live and work in buildings such as barracks for periods of time. The provisions *will not* cover other scenarios where the use of force might be required, for example when people are defending themselves from attack on the street, preventing crime or protecting property; the current law on the use of reasonable force will apply in these situations.

1.4.8.3 Human Rights

Where the common law defences of self-defence, defence of property or the Criminal Law Act 1967 defence of lawful arrest is raised in relation to taking someone's life, the provisions of Article 2 of the European Convention on Human Rights will apply. Under Article 2, the test will be whether the force used was no more than *absolutely necessary* and lethal force will be 'absolutely necessary' only if it is strictly proportionate to the legitimate purpose being pursued. In order to meet those criteria, regard will be had to:

- the nature of the aim being pursued;
- the inherent dangers to life and limb from the situation;
- the degree of risk to life presented by the amount of force employed.

The only circumstances in which lethal force might be permissible here are where the defendant was acting:

- in defence of any person from unlawful violence;
- in order to effect a lawful arrest or to prevent the escape of a person lawfully detained;
- in action lawfully taken for the purpose of quelling a riot or insurrection.

Note that the taking of life *in order to prevent crime* is not mentioned in Article 2.

1.4.8.4 Defence of Property

The ongoing controversy about the use of force by householders confronted by burglars in their own homes was the catalyst for the introduction of the Criminal Justice and Immigration Act 2008. Section 76(2)(aa) makes it clear that the 'common law defence of defence of property' is governed by s. 76 (as well as self-defence, the prevention of crime and making an arrest).

In addition, s. 3(1) of the Criminal Law Act 1967 states reasonable force may be used in the prevention of crime. Therefore, if a person is acting in order to prevent a crime against his/her property, it follows that force can be used to protect property.

Whether such force is reasonable or not will be subject to the requirements of s. 76 of the Criminal Justice and Immigration Act 2008. However, it might be somewhat problematic (if not impossible) to reconcile reasonable force to protect property with the taking of a person's life. It may be that such lethal force would fall foul of s. 76(6) which states that if the force used is disproportionate then it will not be regarded as being reasonable in the circumstances.

Allied to this is the fact that Article 2 of the European Convention on Human Rights does not support the taking of life in the defence of property and it can be seen that such a defence may well fail.

1.4.9 Police Officers

When using force against others, police officers will be criminally liable for any assaults they commit, in the same way as any other person. Apart from the harm done to the victim such assaults can be viewed as a breach of public trust which damages society's confidence in its public services. This approach can be seen in a case involving assaults by prison officers on a prisoner in their charge (*R v Fryer* [2002] EWCA Crim 825). In *Fryer* the Court of Appeal also took account of the relevant ranks and seniority of the officers when passing sentence.

However, just as the same offences and sentences will apply, similarly, the same general *defences* will potentially be available to the officer. One specific issue that can often arise where force is used by a police officer is the technique employed by the officer in applying force or striking someone. This may consist of a particular technique that the officer has been trained to use—either with or without some form of weapon. The issue of whether a particular technique is a 'proper' or 'recognised' one is not the same as the question of the *lawfulness* of any force used on that occasion. Clearly the controlled use of a technique in which an officer has been trained may help a court in determining the issue of the lawfulness or otherwise of the use of force. So too will any training that the officer has (or has not) received in relation to the use of force and personal protection. However, there are times when using an 'authorised technique' will nevertheless be unlawful; conversely there will be circumstances in which the use of an improvised strike or use of an object may be lawful. All will turn on the circumstances of the case.

1.4.10 Infancy

Children under the age of 10 are *irrebuttably* presumed to be incapable of criminal responsibility (*doli incapax*) by virtue of s. 50 of the Children and Young Persons Act 1933.

1.5 | Homicide

1.5.1 Introduction

Homicide covers offences of murder, manslaughter and other occasions where a person causes, or is involved in, the death of another. The common law in relation to homicide is important, not only because of the gravity of the offences themselves, but also because the cases have defined a number of key issues in criminal law applicable to many other offences.

In all cases of homicide the general criminal conduct (*actus reus*) is the same—the killing of another person.

1.5.2 Murder

OFFENCE: **Murder—*Common Law***
- Life imprisonment (mandatory)

Murder is committed when a person unlawfully kills another human being under the Queen's Peace, with malice aforethought.

KEYNOTE

A conviction for murder carries a mandatory sentence of life imprisonment (if the offence is committed by a person aged 18 but under 21 the sentence is 'custody for life' (also mandatory) and in the case of a defendant who is under 18, 'detention at Her Majesty's pleasure': Powers of Criminal Courts (Sentencing) Act 2000, s. 90).

'Unlawful killing' means actively causing the death of another without justification. 'Unlawfully' can be taken to exclude killings for which the accused has a complete and valid justification, such as killing (reasonably) in self-defence. It also includes occasions where someone fails to act after creating a situation of danger (see chapter 1.2).

'Another human being' includes a baby who has been born alive and has an existence independent of its mother. 'Existence independent of its mother' means that the child is fully expelled from the womb; the umbilical cord need not be cut. If a person injures a baby while it is in its mother's womb and it subsequently dies from those injuries *after being born*, it may be appropriate to bring a charge of murder if the defendant intended to kill the mother when he attacked her. It would certainly be appropriate to charge a person with the murder of the child if he/she intended the child to die after having been born alive. If the defendant intended only to cause serious injury to the mother, that intention cannot support a charge of *murder* in respect of the baby if it goes on to die after being born alive. It may, however, support a charge of *manslaughter*. In *Attorney-General's Reference (No. 3 of 1994)* [1998] AC 245 the House of Lords ruled that the doctrine of 'transferred *mens rea*' does not fully apply in cases of unborn children (*in utero*) and therefore any liability of the defendant for the subsequent death of a child that he/she injured before it was born alive will depend on the defendant's intentions at the time of causing the injury.

'Under the Queen's Peace' appears to exclude deaths caused during the legitimate prosecution of warfare (War Crimes Act 1991).

Under the provisions of the Offences Against the Person Act 1861 (s. 9) any British citizen who commits a murder anywhere in the world may be tried in England or Wales. It does not matter what nationality the victim was or where in the world the act took place—all that matters is that at the time the offence was committed, the defendant was a British citizen.

It should be noted that the only state of mind or *mens rea* that will support a charge of attempted murder is an *intention to kill*. Nothing less will suffice.

Where a charge of murder is brought there may be specific restrictions on the applicability of a defence that might otherwise be available. For example, a claim of self-defence based on a mistake arising out of voluntary drunkenness will not be allowed in a prosecution for murder (or manslaughter)—see para. 1.4.3.

1.5.2.1 Malice Aforethought

The cases of *R* v *Moloney* [1985] AC 905 and *R* v *Hancock* [1986] AC 455 identify the *mens rea* required for murder as an intention:

- to kill, or
- to cause grievous bodily harm.

Murder is therefore a crime of 'specific intent'.

The term 'malice aforethought' is often associated with some form of premeditation; this is not required.

1.5.2.2 Year and a Day

Section 1 of the Law Reform (Year and a Day Rule) Act 1996 abolished the limitation that death had to occur within a year and a day of the infliction of injury.

However, by s. 2 of the Act, the consent of the Attorney-General is required before proceedings can be instituted for a 'fatal offence' where either:

(a) the injury alleged to have caused the death was sustained more than three years before death occurred, or

(b) the person has previously been convicted of an offence committed in circumstances alleged to be connected to the death.

1.5.3 Voluntary Manslaughter and 'Special Defences'

As a conviction for murder leaves a judge no discretion in sentencing a defendant, a number of 'special defences' have developed around the offence (diminished responsibility, loss of control and suicide pact). Rather than securing an acquittal, they allow for a conviction of 'voluntary manslaughter' instead of murder (hence the term 'partial' defence to murder). Consequently, voluntary manslaughter is more a finding by a court than an offence with which a person can be charged. It should be noted that these 'special defences' are only available to a defendant who is charged with an offence of murder—they cannot be used in answer to any other charge, e.g. attempted murder.

1.5.3.1 Diminished Responsibility

The Homicide Act 1957, s. 2 states:

(1) A person ('D') who kills or is a party to a killing of another is not to be convicted of murder if D was suffering from an abnormality of mental functioning which—

(a) arose from a recognised medical condition,

(b) substantially impaired D's ability to do one or more of the things mentioned in subsection (1A), and

(c) provides an explanation for D's acts and omissions in doing or being party to the killing.

(1A) Those things are—

(a) to understand the nature of D's conduct;

(b) to form a rational judgment;

(c) to exercise self-control.

(1B) For the purposes of subsection (1)(c), an abnormality of mental functioning provides an explanation for D's conduct if it causes, or is a significant contributory factor in causing, D to carry out that conduct.

(2) On a charge of murder, it shall be for the defence to prove that the person charged is by virtue of this section not liable to be convicted of murder.

(3) A person who but for this section would be liable, whether as principal or as accessory, to be convicted of murder shall be liable instead to be convicted of manslaughter.

(4) The fact that one party to a killing is by virtue of this section not liable to be convicted of murder shall not affect the question whether the killing amounted to murder in the case of any other party to it.

KEYNOTE

The definition requires that the abnormality *substantially* impaired the defendant's ability to do one (or more) of three things and also provides that the defendant's abnormality of mental functioning should be of at least a significant contributory factor in causing the defendant's acts or omissions. Whether the 'impairment of mental responsibility' is 'substantial' or not will be a question of fact for the jury to decide. Minor lapses of lucidity will not be enough.

The abnormality must arise from a *recognised medical condition*. 'Abnormality of mind' has been held to be 'a state of mind so different from that of ordinary human beings that the reasonable man would term it abnormal' (*R* v *Byrne* [1960] 2 QB 396). This includes the mental inability to exert control over one's behaviour and to form rational judgment.

There may be any number of causes of the 'abnormality' of the mind. Examples include post-natal depression and pre-menstrual symptoms (*R* v *Reynolds* [1988] Crim LR 679) and 'battered wives' syndrome' (*R* v *Hobson* [1998] 1 Cr App R 31). In *R* v *Dietschmann* [2003] UKHL 10 the House of Lords accepted that a mental abnormality caused by a grief reaction to the recent death of an aunt with whom the defendant had had a physical relationship could suffice. In that case their lordships went on to hold that there is no requirement to show that the 'abnormality of mind' was the *sole* cause of the defendant's acts in committing the killing.

The burden of proving these features lies with the defence and the standard required is one of a balance of probabilities.

1.5.3.2 Loss of Control

The Coroners and Justice Act 2009, s. 54 states:

(1) Where a person ('D') kills or is a party to the killing of another ('V'), D is not to be convicted of murder if—

   (a) D's acts and omissions in doing or being a party to the killing resulted from D's loss of self-control,

   (b) the loss of self-control had a qualifying trigger, and

   (c) a person of D's sex and age, with a normal degree of tolerance and self-restraint and in the circumstances of D, might have reacted in the same or in a similar way to D.

(2) For the purposes of subsection (1)(a), it does not matter whether or not the loss of control was sudden.

(3) In subsection (1)(c) the reference to 'the circumstances of D' is a reference to all of D's circumstances other than those whose only relevance to D's conduct is that they bear on D's general capacity for tolerance or self-restraint.

(4) Subsection (1) does not apply if, in doing or being a party to the killing, D acted in a considered desire for revenge.

(5) On a charge of murder, if sufficient evidence is adduced to raise an issue with respect to the defence under subsection (1), the jury must assume that the defence is satisfied unless the prosecution proves beyond reasonable doubt that it is not.

(6) For the purposes of subsection (5), sufficient evidence is adduced to raise an issue with respect to the defence if evidence is adduced on which, in the opinion of the trial judge, a jury, properly directed, could reasonably conclude that the defence might apply.

(7) A person who, but for this section, would be liable to be convicted of murder is liable instead to be convicted of manslaughter.

(8) The fact that one party to a killing is by virtue of this section not liable to be convicted of murder does not affect the question whether the killing amounted to murder in the case of any other party to it.

In *R* v *Asmelash* [2013] EWCA Crim 157, the Court of Appeal confirmed that, in considering the question under s. 54(1)(c) of whether 'a person of D's sex and age, with a normal degree of tolerance and self-restraint and in the circumstances of D, might have reacted in the same or similar way to D' the fact that the accused had voluntarily consumed alcohol was *not* to be included in D's circumstances.

The loss of control *need not be sudden* (s. 54(2)) Although subs. (2) in the partial defence states that *it is not a requirement* for the partial defence that the loss of self-control be sudden, it will remain open for the judge (in deciding whether to leave the defence to the jury) and the jury (in determining whether the killing did in fact result from a loss of self-control and whether the other aspects of the partial defence are satisfied) to take into account any delay between a relevant incident and the killing.

Section 54(3) supplements s. 54(1)(c) by clarifying that the reference to the defendant's circumstances in that subsection means all of those circumstances except those whose only relevance to the defendant's conduct is that they impact upon the defendant's general level of tolerance and self-restraint. Thus, a defendant's history of abuse at the hands of the victim could be taken into account in deciding whether an ordinary person might have acted as the defendant did, whereas the defendant's generally short temper could not. Consequently, when applying the test in s. 54(1)(c) the jury will consider whether a person of the defendant's sex and age with an ordinary level of tolerance and self-restraint and in the defendant's specific circumstances (in the sense described earlier in this paragraph) might have acted as the defendant did.

Those acting in a considered desire for revenge cannot rely on the partial defence, even if they lose self-control as a result of a qualifying trigger.

Qualifying Trigger

Section 55 of the Coroners and Justice Act 2009, explains the phrase 'qualifying trigger' mentioned in s. 54(1)(b). The loss of self-control must be attributable to:

* *The defendant's fear of serious violence from the victim against the defendant or another identified person.* This will be a subjective test and the defendant will need to show that he/she lost self control because of a genuine fear of serious violence, whether or not the fear was in fact reasonable. The fear of serious violence needs to be in respect of violence against the defendant or against another identified person. For example, the fear of serious violence could be in respect of a child of the defendant, but it could not be a fear that the victim would in the future use serious violence against people generally.

* *To a thing or things done or said (or both) which constituted circumstances of an extremely grave character and caused the defendant to have a justifiable sense of being seriously wronged.* Whether a defendant's sense of being seriously wronged is justifiable will be an objective question for a jury to determine. This sets a high threshold for the circumstances in which a partial defence is available where a person loses self-control in response to words or actions. It effectively restricts the potential availability of a partial defence in cases where a loss of control is attributable to things done or said.

* *A combination of the above two factors.*

Section 55(6) states that in determining whether a loss of self-control had a qualifying trigger:

* the defendant's fear of serious violence is to be disregarded to the extent that it was caused by a thing which the defendant incited to be done or said for the purpose of providing an excuse to use violence;

* a sense of being seriously wronged by a thing done or said is not justifiable if the defendant incited the thing to be done or said for the purpose of providing an excuse to use violence;

* the fact that a thing done or said constituted sexual infidelity is to be disregarded.

1.5.3.3 Suicide Pact

The Homicide Act 1957, s. 4 states:

> (1) It shall be manslaughter, and shall not be murder, for a person acting in pursuance of a suicide pact between him and another to kill the other or be a party to the other being killed by a third person.

1.5.4 Involuntary Manslaughter

Involuntary manslaughter occurs where the defendant causes the death of another but is not shown to have had the required *mens rea* for murder. As with murder, defendants on a charge of manslaughter cannot rely on a mistake induced by their own voluntary intoxication in claiming self-defence.

OFFENCE: **Manslaughter—*Common Law***
- Triable on indictment • Life imprisonment

Involuntary manslaughter, that is, those cases which do not involve the 'special defences' under the Homicide Act 1957 or Coroners and Justice Act 2009, can be separated into occasions where a defendant:

- kills another by an *unlawful* act which was *likely to cause bodily harm*, or
- kills another by *gross negligence*.

1.5.4.1 Manslaughter by Unlawful Act

In order to prove manslaughter by an unlawful act (also called constructive manslaughter), you must prove:

- An unlawful act by the defendant, that is, an act which constitutes *a criminal offence in its own right*, irrespective of the fact that it ultimately results in someone's death.
- The act must be *inherently* unlawful. An act that only becomes unlawful by virtue of the way in which it is carried out will not be enough. For instance, 'driving' is clearly not an inherently unlawful act but becomes so if done dangerously or carelessly on a road or public place. If someone drives dangerously and thereby causes the death of another, the act of driving, albeit carried out in a way that attracts criminal liability, is *not* an 'unlawful act' for the purposes of constructive manslaughter (*Andrews* v *DPP* [1937] AC

576). Hence the existence of statutory offences addressing most instances of death that are caused by poor standards of driving.

- The inherently unlawful act need not be directed or aimed at anyone and can include acts committed against or towards property such as criminal damage or arson (*R* v *Goodfellow* (1986) 83 Cr App R 23).

- Generally, if the actions of the victim break the chain of causation between the defendant's unlawful act and the cause of death, the defendant will not be responsible for the death of that victim (**see chapter 1.2**). This is why drug dealers who supply controlled drugs cannot generally be held liable for the ultimate deaths of their 'victims' unless they have done far more than just supply a drug (*R* v *Dalby* [1982] 1 WLR 425 and *R* v *Armstrong* [1989] Crim LR 149). This view was affirmed in the case of *R* v *Kennedy* [2007] UKHL 38. The circumstances were that the defendant had prepared a dose of heroin for the deceased and had given the syringe to the deceased before leaving the room they were both in. The deceased injected the drug and as a result died. The House of Lords ruled that a supplier of a drug is not guilty of manslaughter where the deceased freely and voluntarily self-administered the drug.

- An *omission* to do something will not suffice as manslaughter by unlawful act requires *an act*.

- That *the act* involved a risk of bodily harm. That risk will be judged *objectively*, that is: would the risk be apparent to a reasonable and sober person watching the act? (*R* v *Church* [1966] 1 QB 59.) Such acts might include dropping a paving stone off a bridge into the path of a train (*DPP* v *Newbury* [1977] AC 500), setting fire to your house (*Goodfellow*) or firing a gun at police officers and then holding someone else in front of you when the officers return fire (*R* v *Pagett* (1983) 76 Cr App R 279).

- 'Harm' must be physical; the risk of emotional or psychological harm does not appear to be enough (*R* v *Dawson* (1985) 81 Cr App R 150). In *R* v *Carey* [2006] EWCA Crim 17 the deceased, aged 15, had been out walking with friends and had met the defendants who had been drinking alcohol all afternoon. The defendants were verbally abusive and threatening to the deceased and her group. One defendant punched one of the deceased's group and another attacked the deceased herself, pulling her hair back and punching her in the face. Two boys intervened and stopped the attack, at which point the deceased ran off but collapsed and died later that night. The medical evidence showed that, unknown to her doctors or her family, the deceased had a severely diseased heart, and that she might not have died had she not been running.

- On appeal it was held that the manslaughter charge (of which the first defendant was convicted) should have been withdrawn from the jury. Although the attack was unpleasant and accompanied by bullying, any injuries caused had been slight. None of the defendants had intended to cause really serious harm to any of the victims and they did not intend that the deceased should die. The Court of Appeal reiterated the general principle that a person who inflicts a slight injury that unforeseeably leads to the death of the victim nevertheless commits manslaughter (*R* v *Church* [1966] 1 QB 59). However, to hold the defendants liable for the deceased's death in the circumstances of this case would have involved an 'unwarranted extension of the law'. The court observed that the law of unlawful act manslaughter required the commission of an unlawful act which was recognised, by a sober and reasonable person, as being *dangerous* and likely to subject the victim to the risk of *some physical harm which in turn caused the victim's death*. *Carey* was considered a clear case where a sober and reasonable bystander would not have recognised a risk of shock leading to a heart attack in the case of an apparently healthy 15-year-old girl. In addition, the only act committed against the deceased that was 'dangerous' was the assault and the physical harm resulting from it did not cause her death.

- That the defendant had the required *mens rea* for the 'unlawful act' (e.g. for an assault or criminal damage) which led to the death of a victim. If he/she did not have that *mens rea*, the offence of manslaughter will not be made out.

- For example, in *R v Lamb* [1967] 2 QB 981 the defendant pretended to fire a revolver at his friend. Although the defendant believed that the weapon would not fire, the chamber containing a bullet moved round to the firing pin and the defendant's friend was killed. Lamb was charged with manslaughter by unlawful act (the unlawful act being assault) but it could not be proved that Lamb had the *mens rea* required (an intent or recklessness to cause a person to apprehend immediate unlawful violence) for an assault (**see chapter 1.9**) and his conviction for manslaughter was quashed.

The accused cannot rely on his/her lack of *mens rea* induced by voluntary intoxication, as manslaughter is a crime of basic intent (*R v Lipman* [1970] 1 QB 152). This was an extreme case in many ways, in which the accused killed his girlfriend while suffering LSD-induced hallucinations that he was at the centre of the earth being attacked by snakes. If the unlawful act alleged were to be a crime of specific intent, then the accused's intoxication should be relevant.

If a defendant uses a motor vehicle as a means to commit an 'unlawful act' (e.g. an assault), he/she can be charged with manslaughter as long as the 'act' goes beyond poor driving. The CPS has published a policy document which sets out the way in which it will deal with cases of bad driving. Unlawful act manslaughter will be considered the most appropriate charge when there is evidence to prove that the vehicle was used as an instrument of attack (but where the necessary intent for murder was absent), or to cause fright, and death resulted. There are, however, reasons of policy (*R v Lawrence* [1982] AC 510) why, in all but the most deliberate of cases, the offences under the Road Traffic Act 1988 should be used (see *Road Policing*, **chapter 3.3**).

1.5.4.2 Manslaughter by Gross Negligence

Manslaughter is the only criminal offence at common law capable of being committed by negligence. The degree of that negligence has been the source of debate over the years and problems have arisen in trying to distinguish the level of negligence required for manslaughter and that required to prove 'recklessness'.

A charge of manslaughter may be brought where a person, by an instance of *gross negligence*, has brought about the death of another. The ingredients of this offence essentially consist of death resulting from a negligent breach of a duty of care owed by the defendant to the victim in circumstances so reprehensible as to amount to gross negligence (*R v Misra and Srivastava* [2004] EWCA Crim 2375). The most difficult task in defining the degree of negligence that will qualify as 'gross' falls to the trial judge when addressing the jury. Whether a defendant's conduct will amount to gross negligence is a question of fact for the jury to decide in the light of all the evidence (*R v Bateman* (1925) 19 Cr App R 8).

Although the lack of clarity around this offence has resulted in its being challenged under the European Convention on Human Rights, the Court of Appeal has held that its ingredients are sufficiently certain for those purposes (*R v Misra and Srivastava*). What is clear from the decided cases is that civil liability, although a starting point for establishing the breach of a duty of care, is not enough to amount to 'gross negligence', neither is objective 'recklessness' (*R v Adomako* [1995] 1 AC 171).

The test in *Adomako* as summarised by Lord Mackay seems to provide the leading authority on the area—that test for the jury being: '...whether, having regard to the risk of death involved, the conduct of the defendant was so bad in all the circumstances as to amount in their judgment to a criminal act or omission'.

It is not possible to bring proceedings for gross negligence manslaughter against a company or other organisation to which the offence under the Corporate Manslaughter and Corporate Homicide Act 2007 applies (s. 20 of the Corporate Manslaughter and Corporate Homicide Act 2007).

1.5.5 Corporate Manslaughter and Corporate Homicide Act 2007

An organisation (including a government department) can be convicted of a corporate manslaughter offence if the way in which its activities were managed or organised caused a person's death and amounted to a gross breach of the duty of care owed to the deceased by virtue of that person being held in custody.

OFFENCE: **Corporate Manslaughter—*Corporate Manslaughter and Corporate Homicide Act 2007, s. 1***

> • Triable on indictment • Unlimited fine

The Corporate Manslaughter and Corporate Homicide Act 2007, s. 1 states:

> (1) An organisation to which this section applies is guilty of an offence if the way in which its activities are managed or organised—
>
> (a) causes a person's death, and
>
> (b) amounts to a gross breach of a relevant duty of care owed by the organisation to the deceased.

KEYNOTE

The offence is concerned with the way in which an organisation's activities were managed or organised. Under this test, the courts will examine management systems and practices across the organisation, and whether the adequate standard of care was applied to the fatal activity.

The threshold for the offence is gross negligence. The way in which the activities were managed or organised must have fallen far below what could reasonably have been expected.

The failure to manage or organise activities properly must have caused the victim's death.

A duty of care is an obligation that an organisation has to take reasonable steps to protect a person's safety. These duties exist, for example, in respect of the systems of work and equipment used by employees, the condition of worksites and other premises occupied by an organisation and in relation to products or services supplied to customers. The duty must be a *relevant* one. Relevant duties are set out in s. 2 of the Act and include:

- Employer and occupier duties
- Duties connected to:
  - ✦ Supplying goods and services
  - ✦ Commercial activities
  - ✦ Construction and maintenance work
  - ✦ Using or keeping plant, vehicles or other things
- Duties relating to holding a person in custody.

In relation to policing and law enforcement in the Act, there are some exceptions to the relevant duty of care obligation (s. 5 of the Act), these are in:

- Operations for dealing with terrorism, civil unrest or serious disorder, that involve the carrying on of policing or law-enforcement activities where officers or employees of the public authority in question come under attack, or face the threat of attack or violent resistance, in the course of the operations.
- Activities carried out in preparation for, or directly in support of, such operations as above.
- Training of a hazardous nature or training carried out in a hazardous way in order to improve or maintain the effectiveness of officers or employees of the public authority with respect to such operations as above.

Police services are subject to the Act and could be prosecuted in matters where death relates to the organisation's responsibility *as an employer* (or to others working for the organisation) or as *an occupier of premises.*

The Corporate Manslaughter and Corporate Homicide Act 2007, s. 1 states:

> (2) The organisations to which this section applies are—
>
> (a) a corporation;
>
> (b) a department or other body listed in Schedule 1;
>
> (c) a police force;
>
> (d) a partnership or trade union or employers' association, that is an employer.

The Corporate Manslaughter and Corporate Homicide Act 2007, s. 1 states:

> (3) An organisation is guilty of an offence under this section only if the way in which its activities are managed or organised by its senior management is a substantial element in the breach referred to in subsection (1).

1.5.5.1 Meaning of 'Relevant Duty of Care'

The Corporate Manslaughter and Corporate Homicide Act 2007, s. 2 states:

> (1) A 'relevant duty of care', in relation to an organisation, means any of the following duties owed by it under the law of negligence—
>   (a) a duty owed to its employees or other persons working for the organisation or performing services for it;
>   (b) a duty owed as occupier of premises;
>   (c) a duty owed in connection with—
>   (i) the supply by the organisation of goods or services (whether for consideration or not),
>   (ii) the carrying on by the organisation of any construction or maintenance operations,
>   (iii) the carrying on by the organisation of any other activity on a commercial basis, or
>   (iv) the use or keeping by the organisation of any plant, vehicle or other thing;
>   (d) a duty owed to a person who, by reason of being a person within subsection (2), is someone for whose safety the organisation is responsible.

(2) A person is within this subsection if—

    (a)   he is detained at a custodial institution or in a custody area at a court, a police station or customs premises;

    (aa) he is detained in service custody premises;

    (b)   he is detained at a removal centre or a short-term holding facility or in pre-departure accommodation;

    (c)   he is being transported in a vehicle, or being held in any premises, in pursuance of prison escort arrangements or immigration escort arrangements;

    (d)   he is living in secure accommodation in which he has been placed;

    (e)   he is a detained patient.

KEYNOTE

The Act applies to deaths of persons owed a duty of care by virtue of:

- being detained at a custodial institution, or *in a custody area at a court or police station*, or a removal centre or short-term holding facility or in pre-departure accommodation;
- being transported in a vehicle;
- being held in any premises in pursuance of prison escort arrangements or immigration escort arrangements;
- living in secure accommodation in which the person has been placed; or
- being a detained patient (see s. 2(2)).

This means that it ought to be easier to prosecute organisations who hold people in custody, including government departments, for grossly negligent management failings which cause a death, without the need to identify a 'directing mind' of the organisation. Where the death is not attributable to a breach of such a duty of care the organisation might still be liable under other duties contained in the Act (e.g. a duty owed to employees or as occupier of premises under s. 2(1)(a)–(c)).

The Act will apply to all custody providers, whether public or private (i.e. contracted service providers). Liability will ultimately be determined by the courts, depending on the circumstances of the case and e.g. the terms of the contractual arrangements in place.

The commencement of the custody provisions will not apply retrospectively so any offence committed wholly or partly before 1 September 2011 will be considered under the previous law. This will be the case if any of the conduct or events alleged to constitute the offence occurred before the commencement of the provisions.

It is worth noting that the custody provisions do not create additional duties of care. All custody providers already owe duties of care to detainees, to the same extent that they do to e.g. their staff or the public, by virtue of one of the other duties contained in the Act. The specific duty of care owed to detained persons is relevant for the purposes of the offence in the Act.

1.5.6   Causing or Allowing a Child or Vulnerable Adult to Die or Suffer Serious Physical Harm

This offence came about as a result of the difficulties that arise where a child or other vulnerable person dies or suffers serious physical harm as a result of an unlawful act (or omission) of one of several people but it cannot be shown which of them actually caused the death or allowed it to occur.

OFFENCE: **Causing or Allowing a Child or Vulnerable Adult to Die or Suffer Serious Harm—*Domestic Violence, Crime and Victims Act 2004, s. 5***

    • Triable on indictment • Where the child or vulnerable adult dies, 14 years' imprisonment or a fine or both • Where the child or vulnerable adult suffers serious physical harm, 10 years' imprisonment or a fine or both

The Domestic Violence, Crime and Victims Act 2004, s. 5 states:

(1) A person ('D') is guilty of an offence if—
   (a) a child or vulnerable adult ('V') dies or suffers serious physical harm as a result of the unlawful act of a person who—
      (i) was a member of the same household as V, and
      (ii) had frequent contact with him,
   (b) D was such a person at the time of that act,
   (c) at that time there was a significant risk of serious physical harm being caused to V by the unlawful act of such a person, and
   (d) either D was the person whose act caused the death or serious physical harm—
      (i) D was, or ought to have been, aware of the risk mentioned in paragraph (c),
      (ii) D failed to take such steps as he could reasonably have been expected to take to protect V from the risk, and
      (iii) the act occurred in circumstances of the kind that D foresaw or ought to have foreseen.

KEYNOTE

'Child' means a person under the age of 16 and 'vulnerable adult' means a person aged 16 or over whose ability to protect him/herself from violence, abuse or neglect is significantly impaired through physical or mental disability or illness, through old age or otherwise (s. 5(6)).

It is necessary to prove that the victim died or suffered serious physical harm *as a result of the unlawful act* of a person who fits a number of criteria. For these purposes 'act' includes 'omissions' and an act or omission will generally only be 'unlawful' if it would have amounted to an offence (see s. 5(5) and (6)). It must be shown that the defendant was, *at the time of the act,* a member of the same household as the victim *and* had frequent contact with the victim. For these purposes people will be a member of a particular household if they visit it so often and for such periods of time that it is reasonable to regard them as a member of it *even if they do not actually live there* (s. 5(4)(a)). Where, as often happens, the victim lived in different households at different times, the 'same household' criterion will mean the household in which the victim was living at the time of the act that caused the death or serious physical harm (s. 5(4)(b)).

Finally it must be shown that, at the time, there was a significant risk of serious physical harm being caused to the victim by the unlawful act of a person meeting these criteria. 'Serious harm' means grievous bodily harm for the purposes of the Offences against the Person Act 1861 (**see para. 1.9.7.3**).

Once these elements have been established, the offence is completed in one of two ways: directly (i.e. by the defendant's act causing the victim's death or serious physical harm) or indirectly and the prosecution does not have to prove which alternative applies (see s. 5(2)). However, in cases where indirect causation is suspected, three further things must be shown, namely that:

(1) the defendant was (or ought to have been) aware of the risk of serious physical harm;
(2) the defendant failed to take such steps he/she could reasonably have been expected to take to protect the victim from the risk; *and*
(3) the act occurred in the kind of circumstances that the defendant foresaw (or ought to have foreseen).

Unless the defendant is the mother or father of the victim (a) he/she cannot be charged with an offence under this section if aged under 16 at the time of the act, and (b) restrictions will be made on what steps would have been reasonable for a defendant to have taken while under that age (see s. 5(3)).

1.5.7 Encouraging or Assisting Suicide

There is no defence of 'mercy killing' or formal recognition of euthanasia under the current legal system. However, there is a specific offence of encouraging or assisting another to take their own life.

OFFENCE: **Encouraging or Assisting Suicide—*Suicide Act 1961, s. 2***
   • Triable on indictment • 14 years' imprisonment

The Suicide Act 1961, s. 2 states:

(1) A person ('D') commits an offence if—
    (a) D does an act capable of encouraging or assisting the suicide or attempted suicide of another person, and
    (b) D's act was intended to encourage or assist suicide or an attempt at suicide.
(1A) The person referred to in subsection (1)(a) need not be a specific person (or class of persons) known to, or identified by, D.
(1B) D may commit an offence under this section whether or not a suicide, or an attempt at suicide, occurs.

KEYNOTE

This offence is an alternative verdict on a charge of murder/manslaughter (Suicide Act 1961, s. 2(2)). The person committing the offence need not know, or even be able to identify, the other person. For example, the author of a website promoting suicide who intends that one of more of its readers will commit suicide is guilty of an offence, even though the author may never know the identity of those who access the website. The offence applies whether or not a person commits or attempts suicide.

The consent of the DPP is required to initiate proceedings for this offence (s. 2(4) of the Suicide Act 1961).

1.5.7.1 Acts Capable of Encouraging or Assisting

The Suicide Act 1961, s. 2A states:

(1) If D arranges for a person ('D2') to do an act that is capable of encouraging or assisting the suicide or attempted suicide of another person and D2 does that act, D is also to be treated for the purposes of this Act as having done it.
(2) Where the facts are such that an act is not capable of encouraging or assisting suicide or attempted suicide, for the purposes of this Act it is to be treated as so capable if the act would have been so capable had the facts been as D believed them to be at the time of the act or had subsequent events happened in the manner D believed they would happen (or both).
(3) A reference in this Act to a person ('P') doing an act that is capable of encouraging the suicide or attempted suicide of another person includes a reference to P doing so by threatening another person or otherwise putting pressure on another person to commit or attempt suicide.

KEYNOTE

Section 2A(1) creates a liability when a defendant arranges for another to encourage or assist suicide so that responsibility cannot be avoided by using a third party as a conduit to commit the offence. Note that that third party must actually do the 'act', i.e. he/she must encourage or assist the suicide.

Section 2A(2) has the effect that an act can be capable of encouraging or assisting suicide even if the circumstances are such that it was impossible for the act actually to encourage or assist suicide. An act is therefore treated as capable of encouraging and assisting suicide if it would have been so capable had the facts been as the defendant believed them to be at the time of the act (e.g. if pills provided with the intention that they will assist a person to commit suicide are thought to be lethal but are in fact harmless) or had subsequent events happened as the defendant believed they would (e.g. if lethal pills which were sent to a person with the intention that the person would use them to commit or attempt to commit suicide get lost in the post), or both.

Section 2A(3) clarifies that references to doing an act capable of encouraging or assisting another to commit or attempt suicide include a reference to doing so by threatening another person or otherwise putting pressure on another person to commit or attempt suicide.

An 'act' will include a course of conduct.

Providers of information society services (any service normally provided for remuneration, at a distance, by electronic means and at the individual request of a recipient of services) who are established in England, Wales or Northern Ireland are covered by the offence of encouraging or assisting suicide even when they are operating in other European Economic Area states (sch. 12 to the Coroners and Justice Act 2009). The schedule provides exemptions for Internet Service Providers from the offence in limited circumstances, such as where they are acting as mere conduits for information that is capable, and provided with the intention, of encouraging or assisting suicide or are storing it as caches or hosts.

1.5.8 Solicitation of Murder

OFFENCE: **Encouraging Another to Murder—*Offences Against the Person Act 1861, s. 4***

* Triable on indictment • Life imprisonment

The Offences Against the Person Act 1861, s. 4 states:

> Whosoever shall solicit, encourage, persuade or endeavour to persuade, or shall propose to any person, to murder any other person, whether he be a subject of Her Majesty or not, and whether he be within the Queen's dominions or not, shall be guilty of [an offence].

KEYNOTE

Examples of this offence include *R* v *El-Faisal* [2004] EWCA Crim 343 where the defendant, a minister of Islam, was convicted after creating audio tapes containing public speeches given by him encouraging the killing of non-believers. A further example was in *R* v *Ahmad* [2012] EWCA Crim 959 where the offender published material on a website encouraging the murder of Members of Parliament and providing their personal details.

Although the soliciting must be done from within the jurisdiction, the phrase 'whether he be a subject of Her Majesty or not, and whether he be within the Queen's dominions or not' has been interpreted so that it applies not only to the person to be murdered but also the person being solicited. Thus in *R* v *Abu Hamza* [2007] QB 659 it was no defence that the persons being solicited were of various nationalities and the murders were to take place abroad and that it was not proved that any of those solicited to murder were British nationals.

The proposed victim may be outside the United Kingdom.

It does not matter whether or not the person is in fact encouraged to commit murder, but the offence is not complete until someone is in receipt of the solicitation although the act of sending it can constitute an attempt (*R* v *Krause* (1902) 66 JP 121). Encouraging a pregnant woman to kill her child in the future, after it shall have been born alive, is an offence within this section (*R* v *Shephard* (1919) 2 KB 125).

This offence may be appropriate in cases where a person is trying to arrange a 'contract killing'. In *R* v *Kayani* [1997] 2 Cr App R (S) 313 the defendant was sentenced to 12 years' imprisonment for soliciting the murder of his niece and her husband. He was arrested by an undercover police officer posing as a contract killer, to whom payment of £20,000 was tendered partly in cash and partly in heroin. For this reason this offence may be preferred in cases where the defendant has 'conspired' with *one* other person and that person is an undercover police officer.

1.6 Misuse of Drugs

1.6.1 Introduction

This chapter deals, in the main, with offences created by the Misuse of Drugs Act 1971. As some of the concepts associated with drug offences, e.g. 'possession' and 'supply', are important to assist in understanding the legislation, they are dealt with before any offences associated with them. A methodical approach is then taken by dealing with drug offences in the order of possession, supply and production finishing with an examination of other drug related offences and police powers.

1.6.2 Classification

Drugs that are subject to the provisions of the Misuse of Drugs Act 1971 are listed in parts I, II and III of sch. 2 to the Act. The principal purpose of having three classes of controlled drugs is to identify the level of sentence (*R* v *Ryan and Jenkins* [2014] EWCA Crim 791).

The divisions are made largely on the basis of each substance's potential effects on both the person taking it and society in general. The list of controlled drugs is large, and for full details reference should be made to sch. 2 to the Misuse of Drugs Act 1971. Examples of some of the more commonly encountered drugs include:

- **Class A**—This class includes heroin (diamorphine), methadone, cocaine, LSD, 'Ecstasy' (MDMA) and 'crystal meth' (methylamphetamine). It also includes fungus (of any kind) which contains psilocin (such as 'magic mushrooms').
- **Class B**—This class includes cannabis, cannabis resin, codeine, ketamine and ritalin (methylphenidate).
- **Class C**—This class includes valium (diazepam), khat (the leaves, stems or shoots of the plant of the species Catha edulis) and GHB (gamma hydroxybutyrate).

If the charge alleges possession of one particular drug then that drug must be identified.

Note that, although a substance may appear in sch. 2 to the Act, there may be restrictions on the occasions where possession is treated as an offence (**see para. 1.6.3.7**).

It is not necessary, when prosecuting an offence, to distinguish between the various chemical forms in which a drug exists (i.e. as a salt, ester or other form) (*R* v *Greensmith* [1983] 1 WLR 1124).

A defendant's admission may, in some cases, be relied upon to prove his/her knowledge as to what a particular substance is (*R* v *Chatwood* [1980] 1 WLR 874).

1.6.2.1 Temporary Class Drug Orders

The Home Secretary has the power, under the Misuse of Drugs Act 1971, to make any drug subject to temporary control.

Temporary class drug orders can be made if the following two conditions are met:

(1) the drug is not already controlled under the Act as a Class A, B or C drug;
(2) the ACMD [Advisory Council on the Misuse of Drugs] has been consulted and determined that the order should be made, or the Home Secretary has received a recommendation from the Advisory Council that the order should be made, on the basis that it appears to the Home Secretary that:

(a) the drug is being, or is likely to be, misused; and

(b) the misuse is having, or is capable of having, harmful effects.

The order will come into immediate effect and will last for up to 12 months, subject to Parliament agreeing to it within 40 sitting days of the order being made. The order enables the government to act to protect the public against harmful new psychoactive substances, while expert advice is being prepared.

Such a drug will be referred to as a 'temporary class drug' and will be a 'controlled drug' for the purposes of the Misuse of Drugs Act 1971, and other legislation such as the Proceeds of Crime Act 2002, unless otherwise stated. With the *exception of the possession* offence, all the offences under the Misuse of Drugs Act will apply including possession in connection with an offence or prohibition, under ss. 3, 4 and 5(3) of the Act, i.e. possession with intent to supply. Offences committed under the Act in relation to a temporary class drug are subject to the following maximum penalties:

- 14 years' imprisonment and an unlimited fine on indictment, and
- six months' imprisonment and a £5,000 fine on summary conviction.

Simple possession of a temporary class drug is not an offence under the 1971 Act; however, law enforcement officers have been given the following powers to enable them to take action to prevent possible harm to the individual:

- Search and detain a person (or vehicle etc.) where there are reasonable grounds to suspect that the person is in possession of a temporary class drug.
- Seize, detain and dispose of a suspected temporary class drug.
- Arrest or charge a person who commits the offence of intentionally obstructing an enforcement officer in the exercise of their powers.

1.6.2.2 Cannabis

The Misuse of Drugs Act 1971, s. 37 states:

'cannabis' (except in the expression 'cannabis resin') means any plant of the genus *Cannabis* or any part of any such plant (by whatever name designated) except that it does not include cannabis resin or any of the following products after separation from the rest of the plant, namely—
(a) mature stalk of any such plant,
(b) fibre produced from mature stalk of any such plant, and
(c) seed of any such plant,
'cannabis resin' means the separated resin, whether crude or purified, obtained from any plant of the genus *Cannabis*.

KEYNOTE

Cannabis is a Class B drug. Therefore cannabis, cannabis resin, cannabis oil, cannabinol and its derivatives, any preparations or other product containing these substances and any substance which is an ester or ether either of cannabinol or of a cannabinol derivative are also Class B drugs. As cannabis and cannabis resin are both in the same class for the purposes of the 1971 Act there would be no duplicity if a person is charged with possessing either one or the other in the same charge (*R v Best* (1980) 70 Cr App R 21).

1.6.3 Possession

'Possession' is a neutral concept, not implying any kind of fault, blame or guilt. This is the key feature to recognise before considering specific offences under *any* legislation. There are two elements to possession; the physical element and the mental element (*R v Lambert* [2002] 2 AC 545).

1.6.3.1 Custody or Control

The physical element involves proof that the thing is in the custody of the defendant or subject to his control. For example, if X has a wrap of cocaine in his jacket pocket, X has control of the wrap of cocaine (although *mere custody* does not mean that X is in 'possession' at this stage).

This approach is enlarged by s. 37(3) of the Misuse of Drugs Act 1971 which states that 'For the purposes of this Act the things which a person has in his possession shall be taken to include anything subject to his control which is in the custody of another'.

EXAMPLE

X buys a controlled drug via the Internet, directing that it be sent by post to his home address. X is in possession of that drug from the time it arrives through his letterbox. (*R v Peaston* (1979) 69 Cr App R 203)

1.6.3.2 Knowledge of Possession

The second element involves that the defendant knows that the thing in question is under his/her control. He/she need not know what its nature is, but as long as he/she knows that the thing, whatever it is, is under his/her control, it is in his/her possession.

EXAMPLE

X and Y are walking along a street. X is going through his pockets looking for his wallet and as he is searching for the wallet he hands Y several tablets of Ecstasy and asks him to hold onto them while he continues searching. Y has no idea that the tablets he takes hold of are a controlled drug.

- Y has control of the Ecstasy tablets (they are in his hand)
- Y has knowledge of the presence of the Ecstasy tablets in his hand
- *Therefore Y has possession of the Ecstasy tablets.*

Nobody is suggesting, at this stage, that Y is guilty of an offence. Of course Y could rightly be arrested on *suspicion* of possessing a controlled drug but arresting on suspicion that a person has committed an offence and *proving* guilt in relation to it are two different things. Indeed, Y's lack of knowledge about what the tablets are may afford him a defence (**see para. 1.6.9**). But the fact remains that ignorance of, or mistake as to the quality of the thing in question does not prevent the accused being in possession of it.

What if the thing is inside a container, e.g. a box, a bag or a cigarette packet, and the person claims not to have known the thing was inside the container? In such cases, the common law makes the same requirements; you need to show that the person had custody of the container together with a knowledge that it (the container) contained *something*.

EXAMPLE

X is given a packet of cigarettes by Y. X believes the packet contains cigarettes only. The packet does contain several cigarettes but also contains a wrap of cocaine. X does not know about the wrap of cocaine and puts the pack of cigarettes into his pocket.

- X has custody of the pack of cigarettes (they are in his pocket)
- X has knowledge of the presence of the pack of cigarettes (X put them there)
- X knows that the pack of cigarettes contains *something*
- *Therefore X has* possession *of the wrap of cocaine.*

Nobody is suggesting X is guilty of an offence but he is in 'possession' of the wrap of cocaine.

In *R* v *Forsyth* [2001] EWCA Crim 2926, the defendant argued that there was a distinction between a person carrying something *in* a container and a person carrying *something inside something else* in a container. In that particular case, the defendant was found in possession of a box which contained a safe; inside the safe was a significant quantity of a controlled drug. The defendant argued that this type of possession should be differentiated from the situation where someone simply had possession of a box with drugs in it. The Court of Appeal ruled that there was no difference and the issues of proof were the same.

A person does not possess something of which he/she is completely unaware as there would be no knowledge of possession. If a drug is put into someone's pocket without his/her knowledge, he/she is not in possession of it (*Warner* v *Metropolitan Police Commissioner* [1969] 2 AC 256).

1.6.3.3 Joint Possession

To show that two or more persons are in possession of a controlled drug requires more than a mere ability to control it (*R* v *Kousar* [2009] EWCA Crim 139). Mere knowledge of the presence of a drug in the hands of a confederate is not enough; joint possession must be established (*R* v *Searle* [1971] Crim LR 592). In *Searle* it was stated that this could be established by asking the question 'do the drugs form part of a common pool from which all had the right to draw?' In *R* v *Strong* (1989) *The Times*, 26 January 1990, the prosecution put the case on the basis that there was joint possession, that is, each of the co-accused had control of one or more of the packages of cannabis. The Court of Appeal followed *Searle*, and said that what was being looked for was whether each person had the right to say what should be done with the cannabis. Mere presence in the same vehicle as the drugs, and knowing they were there, was not sufficient.

Further issues that can arise from this view of 'possession' were highlighted in *Adams* v *DPP* [2002] EWHC 438 (Admin) where a small quantity of controlled drugs were found in the defendant's home during the execution of a search warrant. There was no proof that the drugs were owned by the defendant, nor that she was specifically aware of their presence but she *did* know that her home was used by various people who were highly likely to bring controlled drugs into it. She was convicted of possession. In hearing her appeal, the Administrative Court held that, where knowledge of possession of drugs was limited to the fact that a visitor had brought drugs into the defendant's home intending to take them, that was not sufficient evidence from which it was appropriate to infer that she had control over the drugs.

The court also held that giving consent (explicitly or impliedly) for the use of a controlled drug did not of itself constitute possession. Similarly, an inference that the defendant knew whose drugs had been found in her home did not amount to evidence of control over the drug itself even though she may well have been able to exercise control over what actually took place in her home.

1.6.3.4 Points to Prove

Once 'possession' has been proved it is then necessary to prove that what the defendant possesses is, in fact, a controlled drug. If this is established then the defendant has a case to answer in relation to the offence of possession of a controlled drug.

....

EXAMPLE

X is subject to a stop and search procedure under s. 23 of the Misuse of Drugs Act 1971 (see para. 1.6.17.1). During the search several packets containing cannabis resin are found in X's coat pocket.

In order to prove 'possession' of the cannabis for the purpose of the possession of a controlled drug offence, you must show:

- that X possessed the cannabis (X has custody/control of it and he knows it is in his possession) and
- that the contents of the packets contain a controlled drug.

....

1.6.3.5 Quality

In the above example, *you would not have to show that X knew what the resin was*. That is, you do not need to show that X knew the *quality* of what he possessed to prove that X 'possessed' it.

If the defendant admits to knowing that the cannabis resin was there but thought it was chocolate, he is in possession of it (*R v Marriott* [1971] 1 WLR 187).

Therefore if a defendant had a packet of cigarettes with him and admitted to knowing that he had them, he would be in possession of a controlled drug if one cigarette was shown to have contained cannabis. The fact that the defendant thought they contained tobacco would be irrelevant to the 'possession' concept (*R v Searle* [1971] Crim LR 592) (although he may have a defence under s. 28: **see para. 1.6.9**).

1.6.3.6 Quantity

The *quantity* of a controlled drug, however, may be so small that the defendant could not possibly have known about it; therefore it could not be 'possessed'.

The House of Lords suggested that if something is 'visible, tangible and measurable', that may be sufficient (*R v Boyesen* [1982] AC 768). If the amount recovered is too small to support a charge of possession, it might be used to prove earlier possession of the drug (*R v Graham* [1970] 1 WLR 113 and *Hambleton* v *Callinan* [1968] 2 QB 427 where traces of a controlled drug in a urine sample were held to be possible evidence of earlier possession of that drug).

Quantity is not only relevant to the fact of possession; it is also relevant to the intention of the person in whose possession the drug is found. Larger quantities (particularly if they are also divided into smaller amounts) may indicate an intention to supply and may be proof of that intention in some circumstances.

1.6.3.7 Possession of a Controlled Drug

OFFENCE: **Possession of Controlled Drug—*Misuse of Drugs Act 1971, s. 5***
- Triable either way • Class A (seven years' imprisonment and/or a fine on indictment; six months' imprisonment and/or prescribed sum summarily) • Class B (five years' imprisonment and/or a fine on indictment; three months' imprisonment and/or a fine summarily) • Class C (two years' imprisonment and/or a fine on indictment; three months' imprisonment and/or a fine summarily) • See Keynote for possession of cannabis or cannabis resin

The Misuse of Drugs Act 1971, s. 5 states:

(2) Subject to section 28 of this Act and to subsection (4) below, it is an offence for a person to have a controlled drug in his possession in contravention of subsection (1)...

KEYNOTE

Section 28 provides a general defence to certain drugs offences and is examined at **para. 1.6.9**.

Where the controlled drug involved is a fungus containing psilocin (a class A drug) or an ester of psilocin (commonly known as magic mushrooms) possession will not be unlawful in certain circumstances. In summary, those circumstances are generally where the fungus is growing *uncultivated* and it:

- is picked by a person already in *lawful possession* of it (e.g. the landowner on whose land the mushrooms are growing) for the purpose of delivering it (as soon as is reasonably practicable) into the custody of a person lawfully entitled to take custody of it and it remains in that person's possession for (and in accordance with) that purpose; or
- it is picked by anyone either for the purpose of delivering it (as soon as reasonably practicable) into the custody of a person lawfully entitled to take custody of it or destroying it (as soon as is reasonably practicable) and it is held for that purpose.

Possession of cannabis can be dealt with under the Penalty Notice for Disorder (PND) Scheme. PNDs cannot be issued for any other drug related offences other than possession of cannabis or cannabis derivatives. PNDs may be issued to any adult found in possession of cannabis for personal use; they are not appropriate for offenders under the age of 18.

Possession of a 'temporary class drug' (see para. 1.6.2.1) is not an offence under this section (s. 5(2A)).

1.6.3.8   Section 5—The Defence to Unlawful Possession

Section 5 provides a defence to an offence of unlawful possession:

(4) In any proceedings for an offence under subsection (2) above in which it is proved that the accused had a controlled drug in his possession, it shall be a defence for him to prove—
   (a) that, knowing or suspecting it to be a controlled drug, he took possession of it for the purpose of preventing another from committing or continuing to commit an offence in connection with that drug and that as soon as possible after taking possession of it he took all such steps as were reasonably open to him to destroy the drug or to deliver it into the custody of a person lawfully entitled to take custody of it; or
   (b) that, knowing or suspecting it to be a controlled drug, he took possession of it for the purpose of delivering it into the custody of a person lawfully entitled to take custody of it and that as soon as possible after taking possession of it he took all such steps as were reasonably open to him to deliver it into the custody of such a person.

KEYNOTE

Defence under s. 5(4)(a)

The purpose in taking possession of the controlled drug under s. 5(4)(a) must be to prevent *another* from committing (in the future) or continuing to commit an offence in connection with *that* drug.

This situation might arise where a parent finds a child in possession of something which appears to be a controlled drug. Provided that that person takes all reasonable steps to destroy the drug or to take it to someone lawfully entitled to possess it (like a police officer), *as soon as possible after taking possession of it*, he/she would be able to use the defence under s. 5(4)(a).

When the accused buried drugs (cannabis) it was not sufficient to satisfy the defence under s. 5(4)(a) that the forces of nature might or would destroy the drug eventually: rather it was for the accused to show that he took all such reasonable steps as were reasonably open to him to destroy them and the acts of destruction must be his (*R* v *Murphy* [2002] EWCA Crim 1587).

Defence under s. 5(4)(b)

The second situation (under s. 5(4)(b)) may arise where a person finds what he/she believes to be a controlled drug and he/she takes possession of it *solely for the purpose of delivering it to a person lawfully entitled to take custody of it*. The defendant must prove that this was his/her intention at the time of taking possession (*R* v *Dempsey* (1986) 82 Cr App R 291).

Section 5(4) will not provide a defence to any other offence connected with the controlled drug (e.g. supplying or offering to supply).

Duress of circumstances is not a defence to this, or any other, offence under the Misuse of Drugs Act 1971 (see para. 1.4.7).

1.6.4 Supplying

In *R* v *Maginnis* [1987] AC 303, the House of Lords held that 'supply' involves more than a mere transfer of physical control of the item from one person to another but includes a further concept, namely that of 'enabling the recipient to apply the thing handed over to purposes for which he desires or has a duty to apply it'. In other words *the person to whom the drug is given must derive some benefit from being given the drug.*

Supplying Explained

So the key to working out if there has been a 'supply' is to ask 'Does being given the drug benefit the person to whom the drug has been given?' If the answer is 'Yes' then the person *giving the drug* is 'supplying' it.

KEYNOTE

In *R* v *Dempsey* (1986) 82 Cr App R 291, a registered drug addict (A) was in lawful possession of a drug. A asked his partner (B) to hold on to some of that drug while he went to administer the remainder of it to himself in a gents' toilet. Both A and B were arrested, A being subsequently charged with 'supplying' B with the drug.

There is no 'supply' from A to B as when A gives the drug to B, B *does not benefit* from the action; B is simply holding on to the drug (although, of course, B would be in unlawful possession of the drug at this stage). If A had given the drug to B for B to use, there would be a 'supply' by A to B as B *is benefiting* from the action; B gets to use the drug. If B intends to give back the drug to A then B would commit the offence of possession with intent to supply.

In *R* v *Maginnis* [1987] AC 303, a drug trafficker (A) temporarily left drugs with (B); B expected A to pick up the drugs the following day and was charged and convicted of possession with intent to supply. The same approach taken with *Dempsey* applies. In *Maginnis* when A gives the drugs to B, B does not benefit from it and there is no 'supply' from A to B; if B returns the drugs to A there is a 'supply' from B to A as A benefits from being given the drug (to sell or use). As B intends to return the drug to A, B is in possession with intent to supply.

If the drug trafficker in *Maginnis* had given the custodian of the drug £50 as a reward for holding the drug then there would have been a 'supply' from A to B as B would benefit from holding the drug (he has been paid £50, benefiting financially from being given the drug).

The issue has been further explored in a case involving a person who claimed that he had been coerced into holding controlled drugs for unnamed dealers. When found in possession of the drugs, the defendant claimed the defence of duress (as to which, **see chapter 1.4**) and said that he had only been an 'involuntary custodian' of them, intending to return them at a later date. The Court of Appeal decided that it was irrelevant whether a person was a voluntary or involuntary custodian of the drugs and that an intention to return them to their depositor amounted to an 'intention to supply' (*R* v *Panton* [2001] EWCA Crim 611).

Dividing up controlled drugs which have been jointly purchased and then handing them out so that persons may use the drug will amount to 'supplying' (*R* v *Buckley* (1979) 69 Cr App R 371).

If a police informer provides a controlled drug to another in order that the other be arrested, there will still be a 'supplying' of the drug (*R* v *X* [1994] Crim LR 827).

Injecting Others

Injecting another with that person's own controlled drug has been held *not to amount* to 'supplying' in a case where the defendant assisted in pushing down the plunger of a syringe that the other person was already using (*R* v *Harris* [1968] 1 WLR 769). It may amount to an offence of 'poisoning' under s. 23 of the Offences Against the Person Act 1861 (**see chapter 1.10**). The problem with charging the supplier of drugs for self-injection by someone who then dies as a result lies in the issues of causation. While there are some authorities which say that supply of a drug for self-injection which leads to the death of the recipient *can potentially* amount to unlawful act manslaughter, difficulties have arisen and the general view is that the supplier is unlikely to be held liable for *causing* death in such a case (*R v Dias* [2001] EWCA Crim 2986). Where the defendant *actually carries out* the injection, liability for causing the death of another in this way can be made out even if the drug injected is not a controlled drug (*R v Andrews* [2002] EWCA Crim 3021, involving an injection of insulin with consent).

1.6.4.1 Supplying a Controlled Drug

OFFENCE: **Supplying Controlled Drug—*Misuse of Drugs Act 1971, s. 4(3)***
• Triable either way • Class A (life imprisonment and/or a fine on indictment; six months' imprisonment and/or prescribed sum summarily) • Class B (14 years' imprisonment and/or a fine on indictment; six months' imprisonment and/or prescribed sum summarily) • Class C (14 years' imprisonment and/or a fine on indictment; three months' imprisonment and/or a fine summarily)

The Misuse of Drugs Act 1971, s. 4 states:

(3) Subject to section 28 of this Act, it is an offence for a person—
  (a) to supply or offer to supply a controlled drug to another in contravention of subsection (1) above; or
  (b) to be concerned in the supplying of such a drug to another in contravention of that subsection; or
  (c) to be concerned in the making to another in contravention of that subsection of an offer to supply such a drug.

KEYNOTE

The three ingredients of this offence were set out in *R v Hughes* (1985) 81 Cr App R 344:

(a) the supply of a drug to another, or as the case may be, the making of an offer to supply the drug to another in contravention of s. 4(1) of the Misuse of Drugs Act 1971;

(b) participation by the accused in an enterprise involving such supply or, as the case may be, such an offer to supply; and

(c) knowledge by the accused of the nature of the enterprise, i.e. that it involved supply of a drug or, as the case may be, offering to supply a drug.

Proof of actual supply is a prerequisite for an offence charged under s. 4(3)(b).
'Supplying' includes distributing (s. 37(1)).

Offering to Supply

An offer may be by words or conduct. If by words, it must be ascertained whether an offer to supply a controlled drug was made. If words are used, the defence under s. 28 (**see para. 1.6.9**) does not appear to apply (*R v Mitchell* [1992] Crim LR 723).

Whether the accused had a controlled drug in his/her possession, had access to controlled drugs or whether the substance in his/her possession was a controlled drug at all is immaterial (*R v Goodward* [1992] Crim LR 588). The offence is committed whether or not the offer is genuine and once an offer is made the offence is complete; it cannot be withdrawn. If the offer is made to an undercover police officer, the offence is still committed and the defendant cannot claim that such an offer was not a 'real' offer (*R v Kray* [1998] EWCA Crim 3211).

If the offer is made by conduct alone (i.e. without any words), it may be difficult to prove this offence.

If the object of a conspiracy (**see chapter 1.3**) is to supply a controlled drug to a co-conspirator, any subsequent charge must make that clear; stating that the defendants conspired to supply the drug to 'another' implies that the supply was to be made to someone *other than any of the conspirators* (*R* v *Jackson* [2000] 1 Cr App R 97).

1.6.4.2 Specific Situations

Section 4A of the Misuse of Drugs Act 1971 requires courts to treat certain conditions as 'aggravating' factors when considering the seriousness of the offence under s. 4(3) if committed by a person aged 18 or over.

The conditions are either:

(1) that the offence was committed on or in the vicinity of school premises at a relevant time. 'Vicinity' is not defined and will be left to each court relying on its local knowledge. Other buildings and premises (e.g. cafes and shopping centres) can fall within this description and courts may decide that a route used to get to or from a school or a place where schoolchildren gather (even if trespassing) may be in the 'vicinity'. School premises are land used for the purposes of a school but *excluding* any land occupied solely as a dwelling *by a person employed at the school* (s. 4A(8)). A 'relevant time' is any time when the school premises are in use by people under the age of 18 (and one hour before the start/after the end of any such time) (s. 4A(5)); or

(2) that in connection with the commission of the offence the offender used a 'courier' who, at the time the offence was committed, was under the age of 18. A person uses a courier if he/she causes or permits another person (the courier):
   (a) to deliver a controlled drug to a third person, or
   (b) to deliver a 'drug related consideration' (basically any money, goods etc. obtained or intended to be used in connection with the supply of a controlled drug) to him/herself or a third person (s. 4A(6) and (7)).

1.6.5 Possession with Intent to Supply

This is an offence that brings the concepts of 'possession' and 'supply' together.

OFFENCE: **Possession with Intent to Supply—*Misuse of Drugs Act 1971, s. 5(3)***
• Triable either way • Class A (life imprisonment and/or a fine on indictment; six months' imprisonment and/or a prescribed sum summarily) • Class B (14 years' imprisonment and/or a fine on indictment; six months' imprisonment and/or prescribed sum summarily) • Class C (14 years' imprisonment and/or a fine on indictment; three months' imprisonment and/or a fine summarily)

The Misuse of Drugs Act 1971, s. 5 states:

(3) Subject to section 28 of this Act, it is an offence for a person to have a controlled drug in his possession, whether lawfully or not, with intent to supply it to another in contravention of section 4(1) of this Act.

KEYNOTE

The lawfulness or otherwise of the *possession* is irrelevant; what matters is the lawfulness of the intended supply. If a police officer is in lawful possession of a controlled drug but intends to supply it unlawfully to another, the offence is committed.

You must show that the intention was that the *person in possession of the controlled drug* (rather than some third party) would supply it at some point in the future (*R* v *Greenfield* [1984] 78 Cr App R 179).

If more than one person has possession of the relevant controlled drug, you must show an individual intention to supply it by each person charged; it is not enough to show a joint venture whereby one or more parties simply knew of another's intent (*R* v *Downes* [1984] Crim LR 552). Given the decision of the Court of Appeal in *Kray* [1998] EWCA Crim 3211 (**see para. 1.6.4.1**), possession with intent to supply a controlled

---

drug to a person who is in fact an undercover police officer would appear to amount to an offence under this section.

All that is necessary in proving the offence under s. 5(3) is to show that the defendant had a controlled drug in his possession and intended to supply that substance to another. If the substance in the defendant's possession is a Class A drug and he intended to supply it to another person, the fact that he thought the drug was some other type of drug does not matter (*R v Leeson* [2000] 1 Cr App R 233).

Possession of drugs paraphernalia (e.g. clingfilm, contact details, etc.) will be relevant evidence to show that a defendant was an active dealer in drugs but it does not prove the intention to supply and the trial judge will give a jury careful directions as to the probative value of such items found in the defendant's possession (*R v Haye* [2002] EWCA Crim 2476).

Where a Rastafarian was prosecuted for possessing cannabis with intent to supply others as part of their religious worship, he claimed that his rights under Articles 8 and 9 of the European Convention on Human Rights had been unnecessarily and disproportionately interfered with. The Court of Appeal, while reducing the sentence, held that such a prosecution had been properly brought (*R v Taylor* [2001] EWCA Crim 2263).

In proving an intention to supply you may be able to adduce evidence of the defendant's unexplained wealth (*R v Smith (Ivor)* [1995] Crim LR 940) or the presence of large sums of money with the drugs seized (*R v Wright* [1994] Crim LR 55).

For the purposes of the offence under s. 4 (supplying a controlled drug) and this offence, the 'another' cannot be someone charged in the same count, but can be someone charged in other counts in the same indictment.

1.6.6 Supply of Articles

OFFENCE: **Supplying Articles for Administering or Preparing Controlled Drugs—**
Misuse of Drugs Act 1971, s. 9A
- Triable summarily • Six months' imprisonment and/or a fine

The Misuse of Drugs Act 1971, s. 9A states:

(1) A person who supplies or offers to supply any article which may be used or adapted to be used (whether by itself or in combination with another article or other articles) in the administration by any person of a controlled drug to himself or another, believing that the article (or the article as adapted) is to be so used in circumstances where the administration is unlawful, is guilty of an offence.

(2) ...

(3) A person who supplies or offers to supply any article which may be used to prepare a controlled drug for administration by any person to himself or another believing that the article is to be so used in circumstances where the administration is unlawful is guilty of an offence.

KEYNOTE

This offence is designed to address the provision of drug 'kits'. Hypodermic syringes, or parts of them, are not covered by this offence (s. 9A(2)).

The administration for which the articles are intended must be 'unlawful'. Section 9A states:

(4) For the purposes of this section, any administration of a controlled drug is unlawful except—
  (a) the administration by any person of a controlled drug to another in circumstances where the administration of the drug is not unlawful under section 4(1) of this Act, or
  (b) the administration by any person of a controlled drug, other than a temporary class drug, to himself in circumstances where having the controlled drug in his possession is not unlawful under section 5(1) of this Act, or.
  (c) the administration by any person of a temporary class drug to himself in circumstances where having the drug in his possession is to be treated as excepted possession for the purposes of this Act (see s. 7A(2)(c)).

(5) In this section, references to administration by any person of a controlled drug to himself include a reference to his administering it to himself with the assistance of another.

For the law relating to temporary class drugs, see para. 1.6.2.1.

1.6.7 Production of a Controlled Drug

OFFENCE: **Producing Controlled Drug—*Misuse of Drugs Act 1971, s. 4(2)***
* Triable either way • Class A (life imprisonment and/or a fine on indictment; six months' imprisonment and/or prescribed sum summarily) • Class B (14 years' imprisonment and/or a fine on indictment; six months' imprisonment and/or prescribed sum summarily) • Class C (five years' imprisonment and/or a fine on indictment; three months' imprisonment and/or a fine summarily)

The Misuse of Drugs Act 1971, s. 4 states:

(2) Subject to section 28 of this Act, it is an offence for a person—
  (a) to produce a controlled drug in contravention of subsection (1)...; or
  (b) to be concerned in the production of such a drug in contravention of that subsection by another.

KEYNOTE

'Produce' means producing by manufacture, cultivation or any other method and 'production' has a corresponding meaning (Misuse of Drugs Act 1971, s. 37).

Converting one form of a Class A drug into another is 'producing' (*R* v *Russell* (1991) 94 Cr App R 351), as is harvesting, cutting and stripping a cannabis plant (*R* v *Harris* [1996] 1 Cr App R 369).

The addition of adulterants or bulking agents can amount to the production of a controlled drug (*R* v *Williams* [2011] EWCA Crim 232).

Being 'concerned in the production' requires evidence that the accused played an identifiable role in the production of the drug in question. This was not satisfied where the accused simply permitted two others who were producing drugs to use his kitchen (*R* v *Farr* [1982] Crim LR 745).

1.6.8 Cultivation of Cannabis

OFFENCE: **Cultivation of Cannabis—*Misuse of Drugs Act 1971, s. 6***
* Triable either way • 14 years' imprisonment and/or a fine on indictment
* Six months' imprisonment and/or prescribed sum summarily

The Misuse of Drugs Act 1971, s. 6 states:

(1) Subject to any regulations under section 7 of this Act for the time being in force, it shall not be lawful for a person to cultivate any plant of the genus *Cannabis*.
(2) Subject to section 28 of this Act, it is an offence to cultivate any such plant in contravention of subsection (1) above.

KEYNOTE

The definition of 'cannabis' provided by s. 37(1) of the Misuse of Drugs Act 1971 (**see para. 1.6.2.2**) does not apply to the use of the word 'cannabis' in s. 6 of the Act, since the context of the instant offence clearly requires that the plant itself be cultivated.

'Cultivate' is not defined but it appears that you need to show some element of attention (e.g. watering) to the plant by the defendant in order to prove this offence. This offence does not permit police officers to tend plants which have been seized as evidence in order to preserve them as exhibits for court.

You need only show that the plant is of the genus *Cannabis* and that the defendant cultivated it; you need not show that the defendant knew it to be a cannabis plant (*R* v *Champ* [1981] 73 Cr App R 367).

1.6.9   General Defence under Section 28

There is a general defence (available under s. 28 of the Misuse of Drugs Act 1971), to a defendant charged with certain drugs offences. Section 28 applies to offences of:

- unlawful production (s. 4(2))
- unlawful supply (s. 4(3))
- unlawful possession (s. 5(2))
- possession with intent to supply (s. 5(3))
- unlawful cultivation of cannabis (s. 6(2))
- offences connected with opium (s. 9) (not covered in the Part I OSPRE syllabus).

The defences under s. 28 are *not* available in cases of conspiracy as conspiracy is not an offence under the 1971 Act (*R* v *McGowan* [1990] Crim LR 399).

The Misuse of Drugs Act 1971, s. 28 states:

(2) Subject to subsection (3) below, in any proceedings for an offence to which this section applies it shall be a defence for the accused to prove that he neither knew of nor suspected nor had reason to suspect the existence of some fact alleged by the prosecution which it is necessary for the prosecution to prove if he is to be convicted of the offence charged.

(3) Where in any proceedings for an offence to which this section applies it is necessary, if the accused is to be convicted of the offence charged, for the prosecution to prove that some substance or product involved in the alleged offence was the controlled drug which the prosecution alleges it to have been, and it is proved that the substance or product in question was that controlled drug, the accused—

(a) shall not be acquitted of the offence charged by reason only of proving that he neither knew nor suspected nor had reason to suspect that the substance or product in question was the particular controlled drug alleged; but

(b) shall be acquitted thereof—

(i) if he proves that he neither believed nor suspected nor had reason to suspect that the substance or product in question was a controlled drug; or

(ii) if he proves that he believed the substance or product in question to be a controlled drug, or a controlled drug of a description, such that, if it had in fact been that controlled drug, or a controlled drug of that description, he would not at the material time have been committing any offence to which this section applies.

KEYNOTE

This defence envisages three distinct situations:

- a lack of knowledge by the defendant of some fact which is alleged by the prosecution;
- a general lack of knowledge by the defendant about the drug in question;
- a conditional belief held by the defendant about the drug in question.

1.6.9.1   Lack of Knowledge of Some Alleged Fact

Section 28(2) allows a defence where the defendant did not *know, suspect* or *have reason to suspect* the existence of some fact which is essential to proving the case.

....

EXAMPLE

X is stopped in the street by Y who asks him to drop off a letter in an envelope at a nearby address in exchange for £10. As X approaches the address he is arrested for possessing a controlled drug (which is inside the envelope), with intent to supply.

X is in 'possession' of the drug as he has custody of it and knows that the envelope contains *something*; what s. 28(2) does is to allow X a defence. X can discharge the evidential burden by showing that he neither knew, nor suspected that the envelope contained a controlled drug, and that he neither knew nor suspected that he was supplying it to another. Both of these elements would be facts which the prosecution would have to allege to prove the offence.

If X knew the person to be a local drug dealer, or the reward for his errand was disproportionately large, say £1000, then he may not be able to discharge this evidential burden.

The test for 'reason to suspect' is an *objective* one (*R* v *Young* [1984] 1 WLR 654). Consequently, where a 'reason to suspect' was not apparent to a defendant because he/she was too intoxicated to see it, the defence will not apply.

1.6.9.2 General Lack of Knowledge about Drug in Question

The wording of s. 28(3)(a) prevents defendants from claiming a 'defence' when what they thought was one type of controlled drug was in fact another, different controlled drug.

Section 28(3)(b) however, has two strands, one concerned with the defendant's general lack of knowledge about the drug in question and the other (**see para. 1.6.9.3**) concerning the defendant's conditional belief.

Section 28(3)(b)(i) will allow defendants to prove that they did not believe or suspect the substance in question to be a controlled drug and that they had no reason so to suspect.

This clearly overlaps with s. 28(2) and X in the above example would also be able to claim this lack of knowledge. If he believed the envelope to contain amphetamine when it turned out to contain heroin, however, this lack of knowledge would not be permitted as a defence under s. 28(3).

1.6.9.3 Conditional Belief about Drug in Question

In contrast to s. 28(3)(a), the second strand of s. 28(3)(b)(ii) allows defendants to discharge the evidential burden by showing that they *did* believe the drug in question to be a particular controlled drug. It is then open to defendants to claim that, had the drug in question actually been the drug which they believed it to be, then they would not have committed any offences in relation to that drug.

EXAMPLE

A registered heroin addict is prescribed methadone. She collects her prescription from a chemist but is mistakenly given pethidine instead. She may be able to discharge the evidential burden by showing that she *believed* the drug in question to be methadone *and* that, if it had been, she would not have committed an offence by possessing it.

1.6.10 Regulated Possession and Supply of Controlled Drugs

The statutory framework governing controlled drugs does not simply ban substances and their possession outright. People working at various levels within the system need to be able to access, analyse and prescribe substances that are controlled by the 1971 Act. To that end, the framework takes account of the differing legitimate activities that may be relevant to individual people or particular circumstances. The majority of the exceptions and conditions imposed on this lawful possession and use can be found in the Misuse of Drugs Regulations 2001 and also in the Misuse of Drugs and Misuse of Drugs (Safe Custody) (Amendment) Regulations (SI 2007/2154).

The importance of the 2001 Regulations lies in the fact that they exempt certain drugs and certain people (pharmacists, laboratory workers and police officers etc.) from the main offences of possession, supply and importation *as long as they are reacting lawfully within the parameters set out by those regulations.* A person in such an occupation who possesses, supplies or imports a controlled drug outside the terms of the exemptions will commit an offence.

Among the key regulations (SI 2001/3998) are:

- Regulation 4—which sets out those controlled drugs which will be exempted from the main offences of importation/exportation when they are contained in medicinal products.
- Regulation 5—allowing people holding a licence issued by the Secretary of State to produce, supply, offer to supply or have in their possession a controlled drug.
- Regulation 6—this allows anyone who is *lawfully* in possession of a controlled drug to give the drug back to the person from whom he/she obtained it and would cover registered heroin addicts properly returning methadone to a chemist. Regulation 6 also allows others to possess and supply certain controlled drugs under strict conditions. Regulation 6 allows police constables to have any controlled drug in their possession, or to supply such a drug to anyone who is lawfully allowed to have it (reg. 6(5)–(7)). These exemptions only apply where constables are *acting in the course of their duty as such.*

Other people who are given the same protection are customs and excise officers, postal workers and people engaged in conveying the drug to someone who may lawfully possess it. This last category would include civilian support staff, exhibits officers and others who, although not police constables, are nevertheless properly engaged in conveying controlled drugs to others.

The remainder of the regulations are generally concerned with exemptions for doctors, vets and others who may need to store or supply controlled drugs; the 2001 Regulations also impose requirements on some such people in relation to record keeping and the provision of information when requested.

1.6.11 Occupiers, etc.

OFFENCE: **Occupier or Manager of Premises Permitting Drug Misuse—*Misuse of Drugs Act 1971, s. 8***

- Triable either way • Class A or B (14 years' imprisonment and/or a fine on indictment; six months' imprisonment and/or prescribed sum summarily) • Class C (14 years' imprisonment and/or a fine on indictment; three months' imprisonment and/or a fine summarily)

The Misuse of Drugs Act 1971, s. 8 states:

A person commits an offence if, being the occupier or concerned in the management of any premises, he knowingly permits or suffers any of the following activities to take place on those premises, that is to say—

(a) producing or attempting to produce a controlled drug in contravention of section 4(1) of this Act;

(b) supplying or attempting to supply a controlled drug to another in contravention of section 4(1) of this Act, or offering to supply a controlled drug to another in contravention of section 4(1);

(c) preparing opium for smoking;

(d) smoking cannabis, cannabis resin or prepared opium.

KEYNOTE

Occupier

A person does not have to be a tenant, or to have estate in land, in order to be an 'occupier'. The term 'occupier' should be given a 'common sense' interpretation (*R* v *Tao* [1977] QB 141). For the purposes of s. 8, a person is in occupation of premises, whatever his/her legal status, if the prosecution can show that the accused exercised control, or had the authority of another, to exclude persons from the premises or to prohibit any of the activities referred to in s. 8 (*R* v *Coid* [1998] Crim LR 199).

Concerned in the Management

To be a manager, the accused must run, organise and plan the use of the premises (*R* v *Josephs* (1977) 65 Cr App R 253) and so must be involved in more than menial or routine duties.

'Premises' is not defined.

The permitting or suffering of these activities requires a degree of *mens rea* (*Sweet* v *Parsley* [1970] AC 132) even if that degree is little more than wilful blindness (*R* v *Thomas* (1976) 63 Cr App R 65). For the purposes of s. 8(b), and therefore presumably s. 8(a), it is not necessary to show that the defendant knew exactly which drugs were being produced, supplied etc.; only that they were 'controlled drugs' (*R* v *Bett* [1999] 1 WLR 2109).

However, the precise activities that are described under s. 8 will need to be proved. So, for instance, if the offence charged is one of knowingly permitting the smoking of cannabis (under subs. (d)), it must be shown that this actually took place; it is not enough that the owner/occupier had given permission for this to happen (*R* v *Auguste* [2003] EWCA Crim 3929). This is also the case when the offence charged is one of supplying or attempting to supply a controlled drug to another (under s. 8(b)), i.e. it must be shown that the supply or attempted supply actually took place (*R* v *McGee* [2012] EWCA Crim 613).

An occupier who permits the growing of cannabis plants commits this offence (*Taylor* v *Chief Constable of Kent* [1981] 1 WLR 606).

1.6.12 Community Protection Notices

Section 1 of the Anti-social Behaviour Act 2003 (which provided a power allowing the police to close premises where drugs offences take place accompanied by disorder or nuisance) was repealed by and replaced with Community Protection Notices (under part 4 of the Anti-social Behaviour, Crime and Policing Act 2014). This area of law is dealt with in *General Police Duties,* chapter 4.8.

1.6.13 Assisting or Inducing Offence Outside United Kingdom

OFFENCE: **Assisting or Inducing Misuse of Drugs Offence Outside UK—*Misuse of Drugs Act 1971, s. 20***

> • Triable either way • 14 years' imprisonment and/or a fine on indictment • Six months' imprisonment and/or a fine summarily

The Misuse of Drugs Act 1971, s. 20 states:

> A person commits an offence if in the United Kingdom he assists in or induces the commission in any place outside the United Kingdom of an offence punishable under the provisions of a corresponding law in force in that place.

KEYNOTE

In order to prove this offence, you must show that the offence outside the United Kingdom actually took place. This offence may overlap with the offences of importation/exportation.

'Assisting' includes taking containers to another country in the knowledge that they would later be filled with a controlled drug and sent on to a third country (*R* v *Evans* (1977) 64 Cr App R 237). For an offence to amount to one under 'corresponding law' for these purposes, a certificate relating to the domestic law concerned with the misuse of drugs must be obtained from the government of the relevant country (s. 36).

1.6.14 Incitement

OFFENCE: Incitement—*Misuse of Drugs Act 1971, s. 19*

• Triable and punishable as for substantive offence incited

The Misuse of Drugs Act 1971, s. 19 states:

> It is an offence for a person to incite another to commit an offence under any other provision of this Act.

KEYNOTE

A person inciting an undercover police officer may commit an offence under s. 19 even though there was no possibility of the officer actually being induced to commit the offence (*DPP* v *Armstrong* [2000] Crim LR 379).

1.6.15 Importation of Controlled Drugs

Section 3 of the Misuse of Drugs Act 1971 *prohibits* the import or export of a controlled drug unless authorised by the regulations made under the Act. The relevant offences and respective penalties are contained in the Customs and Excise Management Act 1979 which provides the following penalties for the improper importation or exportation of controlled drugs:

• Class A—life imprisonment
• Class B—14 years' imprisonment
• Class C—14 years' imprisonment.

1.6.16 Travel Restriction Orders

The Criminal Justice and Police Act 2001 allows courts (in practice the Crown Court) to impose travel restrictions on offenders convicted of drug trafficking offences. Travel restriction orders prohibit offenders from leaving the United Kingdom at any time during the period beginning from their release from custody (other than on bail or temporary release for a fixed period) and up to the end of the order. The minimum period for such an order is two years (s. 33(3)); there is no maximum period prescribed in the legislation.

Where a court

• has convicted a person of a drug trafficking offence
• and it has determined that a sentence of four years or more is appropriate

it is under a *duty* to consider whether or not a travel restriction order would be appropriate (s. 33). If the court decides not to impose an order, it must give its reasons for not doing so.

Offenders may also be required to surrender their UK passport as part of the order.

The offences which are covered by travel restriction orders include the production and supply of controlled drugs, the importation/exportation offences under s. 3 (**see para. 1.6.15**) along with inciting under the Misuse of Drugs Act 1971, s. 19. Possession of a Class A drug with intent to supply is *not* covered by travel restriction order legislation.

An offender may apply to the court that made a restriction order to have it revoked or suspended (s. 35) and the court must consider the strict criteria set out in s. 35 when considering any such suspension or revocation. If an order is suspended, the offender has a legal obligation to be back in the United Kingdom when the period of suspension ends (s. 35(5)(a)).

OFFENCE: **Contravening a Travel Restriction Order—*Criminal Justice and Police Act 2001, s. 36***

　　　• Triable either way　• Five years' imprisonment and/or a fine on indictment　• Six months' imprisonment and/or a fine summarily

The Criminal Justice and Police Act 2001, s. 36 states:

(1) A person who leaves the United Kingdom at a time when he is prohibited from leaving it by a travel restriction order is guilty of an offence…

(2) A person who is not in the United Kingdom at the end of a period during which a prohibition imposed on him by a travel restriction order has been suspended shall be guilty of an offence…

KEYNOTE

These offences do not require a particular state of mind.

The first offence requires proof of two things: (i) that there was an order in existence in respect of the offender, and (ii) that he/she left the United Kingdom during the time it was in force. There is no requirement that the person leave the United Kingdom *voluntarily* in order to be guilty (although he/she would have a good argument if he/she were taken out of the jurisdiction against his/her will or without his/her knowledge).

Travel restriction orders do not prevent the proper exercise of any prescribed power to remove a person from the United Kingdom (s. 37). So if the Secretary of State deports someone who is under a travel restriction order, that person would not commit the above offence.

The second offence requires proof that there was a suspended order in existence in respect of the offender and that, at the end of the suspension period, the offender was not in the United Kingdom.

Failing to deliver up a passport when required by an order is a summary offence (six months' imprisonment and/or a fine (s. 36(3)).

1.6.17　Police Powers

The 1971 Act provides a number of specific enforcement powers.

1.6.17.1　Powers of Entry, Search and Seizure

The Misuse of Drugs Act 1971, s. 23 states:

(1) A constable or other person authorised in that behalf by a general or special order of the Secretary of State (or in Northern Ireland either of the Secretary of State or the Ministry of Home Affairs for Northern Ireland) shall, for the purposes of the execution of this Act, have power to enter the premises of a person carrying on business as a producer or supplier of any controlled drugs and to demand the production of, and to inspect, any books or documents relating to dealings in any such drugs and to inspect any stocks of any such drugs.

(2) If a constable has reasonable grounds to suspect that any person is in possession of a controlled drug in contravention of this Act or of any regulations or orders made thereunder, the constable may—

　(a) search that person, and detain him for the purpose of searching him;

　(b) search any vehicle or vessel in which the constable suspects that the drug may be found, and for that purpose require the person in control of the vehicle or vessel to stop it;

　(c) seize and detain, for the purposes of proceedings under this Act, anything found in the course of the search which appears to the constable to be evidence of an offence under this Act.

In this subsection 'vessel' includes a hovercraft within the meaning of the Hovercraft Act 1968; and nothing in this subsection shall prejudice any power of search or any power to seize or detain property which is exercisable by a constable apart from this subsection.

(3) If a justice of the peace (or in Scotland a justice of the peace, a magistrate or a sheriff) is satisfied by information on oath that there is reasonable ground for suspecting—

　(a) that any controlled drugs are, in contravention of this Act or of any regulations or orders made thereunder, in the possession of a person on any premises; or

(b) that a document directly or indirectly relating to, or connected with, a transaction or dealing which was, or an intended transaction or dealing which would if carried out be, an offence under this Act, or in the case of a transaction or dealing carried out or intended to be carried out in a place outside the United Kingdom, an offence against the provisions of a corresponding law in force in that place, is in the possession of a person on any premises,

he may grant a warrant authorising any constable at any time or times within one month from the date of the warrant, to enter, if need be by force, the premises named in the warrant, and to search the premises and any persons found therein and, if there is reasonable ground for suspecting that an offence under this Act has been committed in relation to any controlled drugs found on the premises or in the possession of any such persons, or that a document so found is such a document as is mentioned in paragraph (b) above, to seize and detain those drugs or that document, as the case may be.

KEYNOTE

Where police officers are on premises under the authority of a warrant obtained under s. 23, it will be important to have established the precise extent of the warrant. If such a warrant authorises the search of *premises only*, that in itself will not give the officers authority to search *people* found on those premises unless the officer can point to some other power authorising the search (*Hepburn* v *Chief Constable of Thames Valley* [2002] EWCA Civ 1841).

However, where the warrant authorises the search of premises *and* people, the Divisional Court has held that it is reasonable to restrict the movement of people within the premises to allow the search to be conducted properly (*DPP* v *Meaden* [2003] EWHC 3005 (Admin)).

For the procedure involved in applying for, and executing warrants, see *General Police Duties*, chapter 4.7.

PACE Code A (see *General Police Duties*) applies to the exercise of any power to search people for controlled drugs specifically included in a warrant issued under s. 23.

A warrant issued under s. 23 of the Act lasts for a period of *one month* from the date of issue.

1.6.17.2   Obstruction

OFFENCE: **Obstruction—*Misuse of Drugs Act 1971, s. 23(4)***
   • Triable either way • Two years' imprisonment and/or a fine on indictment • Six months' imprisonment and/or a fine summarily

The Misuse of Drugs Act 1971, s. 23 states:

   (4) A person commits an offence if he—
      (a) intentionally obstructs a person in the exercise of his powers under this section; or
      (b) conceals from a person acting in the exercise of his powers under subsection (1) above any such books, documents, stocks or drugs as are mentioned in that subsection; or
      (c) without reasonable excuse (proof of which shall lie on him) fails to produce any such books or documents as are so mentioned where their production is demanded by a person in the exercise of his powers under that subsection.

KEYNOTE

The offence of obstructing a person in the exercise of his/her powers is only committed if the obstruction was intentional (*R* v *Forde* (1985) 81 Cr App R 19).

1.6.18   Intoxicating Substances

OFFENCE: **Supply of Intoxicating Substance—*Intoxicating Substances (Supply) Act 1985, s. 1***
   • Triable summarily • Six months' imprisonment and/or a fine

The Intoxicating Substances (Supply) Act 1985, s. 1 states:

(1) It is an offence for a person to supply or offer to supply a substance other than a controlled drug—
   (a) to a person under the age of 18 whom he knows, or has reasonable cause to believe, to be under that age; or
   (b) to a person—
      (i) who is acting on behalf of a person under that age; and
      (ii) whom he knows, or has reasonable cause to believe, to be so acting,

if he knows or has reasonable cause to believe that the substance is, or its fumes are, likely to be inhaled by the person under the age of 18 for the purpose of causing intoxication.

KEYNOTE

Retailers who sell solvents to people apparently under 18, or to people apparently acting on the behalf of someone under 18, would commit this offence.

It is a defence for persons charged with this offence to show that at the time they made the supply or offer they were both:

- under the age of 18 and
- acting otherwise than in the course or furtherance of a business (s. 1(2)).

OFFENCE: **Supply of Butane Lighter Refill to Person under 18—*Cigarette Lighter Refill (Safety) Regulations 1999, reg. 2***
   • Triable summarily • Six months' imprisonment and/or a fine

The Cigarette Lighter Refill (Safety) Regulations 1999 (SI 1999/1844), reg. 2 states:

No person shall supply any cigarette lighter refill canister containing butane or a substance with butane as a constituent part to any person under the age of eighteen years.

KEYNOTE

There is no requirement that the person believed or even suspected the person to be under 18. The 1999 Regulations are made under the Consumer Protection Act 1987, s. 11.

1.7 | Firearms and Gun Crime

1.7.1 Introduction

The key piece of legislation governing firearms is the Firearms Act 1968. The Act covers numerous activities involving firearms and also deals with serious offences involving the criminal use of firearms.

1.7.2 Definitions—Firearm, Ammunition and Imitation Firearm

Before examining any offences relating to firearms, it is useful to begin with some basic definitions.

1.7.2.1 Firearms

The Firearms Act 1968, s. 57 states:

(1) In this Act, the expression 'firearm' means a lethal barrelled weapon of any description from which any shot, bullet or other missile can be discharged, and includes—
   (a) any prohibited weapon, whether it is such a lethal weapon as aforesaid or not; and
   (b) any component part of such a lethal or prohibited weapon; and
   (c) any accessory to any such weapon designed or adapted to diminish the noise or flash caused by firing the weapon.

KEYNOTE

'Lethal barrelled weapon' is not defined under the 1968 Act. In *Grace* v *DPP* [1989] Crim LR 365, it was held that the prosecution must prove the following to satisfy the definition:

(a) whether the weapon was one from which any shot, bullet or other missile could be discharged or whether it could be adapted so as to be capable of discharging such a missile, and
(b) if satisfied, whether it was a lethal barrelled weapon.

An item which could only discharge a missile in combination with other tools extraneous to it would not be a lethal barrelled weapon. The opening words of s. 57(1) refer to the capacity of an item and not to its capacity in combination with other equipment. Thus, an old and damaged starting pistol with a partially drilled barrel could not be regarded as a 'prohibited weapon' and thus a firearm within s. 57, merely because it could be made to discharge a pellet with the aid of a vice-clamp, a mallet and a metal punch (*R* v *Bewley* [2012] EWCA Crim 1457).

A weapon is a lethal barrelled weapon if it is capable of causing injury, irrespective of the intentions of its maker (*Read* v *Donovan* [1947] KB 326). In determining whether a firearm is in fact a lethal barrelled weapon from which missiles can be discharged a court need not consider any specific evidence of someone who has seen the effects of it being fired. Therefore, where magistrates had heard evidence from a gun shop assistant that an air rifle was in working order, they were entitled to conclude that it fell within the definition even though no evidence was given as to the actual effects of the gun being fired (*Castle* v *DPP* (1998) *The Times*, 3 April).

Air pistols (*R* v *Thorpe* [1987] 1 WLR 383) and imitation revolvers (*Cafferata* v *Wilson* [1936] 3 All ER 149) have been held to be lethal barrelled weapons. A signalling pistol which fired explosive magnesium and phosphorous flares capable of killing at short range has been held to be lethal (*Read* v *Donovan*). That is not to say, however, that they will always be so; each case must be determined in the light of the evidence available.

The effect of s. 57(1) (a) is to make a prohibited weapon a firearm whether it is lethal barrelled or not. It follows that *all prohibited weapons are firearms* although not all firearms will be prohibited weapons.

Component parts are not defined but in *R* v *Rogers* [2011] EWCA Crim 1459, the Court of Appeal ruled that in the absence of a cylinder appropriate for a firearm, an unblocked barrel, frame and trigger could *not* be regarded as components of a firearm.

While silencers and flash eliminators are accessories, a silencer or a flash eliminator *on its own* is not a firearm. However, if a defendant is found in possession of a silencer or flash eliminator which has been manufactured for a weapon *that is also in the defendant's possession*, that will be enough to bring the silencer or flash eliminator under s. 57(1). If the silencer is made for a different weapon, it may still come under the s. 57 definition but the prosecution will have to show it could be used with the defendant's weapon and that he/she had it for that purpose (*R* v *Buckfield* [1998] Crim LR 673). Section 57(1) does not include telescopic sights or magazines.

1.7.2.2 Deactivation of Firearms

A weapon ceases to be a firearm if it is deactivated in line with the provisions of the Firearms (Amendment) Act 1988, s. 8 which states:

> For the purposes of the principal Act and this Act it shall be presumed, unless the contrary is shown, that a firearm has been rendered incapable of discharging any shot, bullet or other missile, and has consequently ceased to be a firearm within the meaning of those Acts, if—
> (a) it bears a mark which has been approved by the Secretary of State for denoting that fact and which has been made either by one of the two companies mentioned in section 58(1) of the principal Act or by such other person as may be approved by the Secretary of State for the purposes of this section; and
> (b) that company or person has certified in writing that work has been carried out on the firearm in a manner approved by the Secretary of State for rendering it incapable of discharging any shot, bullet or other missile.

KEYNOTE

A deactivated weapon must remain in its complete state. Where it is disassembled the parts that are then made available are capable of being reassembled into a working weapon and are therefore component parts of a firearm (*R* v *Ashton* [2007] EWCA Crim 234).

The 'two companies' referred to in s. 8(a) are the Society of the Mystery of Gunmakers of the City of London and the Birmingham Proof House.

1.7.2.3 Ammunition

Ammunition is defined by s. 57 of the Firearms Act 1968 which states:

> (2) In this Act, the expression 'ammunition' means any ammunition for any firearm and includes grenades, bombs and other like missiles, whether capable of use with a firearm or not, and also includes prohibited ammunition.

KEYNOTE

The definition of ammunition does not include ingredients and components of ammunition; it is only assembled ammunition that is controlled under the Act. Empty cartridge cases, for example, are not 'ammunition'. The exception to this is missiles for ammunition prohibited under s. 5 of the Act, for example expanding or armour-piercing bullets. Such missiles are themselves regarded as 'ammunition' and are subject to control accordingly (s. 5(1A)(g)).

1.7.2.4 Imitation Firearm

Some, though not all, offences which regulate the use of firearms will also apply to *imitation* firearms. Whether they do so can be found either in the specific wording of the offence, or by virtue of the Firearms Act 1982.

There are two types of imitation firearms:

- general imitations—those which have the appearance of firearms (which are covered by s. 57 of the Firearms Act 1968); and
- imitations of section 1 firearms—those which both have the appearance of a section 1 firearm and which can be readily converted into such a firearm (which are covered by ss. 1 and 2 of the Firearms Act 1982).

> **KEYNOTE**
>
> The 'general imitation' firearm definition is the most commonly used in firearms legislation. That definition is 'anything which has the appearance of being a firearm … whether or not it is capable of discharging any shot, bullet or other missile'.
>
> For that reason, the definition of an imitation of a section 1 firearm will be considered separately and dealt with later in this chapter. Therefore, when imitation firearms are referred to in legislation or future Keynotes, think of it as a 'general imitation' unless otherwise stated.

It has been held that the definition in s. 57 requires the defendant to be carrying a 'thing' which is separate and distinct from the person and therefore capable of being possessed (*R* v *Bentham* [2005] UKHL 18). Holding your fingers under your coat and pretending that this is a firearm (*Bentham*) will not therefore amount to an imitation firearm for the relevant offences as an unsevered hand or finger was part of oneself and therefore could not be 'possessed' in the way envisaged by the Act. The 'imitation' must have the appearance of a firearm and it is not necessary for any object to have been constructed, adapted or altered so as to resemble a firearm (*R* v *Williams* [2006] EWCA Crim 1650). In *K* v *DPP* [2006] EWHC 2183 (Admin) it was held that in some circumstances a realistic toy gun, in this case a plastic ball bearing gun, could become an imitation firearm. This category does not include anything which resembles a prohibited weapon that is designed or adapted to discharge noxious liquid etc.

Whether or not something has the appearance of being a firearm will be a question of fact for the jury/magistrate(s) to decide in each case.

1.7.3 Categories of Firearms and Related Offences

The law regulating firearms classifies weapons into several categories, each of which is specifically defined. These definitions have associated offences dealing with activities such as their possession etc. Alongside these offences are exemptions which allow those activities to be lawful.

1.7.4 Prohibited Weapon

A prohibited weapon is defined under the Firearms Act 1968, s. 5. The definition covers the more powerful or potentially destructive firearms and their ammunition (such as automatic weapons and specialist ammunition) and also small firearms.

The test as to whether a weapon is a 'prohibited' weapon is a purely objective one and is not affected by the intentions of the defendant. Therefore, where a firearm was capable of successively discharging two or more missiles without repeated pressure on the trigger, that weapon was 'prohibited' irrespective of the intentions of the firearms dealer who was in possession of it (*R v Law* [1999] Crim LR 837).

1.7.4.1 List of Prohibited Weapons and Ammunition

The full list of prohibited weapons and ammunition is contained in s. 5(1) and (1A) of the Firearms Act 1968. This list often (but not always) relates to weapons used in a military context and includes:

- automatic weapons
- most self-loading or pump-action weapons
- any firearm which either has a barrel less than 30 cm in length or is less than 60 cm in length overall, other than an air weapon, a muzzle-loading gun or a firearm designed as signalling apparatus
- most smooth bore revolvers
- any weapon, of whatever description, designed or adapted for the discharge of any noxious liquid, gas or other thing
- any air rifle, air gun or air pistol which uses, or is designed or adapted for use with, a self-contained gas cartridge system
- any cartridge with a bullet designed to explode on or immediately before impact
- if capable of being used with a firearm of any description, any grenade or bomb (or other like missile) or rocket or shell designed to explode on or immediately before impact.

KEYNOTE

In relation to weapons designed or adapted for the discharge of any noxious liquid, gas or other thing, taking an empty washing-up bottle and filling it with hydrochloric acid does not amount to adapting it, neither is such a thing a 'weapon' for the purposes of s. 5 (*R v Formosa, R v Upton* [1991] 2 QB 1). This is because to do so does not change the nature of the washing-up bottle itself as the bottle has not been adapted or altered and is therefore not a weapon 'designed or adapted' for the discharge of any noxious liquid etc. The same logic applies to a water pistol filled with ammonia (*R v Titus* [1971] Crim LR 279). Any other approach could be problematic to say the least. In the words of Lloyd LJ (in *Formosa*), '[this] would mean that a householder who filled a milk bottle with acid in order to destroy a wasps' nest would be in possession of a weapon adapted for the discharge of a noxious liquid and would therefore be guilty of the offence of possessing a prohibited weapon; until, of course, he had used the acid for the purpose in question when the milk bottle would revert to its pristine innocence. That could not be right.'

An electric 'stun gun' has been held to be a prohibited weapon as it discharges an electric current (*Flack* v *Baldry* [1988] 1 WLR 393) and it continues to be such even if it is not working (*Brown* v *DPP* (1992) *The Times*, 27 March).

1.7.4.2 Possessing or Purchasing Prohibited Weapons or Ammunition

OFFENCE: **Possessing or Purchasing Prohibited Weapons or Ammunition—**
Firearms Act 1968, s. 5
- Triable either way • 10 years' imprisonment and/or a fine on indictment
- Six months' imprisonment and/or a fine summarily

The Firearms Act 1968, s. 5 states:

(1) A person commits an offence if, without the authority of the Secretary of State or the Scottish Ministers, he has in his possession, or purchases, or acquires [a prohibited weapon or ammunition]...

> **KEYNOTE**
>
> A person may still be in possession of a prohibited weapon even when it is in parts and the accused is in possession of those parts (*R* v *Pannell* (1983) 76 Cr App R 53), or where the weapon is missing an essential part such as the trigger (*R* v *Clarke* [1986] 1 WLR 209).

1.7.4.3 Possession

As an offence contrary to s. 5 of the 1968 Act is a strict liability offence, it is irrelevant whether or not a person knew he/she was in possession of a firearm or ammunition (*R* v *Deyemi* [2007] EWCA Crim 2060). In *Sullivan* v *Earl of Caithness* [1976] QB 966, it was held that a person can remain in possession of a firearm even if someone else has custody of it.

There is no need to prove that the accused knew the nature of the thing he/she possessed in order to prove the offence. If an accused is carrying a rucksack and the rucksack contains ammunition for a section 1 firearm, the accused is in 'possession' of the ammunition irrespective of his/her knowledge or ignorance of its presence in the rucksack (*R* v *Waller* [1991] Crim LR 381; *R* v *Cremin* [2007] EWCA Crim 666). Consider possession of a firearm in the same way that you were invited to consider possession of a controlled drug (**see para 1.6.3**).

1.7.4.4 Exemptions

There are two sets of exemptions in respect of s. 5 prohibited weapons. They are:

*   European exemptions—exemptions to conform with the European Weapons Directive.
*   Special exemptions.

European Weapons Directive

The European Weapons Directive (91/477/EEC) creates exemptions in relation to the possession of, or some transactions in, specified firearms and ammunition by people who have the relevant certificates or who are recognised as collectors under the law of another country.

To this end, s. 5A of the Firearms Act 1968 provides for a number of occasions where the authority of the Secretary of State will not be required to possess or deal with certain weapons under certain conditions.

The main areas covered by s. 5A are:

*   authorised collectors and firearms dealers possessing or being involved in transactions of weapons and ammunition;
*   authorised people being involved in transactions of particular ammunition used for lawful shooting and slaughtering of animals, the management of an estate or the protection of other animals and humans.

Special exemptions

There are a number of special exemptions to the offences involving firearms (under s. 5(1)(aba)). The exemptions include:

*   **Slaughterers**—A slaughterer, if entitled under s. 10 of the 1968 Act, may possess a slaughtering instrument. In addition, persons authorised by certificate to possess, buy, acquire, sell or transfer slaughtering instruments are exempt from the provisions of s. 5 (s. 2 of the Firearms (Amendment) Act 1997).
*   **Humane killing of animals**—This exemption allows a person authorised by certificate to possess, buy, acquire or transfer a firearm solely for use in connection with the humane killing of animals (s. 3 of the Firearms (Amendment) Act 1997). When determining whether a firearm falls within the meaning of a 'humane killer', the definition of a 'slaughtering instrument' under s. 57(4) may be referred to (*R* v *Paul (Benjamin)* [1999] Crim LR 79).

- **Shot pistols for vermin**—This exemption allows a person authorised by certificate to possess, buy, acquire or transfer a 'shot pistol' solely for the shooting of vermin (s. 4(1) of the Firearms (Amendment) Act 1997). A 'shot pistol' is a smooth-bored gun chambered for .410 cartridges or 9mm rim-fire cartridges (s. 4(2)).
- **Treatment of animals**—This exemption allows a person authorised by certificate to possess, buy, acquire or transfer a firearm for use in connection with the treatment of animals or for the purpose of tranquillising or otherwise treating any animal (s. 8 of the Firearms (Amendment) Act 1997). This exemption also applies to offences involving firearms under s. 5(1)(b) and (c).
- **Races at athletic meetings**—A person may possess a firearm at an athletic meeting for the purpose of starting races at that meeting (s. 5(a) of the Firearms (Amendment) Act 1997). Similarly, a person authorised by certificate to possess, buy or acquire a firearm solely for the purposes of starting such races may possess, buy, acquire, sell or transfer a firearm for such a purpose (s. 5(b)).
- **Trophies of war**—A person authorised by certificate to do so may possess a firearm which was acquired as a trophy before 1 January 1946 (s. 6 of the Firearms (Amendment) Act 1997).
- **Firearms of historic interest**—Some firearms are felt to be of particular historical, aesthetic or technical interest. Section 7(4) of the Firearms (Amendment) Act 1997 makes detailed provision for the exemption of such firearms, exemptions which exist in addition to the general exemptions under s. 58 of the Firearms Act 1968 (**see para. 1.7.8**).
- **Air weapons**—In relation to air weapons with self-contained gas cartridges, owned before 20 January 2004, owners, if they applied for a firearms certificate before 1 April 2004, may retain their weapons.

1.7.5 Section 1 Firearm

There is a group of firearms which, although not a category defined in the 1968 Act, is subject to a number of offences including s. 1 (see below). Firearms which fall into this group are often referred to as 'section 1 firearms' and include all firearms except shotguns (**see para. 1.7.6**) and conventional air weapons. However, shotguns which have been 'sawn off' (i.e. had their barrels shortened) are section 1 firearms, as are air weapons declared to be 'specially dangerous'.

Section 1 ammunition includes any ammunition for a firearm except:

- cartridges containing five or more shot, none of which is bigger than 0.36 inches in diameter;
- ammunition for an airgun, air rifle or air pistol; and
- blank cartridges not more than one inch in diameter (s. 1(4)).

1.7.5.1 Conversion

Some weapons which began their life as section 1 firearms or prohibited weapons will remain so even after their conversion to a shotgun, air weapon or other type of firearm (s. 7 of the Firearms (Amendment) Act 1988).

1.7.5.2 Possessing etc. Firearm or Ammunition without Certificate

OFFENCE: **Possessing etc. Firearm or Ammunition without Certificate—*Firearms Act 1968, s. 1***
- Triable either way • Five years' imprisonment and/or a fine on indictment
- Six months' imprisonment and/or a fine summarily

The Firearms Act 1968, s. 1 states:

(1) Subject to any exemption under this Act, it is an offence for a person—
  (a) to have in his possession, or to purchase or acquire, a firearm to which this section applies without holding a firearm certificate in force at the time, or otherwise than as authorised by such a certificate;
  (b) to have in his possession, or to purchase or acquire, any ammunition to which this section applies without holding a firearm certificate in force at the time, or otherwise than as authorised by such a certificate, or in quantities in excess of those so authorised.

KEYNOTE

This offence relates to those firearms described above (**see para. 1.7.5**) as section 1 firearms.

If the firearm involved is a sawn-off shotgun, the offence becomes 'aggravated' (under s. 4(4)) and attracts a maximum penalty of seven years' imprisonment.

The Firearms Act 1982 applies to this section and so the 'general definition' of an imitation firearm *does not* apply. For this offence the definition of an imitation firearm is one 'that has the appearance of a section 1 firearm and which can be readily converted into such a firearm' (which is covered by ss. 1 and 2 of the Firearms Act 1982).

The certificate referred to is issued by the chief officer of police under s. 26A. Such certificates may carry significant restrictions on the types of firearms which the holder is allowed, together with the circumstances under which he/she may have them (s. 44(1) of the Firearms (Amendment) Act 1997).

The issue of whether a certificate covers a particular category of weapon is a matter of law for the judge to decide and cannot be affected by the intentions or misunderstanding of the defendant (*R* v *Paul* (*Benjamin*) [1999] Crim LR 79).

A person may hold a European firearms pass or similar document, in which case he/she will be governed by the provision of ss. 32A to 32C of the Firearms Act 1968.

If a person has such a certificate which allows the possession etc. of the firearm in question and under the particular circumstances encountered, no offence is committed.

Acquire will include hiring, accepting as a gift and borrowing, and 'acquisition' is to be construed accordingly (s. 57(4) of the Firearms Act 1968).

The Violent Crime Reduction Act 2006 created a summary offence that restricts the purchase and sale of cap-type primers (primers are components of ammunition designed for use in metallic ammunition for a firearm which contain a chemical compound that detonates on impact) to persons who hold a relevant firearms certificate or who otherwise have lawful authority for having them (s. 35).

1.7.5.3 Shortening Section 1 Firearm

OFFENCE: **Shortening Barrel of Smooth-bore Section 1 Firearm to Less than 24 Inches—*Firearms (Amendment) Act 1988, s. 6(1)***
  • Triable either way • Five years' imprisonment and/or a fine on indictment
  • Six months' imprisonment and/or a fine summarily

The Firearms (Amendment) Act 1988, s. 6 states:

(1) Subject to subsection (2) below, it is an offence to shorten to a length less than 24 inches the barrel of any smooth-bore gun to which section 1 of the principal Act applies other than one which has a barrel with a bore exceeding 2 inches in diameter; . . .

KEYNOTE

The 'principal Act' is the Firearms Act 1968.

Section 6(2) of the Firearms (Amendment) Act 1988 exempts registered firearms dealers from the offence provided the shortening is done *for the sole purpose* of replacing a defective part of the barrel *so as to produce a new barrel having an overall length of at least 24 inches.*

The length of the barrel of a weapon will be measured from its muzzle to the point at which the charge is exploded (s. 57(6)(a) of the 1968 Act).

Once the shortening has taken place, the nature of the firearm will have changed in which case the person will also commit the relevant possession offence unless he/she has the appropriate authorisation.

1.7.6 Shotguns

A shotgun is defined under s. 1(3)(a) of the Firearms Act 1968. Section 1 (amended by the Firearms (Amendment) Act 1988, s. 2) states:

(3) ...

    (a) a shotgun within the meaning of this Act, that is to say a smooth-bore gun (not being an airgun) which—

        (i) has a barrel not less than 24 inches in length and does not have any barrel with a bore exceeding 2 inches in diameter;

        (ii) either has no magazine or has a non-detachable magazine incapable of holding more than two cartridges; and

        (iii) is not a revolver gun...

(3A) A gun which has been adapted to have such a magazine as is mentioned in subsection (3)(a)(ii) above shall not be regarded as falling within that provision unless the magazine bears a mark approved by the Secretary of State for denoting that fact and that mark has been made, and the adaptation has been certified in writing as having been carried out in a manner approved by him, either by one of the two companies mentioned in section 58(1) of this Act or by such other person as may be approved by him for that purpose.

KEYNOTE

When considering the above definition it helps to remember the 'Rule of 2'—a shotgun barrel must be at least 2 feet long (see s. 57(6)(a) in **para 1.7.5.3**), the bore must not exceed 2 inches in diameter and the non-detachable magazine must hold no more than two cartridges.

For the 'two companies' referred to in s. 1(3A) **see para. 1.7.2.2**.

1.7.6.1 Shotgun Offences

OFFENCE: **Possessing Shotgun without Certificate—*Firearms Act 1968, s. 2(1)***
- Triable either way • Five years' imprisonment and/or a fine on indictment
- Six months' imprisonment and/or a fine summarily

The Firearms Act 1968, s. 2 states:

(1) Subject to any exemption under this Act, it is an offence for a person to have in his possession, or to purchase or acquire, a shotgun without holding a certificate under this Act authorising him to possess shot guns.

KEYNOTE

A shotgun certificate is granted by a chief officer of police under s. 26B of the 1968 Act and will have certain conditions attached to it. A person failing to comply with those conditions commits the offence below.

OFFENCE: **Failing to Comply with Conditions of Shot gun Certificate—*Firearms Act 1968, s. 2(2)***
- Triable summarily • Six months' imprisonment and/or a fine

The Firearms Act 1968, s. 2 states:

(2) It is an offence for a person to fail to comply with a condition subject to which a shot gun certificate is held by him.

The conditions and forms used in relation to the grant of shotgun certificates are contained in the Firearms Rules 1998 (SI 1998/1941) and the Firearms (Amendment) Rules 2005 (SI 2005/3344).

1.7.6.2 Shortening a Shotgun Barrel

OFFENCE: **Shortening Barrel of Shotgun to Less than 24 Inches—*Firearms Act 1968, s. 4(1)***
- Triable either way • Seven years' imprisonment and/or a fine on indictment
- Six months' imprisonment and/or a fine summarily

The Firearms Act 1968, s. 4 states:

(1) Subject to this section, it is an offence to shorten the barrel of a shot gun to a length less than 24 inches.

KEYNOTE

The same exclusions as per the offence of shortening a smooth bore section 1 firearm apply to this offence, i.e. registered firearms dealers are excluded from the wording of the conversion offence (s. 6(2) of the Firearms (Amendment) Act 1988) provided the shortening is done *for the sole purpose* of replacing a defective part of the barrel *so as to produce a new barrel having an overall length of at least 24 inches*.

For the length of the barrel see s. 57(6)(a) in **para 1.7.5.3**.

Once the shortening or conversion has taken place, the nature of the firearm will have changed (e.g. from a shotgun into a section 1 firearm), in which case the person will also commit the relevant possession offence unless he/she has the appropriate authorisation.

1.7.7 Air Weapons

Air weapons are defined under s. 1(3)(b) of the Firearms Act 1968. In summary these are air rifles, air guns or air pistols which do not fall within s. 5(1) and which are not of a type declared to be specially dangerous. Any air rifle, air gun or air pistol that uses or is designed or adapted for use with a self-contained gas cartridge system (carbon dioxide is not air) *does* fall within the definition of a prohibited weapon at s. 5(1).

Some air weapons are deemed to be specially dangerous and therefore subject to stricter control than conventional air weapons. Listed in r. 2 of the Firearms (Dangerous Air Weapons) Rules 1969, as amended, they include:

(1) [any] air rifle, air gun or air pistol—
    (a) which is capable of discharging a missile so that the missile has, on being discharged from the muzzle of the weapon, kinetic energy in excess, in the case of an air pistol, of 6ft lb or, in the case of an air weapon other than an air pistol, of 12ft lb, or
    (b) which is disguised as another object.
Note that this does not include a weapon falling within para. (1)(a) and which is designed for use only when submerged in water (r. 2(2)).

1.7.7.1 Air Weapon Offences

Section 32 of the Violent Crime Reduction Act 2006 imposed a 'face to face' requirement on trade transactions by persons selling air weapons.

OFFENCE: **Sales of Air Weapons by Way of Trade or Business to be Face to Face**—*Violent Crime Reduction Act 2006, s. 32*

- Triable summarily • Six months' imprisonment and/or a fine

The Violent Crime Reduction Act 2006, s. 32 states:

(1) This section applies where a person sells an air weapon by way of trade or business to an individual in Great Britain who is not registered as a firearms dealer.
(2) A person is guilty of an offence if, for the purposes of the sale, he transfers possession of the air weapon to the buyer otherwise than at a time when both—
    (a) the buyer, and
    (b) either the seller or a representative of his,
    are present in person.

KEYNOTE

A representative of the seller is a reference to a person who is:

- employed by the seller in his/her business as a registered firearms dealer;
- a registered firearms dealer who has been authorised by the seller to act on his/her behalf in relation to the sale; or
- a person who is employed by a person falling within s. 32(3)(b) in his/her business as a registered firearms dealer.

This allows an air weapon to be sent from one registered firearms dealer to another to make the final transfer in person to the buyer. It also enables someone to buy an air weapon from a dealer in a distant part of the country without one or other party to the transaction having to make a long journey, while still preserving the safeguards of a face-to-face handover.

OFFENCE: **Firing an Air Weapon Beyond Premises**—*Firearms Act 1968, s. 21A*

- Triable summarily • Fine

The Firearms Act 1968, s. 21A states:

(1) A person commits an offence if—
    (a) he has with him an air weapon on any premises; and
    (b) he uses it for firing a missile beyond those premises.
(2) In proceedings against a person for an offence under this section it shall be a defence for him to show that the only premises into or across which the missile was fired were premises the occupier of which had consented to the firing of the missile (whether specifically or by way of a general consent).

KEYNOTE

'Premises' is not defined by the Act other than it 'includes any land'.

This offence makes it an offence for a person of *any* age to fire an air weapon beyond the boundary of premises. A defence is provided to cover the situation where the person shooting has the consent of the occupier of the land over or into which he/she shoots.

OFFENCE: **Failing to Prevent Minors from Having Air Weapons**—*Firearms Act 1968, s. 24ZA*

- Triable summarily • Fine

The Firearms Act 1968, s. 24ZA states:

(1) It is an offence for a person in possession of an air weapon to fail to take reasonable precautions to prevent any person under the age of eighteen from having the weapon with him.

(2) Subsection (1) does not apply where by virtue of section 23 of this Act, the person under the age of eighteen is not prohibited from having the weapon with him.

(3) In proceedings for an offence under subsection (1) it is a defence that the person charged with the offence—

(a) believed the other person to be aged eighteen or over; and

(b) had reasonable ground for that belief.

The offence does not apply to an antique air weapon held as a curiosity or ornament (s. 58(2) of the 1968 Act), nor, under s. 24ZA(2), does it apply in circumstances where young persons are permitted to have an air weapon with them under one of the exceptions set out in s. 23 of the Act (**see para. 1.7.12**).

1.7.8 General Exemptions

The general exemptions apply to the provisions of ss. 1 to 5 of the Firearms Act 1968. They include:

Police permit holders

Under s. 7(1) of the 1968 Act, the chief officer of police may grant a permit authorising the possession of firearms or ammunition under the conditions specified in the permit.

Clubs, athletics and sporting purposes

Section 11 of the 1968 Act provides exemptions for a person:

* borrowing the firearm/ammunition from a certificate holder *for sporting purposes only* but where the person carrying the firearm/ammunition is under 18, this applies only if the other person is aged 18 or over (s. 11(1));
* possessing a firearm at an athletic meeting for the purposes of starting races (s. 11(2));
* in charge of a miniature rifle range buying, acquiring or possessing miniature rifles and ammunition, and using them at such a rifle range (s. 11(4));
* who is a member of an approved rifle club, miniature rifle club or pistol club to possess a firearm or ammunition *when engaged as a club member in target practice* (s. 15(1) of the Firearms (Amendment) Act 1988);
* borrowing a shotgun from the occupier of private premises and using it on those premises *in the occupier's presence* but where the person borrowing the shotgun is under 18, this only applies if the occupier is aged 18 or over (s. 11(5) of the 1968 Act);
* using a shotgun at a time and place approved by the chief officer of police for shooting at artificial targets (s. 11(6)).

Borrowed rifle on private premises

Section 16 of the Firearms (Amendment) Act 1988 allows a person to borrow a rifle from the occupier of private premises, provided:

* the person is on those premises and in the presence of the occupier (or the occupier's servant); and
* the occupier holds a certificate and the borrowing of the rifle complies with that certificate; and
* where the borrower is aged 17, the occupier in whose presence the rifle is used is 18 or over.

The person borrowing the rifle may buy or acquire ammunition for it in accordance with the certificate's conditions.

Visitors' permits

Section 17 of the Firearms (Amendment) Act 1988 provides for the issuing of a visitors' permit by a chief officer of police and for the possession of firearms and ammunition by the holder of such a permit.

Visitors' permits will not be issued to anyone without a European firearms pass. It is a summary offence (punishable with six months' imprisonment) to make a false statement in order to get a visitors' permit, and it is a similar offence to fail to comply with any conditions within such a permit (s. 17(10)).

Antiques as ornaments or curiosities

Section 58(2) of the 1968 Act allows for the sale, buying, transfer, acquisition or possession of antique firearms *as curiosities or ornaments*. Whether a firearm is such an antique will be a question of fact to be determined by the court in each case. Mere belief in the fact that a firearm is an antique will not be enough (*R* v *Howells* [1977] QB 614).

Authorised firearms dealers

Section 8(1) of the 1968 Act provides for registered firearms dealers (or their employees) to possess, acquire or buy firearms or ammunition in the ordinary course of their business without a certificate. If the possession etc. is not in the ordinary course of their business, the exemption will not apply.

1.7.9 Imitation Firearm Offences

OFFENCE: **Converting Imitation Firearm—*Firearms Act 1968, s. 4(3)***
- Triable either way • Five years' imprisonment and/or a fine on indictment
- Six months' imprisonment and/or a fine summarily

The Firearms Act 1968, s. 4 states:

(3) It is an offence for a person other than a registered firearms dealer to convert into a firearm anything which, though having the appearance of being a firearm, is so constructed as to be incapable of discharging any missile through its barrel.

KEYNOTE

This offence involves the conversion of anything which has the appearance of a firearm so that it can be fired. Once the conversion has taken place, the nature of the imitation firearm will have changed, in which case the person will also commit the relevant possession offences unless he/she has the appropriate authorisation.

Sections 36 to 41 of the Violent Crime Reduction Act 2006 created three specific summary offences to deal with the misuse of firearms:

Section 36 makes it an offence to manufacture, import, modify or sell *realistic imitation firearms* as defined in s. 38.

Section 39 makes it an offence to manufacture, modify or import an imitation firearm that does not conform to specifications set out in regulations to be made by the Secretary of State.

Section 40 inserted s. 24A into the 1968 Act and makes it an offence to sell an imitation firearm to a person under 18. It also makes it an offence for a person under 18 to purchase an imitation firearm.

KEYNOTE

For the purposes of the 2006 Act, an 'imitation firearm' is defined as that used in the Firearms Act 1968, i.e. in the 'general sense' (**see para. 1.7.2.4**). A 'realistic imitation firearm' is effectively a 'sub-category' of an imitation firearm in the general sense. A 'realistic imitation firearm' is defined as an imitation firearm which has an appearance that is so realistic as to make it indistinguishable, for all practical purposes, from a real firearm and is neither a deactivated firearm nor itself an antique (s. 38(1)).

An imitation firearm will be regarded as distinguishable if its size, shape or principal colour is unrealistic for a real firearm (s. 38(3)). The Violent Crime Reduction Act 2006 (Realistic Imitation Firearms) Regulations 2007 (SI 2007/2606) provide defences for an offence under s. 36, and make provision in connection with the definition of 'realistic imitation firearm' in s. 38, specifying the sizes and colours which are to be regarded as unrealistic for a real firearm.

1.7.10 Criminal Use of Firearms

There is a series of firearms offences linked to criminal behaviour. The aggravating factor of the presence of a firearm is evidenced by the fact that the majority carry a life imprisonment sentence; those that do not still carry 10 years' imprisonment.

1.7.10.1 Possession with Intent to Endanger Life

OFFENCE: **Possession with intent to Endanger Life—*Firearms Act 1968, s. 16***

- Triable on indictment • Life imprisonment and/or a fine

The Firearms Act 1968, s. 16 states:

It is an offence for a person to have in his possession any firearm or ammunition with intent by means thereof to endanger life or to enable another person by means thereof to endanger life, whether any injury has been caused or not.

KEYNOTE

This offence *cannot be committed by possessing an imitation firearm.*

The offence involves 'possession' so there is no need for the firearm or ammunition to be produced/shown to another.

You will have to show an intention by the defendant to behave in a way that he/she knows will in fact endanger the life of another (*R* v *Brown and Ciarla* [1995] Crim LR 328); the intention *is not* to enable the defendant or another to *kill.* That intent does not have to be an immediate one and it may be conditional, e.g. an intent to shoot someone if they do not do as they are asked (*R* v *Bentham* [1973] QB 357).

The life endangered must be the life of 'another', not the defendant's (*R* v *Norton* [1977] Crim LR 478) so possession with intent to commit suicide would not be covered by the offence. The person whose life is endangered may be outside the United Kingdom (*R* v *El-Hakkaoui* [1975] 1 WLR 396).

The firearm or ammunition must provide the means by which life is endangered; it is not enough to have a firearm or ammunition at the time when life is endangered by some other means (e.g. by dangerous driving).

Self-defence can be raised in answer to a charge under s. 16 of the 1968 Act but such circumstances will be very unusual (*R* v *Georgiades* [1989] 1 WLR 759). This defence could potentially apply where the defendant is carrying a firearm for his own defence anticipating an imminent attack (*R* v *Salih* [2007] EWCA Crim 2750).

1.7.10.2 Possession with Intent to Cause Fear of Violence

OFFENCE: **Possession with Intent to Cause Fear of Violence—*Firearms Act 1968, s. 16A***

> • Triable on indictment • 10 years' imprisonment and/or a fine

The Firearms Act 1968, s. 16A states:

> It is an offence for a person to have in his possession any firearm or imitation firearm with intent—
> (a) by means thereof to cause, or
> (b) to enable another person by means thereof to cause,
> any person to believe that unlawful violence will be used against him or another person.

KEYNOTE

Section 16A is committed by possession, accompanied by an intention to cause fear of violence at or immediately before the defendant's actions which are designed to cause such fear (*R* v *Goluchowski* [2006] EWCA Crim 1972). There is no need for a firearm/imitation firearm to be produced or shown to anyone, though it must provide the 'means' of the threat. Possession of a firearm/imitation firearm while making a general threat to someone who does not know of its presence is unlikely to fall within this section.

This offence includes imitation firearms in the general sense (see para. 1.7.2.4). In *K* v *DPP* [2006] EWHC 2183 (Admin), the appellant's submission that the knowledge of all those present, and in particular the complainant, that the gun was an imitation firearm was such as to make the commission of the offence impossible was rejected. K's purpose or intention was to make the complainant fear violence and it was not fatal to the conviction that the complainant was aware that it was an imitation firearm.

1.7.10.3 Using Firearm to Resist Arrest

OFFENCE: **Using Firearm to Resist Arrest—*Firearms Act 1968, s. 17(1)***

> • Triable on indictment • Life imprisonment and/or a fine

The Firearms Act 1968, s. 17 states:

> (1) It is an offence for a person to make or attempt to make any use whatsoever of a firearm or imitation firearm with intent to resist or prevent the lawful arrest or detention of himself or another person.

KEYNOTE

The 'firearm' to which s. 17 refers is that defined at **para. 1.7.2.1**, *except* component parts and silencers/flash diminishers (s. 17(4)). For that reason, while the offence includes imitation firearms in the general sense (see **para. 1.7.2.4**) it does not include imitation component parts, etc.

This offence requires proof, not of possession, but of evidence that the defendant made some *actual use* of the firearm and did so intending to resist/prevent the arrest of him/herself or someone else. Any arrest which the defendant intended to prevent/resist must have been 'lawful'.

1.7.10.4 Having Firearm with Intent to Commit Indictable Offence or Resist Arrest

OFFENCE: **Having Firearm with Intent to Commit an Indictable Offence or Resist Arrest—*Firearms Act 1968, s. 18(1)***

> • Triable on indictment • Life imprisonment and/or a fine

The Firearms Act 1968, s. 18 states:

(1) It is an offence for a person to have with him a firearm or imitation firearm with intent to commit an indictable offence, or to resist arrest or prevent the arrest of another, in either case while he has the firearm or imitation firearm with him.

KEYNOTE

This offence requires the defendant to 'have with him' a firearm. This is a more restrictive expression than 'possession' and requires that the firearm is 'readily accessible' to the defendant. In *R* v *Pawlicki* [1992] 1 WLR 827, the Court of Appeal decided that defendants in an auction room had firearms 'with them' which were in a car 50 yards away. Where a defendant left a firearm in his house which was a few miles from the scene of the relevant criminal offence, it was held that this was not enough to meet the requirement of 'having with him' (*R* v *Bradish* [2004] EWCA Crim 1340). Despite this narrower meaning, the defendant does not have to be shown to have been 'carrying' the firearm (*R* v *Kelt* [1977] 1 WLR 1365).

In *R* v *Stoddart* [1998] 2 Cr App R 25, the Court of Appeal made it clear that there are three elements to this offence:

(a) that the accused had with him a firearm or imitation firearm;

(b) that he intended to have it with him; and

(c) that at the same time he had the intention to commit an indictable offence or to resist or prevent arrest.

Proving (b) and (c) is made easier by s. 18(2) of the Act (below).

Intention

In proving the intent for this offence, s. 18 states:

(2) In proceedings for an offence under this section proof that the accused had a firearm or imitation firearm with him and intended to commit an offence, or to resist or prevent arrest, is evidence that he intended to have it with him while doing so.

It is not necessary to show that the defendant intended to *use* the firearm to commit the indictable offence or to prevent/resist the arrest (*Stoddart*).

The mental element is an essential part of this offence so if the defendant only formed the intent as a result of duress (as to which see chapter 1.4), this ingredient will not have been established (*R* v *Fisher* [2004] EWCA Crim 1190).

Section 18 does not appear to require that any arrest be 'lawful'.

This offence includes imitation firearms in the general sense (see para. 1.7.2.4).

The power of entry and search under s. 47 of the 1968 Act applies to this offence (see para. 1.7.12).

1.7.10.5 Possessing Firearm while Committing a Schedule 1 Offence

OFFENCE: **Possessing Firearm while Committing or Being Arrested for sch. 1 Offence—*Firearms Act 1968, s. 17(2)***
• Triable on indictment • Life imprisonment and/or a fine

The Firearms Act 1968, s. 17 states:

(2) If a person, at the time of his committing or being arrested for an offence specified in schedule 1 to this Act, has in his possession a firearm or imitation firearm, he shall be guilty of an offence under this subsection unless he shows that he had it in his possession for a lawful object.

KEYNOTE

This offence may be committed in two ways; either by being in possession of the weapon *at the time of committing* the sch. 1 offence or by being in possession of it *at the time of being arrested* for such an offence. In the second case there may be some time between actually committing the sch. 1 offence and being arrested for it. Nevertheless, if the defendant is in possession of the firearm at the time of his/her arrest, the offence is committed (unless he/she can show that it was for a lawful purpose).

There is no need for the defendant to be subsequently *convicted* of the sch. 1 offence, nor even to prove that it has been committed; all that is needed is to show that the defendant, at the time of the commission of the sch. 1 offence and/or of his/her arrest for a sch. 1 offence, had a firearm/imitation firearm in his/her possession (*R* v *Nelson* [2001] QB 55).

It is for the defendant to prove that the firearm was in his/her possession for a lawful purpose.

This offence includes imitation firearms in the general sense (**see para. 1.7.2.4**).

Schedule 1 Offences

There are a number of offences contained in sch. 1 but the *main* offences may be remembered by using the mnemonic ACTOR:

- Abduction—part I of the Child Abduction Act 1984 (child abduction).
- Criminal damage—s. 1 of the Criminal Damage Act 1971.
- Theft, robbery, burglary, blackmail and taking a conveyance—Theft Act 1968.
- Offences against the person—assaults and woundings (ss. 20 and 47 of the Offences Against the Person Act 1861), assault on police (s. 89 of the Police Act 1996) and civilian custody officers (s. 90(1) of the Criminal Justice Act 1991 and s. 13(1) of the Criminal Justice and Public Order Act 1994).
- Rape and other sexual/abduction offences—the following offences under the Sexual Offences Act 2003: s. 1 (rape), s. 2 (assault by penetration), s. 4 (causing a person to engage in sexual activity without consent), where the activity caused involved penetration within subs. (4)(a)–(d) of that section, s. 5 and s. 6 (rape and assault of a child under 13), s. 8 (causing or inciting a child under 13 to engage in sexual activity), where an activity involving penetration within subs. (2)(a)–(d) of that section was caused, s. 30 and s. 31 (sexual activity with/causing or inciting a person with a mental disorder impeding choice), where the touching involved or activity caused penetration within subs. (3)(a)–(d) of that section. Also offences under part I of the Child Abduction Act 1984.

Although covering several types of assault, sch. 1 does not extend to wounding/causing grievous bodily harm with intent (s. 18 of the Offences Against the Person Act 1861). Schedule 1 also covers the aiding, abetting or attempting to commit such offences.

1.7.10.6 Using Someone to Mind a Weapon

OFFENCE: **Using Someone to Mind a Weapon—*Violent Crime Reduction Act 2006, s. 28(1)***
- Triable on indictment • 10 years' imprisonment and/or a fine (firearms, etc.)
- Four years' imprisonment and/or a fine (offensive weapons, etc.)

The Violent Crime Reduction Act 2006, s. 28 states:

(1) A person is guilty of an offence if—
    (a) he uses another to look after, hide or transport a dangerous weapon for him; and
    (b) he does so under arrangements or in circumstances that facilitate, or are intended to facilitate, the weapon's being available to him for an unlawful purpose.
(2) For the purposes of this section the cases in which a dangerous weapon is to be regarded as available to a person for an unlawful purpose include any case where—
    (a) the weapon is available for him to take possession of it at a time and place; and
    (b) his possession of the weapon at that time and place would constitute, or be likely to involve or to lead to, the commission by him of an offence.

1.7.11 Further Firearms Offences

Alongside offences associated with the criminal use of firearms are several offences dealing with an offender 'having with him' a firearm in a public place and whilst trespassing.

1.7.11.1 Having Firearm or Imitation Firearm in Public Place

OFFENCE: **Having Firearm/Imitation Firearm in Public Place—*Firearms Act 1968, s. 19***

- Triable either way • Seven years' imprisonment and/or a fine on indictment (if the weapon is an imitation firearm 12 months' imprisonment and/or a fine)
- If the weapon is an air weapon six months' imprisonment and/or a fine

The Firearms Act 1968, s. 19 states:

A person commits an offence if, without lawful authority or reasonable excuse (the proof whereof lies on him), he has with him in a public place—

(a) a loaded shot gun,

(b) an air weapon (whether loaded or not),

(c) any other firearm (whether loaded or not) together with ammunition suitable for use in that firearm, or

(d) an imitation firearm.

KEYNOTE

The offence is triable only summarily when the firearm is an air weapon. The s. 19 offence may be committed whether the air weapon is lethal barrelled or not (*Street* v *DPP* [2003] EWHC 86 (Admin)).

A 'public place' includes any highway and any other premises or place to which, at the material time, the public have or are permitted to have access whether on payment or otherwise (s. 57(4) of the Act).

If the weapon is a shotgun it must be loaded. 'Loaded' means there is ammunition in the chamber or barrel (or in any magazine or other device) whereby the ammunition can be fed into the chamber or barrel by the manual or automatic operation of some part of the weapon (see s. 57(6)(b)). If the weapon is an imitation firearm (see para. 1.7.2.4) or an air weapon the offence is committed by the defendant having it with him/her. In the case of other firearms the offence is committed by the defendant having the firearm with him/her together with ammunition suitable for use in it.

For the meaning of 'has with him', see para. 1.7.10.4.

This offence is one of strict liability. If you can show that the defendant knew he had something with him and that the 'something' was a loaded shotgun, an air weapon, an imitation firearm, or another firearm with ammunition, the offence is complete (*R* v *Vann and Davis* [1996] Crim LR 52). It is for the defendant to show lawful authority or reasonable excuse; possession of a valid certificate does not of itself provide lawful authority for having the firearm/ammunition in a public place (*Ross* v *Collins* [1982] Crim LR 368).

1.7.11.2 Trespassing with Firearms

OFFENCE: **Trespassing with Firearm in Building—*Firearms Act 1968, s. 20(1)***
   • Triable either way (unless imitation firearm or air weapon) • Seven years' imprisonment and/or a fine on indictment • Six months' imprisonment and/or a fine summarily

The Firearms Act 1968, s. 20 states:

(1) A person commits an offence if, while he has a firearm or imitation firearm with him, he enters or is in any building or part of a building as a trespasser and without reasonable excuse (the proof whereof lies on him).

> **KEYNOTE**
>
> This offence is committed either by entering a building/part of a building or simply by *being* in such a place, in each case as a trespasser while having the firearm. As there is no need for the defendant to have 'entered' the building as a trespasser in every case, the offence might be committed after the occupier has withdrawn any permission for the defendant to be there.
>
> For the interpretation of 'has with him', **see para. 1.7.10.4.**
>
> It will be for defendants to prove that they had reasonable excuse (on the balance of probabilities).
>
> If the relevant firearm is an imitation or an air weapon, the offence is triable summarily.
>
> This offence includes imitation firearms in the general sense (**see para. 1.7.2.4**). If the relevant firearm is an imitation or an air weapon, the offence is triable summarily.
>
> The power of entry and search under s. 47 of the 1968 Act applies to this offence (**see para. 1.7.12**).

OFFENCE: **Trespassing with Firearm on Land—*Firearms Act 1968, s. 20(2)***
   • Triable summarily • Three months' imprisonment and/or a fine

The Firearms Act 1968, s. 20 states:

(2) A person commits an offence if, while he has a firearm or imitation firearm with him, he enters or is on any land as a trespasser and without reasonable excuse (the proof whereof lies on him).

> **KEYNOTE**
>
> The elements of this offence are generally the same as those for the s. 20(1) offence (**see para. 1.7.11.2**).
>
> There is no requirement that the defendant had the firearm/imitation firearm with him/her when entering onto the land.
>
> 'Land' for these purposes will include land covered by water (s. 20(3)).
>
> This offence includes imitation firearms in the general sense (**see para. 1.7.2.4**).
>
> The power of entry and search under s. 47 of the 1968 Act applies to this offence (**see para. 1.7.12**).

1.7.12 Police Powers

The Firearms Act 1968, s. 47 states:

(1) A constable may require any person whom he has reasonable cause to suspect—
   (a) of having a firearm, with or without ammunition, with him in a public place; or
   (b) to be committing or about to commit, elsewhere than in a public place, an offence relevant for the purposes of this section,
   to hand over the firearm or any ammunition for examination by the constable.

1.7.12.1 Power to Demand Documentation

The Firearms Act 1968, s. 48 states:

(1) A constable may demand, from any person whom he believes to be in possession of a firearm or ammunition to which section 1 of this Act applies, or of a shot gun, the production of his firearm certificate or, as the case may be, his shot gun certificate.

1.7.13 Possession or Acquisition of Firearms by Convicted Persons

Section 21 of the Firearms Act 1968 places restrictions on convicted persons in respect of their possession of firearms and/or ammunition.

Any person who has been sentenced to:

- custody for *life*, or
- to preventive detention, imprisonment, corrective training, youth custody or detention in a young offender institution for *three years or more*

must not, *at any time*, have a firearm or ammunition in his/her possession, i.e. a lifetime ban.

Section 21 goes on to provide that any person who has been sentenced to imprisonment, youth custody, detention in a young offender institution or a secure training order for *three months or more, but less than three years*, must not have a firearm or ammunition in his/her possession at any time before the end of a five-year period beginning on the date of his/her release.

Date of release means, for a sentence partly served and partly suspended, the date on which the offender completes the part to be served and, in the case of a person subject to a secure training order, the date on which he/she is released from detention (under the various relevant statutes) or the date halfway through the total specified by the court making the order, whichever is the latest (s. 21(2A)).

Section 110 of the Anti-social Behaviour, Crime and Policing Act 2014 extends the definition of a prohibited person to include persons with suspended sentences of three months or more. The period of five years will begin on the second day after the date on which sentence has been passed. A suspended sentence can only be for a maximum of two years so the permanent prohibition will not apply.

A person holding a licence under the Children and Young Persons Act 1933 or a person subject to a recognizance to keep the peace or be of good behaviour with a condition relating to the possession of firearms, must not, *at any time during the licence or the recognizance*, have a firearm or ammunition in his/her possession (s. 21(3)).

Where sentences or court orders are mentioned, their Scottish equivalents will also apply and a person prohibited in Northern Ireland from possessing a firearm/ammunition will also be prohibited in Great Britain (s. 21(3A)).

Section 21 *does not apply to imitation firearms* as there is no express reference to them in the section and because the reference in the Firearms Act 1982 does not apply.

Section 21(6) provides that a person prohibited under this section from having in his possession a firearm or ammunition, may apply to the Crown Court for a removal of the prohibition and if the application is granted that prohibition shall not then apply to him.

1.7.13.1 Supplying Firearm to Person Prohibited by Section 21

OFFENCE: **Selling or Transferring Firearm to Person Prohibited by s. 21—*Firearms Act 1968, s. 21(5)***

- Triable either way • Five years' imprisonment and/or a fine on indictment
- Six months' imprisonment and/or a fine summarily

The Firearms Act 1968, s. 21 states:

(5) It is an offence for a person to sell or transfer a firearm or ammunition to, or to repair, test or prove a firearm or ammunition for, a person whom he knows or has reasonable ground for believing to be prohibited by this section from having a firearm or ammunition in his possession.

KEYNOTE

Given that all people are presumed to know the law once it is published, it would seem that the knowledge or belief by the defendant would apply to the *convictions* of the other person, not the fact that possession by that person was an offence.

1.7.14 Other Restrictions on Possession or Acquisition

Sections 22 to 24 of the Firearms Act 1968 create a number of summary offences restricting the involvement of people of various ages in their dealings with certain types of firearm and ammunition.

In summary the age restrictions are as follows:

- a person under 18:
  + must not purchase or hire any firearm or ammunition (s. 22(1)(a));
  + must not have with him/her an air weapon or ammunition for an air weapon (s. 22(4)). An exception to this is where the person is under the supervision of another who is at least 21 years old. However, if the person under 18 fires the weapon beyond the relevant premises, he/she will commit an offence under s. 21A (**see para. 1.7.7.1**) and the person supervising him/her will be guilty of an offence under s. 23(1). It is not an offence under this section for a person aged 14 or over to have with him/her an air weapon or ammunition on private premises with the consent of the occupier (s. 23(3));
  + it is an offence to sell or let on hire an air weapon or ammunition for an air weapon to a person under the age of 18 (s. 24(1)(a)), or to make a gift/part with possession of an air weapon or ammunition for an air weapon to such a person (unless under the permitted circumstances above) (s. 24(4));
  + it is an offence to sell an imitation firearm to a person under the age of 18 (s. 24A(2)), or for a person under 18 to purchase one (s. 24A(1)). It is a defence to show that the vendor believed that the purchaser was 18 or over and had reasonable grounds for that belief (s. 24A(3));
- a person under 15:
  + must not have with him/her an assembled shotgun unless supervised by a person aged at least 21 or while the shotgun is securely covered so it cannot be fired (s. 22(3)); and
  + it is an offence to make a gift of a shotgun/ammunition to such a person (s. 24(3));
- a person under 14:
  + must not have in his/her possession a section 1 firearm or ammunition (s. 22(2));
  + must not part with possession of any firearm or ammunition to which s. 15 of the Firearms (Amendment) Act 1988 applies, except in circumstances where under s. 11(1), (3) or (4) of this Act, he/she is entitled to have possession of it without holding a firearm certificate; and
  + it is an offence to make a gift or lend or part with possession of such a firearm/ammunition to such a person (s. 24(2)) (subject to some exceptions relating to sports and shooting clubs—see s. 11 of the Firearms Act 1968 and s. 15 of the Firearms (Amendment) Act 1988).

There is a further provision creating an offence for a person under 18 who is the holder of a certificate using a firearm for a purpose not authorised by the European Weapons Directive (s. 22(1A)).

KEYNOTE

For the full extent of these restrictions and their exemptions, reference should be made to the 1968 and 1988 Acts. Note that s. 24(5) of the Firearms Act 1968 provides that it is a defence to prove that the person charged with an offence believed that other person to be of or over the age mentioned and had reasonable grounds for the belief.

It is a summary offence (punishable by one month's imprisonment and/or a fine) to be in possession of *any* loaded firearm when drunk (s. 12 of the Licensing Act 1872). There is no requirement that the person be in a public place.

1.7.15 Restrictions on Transfer of Firearms

The Firearms (Amendment) Act 1997 created a number of offences concerned with the transfer, lending, hiring etc. of firearms and ammunition. It is an offence to fail to comply with these requirements (ss. 32 to 35). The mode of trial and punishment depends on whether the weapon is a section 1 firearm or a shotgun.

In brief, a person 'transferring' (that is, selling, letting on hire, lending or giving) a section 1 firearm or ammunition to another must:

- produce a certificate or permit entitling him/her to do so (s. 32(2)(a)),
- they must comply with all the conditions of that certificate or permit (s. 32(2)(b)), and
- the transferor must personally hand the firearm or ammunition over to the receiver (s. 32(2)(c)).

The 1997 Act also requires that any person who is the holder of a certificate or permit who is involved in such a transfer (which includes lending a shotgun for a period of more than 72 hours) shall within seven days of the transfer give notice to the chief officer of police who granted the certificate or permit (s. 33(2)).

Notice is also required of certificate or permit holders where a firearm is lost, deactivated or destroyed or where ammunition is lost, or where firearms are sold outside Great Britain (see ss. 34 and 35).

OFFENCE: **Trade Transactions by Person not Registered as Firearms Dealer— _Firearms Act 1968, s. 3(1)_**
  - Triable summarily • Six months' imprisonment and/or a fine

The Firearms Act 1968, s. 3 states:

(1) A person commits an offence if, by way of trade or business, he—
  (a) manufactures, sells, transfers, repairs, tests or proves any firearm or ammunition to which section 1 of this Act applies, or a shot gun;
  (b) exposes for sale or transfer, or has in his possession for sale, transfer, repair, test or proof any such firearm or ammunition, or a shot gun, or
  (c) sells or transfers an air weapon, exposes such a weapon for sale or transfer or has such a weapon in his possession for sale or transfer,

  without being registered under this Act as a firearms dealer.

KEYNOTE

A registered firearms dealer is a person who, by way of trade or business, manufactures, sells, transfers, repairs, tests or proves firearms or ammunition to which s. 1 of this Act applies, or shotguns, or sells or transfers air weapons.

If the person undertakes the repair, proofing etc. of a section 1 firearm or ammunition or a shotgun otherwise than as a trade or business, he/she commits an offence (which is triable either way and is punishable by five years' imprisonment and/or a fine on indictment or by six months' imprisonment and/or a fine summarily) under s. 3(3) unless he/she can point to some authorisation under the Act allowing him/her to do so.

Section 3 goes on to create further either way offences of selling or transferring a firearm or ammunition to someone other than a registered firearms dealer or someone otherwise authorised under the Act to buy or acquire them and of falsifying certificates with a view to acquiring firearms.

Registration is under s. 33 of the 1968 Act.

'Transferring' is also defined under s. 57(4) and includes letting on hire, giving, lending and parting with possession.

Section 9(2) of the 1968 Act exempts auctioneers from the restrictions on selling and possessing for the purposes of sale of firearms and ammunition where the auctioneer has a permit from the chief officer of police. There are further defences provided by s. 9 (for carriers and warehouse staff) and also under s. 8 (transfer to people authorised to possess firearms without a certificate).

1.8 | Racially and Religiously Aggravated Offences

1.8.1 Introduction

The Crime and Disorder Act 1998 takes existing offences and sets out circumstances in which those existing offences become racially or religiously aggravated. The 'aggravated' form of the offence carries a higher maximum penalty than the ordinary form of the offence. Those offences are dealt with in the relevant chapters of the Manuals—the first group is assaults and follows this chapter.

1.8.2 Offences Covered by the Legislation

The offences that can become racially or religiously aggravated can be grouped in four categories:

- Assaults
    - wounding or grievous bodily harm—Offences Against the Person Act 1861, s. 20
    - causing actual bodily harm—Offences Against the Person Act 1861, s. 47
    - common assault—Criminal Justice Act 1988, s. 39 (**see chapter 1.9**)
- Criminal Damage
    - 'simple' criminal damage—Criminal Damage Act 1971, s. 1(1) (**see chapter 1.16**)
- Public Order
    - causing fear or provocation of violence—Public Order Act 1986, s. 4
    - intentional harassment, alarm or distress—Public Order Act 1986, s. 4A
    - causing harassment, alarm or distress—Public Order Act 1986, s. 5 (see *General Police Duties*, **chapter 4.11**)
- Harassment
    - harassment—Protection from Harassment Act 1997, s. 2
    - stalking—Protection from Harassment Act 1997, s. 2A
    - putting people in fear of violence—Protection from Harassment Act 1997, s. 4
    - stalking involving fear of violence or serious alarm or distress—Protection from Harassment Act 1997, s. 4A (see *General Police Duties*, **para. 4.8.4**).

KEYNOTE

The *basic offence must* have been committed. Only when that is accomplished should consideration then be given as to whether the offence is aggravated *within the meaning of s. 28 of the Act* (**see para. 1.8.3**). While the definition of a 'racist' incident is of critical importance to police officers, that definition ('a racist incident is any incident which is perceived to be racist by the victim or any other person') must not be confused with the definition of a 'racially or religiously aggravated' offence under s. 28 of the Act. A 'racist' incident *does not automatically* become a racially or religiously aggravated offence.

1.8.3 'Racially or Religiously Aggravated'

Section 28 of the Crime and Disorder Act 1998 states:

(1) An offence is racially or religiously aggravated for the purposes of sections 29 to 32...if—

    (a) at the time of committing the offence, or immediately before or after doing so, the offender demonstrates towards the victim of the offence hostility based on the victim's membership (or presumed membership) of a racial or religious group; or

    (b) the offence is motivated (wholly or partly) by hostility towards members of a racial or religious group based on their membership of that group.

(2) In subsection (1)(a) above—

'membership', in relation to a racial or religious group, includes association with members of that group;

'presumed' means presumed by the offender.

(3) It is immaterial for the purposes of paragraph (a) or (b) of subsection (1) above whether or not the offender's hostility is also based, to any extent, on any other factor not mentioned in that paragraph.

(4) In this section 'racial group' means a group of persons defined by reference to race, colour, nationality (including citizenship) or ethnic or national origins.

(5) In this section 'religious group' means a group of persons defined by reference to religious belief or lack of religious belief.

1.8.3.1 Timing of the Hostility

A racial insult uttered moments before an assault on a doorman was enough to make the offence racially aggravated for the purposes of s. 29 of the Crime and Disorder Act 1998 (*DPP* v *Woods* [2002] EWHC 85 (Admin)). In *DPP* v *McFarlane* [2002] EWHC 485 (Admin) it was decided that, where the expressions 'jungle bunny', 'black bastard' and 'wog' were used, the offence was made out as the words were used immediately before and at the time of the commission of the offence (contrary to s. 4 of the Public Order Act 1986).

The word 'immediately' in s. 28(1) not only means immediately before but also *immediately after* the commission of the offence.

The need for any such hostility to be demonstrated *immediately* means that it must be shown to have taken place in the immediate context of the basic offence. In *Parry* v *DPP* [2004] EWHC 3112 (Admin) the defendant had caused damage to a neighbour's door by throwing nail polish over it. The police attended 20 minutes after the damage had occurred and spoke to the defendant who was, by that time, sitting in his own house. The defendant made comments demonstrating hostility based on the victim's membership of a racial group. The defendant was convicted of racially aggravated criminal damage but appealed and the conviction was quashed. The court held that the wording of the statute meant that any hostility had to be demonstrated *immediately* before or *immediately* after the substantive offence and that the courts below (magistrates') had not been entitled to consider the retrospective effect of the comments made later by the defendant.

1.8.3.2 Demonstration of Hostility

Section 28(1)(a) requires that the defendant demonstrate hostility immediately before, during or after committing the offence. This is not to establish the accused's state of mind, but what he *did* or *said* so as to demonstrate hostility towards the victim. The demonstration will often be by way of words, shouting, holding up a banner etc. or by adherence to a group that is demonstrating racial hostility.

In the context of criminal damage, the Divisional Court has confirmed that the relevant hostility can be demonstrated even if the victim is no longer present or is not present (*Parry*). However, the need for any such hostility to be demonstrated *immediately* means that it must be shown to have taken place in the immediate context of the offence.

1.8.3.3 Hostility

Common to both factors under s. 28(1)(a) and (b) is the notion of 'hostility' which is not defined by the Act. The *Oxford English Dictionary* defines 'hostile' as 'of the nature or disposition of an enemy; unfriendly, antagonistic'. It would seem relatively straightforward to show that someone's behaviour in committing the relevant offences was 'unfriendly or antagonistic'.

1.8.3.4 Victim

The demonstration of hostility will be towards the *victim* based on the *victim's* membership or presumed membership of a racial or religious group (under s. 28(1)(a)). This causes no difficulty where the offence is one of assault, public order or harassment where the victim is a person or where the offence is a criminal damage matter and the property is owned by a person (s. 30(3) of the Act provides that the person to whom the property belongs or is treated as belonging, will be treated as the victim). However, there are problems where the victim of criminal damage is a corporate body, e.g. where a bus shelter belonging to a transport company is damaged by racist graffiti. Of course the transport company may have a legal personality but it is impossible for it to have a race or a religion. Therefore it cannot be possible to prove the offence under s. 28(1)(a) as it must be based on the victim's membership or presumed membership of a racial or religious group. In these circumstances the most suitable charge will be under s. 28(1)(b) of the Act (motivation).

Police officers can be victims of these offences and are entitled to the same protection under the legislation as anyone else (*R* v *Jacobs* [2001] 2 Cr App R (S) 38).

> **KEYNOTE**
>
> The victim's perception of the incident (whatever it is) is totally irrelevant.

1.8.3.5 Motivation by Hostility

Section 28(1)(b) is concerned with the accused's motivation, which does concern his subjective state of mind. It will often be the case that the kind of demonstration referred to in **para. 1.8.3.2** would be evidence of such motivation. In *Taylor* v *DPP* [2006] EWHC 1202 (Admin), it was decided that use of phrases such as 'fucking nigger' and 'fucking coon bitch', patently not used in a jesting manner, must, in the circumstance of the case, have led any judge to find that the offence (in this case, the Public Order Act 1986, s. 5(1)(a)) was motivated, at least in part, by racial hostility as described in s. 28(1)(b). The fact that the offence is motivated only in part by such hostility would not alter the fact that the offence has been committed (motivated wholly or *partly* by such hostility).

1.8.3.6 Racial Groups

Section 28(4) of the Crime and Disorder Act 1998 states that a 'racial group' means a group of persons defined by reference to race, colour, nationality (including citizenship) or ethnic or national origins.

In determining whether or not a group is defined by *ethnic origins*, the courts will have regard to the judgment in the House of Lords in *Mandla* v *Dowell Lee* [1983] 2 AC 548. In that case their lordships decided that Sikhs were such a group after considering whether they as a group had:

- a long shared *history*;
- a *cultural tradition* of their own, including family and social customs and manners, often, but not necessarily, associated with religious observance;
- either a *common geographical origin* or descent from a small number of *common ancestors*;

- a *common language*, not necessarily peculiar to that group;
- a *common literature* peculiar to that group;
- a *common religion* different from that of neighbouring groups or the general community surrounding the group; and
- the characteristic of being a *minority* or an *oppressed* or a *dominant* group within a larger community.

Lord Fraser's dictum in *Mandla* suggests that the first two characteristics above are essential in defining an 'ethnic group', while the others are at least relevant. His lordship also approved a decision from New Zealand to the effect that Jews are a group with common ethnic origins (*King-Ansell* v *Police* [1979] 2 NZLR 531).

KEYNOTE

When considering whether an offence was racially motivated under s. 28, hostility demonstrated to people who were foreign nationals simply because they were 'foreign' can be just as objectionable as hostility based on some more limited racial characteristic. In *DPP* v *M* [2004] EWHC 1453 (Admin) a juvenile used the words 'bloody foreigners' immediately before smashing the window of a kebab shop. The Divisional Court held that this was capable of amounting to an expression of hostility based on a person's membership or presumed membership of a racial group for the purposes of s. 28(1)(a) of the Crime and Disorder Act 1998. Although the statutory wording used the expression 'a racial group', the court held that a specific and inclusive definition of such a group had to be used by the defendant (e.g. the defendant did not have to single out a specific nationality) and the size of group referred to by a defendant (such as all 'foreigners') was irrelevant. In *R* v *Rogers* [2005] EWCA Crim 2863 the defendant had called three Spanish women 'bloody foreigners' and told them to 'go back to your own country'. The prosecution case was that the defendant had demonstrated hostility based on the women's membership of a racial group. The court's decision clarifies the position that, for an offence to be aggravated under s. 28, the defendant has first to form a view that the victim is a member of a racial group (within the definition in s. 28(4)) and then has to say (or do) something that demonstrates hostility towards the victim based on membership of that group. However, the Court of Appeal noted that the very wide meaning of racial group under s. 28(4) gives rise to a danger of aggravated offences being charged where mere 'vulgar abuse' had included racial descriptions that did not truly indicate hostility to the race in question. Consequently, s. 28 should not be used unless the prosecuting authority is satisfied that the facts truly suggest that the offence was aggravated (rather than simply accompanied) by racism.

The Divisional Court has held that the words 'white man's arse licker' and 'brown Englishman' when used to accompany an assault on an Asian victim did not necessarily make the assault 'racially aggravated' and that the prosecution had not done enough to show that the assailants' behaviour fell under the definition set out in s. 28 of the 1998 Act (*DPP* v *Pal* [2000] Crim LR 756), a case that is hard to reconcile with s. 28(2).

Traditional Romany gypsies are capable of being a racial group on the basis of ethnic origin (*Commission for Racial Equality* v *Dutton* [1989] QB 783). The term 'Travellers' would not be covered, although in *O'Leary* v *Allied Domecq* (2000) 29 August, unreported (Case No 950275-79) it was held that 'Irish Travellers' were a distinct group for the purposes of the Race Relations Act 1976. However, it should be noted that this decision is only 'persuasive' (as it was a county court decision) and our courts have yet to decide firmly whether 'Irish Travellers' are a 'racial group' for the purposes of the Crime and Disorder Act 1998. It is likely that the 'Irish' element would be covered anyway as English and Scottish people have been held to constitute groups defined by reference to national origins and thus as members of 'racial groups' in the broad sense as defined and protected from discrimination under the Race Relations Act 1976 (now the Equality Act 2010) (*Northern Joint Police Board* v *Power* [1997] IRLR 610). This decision ought logically to extend to Irish and Welsh people. This does not mean that 'travellers' are entirely excluded from the protection the Act offers as, for example, if a 'New-Age' traveller were subject to a trigger offence accompanied by a demonstration of hostility based on his/her skin colour or religion as opposed to being simply a 'New-Age' traveller, the offence would be committed.

In *Attorney-General's Reference (No. 4 of 2004), sub nom Attorney-General* v *D* [2005] EWCA Crim 889 the use of the word 'immigrant', in its simple implication that a person was 'non-British', was specific enough to denote membership of a 'racial group' within its meaning in s. 28(4) of the Crime and Disorder Act 1998.

1.8.3.7 Religious Groups

A 'religious group' may, for the purposes of the Act, include a group defined by its lack of religious beliefs. If, for example, D assaults V and at the time of the assault D demonstrates hostility towards V because V is an atheist or humanist who rejects religious beliefs, D must be guilty of a religiously aggravated offence. The same could be said of an assault on an agnostic.

A purely religious group such as Rastafarians (who have been held not to be members of an ethnic group *per se* (*Dawkins* v *Crown Suppliers* (*Property Services Agency*) [1993] ICR 517) are covered by the aggravated forms of offences as they are a religious group. In reality, a number of racial groups will overlap with religious groups in any event; Rastafarians would be a good example. An attack on a Rastafarian might be a racially aggravated offence under s. 28 because it was based on the defendant's hostility towards a *racial group* (e.g. African-Caribbeans) into which many Rastafarians fall. Alternatively, an attack might be made on a white Rastafarian based on the victim's religious beliefs (or lack of religious beliefs), i.e. his 'membership of a religious group'. Muslims have also been held not to be a racial group (*JH Walker* v *Hussain* [1996] ICR 291) but Muslims are clearly members of a religious group and, as such, are covered by the Act.

KEYNOTE

To be guilty of an offence that is racially or religiously aggravated, it is not necessary that the accused be of a different racial, national or ethnic (or religious) group from the victim (*R* v *White* [2001] EWCA Crim 216).

1.8.3.8 Membership

An important extension of 'racial or religious groups' is the inclusion of people who associate with members of that group. 'Membership' *for the purposes of s. 28(1)(a)* will include *association* with members of that group (s. 28(2)). This means that a white man who has a black female partner would potentially fall within the category of a 'member' of her racial group and vice versa. Moreover, people who work within certain racial or religious groups within the community could also be regarded as members of those groups for these purposes.

For the purposes of s. 28(1)(a), 'membership' will also include anyone *presumed by the defendant* to be a member of a racial or religious group. Therefore, if a defendant wrongly presumed that a person was a member of a racial or religious group, say a Pakistani Muslim, and assaulted that person as a result, the defendant's *presumption* would be enough to make his/her behaviour 'racially or religiously aggravated', even though the victim was in fact an Indian Hindu.

Such a presumption would not extend to the aggravating factors under s. 28(1)(b). The only apparent reason for this would seem to be that the s. 28(1)(a) offence requires hostility to be demonstrated towards a particular person ('the victim') while the offence under s. 28(1)(b) envisages hostility towards members of a racial or religious group generally and does not require a specific victim.

Section 28(3) goes on to provide that it is immaterial whether the defendant's hostility (in either case under s. 28(1)) is also based to any extent on *any other factor*. This concession in s. 28(3) only prevents the defendant pointing to another *factor* in order to explain his/her behaviour in committing the relevant offence (assault, criminal damage, etc.). Although it removes the opportunity for a defendant to argue that his/her behaviour was as a result of other factors (e.g. arising out of a domestic dispute), the subsection does not remove the burden on the prosecution to show that the defendant either demonstrated racial or religious hostility or was motivated by it.

1.9 Non-Fatal Offences Against the Person

1.9.1 Introduction

Non-fatal offences against the person are common, so officers need to be able to consider what type of assault they are dealing with. This chapter begins by explaining some of the basic areas of assault law before moving on to deal with more serious assault crimes.

1.9.2 Assault

An assault is any act which intentionally or recklessly causes another to apprehend immediate unlawful violence (*Fagan* v *Metropolitan Police Commissioner* [1969] 1 QB 439). The mental elements involved, i.e. the intention or recklessness on the part of the defendant and the 'apprehension' on the part of the victim, means that *no physical contact* between the offender and victim is required. If X shouts at Y 'I'm going to kick your head in!', intending Y to believe the threat and Y does believe it, an assault has been committed by X against Y. Assault can only be committed by carrying out an act; it cannot be committed by an omission.

1.9.2.1 Mental Elements of Assault

On the part of the defendant, the *mens rea* needed to prove assault is either:

- the intention to cause apprehension of immediate unlawful violence; or
- subjective recklessness as to that consequence.

The victim must 'apprehend' (believe) that he/she is going to be subjected to immediate unlawful violence, so the state of mind of the *victim* in an assault is relevant. If X threatened to shoot Y with an imitation pistol then X could be charged with assault provided Y believed that the pistol was real and that he/she was going to be shot (apprehending unlawful violence). The fact that the pistol was an imitation and could never actually physically harm Y is not important as X has caused Y to apprehend immediate violence being used (*Logdon* v *DPP* [1976] Crim LR 121). If Y knew that the pistol was an imitation and that it could not be fired to hurt him, then Y would not believe the threat and would not 'apprehend' immediate unlawful violence and there would be no assault committed by X. Likewise, if X threw a stone at Y, who has his back to X when the stone is thrown, and the stone sails past Y's head without Y noticing it, there would be no assault as Y did not 'apprehend' unlawful violence.

'Apprehension' does not mean 'fear' so there is no need to show that the victim was actually in fear. So if V is threatened with violence by D and V does apprehend the threat of immediate violence, it does not matter whether he/she is frightened by it. He/she may relish the opportunity to teach D a lesson, and yet still be regarded as the victim of D's assault. The violence apprehended by the victim does not have to be a 'certainty'. Causing a fear of some possible violence can be enough (*R* v *Ireland* [1998] AC 147) provided that the violence feared is about to happen in the *immediate* future (*R* v *Constanza* [1997] 2 Cr App R 492).

1.9.2.2 What is 'Immediate'?

Although the force threatened must be immediate, that immediacy is somewhat elastic. Courts have accepted that, where a person makes a threat from outside a victim's house to the victim inside, an assault is committed even though there will be some time lapse before the defendant can carry out the threat.

In *Ireland* the House of Lords suggested that a threat to cause violence 'in a minute or two' might be enough to qualify as an assault; a threat to provoke some apprehension of violence in the more distant future would not suffice.

The victim must be shown to have feared the use of *force*; it will not be enough to show that a person threatened by words (or silence) feared more words or silence.

1.9.2.3 Words

Words (and silence) can amount to an assault provided they are accompanied by the required *mens rea*. In *Ireland* it was held that telephone calls to a victim, followed by silences (which led the victims to fear that unlawful force would be used against them), could fulfil the requirements for the *actus reus* of assault if it brought about the desired consequences (e.g. fear of the immediate use of unlawful force). It was accepted that 'a thing said is also a thing done' and the view that words can never amount to an assault was rejected.

Where the words threatening immediate unlawful force come in the form of letters, it has been held that an assault may have been committed (*Constanza* at **para. 1.9.2.1**). It is natural to assume that *any form of communication* can be used as a method for an assault. Thus it would be possible to assault someone via an email or a text message.

1.9.2.4 Conditional Threats

Words can *negate* an assault if they make a conditional threat, e.g., where you attend an incident and one person says to another '*If these officers weren't here I'd chin you!*'. In this situation the defendant is making a *hypothetical* threat and is really saying 'if it weren't for the existence of certain circumstances, I would assault you' (*Tuberville* v *Savage* (1669) 1 Mod Rep 3). This should be contrasted with occasions where the defendant makes an immediate threat conditional upon some real circumstance, e.g. '*If you don't cross the road, I'll break your neck*'. Such threats have been held, in a civil case, to amount to an assault (*Read* v *Coker* (1853) 138 ER 1437).

1.9.3 Battery

A battery is committed when a person intentionally or recklessly (subjectively) inflicts unlawful force on another (*Fagan* v *Metropolitan Police Commissioner* [1969] 1 QB 439). Battery *requires physical contact* with the victim, so the offence could not be carried out via the phone (causing psychiatric injury (*R* v *Ireland* [1998] AC 147)). It is sufficient to constitute battery that the defendant attacks the clothing which another is wearing (*R* v *Day* (1845) 1 Cox CC 207).

Battery need not be preceded by an assault. A blow may, for example, be struck from behind, without warning.

A very small degree of physical contact will be enough, not, as many think, an act involving serious violence.

That force can be applied directly or indirectly. For example, where a defendant punched a woman causing her to drop and injure a child she was holding, he was convicted of the offence against that child (*Haystead* v *Chief Constable of Derbyshire* [2000] 3 All ER 890). In *DPP* v *Santa-Bermudez* [2003] EWHC 2908 (Admin), the defendant was held to have committed a battery against a police officer when he falsely assured her that he had no 'sharps' in his possession, and thus caused her to stab herself on a hypodermic needle as she searched him.

1.9.4 Assault or Battery?

Although the terms 'assault' and 'battery' have distinct legal meanings, they are often referred to as simply 'assaults' or 'common assault'. It is, however, important to separate the two expressions when charging or laying an information against a defendant as to include both may be bad for duplicity (*DPP* v *Taylor* [1992] QB 645). In *Taylor*, the Divisional Court held that all common assaults and batteries are now offences contrary to s. 39 of the Criminal Justice Act 1988 (**see para. 1.9.7.1**), and that the information must include a reference to that section.

1.9.5 Consent

A key element in proving an assault is the *unlawfulness* of the force used or threatened. Although the courts have accepted consent as a feature which negates any offence, they have been reluctant to accept this feature in a number of cases. The two principal questions that may arise in this context are:

* did the alleged victim in fact consent (expressly or by implication) to what was done; and
* if so, do public policy considerations invalidate that consent?

1.9.5.1 Legitimate Consent to Risk of Injury

One of the more straightforward policy considerations would include the implied consent to contact with others during the course of everyday activities. We are all 'deemed' to consent to various harmless and unavoidable contact such as brushing against another on a crowded train. In such a case it will be a matter of fact to decide whether the behaviour complained of went beyond what was acceptable in those particular circumstances.

There are times when a person may consent to even serious harm such as during properly conducted sporting events (*Attorney-General's Reference (No. 6 of 1980)* [1981] QB 715), tattooing and medical operations. Participants in contact sports such as football are deemed to consent to the risk of clumsy or mistimed tackles or challenges; but this does not include tackles that are deliberately late or intended to cause harm (e.g. in an off-the-ball incident (*R* v *Lloyd* (1989) 11 Cr App R (S) 36)). Injuries caused in an unauthorised prize fight could not be consented to as this would not be a properly conducted sporting event. In *R* v *Barnes* [2004] EWCA Crim 3246 the defendant appealed against his conviction for inflicting grievous bodily harm after he caused a serious leg injury by way of a tackle during a football match. The tackle took place after the victim had kicked the ball into the goal but, while accepting that the tackle was hard, the defendant maintained that it had been a fair challenge and that the injury caused was accidental. The Court of Appeal held that where injuries were sustained in the course of contact sports, public policy limited the availability of the defence of consent to situations where there had been implicit consent to what had occurred. Whether conduct reached the required threshold to be treated as 'criminal' would depend on all the circumstances. The fact that the actions of the defendant had been within the rules and practice of the game would be a firm indication that what had occurred was not criminal, although in highly competitive sports even conduct *outside the rules* could be expected to occur in the heat of the moment, and such conduct still might not reach the threshold level required for it to be criminal. The court held that the threshold level was an objective one to be determined by the type of sport, the level at which it was played, the nature of the 'act', the degree of force used, the extent of the risk of injury and the state of mind of the defendant.

Teachers who are employed at schools for children with special needs, including behavioural problems, do not impliedly consent to the use of violence against them by pupils (*H* v *CPS* [2010] EWHC 1374 (Admin)).

What of the situation where the consent of the victim has been obtained by fraud? In *R* v *Richardson* [1999] QB 444 a dentist (Diane Richardson), who had been suspended by the General Dental Council, continued practising dentistry. The circumstances came to light and charges of assault were brought. Although initially convicted, the Court of Appeal quashed the conviction on the basis that fraud will only negate consent if it relates to the identity of the person or to the nature and quality of the act. Richardson did not lie about her identity (she did not lie about her name) nor about the nature and quality of the act (the dentistry carried out). While her behaviour was reprehensible, it did not amount to an offence. This does not mean that persons without appropriate qualifications sneaking into a surgery and putting on a white coat and calling themselves 'Doctor' followed by their true name could avoid liability if they then made physical contact with another in the guise of providing treatment. While there is no fraud as to identity, any treatment carried out would be caught by a fraud in respect of the quality of the act. Consent would also be negated if a genuine doctor indecently touched his patients on the basis that this was part of a routine medical examination when its true purpose was for sexual gratification (*R* v *Tabassum* [2000] 2 Cr App R 328).

1.9.5.2 Consent to Sado-masochistic Injuries

Where actual bodily harm (or worse) is deliberately inflicted, consent to it will ordinarily be deemed invalid on the grounds of public policy even if 'victims' know exactly what they are consenting to.

An example of this approach can be seen in the case of *R* v *Brown* [1994] 1 AC 212. That case involved members of a sado-masochist group who inflicted varying degrees of injuries on one another (under ss. 47 and 20 of the Offences Against the Person Act 1861) for their own gratification. The group claimed that they had consented to the injuries and therefore no assault or battery had taken place. Their lordships followed an earlier policy that *all assaults which result in more than transient harm will be unlawful unless there is good reason for allowing the plea of 'consent'*. Good reason will be determined in the light of a number of considerations:

- the practical consequences of the behaviour
- the dangerousness of the behaviour
- the vulnerability of the 'consenting' person.

Sado-masochistic injury may justifiably be made the subject of criminal law on grounds of the 'protection of health'. It was for this reason that the European Court of Human Rights held that there had been no violation of the defendants' right to respect for private and family life (under Article 8) in *Brown*.

Further issues in clarifying what will amount to 'true' or effective consent were added by the decision of the Court of Appeal in *R* v *Wilson* [1997] QB 47. In that case the court accepted that a husband might lawfully brand his initials on his wife's buttocks with a hot knife provided she consented (as she appeared to have done). The reasoning behind the judgment seems to be based on the fact that the branding was similar to a form of tattooing, but also on the policy grounds that consensual activity between husband and wife is not a matter for criminal investigation. Therefore, if a situation arose where a husband and wife took part in mutual branding in the privacy of their home, their criminal liability would arguably depend on whether they caused the harm for purposes of sado-masochistic pleasure or out of some affectionate wish to be permanently adorned with the mark of their loved one.

1.9.6　Lawful Chastisement

The School Standards and Framework Act 1998 outlaws corporal punishment in *all* British schools, including independent schools, although staff may use reasonable force in restraining violent or disruptive pupils. The Divisional Court has held that this legislation removes entirely the defence of lawful chastisement from any teacher when they are acting as such (*R* (*on the application of Williamson*) v *Secretary of State for Education and Employment* [2001] EWHC Admin 960, later affirmed by the House of Lords [2005] UKHL 15).

Section 58 of the Children Act 2004 removes the defence of lawful chastisement for parents or adults acting *in loco parentis* (meaning 'in place of the parent') where the accused person is charged with assault occasioning actual bodily harm (Offences Against the Person Act 1861, s. 47), wounding or causing grievous bodily harm (Offences Against the Person Act 1861, s. 18 or 20) or child cruelty (Children and Young Persons Act 1933, s.1) to persons less than 18 years of age. However, the lawful chastisement defence remains available for parents and adults acting *in loco parentis* charged with common assault under the Criminal Justice Act 1988, s. 39. CPS charging standards state that if an injury to a child amounts to no more than reddening of the skin, and the injury is transient and trifling, a charge of common assault may be laid against the defendant for whom the lawful chastisement defence remains available. Whether the actions of the defendant are 'reasonable' will be important; physical punishment where a child is hit (causing injury reddening to the skin) with an implement such as a cane may well be considered 'unreasonable'. It is important to note that the law does not rule out physical chastisement by a parent etc. but that chastisement should only constitute 'mild smacking' rather than cause injuries subject to assault charges.

1.9.7　Assault Offences

Having considered the key common elements in this area, the specific offences are set out below.

1.9.7.1　Common Assault and Battery

OFFENCE: **Common Assault/Battery—*Criminal Justice Act 1988, s. 39***
- Triable summarily • Six months' imprisonment

OFFENCE: **Racially or Religiously Aggravated—*Crime and Disorder Act 1998, s. 29(1)(c)***
- Triable either way • Two years' imprisonment and/or a fine on indictment
- Six months' imprisonment and/or a fine summarily

KEYNOTE

The racially or religiously aggravated offence can be tried on indictment without having to be included alongside another indictable offence as is the case with common assaults generally (Criminal Justice Act 1988, s. 40).

CPS Charging Standards state that a charge under s. 39 of the Act is appropriate where *no injury or injuries which are not serious* occur. In determining the seriousness of injury, relevant factors may include the fact that there has been significant medical intervention and/or permanent effects have resulted (whereby a charge of s. 47 assault may be more appropriate).

The injury sustained by the victim should always be considered first, and in most cases the degree of injury will determine what the appropriate charge is.

1.9.7.2 Assault Occasioning Actual Bodily Harm

OFFENCE: **Assault Occasioning Actual Bodily Harm—***Offences Against the Person Act 1861, s. 47*
* Triable either way * Five years' imprisonment on indictment * Six months' imprisonment and/or a fine summarily

OFFENCE: **Racially or Religiously Aggravated—***Crime and Disorder Act 1998, s. 29(1)(b)*
* Triable either way * Seven years' imprisonment and/or a fine on indictment
* Six months' imprisonment and/or a fine summarily

The Offences Against the Person Act 1861, s. 47 states:

> Whosoever shall be convicted...of any assault occasioning actual bodily harm shall be liable...to be kept in penal servitude...

KEYNOTE

The state of mind required is the same as that for an assault or battery.

It must be shown that 'actual bodily harm' was a consequence, directly or indirectly, of the defendant's actions. Such harm can include shock (*R* v *Miller* [1954] 2 QB 282) and mental 'injury' (*R* v *Chan-Fook* [1994] 1 WLR 689).

So what is 'actual bodily harm'? In *DPP* v *Smith* [1961] AC 290, it was noted that the expression needed 'no explanation' and, in *Chan-Fook*, the court advised that the phrase consisted of 'three words of the English language which require no elaboration and in the ordinary course should not receive any. While the phrase 'bodily harm' has its ordinary meaning, it has been said to include any hurt calculated to interfere with the health or comfort of the victim: such hurt need not be permanent, but must be more than transient and trifling (*R* v *Miller*).

The Administrative Court has accepted that a momentary loss of consciousness caused by a kick but without any physical injury can be 'actual harm' because it involved an injurious impairment of the victim's sensory abilities which did not fall within the 'trifling' category described in *R* v *Miller* (*T* v *DPP* [2003] EWHC 266 (Admin)).

It was held in *DPP* v *Smith* (*Ross Michael*) [2006] EWHC 94 (Admin), that the *substantial* cutting of a person's hair against his/her will could amount to actual bodily harm even though no pain or other injury may be involved. In *Smith* the defendant cut off his ex-partner's ponytail, deliberately and without her permission. Even though medically and scientifically speaking, the hair above the surface of the scalp is no more than dead tissue, it remains part of the body and is attached to it. While it is so attached, it falls within the meaning of 'bodily' in the phrase 'actual bodily harm' as it is concerned with the body of the individual victim. Therefore the same would be true of fingernails.

CPS charging standards state that ABH should generally be charged where injuries and overall circumstances indicate that the offence merits clearly more than six months' imprisonment and where the prosecution intend to represent that the case is not suitable for summary trial. Examples may include cases where there is a need for a number of stitches (but not superficial application of steri-strips) or a hospital procedure under anaesthetic.

Where psychiatric injury is relied upon as the basis for an allegation of assault occasioning actual bodily harm, and the matter is not admitted by the defence, then expert evidence must be called by the prosecution (*R* v *Chan-Fook* [1994] 1 WLR 689).

1.9.7.3 Wounding or Inflicting Grievous Bodily Harm

OFFENCE: **Wounding or Inflicting Grievous Bodily Harm—***Offences Against the Person Act 1861, s. 20*
* Triable either way * Five years' imprisonment on indictment
* Six months' imprisonment and/or a fine summarily

OFFENCE: **Racially or Religiously Aggravated—*Crime and Disorder Act 1998, s. 29(1)(a)***

- Triable either way • Seven years' imprisonment and/or a fine on indictment
- Six months' imprisonment and/or a fine summarily

The Offences Against the Person Act 1861, s. 20 states:

> Whosoever shall unlawfully and maliciously wound or inflict any grievous bodily harm upon any other person, either with or without any weapon or instrument, shall be guilty of a misdemeanour...

KEYNOTE

Although the word maliciously suggests some form of evil premeditation, 'malice' here amounts to *subjective recklessness*. It means that the defendant must realise that there is a risk of *some harm* being caused to the victim but took the risk anyway. The defendant does not need to foresee the degree of harm which is eventually caused, only that his/her behaviour may bring about some harm to the victim.

Wounding requires the breaking of the continuity of the whole of the skin (dermis and epidermis) or the breaking of the inner skin within the cheek, lip or urethra. A cut which breaks all the layers of a person's skin, whether caused externally (e.g. a knife wound) or internally (e.g. a punch causing a tooth to puncture the cheek), will amount to a wound. It does not include the rupturing of internal blood vessels.

The definition of wounding may encompass injuries that are relatively minor in nature, e.g. a small cut. An assault resulting in such minor injuries should more appropriately be charged contrary to s. 47 of the Act. An assault contrary to s. 20 should be reserved for the type of wounds considered to be serious (thus equating the offence with the infliction of grievous, or serious, bodily harm). For example, a cut on the back of a person's hand requiring two stitches and not resulting in 'serious or really serious harm' is likely to be considered as a s. 39 or perhaps a s. 47 assault. If the same injury were across the surface of the eye causing loss of sight in the eye and thereby resulting in 'serious or really serious harm', a charge of s. 20 or s. 18 assault may be appropriate.

In *R v Ireland* [1998] AC 147 it was stated that no 'assault' is needed for this offence and that harm could be 'inflicted' indirectly (in this case by menacing telephone calls inflicting psychiatric harm). Therefore there is now little if any difference between inflicting harm and 'causing' harm. It should be enough to show that the defendant's behaviour brought about the resulting harm to the victim.

In *R v Saunders* [1985] Crim LR 230 it was held that 'grievous bodily harm' meant 'serious or really serious harm'. This harm will include psychiatric harm (*Ireland*). Examples of what will amount to 'grievous bodily harm' can be found in the CPS Charging Standards and include:

- injury resulting in some permanent disability or visible disfigurement
- broken or displaced limbs or bones
- injuries requiring blood transfusion or lengthy treatment.

A case involving a visible disfigurement is *R v Marsh* [2011] EWCA Crim 3190 where the female offenders became involved in a fight with a 16-year-old girl. One held the girl's arms behind her back while the second cut the girl's face with a key, causing a 4cm laceration which would leave a permanent scar; the offenders were convicted of a s. 20 offence.

There is no definitive list of the kind of injuries that may be considered to be serious, but in *R v Birmingham* [2002] EWCA Crim 2608, it was held that a large number of minor wounds were capable of amounting to grievous bodily harm on a charge of aggravated burglary.

Following *R v Dica* [2004] EWCA Crim 1103, there was an acceptance that the deliberate infection of another with the HIV virus could amount to grievous bodily harm, although there were still significant difficulties with regard to 'consent' if the infection had taken place as a result of consensual sexual activity. This issue was explored further in *R v Konzani* [2005] EWCA Crim 706. In that case the defendant appealed against convictions for inflicting grievous bodily harm on three women contrary to s. 20. The defendant had unprotected consensual sexual intercourse with the women, but without having disclosed that he was HIV positive. The women subsequently contracted the HIV virus. The Court of Appeal held that there was a critical distinction between taking a risk as to the various potentially adverse (and possibly problematic) consequences of unprotected consensual intercourse, and the giving of informed consent *to the risk of infection with a fatal disease*. Before consent to the risk of contracting HIV could provide a defence, that consent had to be an *informed* consent in this latter sense (*Dica*). Therefore, simply having an honestly held belief that the other person was consenting would only help if that consent would itself have provided a defence to the passing of the infection.

This approach was confirmed in *R* v *B* [2006] EWCA Crim 2945, where the Court of Appeal stated that, while a defendant's condition (being HIV positive) was immaterial in relation to the consent issue in an offence of rape, the defendant would have no defence to the harm created by the sexual activity merely by virtue of that consent, as the consent related to the sexual activity and not to the disease (but **see para 1.11.2.2** for further considerations in relation to consent and HIV).

1.9.7.4   Wounding or Causing Grievous Bodily Harm with Intent

OFFENCE: **Wounding or Causing Grievous Bodily Harm with Intent—*Offences Against the Person Act 1861, s. 18***

> * Triable on indictment only * Life imprisonment

The Offences Against the Person Act 1861, s. 18 states:

> Whosoever shall unlawfully and maliciously by any means whatsoever wound or cause any grievous bodily harm to any person with intent to do some grievous bodily harm to any person, or with intent to resist or prevent the lawful apprehension or detainer of any person, shall be guilty of felony...

KEYNOTE

An offence under s. 18 may take one of four different forms, namely:

(a) wounding with intent to do grievous bodily harm;

(b) causing grievous bodily harm with intent to do so;

(c) maliciously wounding with intent to resist or prevent the lawful apprehension etc. of any person; or

(d) maliciously causing grievous bodily harm with intent to resist or prevent the lawful apprehension etc. of any person.

Although there are similarities with the offence under s. 20 (**see para. 1.9.7.3**), you must show the appropriate *intent* (e.g. to do grievous bodily harm to *anyone* or to resist/prevent the lawful apprehension/detention of *anyone*). Factors that may indicate such a specific intent include:

* a repeated or planned attack
* deliberate selection of a weapon or adaptation of an article to cause injury, such as breaking a glass before an attack
* making prior threats
* using an offensive weapon against, or kicking a victim's head.

In form (a) or (b), where the intent was to cause grievous bodily harm, the issue of 'malice' will not arise. However, where the intent was to resist or prevent the lawful arrest of someone (in form (c) or (d)), the element of maliciousness (subjective recklessness) as set out above (**see para. 1.9.7.3**) will need to be proved. In addition, where it is alleged that D acted with the intent to avoid or resist the lawful apprehension of any person, it may be his/her own arrest or that of another he/she resisted, but the lawfulness of that arrest or detention must in either event be proved by the prosecution. It does not follow that D must be proved to have known the arrest etc. was lawful, but in a case such as *Kenlin* v *Gardiner* [1967] 2 QB 510, where D mistook the arresting officers for kidnappers, mistaken self-defence may be raised by the defence.

The word 'cause', together with the expression 'by any means whatsoever', seems to give this offence a wider meaning than s. 20. However, the increasingly broad interpretation of the s. 20 offence means that there is little difference in the *actus reus* needed for either offence.

In relation to injuries brought about by driving motor vehicles, the Court of Appeal has held that there is nothing wrong in principle in charging a driver with causing grievous bodily harm as well as dangerous driving in appropriate circumstances (*R* v *Bain* [2005] EWCA Crim 7). It follows that bringing about other forms of significant or lasting injury with a motor vehicle could be dealt with under the offences in this part of the chapter. However, in *Bain* it was held that where a driver was charged with both offences (causing grievous bodily harm and dangerous driving), a court could not impose consecutive terms of imprisonment for both offences arising out of the same incident. The Legal Aid, Sentencing and Punishment of Offenders Act 2012 created a specific offence of causing serious injury by dangerous driving (under s. 143) which may be a far more appropriate charge when the offence has been brought about by driving a mechanically propelled vehicle (see *Road Policing*, para. 3.3.3).

The provisions of ss. 28 and 29 of the Crime and Disorder Act 1998 in relation to racially or religiously aggravated assaults do not apply to this offence. However, the courts must still take notice of any element of racial or religious aggravation when determining sentence (Criminal Justice Act 2003, s. 145—increase in sentences for racial or religious aggravation).

1.9.8 Other Assault Offences

1.9.8.1 Assault with Intent to Resist Arrest

OFFENCE: **Assault with Intent to Resist Arrest—*Offences Against the Person Act 1861, s. 38***
- Triable either way • Two years' imprisonment

The Offences Against the Person Act 1861, s. 38 states:

> Whosoever...shall assault any person with intent to resist or prevent the lawful apprehension or detainer of himself or of any other person for any offence, shall be guilty of a misdemeanour...

KEYNOTE

It must be shown that the defendant intended to resist or prevent the lawful arrest or detention of a person (his/her own arrest/detention or that of another) and that the arrest was lawful (*R* v *Self* [1992] 1 WLR 657). Provided they were acting within their powers, this offence can apply to arrests made, not only by police officers, but also by any person who has a power of arrest, i.e. members of the public.

Once the lawfulness of the arrest is established, the state of mind necessary for the above offence is that required for a common assault coupled with an intention to resist/prevent that arrest/detention. It is irrelevant whether or not the person being arrested/detained had actually committed an offence. These principles were set out by the Court of Appeal in a case where the defendant mistakenly believed that the arresting officers had no lawful power to do so. The court held that such a mistaken belief does not provide a defendant with the defence of 'mistake'. Similarly, a belief in one's own innocence, however genuine or honestly held, cannot afford a defence to a charge under s. 38.

1.9.8.2 Assault on Police

There is an offence which deals specifically with assaults on police officers and those assisting them.

OFFENCE: **Assault Police—*Police Act 1996, s. 89***
- Triable summarily • Six months' imprisonment and/or a fine

The Police Act 1996, s. 89 states:

(1) Any person who assaults a constable in the execution of his duty, or a person assisting a constable in the execution of his duty, shall be guilty of an offence ...

KEYNOTE

This offence requires that the officer was acting in the execution of his/her duty when assaulted. If this is not proved, then part of the *actus reus* will be missing. Even a minor, technical and inadvertent act of unlawfulness on the part of the officer will mean that he/she cannot have been acting in the lawful execution of his/her duty. While the precise limits of a constable's duty remain undefined, it is clear that a police officer may be acting in the course of his/her duty even when doing more than the minimum the law requires (*R* v *Waterfield* [1964] 1 QB 164). It is also clear that any action amounting to assault, battery, unlawful arrest or trespass to property takes the officer outside the course of his/her duty (*Davis* v *Lisle* [1936] 2 KB 434).

A court may infer from all the circumstances that an officer was in fact acting in the execution of his/her duty (*Plowden* v *DPP* [1991] Crim LR 850).

Where the assault is made in reaction to some form of physical act by the officer, it must be shown that the officer's act was not in itself unlawful.

Other than the powers of arrest and detention, police officers have no general power to take hold of people in order to question them or keep them at a particular place while background inquiries are made about them. Therefore, if an officer does hold someone by the arm for questioning without arrest, there may well be a 'battery' by that officer (*Collins* v *Wilcock* [1984] 1 WLR 1172). The courts have accepted, however, that there may be occasions where a police officer is justified in taking hold of a person to attract his/her attention or to calm him/her down (*Mepstead* v *DPP* [1996] COD 13).

Where a prisoner is arrested and brought before a custody officer, that officer is entitled to assume that the arrest has been lawful. Therefore, if the prisoner goes on to assault the custody officer, that assault will be an offence under s. 89(1) even if the original arrest turns out to have been unlawful (*DPP* v *L* [1999] Crim LR 752).

There is no need to show that the defendant knew, or suspected, that the person was in fact a police officer or that the police officer was acting in the lawful execution of his/her duty (*Blackburn* v *Bowering* [1994] 1 WLR 1324). However, if the defendant claims to have been acting in self-defence under the mistaken and honestly held belief that he/she was being attacked, there may not be sufficient *mens rea* for a charge of assault.

These offences are simply a form of common assault upon someone carrying out a lawful function.

1.9.8.3   **Obstructing a Police Officer**

OFFENCE: **Obstruct Police—*Police Act 1996, s. 89***
- Triable summarily   • One month's imprisonment and/or a fine

The Police Act 1996, s. 89 states:

(2) Any person who resists or wilfully obstructs a constable in the execution of his duty, or a person assisting a constable in the execution of his duty, shall be guilty of an offence...

KEYNOTE

No offence under s. 89(2) can be committed unless the officer was acting in the lawful execution of his/her duty.

Resistance suggests some form of physical opposition; obstruction does not and may take many forms, e.g. warning other drivers of a speed check operation (*R (DPP)* v *Glendinning* (2005) EWHC 2333 (Admin)—note that the persons warned about the speed check must be actually committing or about to commit the speeding offence), deliberately providing misleading information (*Ledger* v *DPP* [1991] Crim LR 439), deliberately drinking alcohol before providing a breath specimen (*Ingleton* v *Dibble* [1972] 1 QB 480), or 'tipping off' people who were about to commit an offence (*Green* v *Moore* [1982] QB 1044). Obstruction has been interpreted as making it more difficult for a constable to carry out his/her duty (*Hinchcliffe* v *Sheldon* [1955] 1 WLR 1207). Refusing to answer an officer's questions is not obstruction (*Rice* v *Connolly* [1966] 2 QB 414), neither is advising a person not to answer questions (*Green* v *DPP* (1991) 155 JP 816) unless perhaps the defendant was under some duty to provide information. Any obstruction must be *wilful*, that is the defendant must intend to do it. The obstruction will not be 'wilful' if the defendant was simply trying to help the police, even if that help turned out to be more of a hindrance (*Willmot* v *Atack* [1977] QB 498).

Obstruction can be caused by omission but only where the defendant was already under some duty towards the police or the officer. There is also a common law offence of refusing to go to the aid of a constable when asked to do so in order to prevent or diminish a breach of the peace (*R* v *Waugh* (1986) *The Times*, 1 October).

1.9.9 Threats to Kill

OFFENCE: **Making a Threat to Kill—*Offences Against the Person Act 1861, s. 16***
- Triable either way • 10 years' imprisonment on indictment
- Six months' imprisonment and/or a fine summarily

The Offences Against the Person Act 1861, s. 16 (amended by the Criminal Law Act 1977, s. 65, sch. 12) states:

A person who without lawful excuse makes to another a threat, intending that that other would fear it would be carried out, to kill that other or a third person shall be guilty of an offence ...

KEYNOTE
The proviso that the threat must be made 'without lawful excuse' means that a person acting in self-defence or in the course of his/her duty in protecting life (e.g. an armed police officer) would not commit this offence (provided that his/her behaviour was 'lawful').

A threat can be communicated in any way. In *R* v *Martin* (1993) 14 Cr App R (S) 645 the offender sent two anonymous notes stained with blood to the victim and in *R* v *Patel* [2012] EWCA Crim 2172 the offender threatened his former partner that he would kill their young son and then sent a text message to her that he had done so.

You must show that the threat was made (or implied (*R* v *Solanke* [1970] 1 WLR 1)) with the intention that the person receiving it would fear that it would be carried out. It is the *intention* of the person who makes the threat which is important in this offence. It does not matter whether the person to whom the threat is made *does* fear that the threat would be carried out.

The threat may be to kill another person at some time in the future or it may be an immediate threat, but the threatened action must be directly linked with the defendant. Simply passing on a threat on behalf of a third person *without the necessary intent* would be insufficient for this offence.

A threat to a pregnant woman in respect of her unborn child is not sufficient if the threat is to kill it before its birth (the unborn child is not a 'person'). But if it is a threat to kill the child after its birth, this would appear to be an offence within this section (*R* v *Tait* [1990] 1 QB 290).

Miscellaneous Offences Against the Person

1.10.1 Introduction

In addition to the offences examined in the previous chapter, there are further offences against the person that, while not as prevalent, are nevertheless important.

1.10.2 Torture

OFFENCE: **Torture—*Criminal Justice Act 1988, s. 134***

> • Triable on indictment • Life imprisonment

The Criminal Justice Act 1988, s. 134 states:

(1) A public official or person acting in an official capacity, whatever his nationality, commits the offence of torture if in the United Kingdom or elsewhere he intentionally inflicts severe pain or suffering on another in the performance or purported performance of his official duties.

(2) A person not falling within subsection (1) above commits the offence of torture, whatever his nationality, if—

(a) in the United Kingdom or elsewhere he intentionally inflicts severe pain or suffering on another at the instigation or with the consent or acquiescence—

(i) of a public official; or

(ii) of a person acting in an official capacity; and

(b) the official or other person is performing or purporting to perform his official duties when he instigates the commission of the offence or consents to or acquiesces in it.

(3) It is immaterial whether the pain or suffering is physical or mental or whether it is caused by an act or an omission.

KEYNOTE

This offence can be committed anywhere in the world and by anyone (whatever their nationality).

The consent of the Attorney-General is needed before bringing a prosecution under s. 134. This offence could be committed by police officers in the course of their duties, and may have significant implications for Custody Officers.

Although the offence has a statutory defence of 'lawful authority, justification or excuse' (**see para. 1.10.2.1**), Article 3 of the European Convention on Human Rights contains an absolute prohibition on torture. Irrespective of the circumstances, there can be no derogation from an individual's absolute right under Article 3 to freedom from torture, inhuman or degrading treatment or punishment.

These three features have been identified as having the following broad characteristics:

- Torture—deliberate treatment leading to serious or cruel suffering.
- Inhuman treatment—treatment resulting in intense suffering, both physical and mental.
- Degrading treatment—treatment giving rise to fear and anguish in the victim, causing feelings of inferiority and humiliation.

(*Ireland* v *United Kingdom* (1979–80) 2 EHRR 25.)

Causing mental anguish without any physical assault could be a violation of Article 3 (*Denmark* v *Greece* (1969) 12 YB Eur Conv HR special Vol.).

Article 3 does not only prohibit the deliberate application of pain and suffering, but also a range of other behaviour. Oppressive interrogation techniques such as sleep deprivation, exposure to continuous loud noise and forcing suspects to adopt uncomfortable postures for prolonged lengths of time have been held to fall within the second and third categories of inhuman and degrading treatment (*Ireland* v *United Kingdom*).

In each case, it must be shown that the prohibited behaviour went beyond the 'minimum level of severity'. In determining whether the behaviour did go beyond that level, and under which particular category that behaviour falls, the courts will take into account factors such as the age, sex, state of health and general life experience of the victim. 'Severe pain or suffering' can be mental as well as physical and can be caused by omission.

1.10.2.1 Defence

The Criminal Justice Act 1988, s. 134 states:

(4) It shall be a defence for a person charged with an offence under this section in respect of any conduct of his to prove that he had lawful authority, justification or excuse for that conduct.

1.10.3 Poisoning

OFFENCE: **Poisoning—*Offences Against the Person Act 1861, s. 23***
  • Triable on indictment • 10 years' imprisonment

The Offences Against the Person Act 1861, s. 23 states:

Whosoever shall unlawfully and maliciously administer to or cause to be administered to or taken by any other person any poison or other destructive or noxious thing, so as thereby to endanger the life of such person, or so as thereby to inflict upon such person any grievous bodily harm, shall be guilty of [an offence] . . .

KEYNOTE

In *R* v *Kennedy (No. 2)* [2008] 1 AC 269, the House of Lords held that s. 23 creates three distinct offences:

1. Where D administers the noxious thing directly to V, as by injecting V with the noxious thing, holding a glass containing the noxious thing to V's lips, or spraying a noxious thing (e.g. CS gas or ammonia) in V's face. This might include the use of CS spray by police officers but the 'administering' would also have to be shown to be both unlawful and malicious.

2. Where D does not directly administer a noxious thing to V but causes an innocent third party (T) to administer it to V. If D, knowing a syringe to be filled with poison, instructs T to inject V, when T believes the syringe to contain a legitimate therapeutic substance, D would commit this offence.

3. Where the noxious thing is not administered to V but is taken by him/her, provided D causes the noxious thing to be taken by V and V does not make a voluntary and informed decision to take it. If D puts a noxious thing in food which V is about to eat and V, ignorant of the presence of the noxious thing, eats it, D commits the offence.

The administering must be unlawful. Consent will normally negate unlawfulness, but not where it is procured by deception or where considerations of public policy invalidate that consent. A person cannot, for example, validly consent to being injected with a dangerous drug, such as heroin, unless this is done for bona fide medical reasons (*R* v *Cato* [1976] 1 WLR 110). This offence would certainly cover the administering of a controlled drug to another or inducing another to take a controlled drug.

Other than the requirement for 'malice' (which means subjective recklessness), this offence is mainly concerned with the consequences caused to the victim and not the defendant's intentions (the consequences being that a person's life was endangered or the infliction of grievous bodily harm).

'Causing to be administered' would cover indirect poisoning or even inducing someone to poison him/herself.

Whether a substance is poisonous, destructive or noxious will depend on both its quality and quantity. Some substances may become poisonous or noxious only in large amounts whereas others may be so *per se*.

An example of this offence can be seen in *R* v *MK* [2008] EWCA Crim 425 where a 23-year-old offender pleaded guilty to the offence under s. 23. He had given a three-year-old child in his care a teaspoon full of methadone and planned to obtain a urine sample from the child, which would be free from Class A drugs but positive for methadone. The child suffered a life-threatening illness as a result. The offender did not admit to the doctors treating the child what he had done, so the child's suffering was prolonged; he was sentenced to four and a half years' imprisonment.

1.10.3.1 Poisoning with Intent

OFFENCE: **Poisoning with Intent—*Offences Against the Person Act 1861, s. 24***
  • Triable on indictment • Five years' imprisonment

The Offences Against the Person Act 1861, s. 24 states:

> Whosoever shall unlawfully and maliciously administer to or cause to be administered to or taken by any other person any poison or other destructive or noxious thing, with intent to injure, aggrieve, or annoy any such person, shall be guilty of a misdemeanour...

KEYNOTE

The *actus reus* of this offence is similar to that under s. 23 (administering etc.) but with this offence there is no requirement to prove any consequences of a defendant's actions although the *intent* to injure, aggrieve or annoy must be proved.

Examples of this offence include:

• giving a woman a drink which contained a large quantity of a Class C drug causing her to fall into a deep sleep for a day;
• allowing two young boys to inhale isobutyl nitrate so that they became dizzy and unwell;
• throwing a mixture of chilli, black pepper and turmeric into the face of a victim, causing permanent damage to her eyes.

Section 24 has been used successfully to prosecute defendants who 'spike' their victims' drinks with drugs such as ecstasy (*R* v *Gantz* [2004] EWCA Crim 2862) or who ply children with such drugs for improper purposes. The overstimulation of a victim's metabolism that such action is intended to cause can be viewed as a type of injury (*R* v *Hill* (1986) 83 Cr App R 386 where the offender administered slimming pills to young boys in order to keep them awake).

There is a further, more extreme offence of using noxious substances to cause harm or intimidation under the Anti-terrorism, Crime and Security Act 2001, s. 113. This offence, which carries 14 years' imprisonment on indictment, occurs where a person takes any action which:

• involves the use of a noxious substance or other noxious thing;
• has or is likely to have an effect set out below; and
• is designed to influence the government or to intimidate the public or a section of the public.

The effects are:

• causing serious violence against a person, or serious damage to property, anywhere in the world;
• endangering human life or creating a serious risk to the health or safety of the public or a section of the public; or
• inducing in members of the public the fear that the action is likely to endanger their lives or create a serious risk to their health or safety.

1.10.4 False Imprisonment

OFFENCE: **False Imprisonment—*Common Law***
- Triable on indictment • Unlimited maximum penalty

It is an offence at common law falsely to imprison another person.

KEYNOTE

The elements required for this offence are the unlawful and intentional/reckless restraint of a person's freedom of movement (*R* v *Rahman* (1985) 81 Cr App R 349). Locking someone in a vehicle or keeping him/her in a particular place for however short a time may amount to false imprisonment if done unlawfully. An unlawful arrest may amount to such an offence and it is not uncommon for such an allegation to be levelled at police officers against whom a public complaint has been made. On the other hand, making a *lawful* arrest will mean that the person was lawfully detained and no offence would be committed in such circumstances.

In *R* v *Shwan Faraj* [2007] EWCA Crim 1033, the court stated that there was no reason why a householder should not be entitled to detain someone in his house whom he genuinely believed to be a burglar; he would be acting in defence of his property in doing so (a lawful detention of the person). However, a householder would have to honestly believe he needed to detain the suspect and would have to do so in a way that was reasonable.

1.10.5 Kidnapping

OFFENCE: **Kidnapping—*Common Law***
- Triable on indictment • Unlimited maximum penalty

It is an offence at common law to take or carry away another person without the consent of that person and without lawful excuse.

KEYNOTE

The required elements of this offence are the unlawful taking or carrying away of one person by another by force or fraud (*R* v *D* [1984] AC 778). Force includes the threat of force (*R* v *Archer* [2011] EWCA Crim 2252). These requirements go beyond those of mere restraint needed for false imprisonment. Parents may be acting without lawful excuse, for instance, if they are acting in breach of a court order in respect of their children (**see** chapter 1.13). The 'taking or carrying away' need not involve great distances as a short distance (just a few yards/metres) will suffice (*R* v *Wellard* [1978] 1 WLR 921).

The taking or carrying away of the victim must be without the consent of the victim. If the victim consents to an initial taking but later withdraws that consent, the offence would be complete. If the consent is obtained by fraud, the defendant cannot rely on that consent and the offence will be made out (*R* v *Cort* [2003] EWCA Crim 2149). In *R* v *Hendy-Freegard* [2007] EWCA Crim 1236 the defendant was a confidence trickster who pretended to be an undercover agent working for MI5 or Scotland Yard. He told his victims that he was investigating the activities of the IRA and that his investigations had revealed that they were in danger. This allowed him to take control of their lives for years and in doing so to direct them to move about the country from location to location. The defendant was eventually arrested and convicted of kidnapping on the basis that the offence of kidnapping had occurred as his victims had made journeys around the country which they had been induced to make as a result of the defendant's false story. The defendant successfully appealed against the kidnapping conviction, with the court stating that causing a person to move from place to place *when unaccompanied by the defendant* could not itself constitute either taking or carrying away or deprivation of liberty, which were necessary elements of the offence.

The state of mind required for this offence is the same as that for false imprisonment, indeed the only thing separating the two offences seems to be *actus reus* (*R* v *Hutchins* [1988] Crim LR 379).

1.10.6 Hostage Taking

OFFENCE: **Hostage Taking—*Taking of Hostages Act 1982, s. 1***
- Triable on indictment • Life imprisonment

The Taking of Hostages Act 1982, s. 1 states:

(1) A person, whatever his nationality, who, in the United Kingdom or elsewhere—
    (a) detains any other person ('the hostage'), and
    (b) in order to compel a State, international governmental organisation, or person to do or abstain from doing any act, threatens to kill, injure or continue to detain the hostage, commits an offence.

KEYNOTE

The consent of the Attorney-General is needed before bringing a prosecution for this offence. To be guilty, a defendant must detain a person and threaten to kill, injure or continue to detain him/her with the intentions outlined under s. 1(1)(b). It is therefore an offence of 'specific' intent (**see chapter 1.1**).

1.11 Sexual Offences

1.11.1 Introduction

The majority of offences in this chapter are dealt with under the Sexual Offences Act 2003. The Act provides measures such as the presumptions about consent that will be made by a court under certain circumstances. In many of the mainstream offences, the Act uses the approach of describing actions of a hypothetical offender 'A' towards the victim 'B'. Apart from the offence of rape (under ss. 1 and 5 of the Act) the offences are 'gender neutral', i.e. they can be committed by a male or a female.

It is important to note that there is overlap between many of the offences, for example a mentally disordered person could be raped under s. 1 (because of his/her lack of ability to give true consent) or subjected to sexual activity contrary to s. 30 (due to an inability to refuse). In all circumstances it is essential that the most appropriate option is chosen.

1.11.1.1 Human Rights Considerations

Sexual activities are aspects of a person's 'private life' as protected by Article 8 of the Convention (*Dudgeon* v *United Kingdom* (1981) 3 EHRR 40 and *ADT* v *United Kingdom* [2000] 31 EHRR 33). This concept applies to homosexual and heterosexual relationships (*X* v *United Kingdom* (1997) 24 EHRR 143).

The Sexual Offences Act 2003 and its compatibility with the European Convention on Human Rights were considered in *R* v *G* & *Secretary of State for the Home Department* [2006] EWCA Crim 821. The Court of Appeal held that the imposition of strict liability in relation to the offence under s. 5 of the Act (rape of a child under 13) did not infringe Article 6.2 of the Convention (presumption of innocence).

1.11.1.2 Anonymity

Under the Sexual Offences (Amendment) Act 1992, victims of most sexual offences (including rape, incest, and indecency with children) are entitled to anonymity throughout their lifetime. This means that there are restrictions on the way in which trials and cases may be reported and the courts have powers to enforce these provisions.

1.11.2 Rape

OFFENCE: **Rape—*Sexual Offences Act 2003, s.1***
* Triable on indictment * Life imprisonment

The Sexual Offences Act 2003, s. 1 states:

(1) A person (A) commits an offence if—
  (a) he intentionally penetrates the vagina, anus or mouth of another person (B) with his penis,
  (b) B does not consent to the penetration, and
  (c) A does not reasonably believe that B consents.
(2) Whether a belief is reasonable is to be determined having regard to all the circumstances, including any steps A has taken to ascertain whether B consents.

KEYNOTE

Rape is an offence that can *only* be committed via the use of the penis. Therefore rape (as a principal offender) can only be committed by a man, although a woman who encourages or assists a man to penetrate another person with his penis, not reasonably believing the other person is consenting, may be convicted of aiding and abetting rape (*R* v *Cogan* [1976] QB 217). It can be committed if the defendant penetrates the vagina, anus or mouth of the victim with the penis. 'Vagina' is taken to include the vulva (s. 79(9)). In respect of penetration of the vagina it is not necessary to show that the hymen was ruptured.

You must show that the victim did not in fact consent at the time and that the defendant did not reasonably believe that he/she consented. The wording is supported by the further provision that whether or not the defendant's belief is reasonable will be determined having regard to all the circumstances (s. 1(2)). Section 1(2) does not positively require an accused to have taken steps to ascertain whether the complainant consents. However, this is something a jury will consider when considering the reasonableness of his belief. More steps are likely to be expected where there is no established relationship.

Sections 75 and 76 apply to this offence.

If the victim is a child under 13, a specific offence of 'Rape of a Child Under 13' is committed (s. 5). You simply have to prove intentional penetration and the child's age; *no issue of 'consent' arises*.

Section 103(2)(b) of the Criminal Justice Act 2003 provides that a defendant's propensity to commit offences of the kind with which he is charged may (without prejudice to any other way of doing so) be established by evidence that he has been convicted of an offence of 'the same category'. An offence under s. 1, if committed in relation to a person under the age of 16, or under s. 5 (including aiding, abetting, counselling, procuring, inciting or attempting the commission of such an offence) falls within the relevant sexual offences category. A number of other sexual offences that follow in this chapter are also covered and will fall within the relevant sexual offences category (see the Criminal Justice Act 2003 (Categories of Offences) Order 2004 (SI 2004/3346)).

1.11.2.1 Criminal Conduct

To prove rape you must show that the defendant intentionally penetrated the vagina, mouth or anus of the victim with his penis. Penetration is a continuing act from entry to withdrawal (s. 79(2)). The 'continuing' nature of this act is of importance when considering the issue of consent and the statutory presumptions under ss. 75 and 76. While it is not necessary to prove ejaculation (indeed it is entirely irrelevant to the offence), the presence of semen or sperm may be important in proving the elements of a sexual offence. References to a part of the body (for example, penis, vagina) will include references to a body part which has been surgically constructed, particularly if it is through gender reassignment (s. 79(3)). The offence thus protects transsexuals. It also means, however, that a person who has a surgically constructed penis can commit the offence of rape.

1.11.2.2 Consent

The Sexual Offences Act 2003, s. 74 states:

> For the purpose of this Part, a person consents if he agrees by choice, and has the freedom and capacity to make that choice.

The issue of consent is a question of fact and is critical to proving the offence of rape. As it is potentially the most difficult aspect of the offence to prove, legislation has included some specific situations which allow presumptions and conclusions to be made regarding a lack of consent.

Any consent given must be 'true' consent, not simply a *submission* induced by fear or fraud. Therefore, if the person does not have any real choice in the matter, or the choice is not a genuine exercise of free will, then he/she has not 'consented'.

An example of how 'true' consent operates is the case involving PC Stephen Mitchell who committed a number of sexual offences against vulnerable women over a period of years. On one occasion Mitchell drove one of his victims to a dirt track and told her that if she did not do as he said he would ensure her children were taken away from her for good, and then raped her. Any 'consent' given by the victim could not be 'true' because her choice to participate in the act of sexual intercourse would not be by the genuine exercise of free will (a 'gun to the head'-type scenario).

'Capacity' is an integral part of the definition of consent. A valid consent can only be given by a person who has the capacity to give it. The Sexual Offences Act 2003 does not define 'capacity'. Common-law principles that developed under the old law suggest that complainants will not have had the capacity to agree by choice where their understanding and knowledge were so limited that they were not in a position to decide whether or not to agree (*R v Howard* (1965) 1 WLR 13). Some people are not capable of giving the required consent—these are addressed in further sections of this chapter.

Even if freely given, consent may still be withdrawn at any time. Once the 'passive' party to sexual penetration withdraws consent, any continued activity (for example, penetration in rape: *R v Cooper* [1994] Crim LR 531) can amount to a sexual offence provided all the other ingredients are present.

In *R v B* [2006] EWCA Crim 2945, the Court of Appeal stated that whether an individual had a sexual disease or condition, such as being HIV positive, was not an issue as far as consent was concerned. The case related to a man who was alleged to have raped a woman after they had met outside a nightclub. When arrested, the man informed the custody officer that he was HIV positive, a fact he had not disclosed to the victim prior to sexual intercourse. At the original trial, the judge directed that this non-disclosure was relevant to the issue of consent. On appeal the court stated that this was not the case and that the consent issue for a jury to consider was whether or not the victim consented to sexual intercourse, not whether she consented to sexual intercourse with a person suffering from a sexually transmitted disease. However, in *McNally v R* [2013] EWCA Crim 1051 (**see para. 1.11.2.3**) the Court of Appeal observed that *B* was not an authority that HIV status *could not* vitiate consent. *B* left the issue open and HIV status *could* vitiate consent if, for example, the complainant had been positively assured that the accused was not HIV positive.

KEYNOTE

So the situation with a person who *is HIV positive* and *is aware* of his condition is as follows:

- if the accused makes no mention of his condition this will not be rape (*R v B*). However, it may constitute an offence under the Offences Against the Person Act 1861 (s. 20 or s.18) (see *R v Dica* and *R v Konzani*, at para 1.9.7.3);
- if the accused positively assures the complainant that he is not HIV positive this would constitute rape (*R v McNally*).

1.11.2.3   Conditional Consent

Section 74 has been considered by the High Court and the Court of Appeal in a series of cases where apparent consent in relation to sexual offences was considered *not to be true consent*, either because a condition upon which consent was given was not complied with or because of a material deception (other than one which falls within s. 76 of the Sexual Offences Act 2003 (**see para. 1.11.2.5**)). The judgments identified three sets of circumstances in which the consent to sexual activity might be vitiated where the condition was breached.

In *Assange v Sweden* [2001] EWHC 2489 (Admin) the Divisional Court considered the situation in which A knew B (the complainant) would only consent to sexual intercourse if he used a condom. The court rejected the view that the conclusive presumption in s. 76 of the Sexual Offences Act 2003 would apply and concluded that the issue of consent could be determined under s. 74 rather than s. 76 and stated that it would be open to a jury to hold that if B had made it clear that she would only consent to sexual intercourse if A used a condom then there would be no consent if, without B's consent, A did not use a condom, or removed or tore the condom. A's conduct in having sexual intercourse without a condom in circumstances where B had made it clear that she would only have sexual intercourse if A did use a condom would therefore amount to an offence.

In *R (F) v DPP* [2013] EWHC 945 (Admin), the High Court examined an application for judicial review of the refusal of the DPP to initiate a prosecution for rape and/or sexual assault on B by A (her former partner). 'Choice' and the 'freedom' to make any particular choice must, the court said, be approached in 'a broad commonsense way'. Against what the court described as the 'essential background' of A's 'sexual dominance' of B and B's 'unenthusiastic acquiescence to his demands' the court considered a specific incident when B consented to sexual intercourse only on the clear understanding that A *would not* ejaculate inside her vagina. B believed that A intended and agreed to withdraw before ejaculation, and A knew and understood that this was the *only basis* on which B was prepared to have sexual intercourse with him. When he deliberately ejaculated inside B, the result, the court said, was B being deprived of choice relating to the crucial feature on which her original consent to sexual intercourse was based and accordingly her consent was negated. Contrary to B's wishes, and knowing that she would not have consented, and did not consent to penetration or the continuation of penetration, if B had an inkling of A's intention, A deliberately ejaculated within her vagina. This combination of circumstances falls within the statutory definition of rape.

The third case, *McNally v R* [2013] EWCA Crim 1051, differs from the two cases. Unlike *Assange* and *F*, both of which turned on an express condition, *McNally* was concerned with the material deception of B by A. The unusual facts considered by the court involved the relationship between two girls which, over three years, developed from an Internet relationship to an 'exclusive romantic relationship' that involved their meeting and engaging in sexual activity. From the start, A presented herself to B as a boy, a deception she maintained throughout their relationship. Examining the nature of 'choice' and 'freedom' the court determined that 'deception as to gender can vitiate consent'. The court's reasoning is that while, in a physical sense, the acts of assault by penetration of the vagina are the same whether perpetrated by a male or a female, the sexual nature of the acts is, on any commonsense view, different where the complainant is deliberately deceived by a defendant into believing the latter is male. Assuming the facts to be proved as alleged, B chose to have sexual encounters with a boy and her preference (her freedom to choose whether or not to have a sexual encounter with a girl) was removed by A's deception. Demonstrating that the circumstances in which consent may be vitiated are not limitless, the court explained that, in reality, some deceptions (such as, for example, in relation to wealth) will *obviously not be sufficient* to vitiate consent.

1.11.2.4 Section 75—Evidential Presumptions and Consent

The Sexual Offences Act 2003, s. 75 states:

(1) If in proceedings for an offence to which this section applies it is proved—
  (a) that the defendant did the relevant act,
  (b) that any of the circumstances specified in subsection (2) existed, and
  (c) that the defendant knew that those circumstances existed,
the complainant is to be taken not to have consented to the relevant act unless sufficient evidence is adduced to raise an issue as to whether he consented, and the defendant is to be taken not to have reasonably believed that the complainant consented unless sufficient evidence is adduced to raise an issue as to whether he reasonably believed it.

KEYNOTE

This means that, if the prosecution can show that the defendant carried out the relevant act in relation to certain specified sexual offences (for example, penetration in rape) and that any of the circumstances below existed and the defendant knew they existed, it will be presumed that the victim did not consent. Then the defendant will have to satisfy the court, by reference to evidence, that this presumption should not be made.

Section 75(2) sets out the circumstances in which evidential presumptions *may* apply. They are that:

(a) *any person* was, at the time of the relevant act (or immediately before it began), using violence against *the complainant* or causing *the complainant* to fear that immediate violence would be used against him/her;

(b) *any person* was, at the time of the relevant act or immediately before it began, causing *the complainant* to fear that violence was being used, or that immediate violence would be used, against *another person*;

(c) *the complainant* was, and the defendant was not, unlawfully detained at the time of the relevant act;

(d) *the complainant* was asleep or otherwise unconscious at the time of the relevant act;

(e) because of *the complainant's* physical disability, *the complainant* would not have been able at the time of the relevant act to communicate to the defendant whether the complainant consented;

(f) *any person* had administered to or caused to be taken by the complainant, without the complainant's consent, a substance which, having regard to when it was administered or taken, was capable of causing or enabling the complainant to be stupefied or overpowered at the time of the relevant act.

The 'relevant act' for each offence covered by s. 75 will generally be obvious but is set out specifically at s. 77.

It is important to note that the circumstances set out in s. 75(2) are not exhaustive in terms of deciding when consent will be absent. There may be circumstances that fall outside the situations described in s. 75(2) where consent does not exist. For example, the case of PC Stephen Mitchell (**see para. 1.11.2.2**) did not involve any of the circumstances set out in s. 75(2) and yet he was still guilty of rape as his victim's consent was not *true* consent; it was obtained by a threat to take her children away (submission). This fact that this situation does not appear in the sets of circumstances listed in s. 75(2) merely means that a presumption in relation to consent cannot be made in such a case—*it does not mean that the victim consented to the activity.*

1.11.2.5 Conclusive Presumptions about Consent

Section 76 of the Sexual Offences Act 2003 states:

(1) If in proceedings for an offence to which this section applies it is proved that the defendant did the relevant act and that any of the circumstances specified in subsection (2) existed, it is to be conclusively presumed—

   (a) that the complainant did not consent to the relevant act, and

   (b) that the defendant did not believe that the complainant consented to the relevant act.

(2) The circumstances are that—

   (a) the defendant intentionally deceived the complainant as to the nature or purpose of the relevant act;

   (b) the defendant intentionally induced the complainant to consent to the relevant act by impersonating a person known personally to the complainant.

These provisions deal with situations where the defendant either misrepresents the nature or purpose of what he/she is doing (for example, pretending that inserting a finger into the victim's vagina is for medical reasons) or impersonates the victim's partner. Section 76 requires that a misunderstanding was created by the defendant and that it was done deliberately. Once it is proved, beyond a reasonable doubt, that these circumstances existed then it is conclusive and the defendant cannot argue against them.

In *R* v *B* [2013] EWCA Crim 823 (seven counts of causing his girlfriend to engage in sexual activity without consent under s. 4 of the Sexual Offences Act 2003 (**see para. 1.11.6**)),

B, using pseudonyms, established an online Facebook relationship with his girlfriend so as to persuade and then blackmail her into providing him with photographs of her engaging in sexual activity. The Court of Appeal held that the reliance at trial upon s. 76 was misplaced. The motive behind the conduct was sexual gratification, and there was no deception as to that (i.e. there was no deception as to the purpose of the act). The prosecution would have had forceful arguments under s. 74 on the basis that the victim only complied because she was being blackmailed. In light of s. 76(2), it would appear that deception as to the identity of the recipient would not be sufficient as it was impersonation of a person unknown to the complainant. This case can be contrasted with *R* v *Devonald* [2008] EWCA Crim 527 (another s. 4 offence). In this case the court held that s. 76 did apply; it was open to the jury to conclude that the complainant was deceived into believing he was masturbating for the gratification of a 20-year-old girl via a webcam when in fact he was doing it for the father of a former girlfriend who was teaching him a lesson. Here, 'purpose' has been given a wide meaning in that the deception was not as to sexual gratification, rather it was to the purpose of the masturbation (to teach the victim a lesson).

It is important to emphasise the fact that s. 76 deals with situations where the defendant either:

- deceives the victim regarding the nature and purpose of the act or
- induces the victim to consent to the relevant act by impersonating a person known personally to the complainant.

If the deception/inducement *does not* relate to either of these aims then s. 76 has no application. For example, in *R* v *Jheeta* [2007] EWCA Crim 1699, the defendant deceived the complainant into having sex more frequently than she would have done otherwise. In these circumstances the conclusive presumptions under the Sexual Offences Act 2003 had no relevance as the complainant had not been deceived as to the nature or purpose of the sexual intercourse. Likewise, a false promise to marry made by A to B to encourage B to have sexual intercourse would not be covered, nor would a false promise to pay B in exchange for sexual intercourse.

As with s. 75, the 'relevant act' for each offence covered by s. 76 will generally be obvious but is set out specifically at s. 77.

1.11.3 Sexual Assault

There are several specific offences dealing with types of sexual assault: these are discussed below.

1.11.3.1 Assault by Penetration

OFFENCE: **Assault by Penetration—*Sexual Offences Act 2003, s. 2***
- Triable on indictment • Life imprisonment

The Sexual Offences Act 2003, s. 2 states:

(1) A person (A) commits an offence if—
  (a) he intentionally penetrates the vagina or anus of another person (B) with a part of his body or anything else,
  (b) the penetration is sexual,
  (c) B does not consent to the penetration, and
  (d) A does not reasonably believe that B consents.

1.11.3.2 The Definition of the Term 'Sexual'

Section 78 of the Act defines the term 'sexual' and provides that penetration, touching or any other activity will be sexual if a reasonable person would consider that:

(a) whatever its circumstances or any person's purpose in relation to it, it is sexual by its very nature or,

(b) because of its nature it *may* be sexual and because of its circumstances or the purpose of any person in relation to it, it is sexual.

Therefore, activity under (a) covers things that a reasonable person would always consider to be sexual (for example, masturbation), while activity under (b) covers things that may or may not be considered sexual by a reasonable person depending on the circumstances or the intentions of the person carrying it out (or both). For instance, a doctor inserting his/her finger into the vagina of a patient might be considered sexual by its nature, but if done for a purely medical purpose in a hospital (the circumstances and genuine medical purpose of the doctor in examining the patient), it would not be sexual.

If the activity would not appear to a reasonable person to be sexual, then it will not meet either criterion and, irrespective of any sexual gratification the person might derive from it, the activity will not be 'sexual'. Therefore weird or exotic fetishes that no ordinary person would regard as being sexual or potentially sexual will not be covered. This pretty well follows the common law developments in this area (*R* v *Court* [1989] AC 28 and *R* v *Tabassum* [2000] 2 Cr App R 328).

1.11.3.3 Sexual Assault by Touching

OFFENCE: **Sexual Assault by Touching—*Sexual Offences Act 2003, s. 3***

> • Triable either way • If victim is child under 13—14 years' imprisonment; otherwise 10 years' imprisonment on indictment • Six months' imprisonment summarily

The Sexual Offences Act 2003, s. 3 states:

(1) A person (A) commits an offence if—
   (a) he intentionally touches another person (B),
   (b) the touching is sexual,
   (c) B does not consent to the touching, and
   (d) A does not reasonably believe that B consents.

1.11.3.4 The Definition of the Term 'Touching'

Section 79(8) states that touching includes touching:

- with any part of the body,
- with anything else,
- through anything

and in particular, touching amounting to penetration (this could include kissing).

The part of the body touched does not have to be a sexual organ or orifice. There is no requirement for force or violence so the lightest touching will suffice. 'Touching' for the purposes of an offence under s. 3 (**see para. 1.11.3.3**) includes the touching of a victim's clothing even though the person of the victim is not touched through the clothing (*R* v *H* [2005] EWCA Crim 732). In *H* it was held that it was not Parliament's intention to preclude the touching of a victim's clothing from amounting to a sexual 'assault'. Where touching was not automatically by its nature 'sexual' the test under s. 78(b) applies (**see para. 1.11.3.2**). In a case where that section applies it will be appropriate for a trial judge to ask the jury to determine whether touching was 'sexual' by answering two questions. First, would the jury, as 12 reasonable people, consider that the touching could be sexual and, if so, whether in all the circumstances of the case, they would consider that the purpose of the touching *had in fact been* sexual.

The victim need not be aware of the touching. For example in the case of *R* v *Bounekhla* [2006] EWCA Crim 1217 the accused surreptitiously took his penis out of his trousers and ejaculated onto a woman's clothing when pressed up against her dancing at a nightclub.

If touching does not occur, the offence is not completed, although the circumstances may amount to an attempt. Nevertheless, it remains arguable that ejaculation onto a victim's clothing without contact with any part of the accused's body still constitutes a touching.

1.11.4 Causing Sexual Activity without Consent

OFFENCE: **Causing a Person to Engage in Sexual Activity without Consent—**
Sexual Offences Act 2003, s. 4

- If involves penetration: of the victim's anus or vagina, of victim's mouth with penis, of any other person's anus or vagina with a part of victim's body or by victim, or of any person's mouth by victim's penis—triable on indictment; life imprisonment
- Otherwise triable either way; 10 years' imprisonment on indictment; six months' imprisonment summarily

The Sexual Offences Act 2003, s. 4 states:

(1) A person (A) commits an offence if—
 (a) he intentionally causes another person (B) to engage in an activity,
 (b) the activity is sexual,
 (c) B does not consent to engaging in the activity, and
 (d) A does not reasonably believe that B consents.

KEYNOTE

The offence is committed when A causes B to engage in sexual activity without B's consent, whether or not A also engages in it and whether or not A is present.

The offence can involve a number of permutations, for example a woman making a man penetrate her, a man forcing someone else to masturbate him, a woman making another woman masturbate a third person or even an animal. The shocking circumstances of *R* v *H* [2008] EWCA Crim 1202 are an example of where an animal was used in the commission of the offence where the visibly mentally disabled victim was forced, among other things, to be penetrated in the anus by a dog. It would include causing a person to act as a prostitute. Apart from the defendant and the victim, there may be others involved who also consent—they may be liable for aiding and abetting under the right circumstances.

The term 'activity' is not defined and is capable of being given a wide interpretation, although it must have actually taken place. The activity engaged in must be 'sexual' in accordance with s. 78. It can include engaging someone in a conversation of a sexual nature (*R* v *Grout* [2011] EWCA Crim 299).

This offence overlaps partly with rape in that it deals with vaginal, anal and oral penetration. The offence is wider than rape, in that rape can only be committed by a man, as a principal, and does not involve penetration with an object. The offence can be committed by and against persons of either sex and includes cases of 'female rape', i.e. where A causes B to penetrate her vagina with his penis. Furthermore, the offence makes A criminally liable for causing B to engage in sexual activity where B cannot himself be convicted of any offence because he has a defence such as duress or is under the age of criminal responsibility (see chapter 1.4).

Whether a belief is reasonable is to be determined having regard to all the circumstances, including any steps the defendant has taken to ascertain whether the victim consents (s. 4(2)).

Sections 75 and 76 apply to this offence.

There is a specific offence of causing or *inciting* a child under 13 to engage in sexual activity (s. 8). An individual can commit an offence of incitement even if the activity he/she is encouraging, etc. does not take place. In *R* v *Walker* [2006] EWCA Crim 1907, the Court of Appeal held that s. 8 of the Act created two offences: (i) intentionally causing, and (ii) intentionally inciting a child under 13 to engage in sexual activity. The offence was centred on the concept of incitement and the acts had to be intentional or deliberate, but it was not a necessary ingredient for incitement of sexual activity that the defendant had intended the sexual activity to take place.

1.11.5 Child Sex Offences

The Sexual Offences Act 2003 contains specific offences relating to sexual activity involving or directed towards children. In considering each offence it is important to remember the relevant ages, both of offenders and victims. In addition, the Act makes special exceptions to some offences of aiding, abetting or counselling some offences involving children (**see para. 1.11.5.4** for such an example).

The full list of offences is set out in s. 73(2); basically it covers specific offences against children under 13 and offences involving sexual activity with a child under 16.

1.11.5.1 Sexual Activity with a Child

OFFENCE: **Sexual Activity with a Child—*Sexual Offences Act 2003, s. 9***
  • If involves penetration: of victim's anus or vagina by a part of defendant's body or anything else, of victim's mouth with defendant's penis, of defendant's anus or vagina by a part of victim's body or of defendant's mouth by victim's penis—triable on indictment; 14 years' imprisonment • Otherwise triable either way; 14 years' imprisonment on indictment; six months' imprisonment summarily

The Sexual Offences Act 2003, s. 9 states:

(1) A person aged 18 or over (A) commits an offence if—
  (a) he intentionally touches another person (B),
  (b) the touching is sexual, and
  (c) either—
    (i) B is under 16 and A does not reasonably believe that B is 16 or over, or
    (ii) B is under 13.

KEYNOTE

The person committing this offence must be at least 18. If the defendant is under 18, he/she commits a specific offence, punishable by five years' imprisonment (if tried on indictment) under s. 13. Similarly, if the person committing the offence is in a position of trust in relation to the victim, he/she commits a specific offence under s. 16.

You must show that the defendant intentionally touched the victim sexually and either that the victim was under 13 (in which case the offence is complete) or that the victim was under 16 and that the defendant did not reasonably believe he/she was 16 or over. In either case consent is irrelevant.

There is a further specific offence (s. 10) of a person aged 18 or over intentionally causing or inciting another to engage in the type of sexual activity set out above. The sexual activity caused or envisaged may be with the defendant or with a third person. In the case of incitement there is no need for the sexual activity itself to take place. If the person committing the offence is in a position of trust in relation to the victim, he/she commits a specific offence under s. 17 (**see para. 1.11.5.5**).

1.11.5.2 Sexual Activity in Presence of a Child

OFFENCE: **Engaging in Sexual Activity in the Presence of a Child—*Sexual Offences Act 2003, s. 11***
  • Triable either way • 10 years' imprisonment on indictment
  • Six months' imprisonment summarily

The Sexual Offences Act 2003, s. 11 states:

(1) A person aged 18 or over (A) commits an offence if—
  (a) he intentionally engages in an activity,
  (b) the activity is sexual,
  (c) for the purpose of obtaining sexual gratification, he engages in it—
    (i) when another person (B) is present or is in a place from which A can be observed, and
    (ii) knowing or believing that B is aware, or intending that B should be aware, that he is engaging in it, and
  (d) either—
    (i) B is under 16 and A does not reasonably believe that B is 16 or over, or
    (ii) B is under 13.

The person committing this offence must be at least 18. If the defendant is under 18, he/she commits a specific offence, punishable by five years' imprisonment (if tried on indictment) under s. 13. Similarly, if the person committing the offence is in a position of trust in relation to the victim, he/she commits a specific offence under s. 18.

The activity in which the offender is engaged must be 'sexual' and intentional and must be in order to obtain sexual gratification (for the defendant). The display of sexual images or sexual activity might, in certain circumstances, be appropriate, for example, for medical or educational reasons, hence the requirement that the offence depended on the corrupt purpose of 'sexual gratification'. The offence under s. 12 of the Act does not require that such gratification has to be taken immediately; i.e. the section does not require that the offence can only be committed if the purposed sexual gratification and the viewed sexual act, or display of images, were simultaneous, contemporaneous or synchronised. For example, the defendant may cause a child to watch a sexual act to put the child in a frame of mind for future sexual abuse, as well as where the defendant does so to obtain enjoyment from seeing the child watch the sexual act (*R* v *Abdullahi* [2006] EWCA Crim 2060). The approach to 'sexual gratification' taken in *Abdullahi* appears equally applicable to other offences where this phrase appears (the offence under s. 11 of the Act, for example).

A person under 16 must be present or in a place from which the defendant can be observed and the defendant must know, believe or intend that the child was aware that he/she was engaging in that activity. Therefore, it is not necessary to show that the child was in fact aware of the activity in every case. Because of the wording in s. 79(7), 'observation' includes direct observation or by looking at any image.

In relation to the child you must show that either the child was under 13 (in which case the offence is complete) or that he/she was under 16 and that the defendant did not reasonably believe him/her to be 16 or over.

This offence is aimed at, for example, people masturbating in front of children or performing sexual acts with others where they know they can be seen (or they want to be seen) by children directly or via a camera/video phone etc.

1.11.5.3 Causing a Child to Watch a Sex Act

OFFENCE: **Causing a Child to Watch a Sexual Act—*Sexual Offences Act 2003, s. 12***
- Triable either way • 10 years' imprisonment on indictment
- Six months' imprisonment summarily

The Sexual Offences Act 2003, s. 12 states:

(1) A person aged 18 or over (A) commits an offence if—
  (a) for the purpose of obtaining sexual gratification, he intentionally causes another person (B) to watch a third person engaging in an activity, or to look at an image of any person engaging in an activity,
  (b) the activity is sexual, and
  (c) either—
    (i) B is under 16 and A does not reasonably believe that B is 16 or over, or
    (ii) B is under 13.

The person committing this offence must be at least 18. If the defendant is under 18, he/she commits a specific offence, punishable by five years' imprisonment (if tried on indictment) under s. 13. Similarly, if the person committing the offence is in a position of trust in relation to the victim, he/she commits a specific offence under s. 19.

This offence is concerned with intentionally causing a child to watch a third person engaging in sexual activity or to look at an image of a person *engaging in sexual activity*. 'Image' includes a moving or still image and includes an image produced by any means and, where the context permits, a three-dimensional image (s. 79(4)); it also includes images of an imaginary person (s. 79(5)).

The defendant must have acted for the purposes of obtaining sexual gratification. For issues in relation to the term 'sexual gratification' see the explanation given in **para. 1.11.5.2**. You must show that either the child was under 13 (in which case the offence is complete) or that he/she was under 16 and that the defendant did not reasonably believe him/her to be 16 or over.

1.11.5.4   Arranging Intended Child Sex Offences

OFFENCE: **Arranging or Facilitating Commission of Child Sex Offences—*Sexual Offences Act 2003, s. 14***

- Triable either way • 14 years' imprisonment on indictment
- Six months' imprisonment summarily

The Sexual Offences Act 2003, s. 14 states:

(1) A person commits an offence if—
   (a) he intentionally arranges or facilitates something that he intends to do, intends another person to do, or believes that another person will do, in any part of the world, and
   (b) doing it will involve the commission of an offence under any of sections 9 to 13.

KEYNOTE

The relevant offences are those set out in ss. 9 to 13 of the Act described in the earlier paragraphs of this chapter.

The offence applies to activities by which the defendant intends to commit one of those relevant child sex offences him/herself, or by which the defendant intends or believes another person will do so, in either case in any part of the world. The offence is complete whether or not the sexual activity actually takes place. Examples of the offence would include a defendant approaching a third person to procure a child to take part in sexual activity with him or where the defendant makes travel arrangements for another in the belief that the other person will commit a relevant child sex offence.

This part of the Act specifically excludes the actions of those acting for the child's protection who arrange or facilitate something that they believe another person will do, but that they do not intend to do or intend another person to do. Acting for the child's protection must fall within one of the following:

- protecting the child from sexually transmitted infection,
- protecting the physical safety of the child,
- preventing the child from becoming pregnant, or
- promoting the child's emotional well-being by the giving of advice,

and *not* for obtaining sexual gratification or for causing or encouraging the activity constituting the relevant child sex offence or the child's participation in it. This statutory exception (contained in s. 14(2) and (3)) covers activities such as health workers supplying condoms to people under 16 who are intent on having sex in any event and need protection from infection.

OFFENCE: **Meeting a Child Following Sexual Grooming—*Sexual Offences Act 2003, s. 15***

- Triable either way • 10 years' imprisonment on indictment
- Six months' imprisonment summarily

The Sexual Offences Act 2003, s. 15 states:

(1) A person aged 18 or over (A) commits an offence if—
   (a) A has met or communicated with another person (B) on one or more occasions and subsequently—
      (i) A intentionally meets B,
      (ii) A travels with the intention of meeting B in any part of the world or arranges to meet B in any part of the world, or
      (iii) B travels with the intention of meeting A in any part of the world,

(b) A intends to do anything to or in respect of B, during or after the meeting mentioned in para-graph (a)(i) to (iii) and in any part of the world, which if done will involve the commission by A of a relevant offence,

(c) B is under 16, and

(d) A does not reasonably believe that B is 16 or over.

KEYNOTE

The initial action of the defendant involves either a meeting or a communication with the victim (who must be under 16) on at least one previous occasion. Such meetings or communications can be innocuous, such as family occasions or during the course of youth activities and so on. The only requirement prior to an inten-tional meeting during which an offender intends to do anything to a complainant which, if carried out, would involve the commission by the offender of a relevant offence is a meeting or communication 'on one or more occasions'. There is no requirement that either communication be sexual in nature (*R* v *G* [2010] EWCA Crim 1693).

The communication can include text messaging or interactions in Internet 'chat rooms'. Such contact can have taken place in any part of the world.

Once the earlier meeting or communication has taken place, the offence is triggered by:

- an intentional meeting with the victim;
- a defendant travelling with the intention of meeting the victim;
- a defendant arranging to meet the victim;
- the victim travelling to meet the defendant in any part of the world.

The activity at s. 15(1)(a)(iii) means that an offence will be committed by an adult where a child under 16 travels to meet the adult or the adult arranges to meet the child.

At the time of any of the above activities, the defendant must intend to do anything to or in respect of the victim, during or even after the meeting, that would amount to a relevant offence. A relevant offence here is generally any offence under part I of the Act (all the offences covered in this chapter). Note that the intended offence *does not* have to take place.

You must show that the victim was under 16 and that the defendant did not reasonably believe that he/she was 16 or over.

1.11.5.5   Abuse of Position of Trust

OFFENCE: **Abuse of Position of Trust—*Sexual Offences Act 2003, ss. 16 to 19***
- Triable either way • Five years' imprisonment on indictment
- Six months' imprisonment summarily or a fine not exceeding the statutory maximum or both

Offences under ss. 16 to 19 are exactly the same activities as discussed above (**see paras 1.11.5.1 to 1.11.5.3**), except that they are committed by a person in 'a position of trust' and can be committed against a child aged 16 or 17.

'Position of Trust'

The Sexual Offences Act 2003, s. 21 states:

(1) For the purposes of sections 16 to 19, a person (A) is in a position of trust in relation to another person (B) if—

(a) any of the following subsections applies, or

(b) any condition specified in an order made by the Secretary of State is met.

(2) This subsection applies if A looks after persons under 18 who are detained in an institution by virtue of a court order or under an enactment, and B is so detained in that institution.

(3) This subsection applies if A looks after persons under 18 who are resident in a home or other place in which—

(a) accommodation and maintenance are provided by an authority under section 23(2) of the Children Act 1989 (c. 41)..., or

(b) accommodation is provided by a voluntary organisation under section 59(1) of that Act..., and B is resident, and is so provided with accommodation and maintenance or accommodation, in that place.

(4) This subsection applies if A looks after persons under 18 who are accommodated and cared for in one of the following institutions—

    (a) a hospital,

    (b) in Wales, an independent clinic,

    (c) a care home,

    (d) a community home, voluntary home or children's home, or

    (e) a home provided under section 82(5) of the Children Act 1989,

    and B is accommodated and cared for in that institution.

(5) This subsection applies if A looks after persons under 18 who are receiving education at an educational institution and B is receiving, and A is not receiving, education at that institution.

(6) ...

(7) This subsection applies if A is engaged in the provision of services under, or pursuant, to anything done under—

    (a) sections 8 to 10 of the Employment and Training Act 1973 (c. 50), or

    (b) section 68, 70(1)(b) or 74 of the Education and Skills Act 2008,

    and, in that capacity, looks after B on an individual basis.

(8) This subsection applies if A regularly has unsupervised contact with B (whether face to face or by any other means)—

    (a) in the exercise of functions of a local authority under section 20 or 21 of the Children Act 1989 (c. 41),

    (b) ...

(9) This subsection applies if A, as a person who is to report to the court under section 7 of the Children Act 1989...on matters relating to the welfare of B, regularly has unsupervised contact with B (whether face to face or by any other means).

(10) This subsection applies if A is a personal adviser appointed for B under—

    (a) section 23B(2) of, or paragraph 19C of Schedule 2 to, the Children Act 1989,

    (b) ...

    and, in that capacity, looks after B on an individual basis.

(11) This subsection applies if—

    (a) B is subject to a care order, a supervision order or an education supervision order, and

    (b) in the exercise of functions conferred by virtue of the order on an authorised person or the authority designated by the order, A looks after B on an individual basis.

(12) This subsection applies if A—

    (a) is an officer of the Service or Welsh family proceedings officer (within the meaning given by section 35 of the Children Act 2004) appointed for B under section 41(1) of the Children Act 1989,

    (b) is appointed a children's guardian of B under rule 6 or rule 18 of the Adoption Rules 1984 (S.I. 1984/265), or

    (c) is appointed to be the guardian ad litem of B under rule 9.5 of the Family Proceedings Rules 1991 (S.I. 1991/1247)...

    (d) is appointed to be the children's guardian of B under rule 59 of the Family Procedure (Adoption) Rules 2005 (S.I. 2005/2795) or rule 16.3(1)(ii) or rule 16.4 of the Family Procedure Rules 2010 (S.I. 2010/2955)

    and, in that capacity, regularly has unsupervised contact with B (whether face to face or by any other means).

(13) This subsection applies if—

    (a) B is subject to requirements imposed by or under an enactment on his release from detention for a criminal offence, or is subject to requirements imposed by a court order made in criminal proceedings, and

    (b) A looks after B on an individual basis in pursuance of the requirements.

KEYNOTE

The key to this list lies in establishing whether the defendant looked after people under 18 in the contexts described or the defendant's relationship with the victim fell into one of the other categories at s. 21(7)–(13). Further clarification for the interpretation of these definitions is set out in s. 22.

In summary, positions of trust include the wide range of settings in which a child is being lawfully detained or accommodated, including situations such as foster care or residential care. Those who look after children on an individual basis such as Connexions Personal Advisors and people with unsupervised contact appointed under the relevant parts of the Children Act 1989 will be covered.

There are specific procedures in place for dealing with allegations of abuse made against teachers and educational support staff. These are overseen by the relevant Local Safeguarding Children Boards.

Essentially the above provisions make it a specific offence for a person aged 18 or over in a position of trust to engage in sexual activity which is prohibited by the general child sex offences considered earlier in this chapter (ss. 9 to 12) in relation to a child, namely:

- sexual activity with a child;
- causing or inciting a child to engage in sexual activity;
- sexual activity in the presence of a child;
- causing a child to watch a sexual act.

There are however some key differences. For instance, in such cases involving an abuse of a position of trust, the 'child' victim can be 16 or 17 years old and except in cases where the victim is under 13, it must be shown that the defendant did not reasonably believe that the victim was 18 or over. Once it is proved that the victim was under 18 an evidential burden passes to the defendant. This means that, unless the defendant can point to some evidence to raise an arguable case to the contrary, it will be presumed that he/she did not reasonably believe that the victim was 18 or over.

There are further provisions relating to rebuttable presumptions of knowledge by the defendant. Generally, if the position of trust held by the defendant falls within the first four categories set out in s. 21 (2)–(5) (basically where the defendant looks after children at an institution and the victim is at that institution), there will be a further evidential burden on the defendant. Where the defendant works in an institution where the victim is, it will be presumed that the defendant knew (or could reasonably have been expected to know) that there was a position of trust between him/her and the victim unless he/she can point to some evidence to the contrary.

An exception to the offences under ss. 16 to 19 is where a lawful sexual relationship existed between the defendant and the victim before the position of trust arose (s. 24) and where the defendant and the victim were lawfully married to each other at the time (s. 23).

1.11.5.6   Sex Offences with Family Members

OFFENCE: **Sexual Activity with Child Family Member—*Sexual Offences Act 2003, s. 25***

- Where defendant is 18 or over at the time of the offence and if involves penetration: of victim's anus or vagina by a part of defendant's body or anything else, of victim's mouth with defendant's penis, of defendant's anus or vagina by a part of victim's body or of defendant's mouth by victim's penis—triable on indictment: 14 years' imprisonment • Otherwise triable either way; 14 years' imprisonment on indictment; six months' imprisonment and/or a fine summarily • Or, where defendant is under 18 at the time of the offence; five years' imprisonment on indictment; six months' imprisonment and/or a fine summarily

The Sexual Offences Act 2003, s. 25 states:

(1) A person (A) commits an offence if—
  (a) he intentionally touches another person (B),
  (b) the touching is sexual,
  (c) the relation of A to B is within section 27,
  (d) A knows or could reasonably be expected to know that his relation to B is of a description falling within that section, and
  (e) either—
    (i) B is under 18 and A does not reasonably believe that B is 18 or over, or
    (ii) B is under 13.

KEYNOTE

Where the defendant intentionally incites another person (the victim) to touch him/her or to allow him/herself to be touched by the defendant, there is a specific offence committed under s. 26.

For the relevant definitions of touching and sexual **see paras 1.11.3.4** and *1.11.3.2*.

The further elements that must be proved are the existence of the relevant family relationship between the defendant and the victim, and the age of the victim.

Where the relevant family relationship is proved, it will be presumed that the defendant knew or could reasonably have been expected to know that he/she was related to the victim in that way. Similarly where it is proved that the victim was under 18, there will be a presumption that the defendant did not reasonably believe that the victim was 18 or over. In respect of both the relationship and the age of the defendant under these circumstances, the defendant will have an evidential burden to discharge in that regard (s. 25(2) and (3)).

The relevant family relationships are set out in s. 27. These cover all close family relationships along with adoptive relationships. They are where:

- the defendant or the victim is the other's parent, grandparent, brother, sister, half-brother, half-sister, aunt or uncle or
- the defendant is or has been the victim's foster parent.

Additional categories are where the defendant and victim live or have lived in the same household, or the defendant is or has been regularly involved in caring for, training, supervising or being in sole charge of the victim and:

- one of them is or has been the other's step-parent,
- they are cousins,
- one of them is or has been the other's stepbrother or stepsister, or
- they have the same parent or foster parent.

There are exceptions for situations where the defendant and the victim are lawfully married at the time or where (under certain circumstances) the sexual relationship pre-dates the family one. For example, where two divorcees each have a child of 17 who are engaged in a sexual relationship before their respective parents marry and move all four of them into the same household.

1.11.5.7   Other Offences with Family Members

OFFENCE: **Sex with an Adult Relative: Penetration—*Sexual Offences Act 2003, s. 64***

- Triable either way • Two years' imprisonment on indictment
- Six months' imprisonment and/or a fine summarily

The Sexual Offences Act 2003, s. 64 states:

(1) A person aged 16 or over (A) (subject to subsection 3A)) commits an offence if
   (a) he intentionally penetrates another person's vagina or anus with a part of his body or anything else, or penetrates another person's mouth with his penis,
   (b) the penetration is sexual,
   (c) the other person (B) is aged 18 or over,
   (d) A is related to B in a way mentioned in subsection (2), and
   (e) A knows or could reasonably be expected to know that he is related to B in that way.

OFFENCE: **Sex with an Adult Relative: Consenting to Penetration—*Sexual Offences Act 2003, s. 65***

- Triable either way • Two years' imprisonment on indictment
- Six months' imprisonment and/or a fine summarily

The Sexual Offences Act 2003, s. 65 states:

(1) A person aged 16 or over (A) (subject to subsection 3A)) commits an offence if—
    (a) another person (B) penetrates A's vagina or anus with a part of B's body or anything else, or penetrates A's mouth with B's penis,
    (b) A consents to the penetration,
    (c) the penetration is sexual,
    (d) B is aged 18 or over,
    (e) A is related to B in a way mentioned in subsection (2), and
    (f) A knows or could reasonably be expected to know that he is related to B in that way.

KEYNOTE

For either offence to be committed the penetration must be 'sexual'. This requirement ensures that a penetration for some other purpose, for example where one sibling helps another to insert a pessary for medical reasons, is not caught by this offence.

A 'relative' for ss. 64 and 65 is a parent, grandparent, child, grandchild, brother, sister, half-brother, half-sister, uncle, aunt, nephew or niece.

The Criminal Justice and Immigration Act 2008 amended ss. 64 and 65 so that the offences of sex with an adult relative are committed where an adoptive parent has consensual sex with their adopted child when he/she is aged 18 or over. The adopted person does not commit this offence unless he/she is aged 18 or over.

In both offences, where the relevant relationship is proved, it will be taken that the defendant knew or could reasonably have been expected to know that he/she was related in that way unless sufficient evidence is adduced to raise an issue as to whether he/she knew or could reasonably have been expected to know that he/she was.

1.11.5.8   Sexual Exploitation of Children

OFFENCE: **Paying for Sexual Services of a Child—*Sexual Offences Act 2003, s. 47***
- If victim is child under 13; triable on indictment; life imprisonment
- Where victim is under 16 at the time of the offence and if involves penetration of victim's anus or vagina by a part of defendant's body or anything else, of victim's mouth with defendant's penis, of defendant's anus or vagina by a part of victim's body or by victim with anything else—triable on indictment: 14 years' imprisonment
- Otherwise triable either way: seven years' imprisonment on indictment; six months' imprisonment and/or a fine summarily

The Sexual Offences Act 2003, s. 47 states:

(1) A person (A) commits an offence if—
    (a) he intentionally obtains for himself the sexual services of another person (B),
    (b) before obtaining those services, he has made or promised payment for those services to B or a third person, or knows that another person has made or promised such a payment.

KEYNOTE

If the child is under 13, the offence is complete at this point. If the child is under 18, you must prove that the defendant did not reasonably believe that the child was 18 or over (s. 47(1)(c)).

Payment means any financial advantage, including the discharge of an obligation to pay or the provision of goods or services (including sexual services) gratuitously or at a discount (s. 47(2)). This would include situations where the child victim is given drugs or other goods/services at a cheaper rate in exchange for sexual services from the child.

OFFENCE: **Causing, Inciting, Controlling, Arranging or Facilitating the Sexual Exploitation of Children**—*Sexual Offences Act 2003, ss. 48 to 50*

- Triable either way • 14 years' imprisonment on indictment
- Six months' imprisonment and/or a fine summarily

The Sexual Offences Act 2003, s. 48 states:

(1) A person (A) commits an offence if—
(a) he intentionally causes or incites another person (B) to be sexually exploited, in any part of the world...

The Sexual Offences Act 2003, s. 49 states:

(1) A person (A) commits an offence if—
(a) he intentionally controls any of the activities of another person (B) relating to B's sexual exploitation in any part of the world...

The Sexual Offences Act 2003, s. 50 states:

(1) A person (A) commits an offence if—
(a) he intentionally arranges or facilitates the sexual exploitation in any part of the world of another person (B)...

KEYNOTE

These offences are aimed at those who seek to recruit children for prostitution or to take part in pornography, or otherwise control these activities and arrangements anywhere in the world. For the accused to be guilty of the incitement offence it is not necessary that B actually becomes a prostitute or involves him/herself in pornography.

If the child is under 13, the offences are complete once the relevant conduct of the defendant has been proved and any belief the defendant may have had as to the child's age is irrelevant to guilt. If the child is under 18, you must prove that the defendant did not reasonably believe that the child was 18 or over (see subs. (1)(b) of each).

For the purposes of ss. 48 to 50, a person (B) is sexually exploited if:

- on at least one occasion and whether or not compelled to do so, B offers or provides sexual services to another person in return for payment or a promise of payment to B or a third person, or
- an indecent image of B is recorded

and sexual exploitation is to be interpreted accordingly (s. 51(2)).

Payment means any financial advantage, including the discharge of an obligation to pay or the provision of goods or services (including sexual services) gratuitously or at a discount (s. 51(3)).

These offences would be committed if the child is recruited on a one-off basis, as well as on those occasions where the child is habitually involved. Unlike the general offence of controlling prostitution (see para. 1.11.12.2) there is no need to show that the causing or inciting was done for gain. The expressions used in the sections are deliberately wide and will, in places, overlap. Controlling the activities of the child would include, for example, setting the relevant price or specifying which room or equipment is to be used. Arranging will include taking an active part in the transport or travel arrangements or organising relevant facilities (such as hotel rooms etc.).

1.11.5.9 Indecent Photographs

OFFENCE: **Indecent Photographs**—*Protection of Children Act 1978, ss. 1, 1A and 1B*

- Triable either way • 10 years' imprisonment on indictment
- Six months' imprisonment and/or a fine summarily

The Protection of Children Act 1978, s. 1 states:

1 Indecent photographs of children

(1) Subject to sections 1A and 1B, it is an offence for a person—

    (a) to take, or permit to be taken or to make, any indecent photograph or pseudo-photograph of a child; or

    (b) to distribute or show such indecent photographs or pseudo-photographs; or

    (c) to have in his possession such indecent photographs or pseudo-photographs, with a view to their being distributed or shown by himself or others; or

    (d) to publish or cause to be published any advertisement likely to be understood as conveying that the advertiser distributes or shows such indecent photographs or pseudo-photographs, or intends to do so.

(2) For purposes of this Act, a person is to be regarded as distributing an indecent photograph or pseudo-photograph if he parts with possession of it to, or exposes or offers it for acquisition by, another person.

(3) …

(4) Where a person is charged with an offence under subsection (1)(b) or (c), it shall be a defence for him to prove—

    (a) that he had a legitimate reason for distributing or showing the photographs or pseudo-photographs or (as the case may be) having them in his possession; or

    (b) that he had not himself seen the photographs or pseudo-photographs and did not know, nor had any cause to suspect, them to be indecent.

(5) References in the Children and Young Persons Act 1933 (except in sections 15 and 99) to the offences mentioned in Schedule 1 to that Act shall include an offence under subsection (1)(a) above.

KEYNOTE

For the definition of a 'photograph' or 'pseudo-photograph' see 'What is a Photograph?' below.

The consent of the DPP is needed before prosecuting an offence under the Protection of Children Act 1978.

A person will be a 'child' for the purposes of the Act if it appears from the evidence as a whole that he/she was, at the material time, under the age of 18 (Protection of Children Act 1978, s. 2(3)).

Once the defendant realises, or should realise, that material is indecent, any distribution, showing or retention of the material with a view to its being distributed will result in an offence being committed under the 1978 Act if the person depicted turns out to be a child (*R v Land* [1999] QB 65).

If the impression conveyed by a pseudo-photograph is that the person shown is a child or where the predominant impression is that the person is a child, that pseudo-photograph will be treated for these purposes as a photograph of a child, notwithstanding that some of the physical characteristics shown are those of an adult (s. 7(8) of the 1978 Act).

'Distributing' will include lending or offering to another. Cases will vary significantly and some distinction is needed between the seriousness of different types of material. The Court of Appeal has set out five levels of seriousness which are of use in helping police officers and investigators understand how the offences will be dealt with by the criminal courts and also in explaining this to victims and witnesses. The levels are:

(1) images depicting erotic posing with no sexual activity;

(2) sexual activity between children, or solo masturbation by a child;

(3) non-penetrative sexual activity between adults and children;

(4) penetrative sexual activity between children and adults; and

(5) sadism or bestiality.

(*R v Oliver* [2002] EWCA Crim 2766.)

The Court of Appeal recognised that much of this material involves abuse of the child featuring in it and held that, so far as an offender's involvement was concerned, the seriousness of an offence increased with the offender's proximity to, and responsibility for, the original abuse. In considering all these factors, courts will distinguish between pseudo-photographs which had involved no abuse or exploitation of children, and photographic images that involved real children. The Court of Appeal indicated that imprisonment would normally follow where the material had been shown or distributed to others or where the offender had been in possession of a large amount of level 2 material or a small amount of material of level 3 or above.

Although the offences include video recordings, possession of exposed but undeveloped film (i.e. film in the form in which it is taken out of a camera) does not appear to be covered. The offence at s. 1(1)(b) and (c) of the 1978 Act can only be proved if the defendant showed/distributed the photograph etc. or intended to show or distribute the photograph etc. to someone else (*R* v *Fellows* [1997] 1 Cr App R 244 and *R* v *T* [1999] 163 JP 349). If no such intention can be proved, or if the defendant only had the photographs etc. for his/her own use, the appropriate charge would be under s. 160 of the Criminal Justice Act 1988.

Sections 1 and 2 of the Criminal Evidence (Amendment) Act 1997 apply to an offence under s. 1 of the Protection of Children Act 1978 (and to conspiracies, attempts or incitements in the circumstances set out in the 1997 Act).

A legitimate purpose for possessing such material might be where someone has the material as an exhibits officer or as a training aid for police officers or social workers.

The Protection of Children Act 1978, s. 1A states:

1A Marriage and other relationships

(1) This section applies where, in proceedings for an offence under section 1(1)(a) of taking or making an indecent photograph or pseudo-photograph of a child, or for an offence under section 1(1)(b) or (c) relating to an indecent photograph or pseudo-photograph of a child, the defendant proves that the photograph was of the child aged 16 or over, and that at the time of the offence charged the child and he—
    (a) were married, or civil partners of each other or
    (b) lived together as partners in an enduring family relationship.

(2) Subsections (5) and (6) also apply where, in proceedings for an offence under section 1(1)(b) or (c) relating to an indecent photograph or pseudo-photograph of a child, the defendant proves that the photograph was of the child aged 16 or over, and that at the time when he obtained it the child and he—
    (a) were married, or civil partners of each other or
    (b) lived together as partners in an enduring family relationship.

(3) This section applies whether the photograph or pseudo-photograph showed the child alone or with the defendant, but not if it showed any other person.

(4) In the case of an offence under section 1(1)(a), if sufficient evidence is adduced to raise an issue as to whether the child consented to the photograph or pseudo-photograph being taken or made, or as to whether the defendant reasonably believed that the child so consented, the defendant is not guilty of the offence unless it is proved that the child did not so consent and that the defendant did not reasonably believe that the child so consented.

(5) In the case of an offence under section 1(1)(b), the defendant is not guilty of the offence unless it is proved that the showing or distributing was to a person other than the child.

KEYNOTE

There is a specific defence to offences under s. 1(1)(a), (b) and (c) of the Protection of Children Act 1978 (making, distributing or possessing with a view to distributing) where the defendant can prove that the photograph was of a child aged 16 or over, the photograph only showed the defendant and the child, and that, at the time of the offence, they were married, in a civil partnership or lived together as partners in an enduring family relationship (s. 1A). If the defendant can show these elements, then the following further conditions of the defence will apply:

• In the case of an offence under s. 1(1)(a) (taking or permitting to be taken etc.), the defendant will have an evidential burden of showing that the child consented or that the defendant reasonably believed that the child consented to the making of the photograph (s. 1A(4)).

• In the case of an offence under s. 1(1)(b) (distributing or showing), you must prove that the distributing or showing was to a person other than the child in the photograph (s. 1A(5)).

• In the case of an offence under s. 1(1)(c) (possession with a view to distribution or showing etc.), the defendant will have an evidential burden of demonstrating that the image was to be shown/distributed to no person other than the child and that the child consented to the defendant's possession of the photograph (s. 1A(6)).

The Protection of Children Act 1978, s. 1B states:

1B Exception for criminal proceedings, investigations etc.

(1) In proceedings for an offence under section 1(1)(a) of making an indecent photograph or pseudo-photograph of a child, the defendant is not guilty of the offence if he proves that—

    (a) it was necessary for him to make the photograph or pseudo-photograph for the purposes of the prevention, detection or investigation of crime, or for the purposes of criminal proceedings, in any part of the world,

    (b) at the time of the offence charged he was a member of the Security Service or the Secret Intelligence Service, and it was necessary for him to make the photograph or pseudo-photograph for the exercise of any of the functions of that Service, or

    (c) at the time of the offence charged he was a member of GCHQ, and it was necessary for him to make the photograph or pseudo-photograph for the exercise of any of the functions of GCHQ.

KEYNOTE

There is a limited defence in relation to the making of an indecent photograph or pseudo-photograph contrary to s. 1(1)(a) of the Protection of Children Act 1978 where the defendant proves that:

- it was necessary for the defendant to make the photograph or pseudo-photograph for the purposes of the prevention, detection or investigation of crime or for criminal proceedings in any part of the world, or
- at the time the defendant was a member of the Security Service, Secret Intelligence Service or GCHQ (Government Communications Headquarters) and it was necessary for the exercise of any of the functions of that Service/GCHQ (s. 1B).

In order to assist police officers and prosecutors, ACPO and the CPS have published a Memorandum of Understanding. It sets out factors that will be taken into account in deciding whether the intention of someone accused of an offence under s. 1(1)(a) attracted criminal liability when 'making' a photograph etc. As the Memorandum points out:

> This reverse burden is intended to allow those people who need to be able to identify and act to deal with such images to do so. It also presents a significant obstacle to would-be abusers and those who exploit the potential of technology to gain access to paedophilic material for unprofessional (or personal) reasons.

The purpose of the Memorandum is to reassure those whose duties properly involve the prevention, detection or investigation of this type of crime and also as a warning to others who might claim this defence having taken it upon themselves to investigate such offences. In summary the following criteria will be considered:

- How soon after its discovery the image was reported and to whom.
- The circumstances in which it was discovered.
- The way in which the image was stored and dealt with, and whether it was copied.
- Whether the person's actions were reasonable, proportionate and necessary.

What is a Photograph?

Section 7 of the Protection of Children Act 1978 provides a definition of a photograph for the purposes of the Act (the same definition applies to the offence under s. 160 of the Criminal Justice Act 1988) and states:

(1) The following subsections apply for the interpretation of this Act.

(2) References to an indecent photograph include an indecent film, a copy of an indecent film, and an indecent photograph comprised in a film.

(3) Photographs (including those comprised in a film) shall, if they show children and are indecent, be treated for all purposes of this Act as indecent photographs of children and so as respects of pseudo-photographs.

(4) References to a photograph include—

    (a) the negative as well as the positive version; and

    (b) data stored on a computer disc or by other electronic means which is capable of conversion into a photograph.

(4A) References to a photograph also include—

    (a) a tracing or other image, whether made by electronic or other means (of whatever nature)—

        (i) which is not itself a photograph or pseudo-photograph, but

        (ii) which is derived from the whole or part of a photograph or pseudo-photograph (or a combination of either or both); and

    (b) data stored on a computer disc or by other electronic means which is capable of conversion into an image within paragraph (a);

and subsection (8) applies in relation to such an image as it applies in relation to a pseudo-photograph.

(5) 'Film' includes any form of video-recording.

(6) 'Child', subject to subsection (8), means a person under the age of 18.

(7) 'Pseudo-photograph' means an image, whether made by computer graphics or otherwise howsoever, which appears to be a photograph.

(8) If the impression conveyed by a pseudo-photograph is that the person shown is a child, the pseudo-photograph shall be treated for all purposes of this Act as showing a child and so shall a pseudo-photograph where the predominant impression conveyed is that the person shown is a child notwithstanding that some of the physical characteristics shown are those of an adult.

(9) References to an indecent pseudo-photograph include—

    (a) a copy of an indecent pseudo-photograph; and

    (b) data stored on a computer disc or by other electronic means which is capable of conversion into an indecent pseudo-photograph.

KEYNOTE

'Pseudo-photographs' include computer images and the above offences will cover the situation where part of the photograph is made up of an adult form. The use of the Internet to facilitate such offences has led to a great deal of case law on the subject and what follows is a summary of several key decisions by the courts on these issues:

- Downloading images from the Internet will amount to 'making' a photograph for the purposes of s. 1(1)(a) of the 1978 Act (*R* v *Bowden* [2001] QB 88).

- 'Making' pseudo-photographs includes voluntary browsing through indecent images of children on and from the Internet. Once an image is downloaded, the length of time it remains on the screen is irrelevant (*R* v *Smith and Jayson* [2002] EWCA Crim 683).

- In the same case the Court of Appeal held that a person receiving an unsolicited e-mail attachment containing an indecent image of a child would not commit the offence under s. 1(1)(a) by opening it if he/she was unaware that it contained or was likely to contain an indecent image. This was because s. 1(1)(a) does not create an absolute offence.

- Copying onto a hard drive and storing 'pop-ups' containing indecent images of children amounts to possessing those images (*R* v *Harrison* [2007] EWCA Crim 2976).

- If images have been deleted from a computer so that their retrieval is impossible and, at the material time, a person cannot gain access to them and the images are beyond a person's control, that person cannot be in possession of them (*R* v *Porter* [2006] EWCA Crim 560).

- Evidence indicating an interest in paedophile material generally along with evidence to show how a computer had been used to access paedophile news groups, chat lines etc. can be relevant to show it was more likely than not that a file containing an indecent image of a child had been created deliberately (*R* v *Toomer* [2001] 2 Cr App R(S) 8).

- An image consisting of two parts of two different photographs taped together (the naked body of a woman taped to the head of a child) is not a 'pseudo-photograph'. If such an image were to be photocopied it could be (*Atkins* v *DPP* [2000] 1 WLR 1427).

- Where a defendant had knowledge that images were likely to be accessed by others, any images would be downloaded 'with a view to distribute' (*R* v *Dooley* [2005] EWCA Crim 3093).

OFFENCE: **Indecent Photographs—*Criminal Justice Act 1988, s. 160***

- Triable either way • Five years' imprisonment on indictment
- Six months' imprisonment and/or a fine

The Criminal Justice Act 1988, ss. 160 and 160A state:

160 Possession of indecent photograph of child

(1) Subject to section 160A, it is an offence for a person to have any indecent photograph or pseudo-photograph of a child in his possession.

(2) Where a person is charged with an offence under subsection (1) above, it shall be a defence for him to prove—

    (a) that he had a legitimate reason for having the photograph or pseudo-photograph in his possession; or

    (b) that he had not himself seen the photograph or pseudo-photograph and did not know, nor had any cause to suspect, it to be indecent; or

    (c) that the photograph or pseudo-photograph was sent to him without any prior request made by him or on his behalf and that he did not keep it for an unreasonable time.

160A Marriage and other relationships

(1) This section applies where, in proceedings for an offence under section 160 relating to an indecent photograph or pseudo-photograph of a child, the defendant proves that the photograph or pseudo-photograph was of the child aged 16 or over, and that at the time of the offence charged the child and he—

    (a) were married, or civil partners of each other or

    (b) lived together as partners in an enduring family relationship.

(2) This section also applies where, in proceedings for an offence under section 160 relating to an indecent photograph or pseudo-photograph of a child, the defendant proves that the photograph or pseudo-photograph was of the child aged 16 or over, and that at the time when he obtained it the child and he—

    (a) were married, or civil partners of each other or

    (b) lived together as partners in an enduring family relationship.

(3) This section applies whether the photograph or pseudo-photograph showed the child alone or with the defendant, but not if it showed any other person.

(4) If sufficient evidence is adduced to raise an issue as to whether the child consented to the photograph or pseudo-photograph being in the defendant's possession, or as to whether the defendant reasonably believed that the child so consented, the defendant is not guilty of the offence unless it is proved that the child did not so consent and that the defendant did not reasonably believe that the child so consented.

KEYNOTE

For the meaning of 'photograph' and 'pseudo-photograph' see the previous Keynote.

A person will be a 'child' for the purposes of the Act if it appears from the evidence as a whole that he/she was, at the material time, under the age of 18 (Criminal Justice Act 1988, s. 160(4)).

The statutory defence under s. 160(2)(b) of the 1988 Act requires that the defendant (1) has not seen the material and (2) did not know or have any cause to suspect it was indecent. The defendant will be acquitted of the offence under s. 160 if he/she proves that (1) he/she had not seen the material and (2) did not know (and had no cause to suspect) that it was an indecent photograph of a child. This was confirmed in *R* v *Collier* [2004] EWCA Crim 1411 and arose from an argument where the material relating to children had been among other adult material that the defendant did know was indecent—he just did not know that it was an indecent photograph of a child.

1.11.5.10   **Information About Guests at Hotels**

Section 116 of the Anti-social, Crime and Policing Act 2014 confers a power on a police officer, of at least the rank of inspector, to serve a notice on the owner, operator or manager of a hotel that the officer reasonably believes has been or will be used for the purposes of child sexual exploitation or conduct preparatory to or connected with it.

For the purposes of s. 116, 'child sexual exploitation' is defined at s. 116(8) to include offences under any of the following sections:

An offence under any of the following sections of the Sexual Offences Act 2003—
- sections 1 to 13 (rape, assault and causing sexual activity without consent, rape and other offences against children under 13 and child sex offences);
- sections 16 to 19 (abuse of position of trust);
- sections 25 and 26 (familial child sex offences);
- sections 30 to 41 (persons with a mental disorder impeding choice, inducements etc to persons with a mental disorder, and care workers for persons with a mental disorder);
- sections 47 to 50 (abuse of children through prostitution and pornography);
- section 59A (trafficking people for sexual exploitation);
- section 61 (administering a substance with intent);
- sections 66 and 67 (exposure and voyeurism); and
- an offence under section 1 of the Protection of Children Act 1978 (indecent photographs of children).

The notice must be in writing and specify the hotel to which it relates, the date on which it comes into effect and the date on which it expires. It must also explain the information that a constable may require the person issued with a notice to provide, avenues of appeal against the notice, and the consequences of failure to comply. The notice must also specify the period for which it has effect, which, under s. 116(3), must be no more than six months.

The Anti-social Behaviour, Crime and Policing Act 2014, s. 116 states:

(4) A constable may require a person issued with a notice under this section to provide the constable with information about guests at the hotel.
(5) The only information that a constable may require under subsection (4) is—
    (a) guests' names and addresses;
    (b) other information about guests that—
        (i) is specified in regulations made by the Secretary of State, and
        (ii) can be readily obtained from one or more of the guests themselves.
(6) A requirement under subsection (4)—
    (a) must be in writing;
    (b) must specify the period to which the requirement relates;
    (c) must specify the date or dates on or by which the required information is to be provided.
    The period specified under paragraph (b) must begin no earlier than the time when the requirement is imposed and must end no later than the expiry of the notice under this section.

KEYNOTE

'Guest' means a person who, for a charge payable by that person or another, has the use of a guest room at the hotel in question.

'Hotel' includes any guest house or other establishment of a similar kind at which accommodation is provided for a charge.

Section 118(1) states that an offence is committed by a person who fails without reasonable excuse to comply with a requirement imposed on the person under s. 116(4).

Section 118(2) states that an offence is committed by a person who, in response to a requirement imposed on the person under s. 116(4), provides incorrect information which the person:

(a) did not take reasonable steps to verify or to have verified, or

(b) knows to be incorrect.

A person does not commit an offence under subs. (2)(a) if there were no steps that the person could reasonably have taken to verify the information or to have it verified.

These offences are punishable by a fine.

1.11.5.11 Possession of a Paedophile Manual

OFFENCE: **Possession of a Paedophile Manual—Serious Crime Act 2015, s. 69**

- Triable either way—Three years' imprisonment and/or fine
- Six months imprisonment and/or fine

The Serious Crime Act 2015, s. 69 states:

(1) It is an offence to be in possession of any item that contains advice or guidance about abusing children sexually.

(2) It is a defence for a person (D) charged with an offence under this section—

    (a) to prove that (D) had a legitimate reason for being in possession of the item, and

    (b) to prove that—

        (i) D had not read, viewed or (as appropriate) listened to the item, and

        (ii) D did not know, and had no reason to suspect, that it contained advice or guidance about abusing children sexually; or

    (c) to prove that—

        (i) the item was sent to D without any request made by D or on D's behalf, and

        (ii) D did not keep it for an unreasonable time.

KEYNOTE

This section creates a new offence of possession of a paedophile manual, that is any item containing advice or guidance about abusing children sexually. There are already a number of criminal offences that seek to prevent the possession, creation and distribution of indecent images of children, and the dissemination of obscene material. In particular:

- section 1 of the Protection of Children Act 1978 makes it an offence for a person to take, permit to be taken, make, distribute or show, or have in his or her possession with a view to showing or distributing any indecent photograph or pseudo-photograph of a child;
- section 160 of the Criminal Justice Act 1988 makes it an offence to possess an indecent photograph or pseudo-photograph of a child;
- section 63 of the Criminal Justice and Immigration Act 2008 makes it an offence to possess extreme pornographic images; and
- section 62 of the Coroners and Justice Act 2009 makes it an offence to possess a prohibited image of a child.

These existing offences *do not* criminalise mere possession of material containing advice and guidance about grooming and abusing a child sexually. The new offence plugs this gap in the law.

'Abusing children sexually' means doing anything that constitutes an offence under Part 1 of the Sexual Offences Act 2003 against a person under 16 or doing anything that constitutes an offence under s. 1 of the Protection of Children Act 1978 involving indecent photographs (but not pseudo-photographs) (s. 69(8)).

The term 'item' has a wide meaning and includes both physical and electronic documents (for example, emails or information downloaded to a computer) (s. 69(8)).

Subsection (2) sets out a series of defences to the offence of possession of a paedophile manual. They are the same as for other comparable offences, for example, the possession of indecent images of children under section 160(2) of the Criminal Justice Act 1988. They are:

- that the person had a legitimate reason for being in possession of the item; this would be a question of fact for the jury to decide on the individual circumstances of a case. It could cover, for example, those who can demonstrate that they have a legitimate work reason for possessing the item;
- that the person had not seen (or listened to) the item in his or her possession and therefore neither knew, nor had cause to suspect, that it contained advice or guidance about abusing children sexually; and
- that the person had not asked for the item—it having been sent without request—and that he or she had not kept it for an unreasonable period of time; this will cover those who are sent unsolicited material and who act quickly to delete it or otherwise get rid of it.

The standard of proof in making out the defence is the balance of probabilities.

Proceedings for an offence under s. 69(1) may not be instituted in England and Wales, except by or with the consent of the DPP.

1.11.6 Possession of Prohibited Images of Children

OFFENCE: **Possession of Prohibited Images of Children—*Coroners and Justice Act 2009, s. 62***

- Triable either way • Three years' imprisonment on indictment and/or a fine
- Six months' imprisonment and/or a fine

The Coroners and Justice Act 2009, s. 62 states:

(1) It is an offence for a person to be in possession of a prohibited image of a child.
(2) A prohibited image is an image which—
    (a) is pornographic,
    (b) falls within subsection (6), and
    (c) is grossly offensive, disgusting or otherwise of an obscene character.

KEYNOTE

An image is 'pornographic' if it is of such a nature that it must reasonably be assumed to have been produced solely or principally for the purpose of sexual arousal.

An image falls within subs. (6) if it is an image which focuses solely or principally on a child's genitals or anal region, or portrays any of the acts mentioned below. Those acts are:

- the performance by a person of an act of intercourse or oral sex with or in the presence of a child;
- an act of masturbation by, of, involving or in the presence of a child;
- an act which involves penetration of the vagina or anus of a child with a part of a person's body or with anything else;
- an act of penetration, in the presence of a child, of the vagina or anus of a person with a part of a person's body or with anything else;
- the performance by a child of an act of intercourse or oral sex with an animal (whether dead or alive or imaginary);
- the performance by a person of an act of intercourse or oral sex with an animal (whether dead or alive or imaginary) in the presence of a child.

Penetration is a continuing act from entry to withdrawal.

Section 62(4) of the offence states that where (as found in a person's possession) an individual image forms part of a series of images, the question of whether it is pornographic must be determined by reference both to the image itself and the context in which it appears in the series of images. Where an image is integral to a narrative (for example, a mainstream film) which when it is taken as a whole could not reasonably be assumed to be pornographic, the image itself may not be pornographic, even though if considered in isolation the contrary conclusion might have been reached (s. 62(5)). This is related to the exclusion from the scope of the offence of certain excluded images under s. 63 of the Act.

Proceedings for an offence under s. 62(1) may not be instituted in England and Wales, except by or with the consent of the DPP.

Meaning of 'Image' and 'Child'

Section 65 states that an 'image' includes a moving or still image (produced by any means) such as a photograph or film, or data (stored by any means) which is capable of conversion into a movable or still image such as data stored electronically (as on a computer disk), which is capable of conversion into an image. This covers material available on computers, mobile phones or any other electronic device. It should be noted that the term 'image' *does not* include an indecent photograph, or indecent pseudo-photograph, of a child as these are subject to other controls (see s. 160 of the Criminal Justice Act 1988 at **para. 1.11.5.9**).

A 'child' means a person under the age of 18 (s. 65(5)). Where an image shows a person the image is to be treated as an image of a child if the impression conveyed by the image is that the person shown is a child, or the predominant impression conveyed is that the person shown is a child despite the fact that some of the physical characteristics shown are not those of a child (s. 65(6)).

References to an image of a person include references to an image of an imaginary person. References to an image of a child include references to an image of an imaginary child.

1.11.6.1 Defence

The Coroners and Justice Act 2009, s. 64 states:

(1) Where a person is charged with an offence under section 62(1), it is a defence for the person to prove any of the following matters—
  (a) that the person had a legitimate reason for being in possession of the image concerned;
  (b) that the person had not seen the image concerned and did not know, nor had any cause to suspect, it to be a prohibited image of a child;
  (c) that the person—
     (i) was sent the image concerned without any prior request having been made by or on behalf of the person, and
     (ii) did not keep it for an unreasonable time.

This section sets out a series of defences to the s. 62 offence of possession of prohibited images of children.

1.11.7 Possession of Extreme Pornographic Images

This offence covers a more limited range of material than the Obscene Publications Act. It creates a possession offence in respect of a sub-text of extreme pornographic material which is defined in s. 63 of the Act.

OFFENCE: **Possession of Extreme Pornographic Images—*Criminal Justice and Immigration Act 2008, s. 63***
  • Triable either way • Three years' imprisonment on indictment and/or a fine (where the images contain life-threatening acts or serious injury) • Two years' imprisonment on indictment and/or a fine (where the images contain acts of necrophilia or bestiality) • Six months' imprisonment and/or a fine summarily

The Criminal Justice and Immigration Act 2008, s. 63 states:

(1) It is an offence for a person to be in possession of an extreme pornographic image.

KEYNOTE

Proceedings cannot be instituted without the consent of the DPP.

There are three elements to the offence. An image must come within the terms of *all three elements* before it will fall foul of the offence. Those elements are:

- that the image is pornographic;
- that the image is grossly offensive, disgusting, or otherwise of an obscene character, and
- that the image portrays in an explicit and realistic way, one of the following extreme acts:
  ✦ an act which threatens a person's life (this could include depictions of hanging, suffocation or sexual assault involving a threat with a weapon);

- an act which results in or is likely to result in serious injury to a person's anus, breasts or genitals (this could include the insertion of sharp objects or the mutilation of the breasts or genitals);
- an act involving sexual interference with a human corpse (necrophilia);
- a person performing an act of intercourse or oral sex with an animal (whether dead or alive) (bestiality);
- an act which involves the non-consensual penetration of a person's vagina, anus or mouth by another with the other person's penis;
- an act which involves the non-consensual sexual penetration of a person's vagina or anus by another with a part of the other person's body or anything else

- and a reasonable person looking at the image would think that the people and animals portrayed were real.

An 'extreme pornographic image' is an image which is both pornographic and an extreme image. An image is 'pornographic' if it is of such a nature that it must reasonably be assumed to have been produced solely or principally for the purpose of sexual arousal. Section 63(4) and (5) provides that where an image is integral to a narrative (for example a documentary film) which taken as a whole could not reasonably be assumed to be pornographic, the image itself may be taken not to be pornographic even though if considered in isolation the contrary conclusion would have been reached.

An 'image' means either still images (such as photographs) or moving images (such as those in a film). The term also incorporates any type of data, including that stored electronically (as on a computer disk), which is capable of conversion into an image. This covers material available on computers, mobile phones or any other electronic device. The scope of the definition of image is also affected by the requirement that the persons or animals portrayed in an image must appear to be real. Therefore animated characters, sketches, paintings and the like are excluded (s. 63(8)). References to parts of the body include body parts that have been surgically constructed (s. 63(9)).

Section 64 of the Act provides an exclusion from the scope of the offence under s. 63 for classified films (by the British Board of Film Classification).

1.11.7.1 General Defences

Several defences to the offence are set out in s. 65 of the Act. They are:

- that the person had a legitimate reason for being in possession of the image; this will cover those who can demonstrate that their legitimate business means that they have a reason for possessing the image;
- that the person had not seen the image and therefore neither knew, nor had cause to suspect, that the images held were extreme pornographic images; this will cover those who are in possession of offending images but are unaware of the nature of the images; and
- that the person had not asked for the image—it having been sent without request—and that he/she had not kept it for an unreasonable period of time; this will cover those who are sent unsolicited material and who act quickly to delete it or otherwise get rid of it.

1.11.7.2 Defence: Participation in Consensual Acts

Section 66 of the Act provides an additional defence for those who participate in the creation of extreme pornographic images. The defence is limited and will not cover images relating to bestiality and necrophilia images that depict a real corpse.

To use the defence, a defendant must prove (on the balance of probabilities) that he/she directly participated in the act or acts portrayed in the image and that the act(s) did not involve the infliction of non-consensual harm on any person. Where the image depicts necrophilia the defendant must also prove that the human corpse portrayed was not in fact a corpse. Non-consensual harm is harm which is of such a nature that, in law, a person cannot consent to it being inflicted on him/herself, or harm to which a person can consent but did not in fact consent.

1.11.8 Sexual Offences Against People with a Mental Disorder

The Sexual Offences Act 2003 is centred largely upon the fact that certain mental disorders deprive the sufferer of the ability to refuse involvement in sexual activity. This is different from, and wider than, a lack of consent at the time and focuses on the victim's inability to refuse.

1.11.8.1 Definition of 'Mental Disorder'

The relevant definition of a 'mental disorder' is that of s. 1(2) of the Mental Health Act 1983 which defines mental disorder as meaning any disorder or disability of the mind so a person with learning difficulties finds protection in the Act.

1.11.8.2 Sexual Activity with Mentally Disordered Person

OFFENCE: **Sexual Activity with a Person with a Mental Disorder—*Sexual Offences Act 2003, s. 30***
  • If involves penetration of victim's anus or vagina, of victim's mouth with defendant's penis, or of defendant's mouth by victim's penis—triable on indictment; life imprisonment • Otherwise triable either way; 14 years' imprisonment on indictment; six months' imprisonment and/or a fine summarily

The Sexual Offences Act 2003, s. 30 states:

(1) A person (A) commits an offence if—
  (a) he intentionally touches another person (B),
  (b) the touching is sexual,
  (c) B is unable to refuse because of or for a reason related to a mental disorder, and
  (d) A knows or could reasonably be expected to know that B has a mental disorder and that because of it or for a reason related to it B is likely to be unable to refuse.

> **KEYNOTE**
>
> A person is unable to refuse if:
>
> • he/she lacks the capacity to choose whether to agree to the touching (whether because of a lack of sufficient understanding of the nature or reasonably foreseeable consequences of what is being done, or for any other reason), or
>
> • he/she is unable to communicate such a choice to the defendant.
>
> (s. 30(2))
>
> You must show that the defendant knew or could reasonably have been expected to know both that the victim had a mental disorder *and* that because of it (or for a reason related to it) he/she was likely to be unable to refuse. In *Hulme* v *DPP* [2006] EWHC 1347 (Admin), the Divisional Court examined a decision reached by a magistrates' court in relation to a complainant who was a cerebral palsy sufferer with a low IQ (aged 27). The magistrates' court had decided that the complainant was unable to refuse to be touched sexually; the Divisional Court agreed and the conviction against the defendant (who was 73) was upheld.
>
> If the defendant obtains the victim's agreement to sexual touching by means of any inducement (offered or given), or a threat or deception for that purpose, the defendant commits a specific (and similarly punishable) offence under s. 34. An example would be where the defendant promises to give the victim some reward in exchange for allowing sexual touching. If the defendant uses an inducement, threat or deception to cause the victim to engage in or agree to engage in sexual activity, there is a further specific offence (similarly punishable) under s. 35.
>
> In these specific cases of inducements, threats or deception there is still the need to prove that the defendant knew (or could reasonably have been expected to know) of the victim's mental disorder but *no need to prove that the victim was unable to refuse.*

Causing or inciting a person with a mental disorder impeding choice to engage in sexual activity with another person generally (i.e. without threats, inducements or deception) is a separate offence, punishable in the same way, under s. 31. As that is an 'incomplete' or unfinished offence (as to which **see chapter 1.3**) it is not necessary to prove that the sexual activity took place.

1.11.8.3 Sexual Activity in Presence of Mentally Disordered Person

OFFENCE: **Sexual Activity in Presence of a Person with a Mental Disorder—**
Sexual Offences Act 2003, s. 32
- Triable either way • 10 years' imprisonment on indictment
- Six months' imprisonment and/or a fine summarily

The Sexual Offences Act 2003, s. 32 states:

(1) A person (A) commits an offence if—
  (a) he intentionally engages in an activity,
  (b) the activity is sexual,
  (c) for the purpose of obtaining sexual gratification, he engages in it—
    (i) when another person (B) is present or is in a place from which A can be observed, and
    (ii) knowing or believing that B is aware, or intending that B should be aware, that he is engaging in it,
  (d) B is unable to refuse because of or for a reason related to a mental disorder, and
  (e) A knows or could reasonably be expected to know that B has a mental disorder and that because of it or for a reason related to it B is likely to be unable to refuse.

KEYNOTE

For the requirements in proving the victim's inability to refuse see the previous offence under s. 30.

'Observation' includes direct observation or by looking at any image (s. 79(7)). For the specific offence of causing a person with a mental disorder impeding choice to watch a sexual act or an image of such an act **see para. 1.11.8.4**.

If the victim agrees to be present or in the place referred to in s. 32(1)(c)(i) because of any inducement (offered or given), or a threat or deception practised by the defendant for that purpose, the defendant commits a specific (and similarly punishable) offence under s. 36. For instance where the defendant pays the mentally disordered person to stay in a particular place while the activity occurs. In these specific cases of inducements, threats or deception there is still the need to prove that the defendant knew (or could reasonably have been expected to know) of the victim's mental disorder but _no need to prove that the victim was unable to refuse_.

1.11.8.4 Causing Person with Mental Disorder to Watch Sexual Act

OFFENCE: **Causing a Person with a Mental Disorder to Watch a Sexual Act—**
Sexual Offences Act 2003, s. 33
- Triable either way • 10 years' imprisonment on indictment
- Six months' imprisonment summarily

The Sexual Offences Act 2003, s. 33 states:

(1) A person (A) commits an offence if—
  (a) for the purpose of obtaining sexual gratification, he intentionally causes another person (B) to watch a third person engaging in an activity, or to look at an image of any person engaging in an activity,
  (b) the activity is sexual, and
  (c) B is unable to refuse because of or for a reason related to a mental disorder, and
  (d) A knows or could reasonably be expected to know that B has a mental disorder and that because of it or for a reason related to it B is likely to be unable to refuse.

1.11.8.5 Care Workers

There are specific sexual offences that apply to people who are involved in the care of the mentally disordered victim. These offences follow similar wording to those general offences set out above (engaging in, causing or inciting sexual activity etc.). In proving these offences (which appear in ss. 38 to 41 of the Act) you must show that the person was in a relationship of care as defined at s. 42. These are generally people whose employment has brought them into regular face-to-face contact with the victim in care homes, voluntary homes or hospitals. The offences are similar to those involving a position of trust. In these offences there is no need to prove that the victim was unable to refuse to take part in the activity but you must show that the defendant knew or could reasonably have been expected to know that the victim has a mental disorder. Given that the defendant will be a care worker with direct personal knowledge of the victim's circumstances, there is a presumption against the defendant that he/she had (or could reasonably have been expected to have) such knowledge and defendants will have to discharge an evidential burden in that regard if they are using this issue as part of their defence.

1.11.9 Sexual Displays and Voyeurism

There are several offences that involve sexual 'displays' of some description and of voyeurism.

1.11.9.1 Indecent Exposure

OFFENCE: **Outraging Public Decency—*Common Law***
- Triable either way • Unlimited powers of sentence on indictment
- Six months' imprisonment and/or a fine summarily

It is an offence at common law to commit an act of a lewd, obscene or disgusting nature and outrage public decency.

themselves obscene in public toilets, his motives (to induce young boys to engage in gross indecency with him) did not bring his actions under this offence (*Rowley*). In *Knuller (Publishing, Printing and Promotions) Ltd* v *DPP* [1973] AC 435, Lord Simon said that 'outraging public decency' goes considerably beyond offending the sensibilities of, or even shocking, reasonable people and that the recognised minimum standards of decency were likely to vary from time to time.

The offence can be committed by exposing the penis or engaging in simulated sexual acts (*R* v *Mayling* [1963] 2 QB 717); it is not restricted to offences committed by men.

The act must be committed where it might be seen by the public generally and it must be shown that more than one person could have seen the act take place (*R* v *Walker* [1996] 1 Cr App R 111).

It is not necessary to prove that someone was *in fact* annoyed or insulted (*R* v *May* (1990) 91 Cr App R 157).

OFFENCE: **Exposure—*Sexual Offences Act 2003, s. 66***

- Triable either way • Two years' imprisonment on indictment
- Six months' imprisonment summarily

The Sexual Offences Act 2003, s. 66 states:

(1) A person commits an offence if—
    (a) he intentionally exposes his genitals, and
    (b) he intends that someone will see them and be caused alarm or distress.

KEYNOTE

There is no requirement that the defendant acted for sexual gratification and simply exposing the genitals out of loutish behaviour will suffice if the other ingredients are present.

The offence is not restricted to public places and there is no need to show that anyone saw the genitals or was alarmed or distressed. The offence only applies to the genitals, not the buttocks, so the act of 'mooning' will not be covered. A woman who exposes her breasts will not be guilty of an offence under s. 66.

1.11.9.2 Voyeurism

OFFENCE: **Voyeurism—*Sexual Offences Act 2003, s. 67***

- Triable either way • Two years' imprisonment on indictment
- Six months' imprisonment summarily

The Sexual Offences Act 2003, s. 67 states:

(1) A person commits an offence if—
    (a) for the purpose of obtaining sexual gratification, he observes another person doing a private act, and
    (b) he knows that the other person does not consent to being observed for his sexual gratification.
(2) A person commits an offence if—
    (a) he operates equipment with the intention of enabling another person to observe, for the purpose of obtaining sexual gratification, a third person (B) doing a private act, and
    (b) he knows that B does not consent to his operating equipment with that intention.
(3) A person commits an offence if—
    (a) he records another person (B) doing a private act,
    (b) he does so with the intention that he or a third person will, for the purpose of obtaining sexual gratification, look at an image of B doing the act, and
    (c) he knows that B does not consent to his recording the act with that intention.

A person is doing a private act if he/she is in a place which, in the circumstances, would reasonably be expected to provide privacy, and:

- his/her genitals, buttocks or breasts are exposed or covered only with underwear
- he/she is using a lavatory, or
- he/she is doing a sexual act that is not of a kind ordinarily done in public (s. 68).

The word 'breasts' does not extend to the exposed male chest (*R* v *Bassett* [2008] EWCA Crim 1174).

The three activities described above require proof that the victim does not consent to the observing, recording or operating of the relevant equipment *for the purpose of the defendant's or another's sexual gratification* (i.e. the victim might have consented to being observed, recorded etc. for other reasons).

The first offence involves a defendant observing another doing a private act (which will include looking at an image: s. 79(5)) with the relevant motive of gaining sexual gratification.

The second offence deals with people operating equipment such as hoteliers using webcams to enable others to view live footage of the residents for the sexual gratification of those others. There is no need to show that defendants intended to gain sexual gratification themselves.

The third offence deals with the recording of the private act with the intention that the person doing the recording or another will look at the image and thereby obtain sexual gratification. It does not matter that those who eventually look at the recording know that the victim did not consent, though all elements of the offence would be corroborated by the accompanying material (e.g. the descriptions of the pages on an internet website). In *R* v *Turner* [2006] EWCA Crim 63 the defendant (the manager of a gym) had recorded images of women showering and using the sun beds. The court regarded this as an abuse of the defendant's position of trust which took him 'over the custodial threshold' and he was sentenced (following an appeal) to nine months' imprisonment.

There is also a specific offence under s. 67(4) of installing equipment or adapting structures (e.g. drilling peepholes) with the intention of committing the first offence themselves or enabling others to do so. Structures will include tents, vehicles or vessels or other temporary or movable structures.

The restricted wording of s. 67(4) appears not to cover the situation where the defendant installs equipment to *record* the private act (under s. 67(2)) rather than observing it live.

These offences do not extend to activities such as, for example, covertly filming up women's skirts as they go about the public act of shopping.

1.11.9.3 Sexual Activity in a Public Lavatory

OFFENCE: **Sexual Activity in a Public Lavatory—*Sexual Offences Act 2003, s. 71***
- Triable summarily • Six months' imprisonment and/or a fine

The Sexual Offences Act 2003, s. 71 states:

(1) A person commits an offence if—
  (a) he is in a lavatory to which the public or a section of the public has or is permitted to have access, whether on payment or otherwise,
  (b) he intentionally engages in an activity, and,
  (c) the activity is sexual.

This offence will apply to any lavatory to which the public or a section of it has access. For the purposes of this offence only, an activity is sexual if a reasonable person would, in all the circumstances but regardless of any person's purpose, consider it to be sexual.

1.11.10 Preparatory Offences

There are specific provisions to prevent substantive offences from happening.

1.11.10.1 Administering Substance with Intent

OFFENCE: **Administering Substance with Intent—*Sexual Offences Act 2003, s. 61***
- Triable either way • 10 years' imprisonment on indictment
- Six months' imprisonment and/or a fine summarily

The Sexual Offences Act 2003, s. 61 states:

(1) A person commits an offence if he intentionally administers a substance to, or causes a substance to be taken by, another person (B)—
  (a) knowing that B does not consent, and
  (b) with the intention of stupefying or overpowering B, so as to enable any person to engage in a sexual activity that involves B.

KEYNOTE

This offence is aimed at the use of 'date rape' drugs but is wider than that. It would cover the spiking of a victim's soft drinks with alcohol if done with the relevant intent. The substance could be injected or applied by covering the victim's face with a cloth impregnated with the substance.

The key elements are the defendant's intentionally administering *any* substance, in the knowledge that the victim does not consent and with the intention of overpowering or stupefying the victim in order that *any person* can engage in sexual activity involving the victim.

'Administering or causing to be taken' covers a broader range of conduct than the parallel offences of poisoning. The offence is complete when A persuades a third party, C, to administer a substance to B because C knows B and so is more easily able to do so.

As this is an offence of intent rather than consequence there is no need for the victim to be stupefied or overpowered or for the sexual activity to take place.

So far as proof of the relevant elements is concerned, see para. 1.11.2.2.

1.11.10.2 Committing Criminal Offence with Intent to Commit a Sexual Offence

OFFENCE: **Committing Criminal Offence with Intent to Commit a Sexual Offence—*Sexual Offences Act 2003, s. 62***
- Where the offence committed is kidnapping or false imprisonment—triable on indictment only: life imprisonment • Otherwise triable either way: 10 years' imprisonment on indictment; six months' imprisonment and/or a fine summarily

The Sexual Offences Act 2003, s. 62 states:

(1) A person commits an offence under this section if he commits any offence with the intention of committing a relevant sexual offence.

KEYNOTE

'Relevant sexual offence' means an offence under part I of the Act (virtually all regularly occurring sexual offences) including aiding, abetting, counselling or procuring such an offence (s. 62(2)). It *does not extend* to other sexual offences under the Protection of Children Act 1978.

It is designed to deal with the commission of any criminal offence where the defendant's intention is to commit a relevant sexual offence. In addition to offences of kidnapping and false imprisonment, this would cover an array of possible circumstances where the defendant's ulterior motive in committing the first offence

---

is to carry out the relevant sexual offence. There is no express requirement for there to be any immediate link in time between the two offences. It could cover any situation from the theft of drugs or equipment to be used in the course of the sexual offence and going equipped for burglary, to the taking of a vehicle or even dangerous driving with the intention in each case of committing the further relevant sexual offence.

1.11.10.3 Trespass with Intent to Commit Sexual Offence

OFFENCE: **Trespass with Intent to Commit a Relevant Sexual Offence—***Sexual Offences Act 2003, s. 63*

> • Triable either way • 10 years' imprisonment on indictment
> • Six months' imprisonment and/or a fine summarily

The Sexual Offences Act 2003, s. 63 states:

(1) A person commits an offence if—
  (a) he is a trespasser on any premises,
  (b) he intends to commit a relevant sexual offence on the premises, and
  (c) he knows that, or is reckless as to whether, he is a trespasser.

KEYNOTE

A person is a trespasser if they are on the premises without the owner or occupier's consent, whether express or implied or they are there without a power at law to be there. Generally, defendants ought to know whether they are trespassing or not and recklessness will be enough in that regard.

Premises here will include a structure or part of a structure (including a tent, vehicle or vessel or other temporary or movable structure (s. 63(2)).

Relevant sexual offence has the same meaning as in the s. 62 offence (**see para. 1.11.10.2**).

There is no need to prove that the substantive sexual offence took place.

The defendant must intend to commit the relevant offence *on the premises.*

1.11.11 Offences Outside the United Kingdom

Section 72(1) of the Sexual Offences Act 2003 makes it an offence for a UK national to commit an act outside the United Kingdom which would constitute a relevant sexual offence if done in England and Wales.

1.11.12 Offences Relating to Prostitution

There are numerous offences connected with prostitution. This section begins with the definition of a prostitute before examining some of those offences.

1.11.12.1 Definition of a Prostitute

The Sexual Offences Act 2003 defines prostitution and provides that a prostitute is a person (A) who:

• on at least one occasion and
• whether or not compelled to do so,

- offers or provides sexual services to another person
- in return for payment or a promise of payment to A or a third person.

(s. 51(2).)

This definition applies to both men and women.

OFFENCE: **Causing, Inciting or Controlling Prostitution—*Sexual Offences Act 2003, s. 52***
- Triable either way • Seven years' imprisonment on indictment
- Six months' imprisonment and/or a fine summarily

1.11.12.2 Offence of Causing, Inciting or Controlling Prostitution

The Sexual Offences Act 2003, s. 52 states:

(1) A person commits an offence if—
    (a) he intentionally causes or incites another person to become a prostitute in any part of the world, and
    (b) he does so for or in the expectation of gain for himself or a third person.

The Sexual Offences Act 2003, s. 53 states:

(1) A person commits an offence if—
    (a) he intentionally controls any of the activities of another person relating to that person's prostitution in any part of the world, and
    (b) he does so for or in the expectation of gain for himself or a third person.

KEYNOTE

Where the victim is under 18, the specific offence under s. 48 should be considered (**see para. 1.11.5.8**).

The first offence above is concerned with intentional causing or inciting, the latter being an incomplete offence (**see chapter 1.3**).

The second offence above addresses those who intentionally control the activities of prostitutes (pimps).

Unlike the offence involving persons under 18, you must show the defendant acted for, or in the expectation of, gain for him/herself or another. Gain means any financial advantage, including the discharge of an obligation to pay or the provision of goods or services (including sexual services) gratuitously or at a discount or the goodwill of any person which is or appears likely, in time, to bring financial advantage (s. 54). This definition covers the actions of someone who hopes to build up a relationship with, say, a drug dealer who will eventually give the defendant cheaper drugs as a result of his/her activities. Although you do not need to show that money, goods or financial advantage actually passed to the defendant, you must show that he/she wanted or at least expected that someone would benefit from the conduct.

1.11.12.3 Paying for Sexual Services of a Prostitute Subjected to Force

OFFENCE: **Paying for Sexual Services of a Prostitute Subjected to Force—*Sexual Offences Act 2003, s. 53A***
- Triable summarily • Fine

The Sexual Offences Act 2003, s. 53A states:

(1) A person (A) commits an offence if—
    (a) A makes or promises payment for the sexual services of a prostitute (B),
    (b) a third person (C) has engaged in exploitative conduct of a kind likely to induce or encourage B to provide the sexual services for which A has made or promised payment, and
    (c) C engaged in that conduct for or in the expectation of gain for C or another person (apart from A or B).

(2) The following are irrelevant—
   (a) where in the world the sexual services are to be provided and whether those services are provided,
   (b) whether A is, or ought to be, aware that C has engaged in exploitative conduct.
(3) C engages in exploitative conduct if—
   (a) C uses force, threats (whether or not relating to violence) or any other form of coercion, or
   (b) C practises any form of deception.

KEYNOTE

This offence is committed if someone pays or promises payment for the sexual services of a prostitute who has been subject to exploitative conduct of a kind likely to induce or encourage the provision of sexual services for which the payer has made or promised payment. The person responsible for the exploitative conduct must have been acting for or in the expectation of gain for him/herself or another person, other than the payer or the prostitute.

It does not matter where in the world the sexual services are to be provided. An offence is committed regardless of whether the person paying or promising payment for sexual services knows or ought to know or be aware that the prostitute has been subject to exploitative conduct. In other words the offence is one of *strict liability* and *no mental element* is required in respect of the offender's knowledge that the prostitute was forced, threatened, coerced or deceived.

1.11.12.4 Brothels

There are several summary offences aimed at landlords, tenants and occupiers of premises used as brothels (ss. 34 to 36 of the Sexual Offences Act 1956). The Sexual Offences Act 2003 extended the relevant offences so that they covered brothels used by male prostitutes and created the following offence:

OFFENCE: **Keeping a Brothel Used for Prostitution—*Sexual Offences Act 1956, s. 33A***
   • Triable either way   • Seven years' imprisonment on indictment
   • Six months' imprisonment and/or a fine summarily

The Sexual Offences Act 1956, s. 33A states:

(1) It is an offence for a person to keep, or to manage, or act or assist in the management of, a brothel to which people resort for practices involving prostitution (whether or not also for other practices).

KEYNOTE

A brothel is a place to which people resort for the purposes of unlawful sexual intercourse with more than one prostitute; it is not necessary that full sexual intercourse takes place or is even offered. Homosexual activity is as capable as heterosexual activity of founding the existence of a brothel. A massage parlour where other acts of lewdness or indecency for sexual gratification are offered may be a brothel.

Prostitution means offering or providing sexual services, whether under compulsion or not, to another in return for payment or a promise of payment to the prostitute or a third person (s. 51(2)).

OFFENCE: **Keeping a Disorderly House—*Common Law***
   • Triable on indictment   • Unlimited sentence

It is an offence at common law to keep a disorderly house.

1.11.12.5 Soliciting

OFFENCE: **Soliciting by Persons—*Street Offences Act 1959, s. 1***
- Triable summarily - Fine

The Street Offences Act 1959, s. 1 states:

(1) It shall be an offence for a person aged 18 or over whether male or female persistently to loiter or solicit in a street or public place for the purpose of prostitution.
(2) ...
(3) Repealed
(4) For the purposes of this section:
  (a) conduct is persistent if it takes place on two or more occasions in any period of three months;
  (b) any reference to a person loitering or soliciting for the purposes of prostitution is a reference to a person loitering or soliciting for the purposes of offering services as a prostitute.

OFFENCE: **Soliciting by 'Kerb-crawling'—*Sexual Offences Act 2003, s. 51A***
- Triable summarily - Fine

The Sexual Offences Act 2003, s. 51A, (as amended) states:

(1) It is an offence for a person in a street or public place to solicit another (B) for the purpose of obtaining B's sexual services as a prostitute.
(2) The reference to a person in a street or public place includes a person in a vehicle in a street or public place.

1.11.12.6 Trafficking People for Sexual Offences

OFFENCE: **Trafficking People for Sexual Exploitation—*Sexual Offences Act 2003, s. 59A***

- Triable either way • 14 years' imprisonment on indictment
- 12 months' imprisonment and/or a fine summarily

The Sexual Offences Act 2003, s. 59A states:

(1) A person ('A') commits an offence if A intentionally arranges or facilitates—

    (a) the arrival in, or entry into, the United Kingdom or another country of another person ('B'),

    (b) the travel of B within the United Kingdom or another country, or

    (c) the departure of B from the United Kingdom or another country,

    with a view to the sexual exploitation of B.

(2) For the purposes of subsection (1)(a) and (c) A's arranging or facilitating is with a view to the sexual exploitation of B if, and only if—

    (a) A intends to do anything to or in respect of B, after B's arrival, entry or (as the case may be) departure but in any part of the world, which if done will involve the commission of a relevant offence, or

    (b) A believes that another person is likely to do something to or in respect of B, after B's arrival, entry or (as the case may be) departure but in any part of the world, which if done will involve the commission of a relevant offence.

(3) For the purposes of subsection (1)(b) A's arranging or facilitating is with a view to the sexual exploitation of B if, and only if—

    (a) A intends to do anything to or in respect of B, during or after the journey and in any part of the world, which if done will involve the commission of a relevant offence, or

    (b) A believes that another person is likely to do something to or in respect of B, during or after the journey and in any part of the world, which if done will involve the commission of a relevant offence.

(4) A person who is a UK national commits an offence under this section regardless of—

    (a) where the arranging or facilitating takes place, or

    (b) which country is the country of arrival, entry, travel or (as the case may be) departure.

(5) A person who is not a UK national commits an offence under this section if—

    (a) any part of the arranging or facilitating takes place in the United Kingdom, or

    (b) the United Kingdom is the country of arrival, entry, travel or (as the case may be) departure.

KEYNOTE

Sexual exploitation is the most common form of people trafficking. Section 59A makes it an offence to intentionally arrange or facilitate the arrival in or entry into (s. 59A(1)(a)), travel within (s. 59A(1)(b)), or departure from (s. 59A(1)(c)) the United Kingdom or any other country of another person for the purposes of sexual exploitation.

'Country' includes any territory or other part of the world.

A 'relevant offence' means:

- any offence under the law of England and Wales which is an offence under this part or under s. 1(1)(a) of the Protection of Children Act 1978, or
- anything done outside England and Wales which is not an offence within para. (a) but would be if done in England and Wales.

An offence under part 1 of the Sexual Offences Act is, effectively, any offence under the Act that has been covered in this chapter. The offence under the Protection of Children Act 1978 is taking, permitting to be taken or making any indecent photograph or pseudo-photograph of a child (see para. 1.11.5.9).

A 'UK national' means;

- a British citizen,
- a person who is a British subject by virtue of part 4 of the British Nationality Act 1981 and who has the right of abode in the United Kingdom, or
- a person who is a British overseas territories citizen by virtue of a connection with Gibraltar.

1.12 Control of Sex Offenders

1.12.1 Introduction

Part 2 of the Sexual Offences Act 2003 sets out the notification requirements for sex offenders. It deals with sexual harm prevention orders and sexual risk orders which aim to provide enhanced protection for both the public in the United Kingdom and children and adults abroad.

What follows is a summary of the main practical provisions, but reference should be made to the statutory text and the non-statutory guidance issued by the Home Office on part 2 of the 2003 Act for complete coverage.

1.12.2 Offenders Covered by Notification Requirements

A person is subject to the notification requirements for the period set out in s. 82 (the notification period) if:

- he/she is convicted of an offence listed in sch. 3—this covers most of the commonly occurring sex offences set out elsewhere in **chapter 1.11** (for example, the offences of rape, assault by penetration, sexual touching, sexual offences against children, offences associated with an abuse of a position of trust and familial child sex offences);
- he/she is found not guilty of such an offence by reason of insanity;
- he/she is found to be under a disability and to have done the act charged in respect of such an offence; or
- he/she is cautioned in respect of such an offence, not only in England and Wales but for an offence in Northern Ireland as well (s. 80).

In relation to s. 80 (and part 2 generally) a 'conviction' includes a conviction which results in a conditional but not an absolute discharge: s. 134 provides that in relation to an order for a conditional discharge, the legislation that deems a conviction with an absolute or conditional discharge not to be a conviction, does not apply in relation to this part of the Act.

Where the above findings, convictions or cautions are made, the court or the police may issue a certificate that will be evidence of that fact (s. 92) and the Secretary of State may make regulations setting out the form of certificate to be used.

A person subject to the notification requirements is referred to in the legislation as a 'relevant offender'.

Many sex offenders were already subject to the previous notification requirements under part 1 of the Sex Offenders Act 1997. Some of these people continue to be subject to the notification requirements. For the full details as to these offenders see s. 81.

Some relevant offenders will have attracted that status (and the relevant notification requirements—**see para. 1.12.2.1**) by reason of a conviction etc. for one of the sexual offences abolished by the Sexual Offences Act 2003 (buggery or gross indecency between men under s. 12 or 13 of the Sexual Offences Act 1956). Schedule 4 to the 2003 Act and Home Office Circular 19/2004 deal with the procedure whereby such offenders may apply to the Secretary of State for removal of their notification requirements.

1.12.2.1 The Notification Period

Section 82 sets out the notification period. The indefinite notification period can be reviewed (**see para. 1.12.2.10**). The notification period is as follows:

Where a person is under 18 on the relevant date, references to a period of 10 years, 7 years, 5 years or 2 years are substituted by a reference to half that period (s. 82(2)).

Description of relevant offender	Notification period
A person who, in respect of the offence, is or has been sentenced to imprisonment for a term of 30 months or more	An indefinite period beginning with the relevant date
A person who, in respect of the offence or finding, is or has been admitted to a hospital subject to a restriction order	An indefinite period beginning with that date
A person who, in respect of the offence, is or has been sentenced to imprisonment for a term of more than 6 months but less than 30 months	10 years beginning with that date
A person who, in respect of the offence, is or has been sentenced to imprisonment for a term of 6 months or less	7 years beginning with that date
A person who, in respect of the offence or finding, is or has been admitted to a hospital without being subject to a restriction order	7 years beginning with that date
A person within section 80(1)(d) (cautioned)	2 years beginning with that date
A person in whose case an order for conditional discharge is made in respect of the offence	The period of conditional discharge
A person of any other description	5 years beginning with the relevant date

Meaning of Cautioned

Cautioned means cautioned by a police officer after the person concerned has admitted the offence.

The Act makes specific provisions for offenders who are sentenced for more than one offence and for those who, having been initially found to be under a disability, are later tried for the offence.

1.12.2.2 Initial Notification

A relevant offender must notify the police of certain information within a specified time period from the 'relevant date'. Generally the relevant date will be the date of conviction, finding, caution or, in the case of people covered by the Sex Offenders Act 1997, the appropriate date under that Act.

Section 83(1) states that relevant offenders must, within the period of three days beginning with the relevant date (or, if later, the commencement of part 2 of the Act), notify to the police the information set out in s. 83(5). There are some exceptions made in relation to offenders covered by the earlier legislation and those who have already complied with s. 83(1) at the date of being dealt with by the court.

The information required under s. 83(5) includes (but is not limited to) the relevant offender's:

- date of birth;
- national insurance number;
- name on the relevant date *and* on the date on which notification is given. If the offender used one or more other names on those dates, each of those names;
- home address on the relevant date *and* on the date on which notification is given;
- the address of any other premises in the United Kingdom at which, at the time the notification is given, the offender regularly resides or stays; and

- if the relevant offender holds a passport, the passport number and the full name of the offender as it appears on the passport (if the offender does not hold a passport but holds an alternative form of identity document then a description of the identity document is required along with an issue number (if applicable) and the offender's full name as it appears in the document);
- certain information about their bank account (account numbers, sort codes, validation and expiry dates);
- any prescribed information.

In calculating the time under s. 83(1) account is not generally taken of time remanded in custody by order of a court, detention in a hospital or while out of the United Kingdom (s. 83(6)).

Home address means the address of the relevant offender's sole or main residence in the United Kingdom, or where the offender has no such residence, the address or location of a place in the United Kingdom where he/she can regularly be found and, if there is more than one such place, such one of those places as the person may select (s. 83(7)). This means that, if offenders are of no fixed abode, they can give details of any shelter or other place where they are regularly to be found.

1.12.2.3 Notification Requirements: Changes

Section 84(1) states that within the period of three days beginning with:

- the offender using a name which has not been notified to the police under the relevant legislative provisions;
- any change of home address;
- the offender having resided or stayed, for a 'qualifying period' (seven days *or* two or more periods in any 12 months which together amount to seven days), at any premises in the United Kingdom the address of which has not been notified to the police under the relevant legislative provision; or
- the offender's release from custody pursuant to an order of a court or from imprisonment, service detention or detention in a hospital,

a relevant offender must notify to the police that name, the new home address, the address of those premises or (as the case may be) the fact that he/she has been released, and (in addition) the information set out in s. 83(5).

Any notification under the above requirement can be given in advance of the change, provided the actual change takes place within a given 'margin' of time either side of the notified date. For that reason the relevant offender must also specify the date when the event is expected to occur (s. 84(2)). As long as the change notified in advance takes place no earlier than two days before the date notified or no more than three days after, the offender does not need to notify the police of the actual date when it took place. However, if the change takes place outside this margin, the offender must notify the change as required by s. 84(1), e.g. within three days of the actual change. Similarly, if the change takes place three days or more after the date notified in advance, the offender must also tell the police within six days that the change of which advance notice was given did not occur as specified (s. 84(3) and (4)).

As with the initial notification requirements, account is not generally taken of time spent in custody by order of a court, detention in a hospital or while out of the United Kingdom (s. 84(5)).

The Home Secretary may amend, through secondary legislation, the notification requirements placed on those convicted or cautioned of relevant sexual offences or otherwise subject to the sex offender notification requirements. The Act also allows the Secretary of State to add to the information that sex offenders subject to the notification requirements must notify the police. If the Secretary of State does add to the information required to be notified by a sex offender and there is a change in those details, the offender must notify the police within three days of the change. As occurs with the current information which must be notified, the sex offender can notify the police of an expected change in the prescribed details before the change occurs. The Secretary of State may also provide in regulations that an offender who does not have a sole or main residence in the United Kingdom must notify his/her details to the police more frequently.

1.12.2.4 Notification Requirements: Periodic Notification

Relevant offenders must also re-notify the police of the details in s. 83(5) (see para. 1.12.2.2) within one year of either the initial notification or the notification of the changes unless they have already notified them within that period (under s. 84) as a result of changing circumstances (s. 85). In summary this means that, if a relevant offender does not change his/her name or address, or stay away from home for seven days or more, he/she will have to re-notify the police of the relevant details within a year of the initial notification and every year afterwards. Under s. 85(3), if offenders are detained or are abroad when their periodic notification becomes due, they have until three days after their release/return to the United Kingdom to re-notify.

1.12.2.5 Notification Requirements: Travel Outside the United Kingdom

The Secretary of State has the power to make regulations setting out the notification requirements for relevant offenders who travel outside the United Kingdom (s. 86). The current regulations are the Sexual Offences Act 2003 (Travel Notification Requirements) Regulations 2004 (S1 2004/1220). These regulations were amended by SI 2012/1876.

1.12.2.6 Method of Notification and Related Matters

Relevant offenders comply with the obligations to notify the police set out above by attending at such police station in their local police area as the Secretary of State may by regulations prescribe—see the Sexual Offences Act 2015 (Prescribed Police Stations) Regulations 2015 (SI 2015/82) for a list of specific police stations identified for this purpose (or, if there is more than one, at any of them), and giving an oral notification to any police officer, or to any person authorised for the purpose by the officer in charge of the station (s. 87(1)). 'Local police area' means:

- the police area in which the offender's home address is situated or,
- if the offender does not have a home address, the police area in which the home address last notified is situated or,
- if the offender does not have a home address or in the absence of any such notification, the police area in which the court which last dealt with the offender for a relevant matter is situated (s. 88).

If the notification relates to staying away from home for seven days or more, or to an advance change of address, the offender may give the notification at a police station in the police area of the other address (s. 87(2)).

When the offender gives a notification to the police (other than in relation to travel outside the United Kingdom), the police can fingerprint and/or photograph the offender (s. 87(4)) for the purpose of verifying the identity of the relevant offender. 'Photograph' includes any process by means of which an image may be produced and therefore would include methods such as iris scans (s. 88(2)).

1.12.2.7 Notification Orders

In addition to the above, a chief officer of police may apply to a magistrates' court for an order against a person who has been convicted, cautioned or had another relevant finding recorded against him/her for a relevant offence outside the United Kingdom (s. 97). A relevant offence here means an offence abroad which, had it been committed here, would also have been a sch. 3 offence. This provision applies where the relevant offender lives in the chief officer's police area or where the chief officer believes that the offender is intending to come to that police area. This means that a chief officer can apply to a magistrates' court for a notification order against a foreign national who has been convicted abroad and who is intending to come to the chief officer's police area. Notification orders will, broadly speaking, make the offender subject to the notification requirements, however there are specific differences in relation to the calculation of the relevant periods (s. 97(3) and (4) and s. 98).

1.12.2.8 Interim Notification Orders

In addition, the police may apply for an interim notification order while the application for a full notification order is determined (s. 100). Such an interim order may be necessary because the relevant paperwork is likely to delay the hearing for the main order. Once an interim notification order is granted, the relevant offender becomes subject to the notification requirements above and the notification period starts from the date of service of the order (s. 100(5) and (6)).

An offender has a right of appeal against both interim or full notification orders to the Crown Court (s. 101).

1.12.2.9 Young Offenders: Parental Directions

Section 89 of the Sexual Offences Act 2003 makes provisions for young offenders and allows the courts to direct a person with parental responsibility for the offender to comply with his/her notification requirements instead—until either the young offender reaches 18 or an earlier date specified by the court. Under a parental direction the parent must ensure that the young offender attends at the police station with the parent, when a notification is being given (s. 89(2)(b)).

A chief officer may (by complaint to any magistrates' court whose commission area includes any part of his/her police area) apply for a parental direction in respect of any relevant offender who is under 18 and who resides in that police area, or who the chief officer believes is in or is intending to come to that police area (s. 89(4)). A court may alter or discharge a parental direction order on application by the offender, parent or relevant chief officer (s. 90). A variation or alteration might be needed where, for example, the offender's parents divorce or where they cannot exercise enough control over the offender to ensure compliance with the notification requirements.

1.12.2.10 Review of Requirements

As a result of *R (On the Application of F (by his litigation friend F)) and Thompson (FC) v Secretary of State for the Home Department* [2010] UKSC 17, the Supreme Court made a declaration under s. 4 of the Human Rights Act 1998 that the indefinite notification requirements of the Sexual Offences Act 2003 were incompatible with Article 8 of the European Convention on Human Rights. SI 2012/1883 introduced a remedy in the form of a mechanism whereby a person subject to indefinite notification requirements under the 2003 Act can apply for a review and determination that those requirements shall cease.

The review process is triggered by an offender who is subject to indefinite notification requirements making an application to the police. The offender would be entitled to make an application 15 years following his/her release from custody. The review will be carried out by the police and will be completed on the basis of a range of factors, including the information provided from the Responsible Authority and Duty to Co-operate agencies which operate within the Multi-Agency Public Protection Arrangements (MAPPA) framework (ss. 91A–F of the Sexual Offences Act 2003).

1.12.2.11 Failure to Notify

OFFENCE: **Failing to Comply with Notification Requirements—*Sexual Offences Act 2003, s. 91***

> • Triable either way • Five years' imprisonment on indictment • Six months' and/or a fine summarily

The Sexual Offences Act 2003, s. 91 states:

(1) A person commits an offence if he—

    (a) fails, without reasonable excuse, to comply with section 83(1), 84(1), 84(4)(b), 85(1), 87(4) or 89(2)(b) or any requirement imposed by regulations made under section 86(1); or

    (b) notifies to the police, in purported compliance with section 83(1), 84(1) or 85(1) or any requirement imposed by regulations made under section 86(1), any information which he knows to be false.

KEYNOTE

Reasonable excuse will be a question of fact in all the circumstances for the court to decide. In relation to a parental direction, it is more likely that there will be such an excuse, particularly if parents have done all they can to ensure that the young offender comes with them to the police station.

This is a continuing offence, in that offenders continue to commit it for each and every day that they fail to give notification as required (s. 91(3)). Although offenders can only be prosecuted once for the same continuing failure, if they are convicted for the above offence and then fail again to comply, they commit another offence.

1.12.2.12 Supply of Information for Verification

Section 94 provides that a specified person or body may supply information to the Secretary of State (or a person supplying a relevant function to the Secretary of State) for the purposes of the prevention, detection, investigation or prosecution of offences under part 2 of the Act, for use in verifying that information. The information is that which was notified to the police under ss. 83, 84 or 85 (**see para. 1.12.2.2**) or the equivalent earlier legislation (s. 2(1)–(3) of the Sex Offenders Act 1997). Those people and bodies are:

- a chief officer of police
- the Director General of the National Crime Agency.

Verification and Use

Verifying the information here means checking its accuracy by comparing it with information held by the Secretary of State or bodies responsible for functions such as social security, child support, employment or training, the Identity and Passport Service or the Driver and Vehicle Licensing Agency (DVLA). Checking accuracy includes compiling a report, though this part of the Act does not authorise anything that would amount to a breach of the Data Protection Act 1998. The recipient of the report must be one of the people/bodies set out above and they may use the information only for the purposes of the prevention, detection, investigation or prosecution of an offence under part 2 but can retain it whether or not it is in fact used for that purpose (s. 95).

1.12.2.13 Power of Entry—Risk Assessment of Sex Offenders

Section 96B of the Sexual Offences Act 2003 provides a power of entry and search to risk assess sex offenders subject to the notification requirements.

The power enables the police to gather all the information they need about a relevant offender for the purposes of assessing the risks the offender poses, even if he/she is in apparent compliance with the notification requirements and there are insufficient grounds to believe he/she has committed a new substantive offence.

Under the section, the police are allowed to seek a warrant from a magistrates' court to enter and search, by force if necessary, the last notified address of a registered sex offender (or a place where there are grounds to believe the offender resides or can be regularly found) where there have been two failed attempts to enter a specified premises, for the purpose of assessing the risks the offender poses.

The application must be made by a senior police officer, not below the rank of superintendent. The senior police officer should attend court in person to apply for the warrant.

A warrant will only be issued by magistrates if they are satisfied that the following conditions have been met:

- that the offender is a relevant offender (i.e. an offender subject to the notification requirements)
- that the offender is not: remanded or committed to custody by order of a court; serving a sentence of imprisonment or a term of service detention; detained in hospital; or outside the United Kingdom
- that the address of each set of premises to which the warrant relates is either the home address which was last notified in accordance with part 2 of the Sexual Offences Act 2003, or there are reasonable grounds to believe that the registered sex offender resides there or may regularly be found there
- that it is necessary for the constable to enter and search the premises for the purpose of assessing the risk posed by the offender
- that on at least two occasions, a constable has sought entry to the premises in order to search them for that purpose and has been unable to obtain entry for that purpose.

The warrant may also authorise entry to and search of premises on more than one occasion if, on the application, the magistrate is satisfied that it is necessary to authorise multiple entries for the purpose of risk assessment. When a warrant authorises multiple entries, the number of entries authorised may be unlimited or limited to a maximum.

If more than one address is to be searched, the constable will need to attempt (and fail) to enter each address for which the warrant is sought.

In circumstances where a constable has been allowed into the premises to search for the purposes of risk assessment, but not allowed into parts of the premises (e.g. a particular room), this will count as being 'unable to obtain entry' for the purposes of risk assessment.

As a warrant does not grant a power of seizure, where evidence of a crime is found during the course of a search under such a warrant, constables can use their general power of seizure under s. 19 of the Police and Criminal Evidence Act 1984.

1.12.3 Orders to Control Sex Offenders

Section 113 of and sch. 5 to the Anti-social Behaviour, Crime and Policing Act 2014 amend the Sexual Offences Act 2003 to repeal the Sexual Offences Prevention Order (SOPO), the Foreign Travel Order (FTO) and the Risk of Sexual Harm Order (RoSHO) in England and Wales and replace them with the Sexual Harm Prevention Order (SHPO) and the Sexual Risk Order (SRO).

The grounds on which SHPOs and SROs may be made are wider than their predecessors which means that they can be used to manage risks against adults as well as children. The available prohibitions are wider so, for example, foreign travel restrictions can be imposed under either order. In addition to the police, the National Crime Agency will also have the power to apply for the orders.

Section 136ZB of the Sexual Offences Act 2003 states that where a court in England and Wales makes an order listed in the first column of the table below in relation to a person who is already subject to an order listed opposite it in the second column, the earlier order ceases to have effect (whichever part of the United Kingdom it was made in) unless the court states otherwise.

New order	Earlier order
Sexual harm prevention order	—sexual offences prevention order;
	—foreign travel order.
Sexual risk order	—risk of sexual harm order;
	—foreign travel order.

1.12.4 Sexual Harm Prevention Orders (SHPO)

A SHPO is a civil preventative order designed to protect the public from *sexual harm*.

The Sexual Offences Act 2003, s. 103A states:

(1) A court may make an order under this section (a "sexual harm prevention order") in respect of a person ("the defendant") where subsection (2) or (3) applies to the defendant.

(2) This subsection applies to the defendant where—

   (a) the court deals with the defendant in respect of—

      (i) an offence listed in Schedule 3 or 5, or

      (ii) a finding that the defendant is not guilty of an offence listed in Schedule 3 or 5 by reason of insanity, or

      (iii) a finding that the defendant is under a disability and has done the act charged against the defendant in respect of an offence listed in Schedule 3 or 5,

   and

   (b) the court is satisfied that it is necessary to make a sexual harm prevention order, for the purpose of—

      (i) protecting the public or any particular members of the public from sexual harm from the defendant, or

      (ii) protecting children or vulnerable adults generally, or any particular children or vulnerable adults, from sexual harm from the defendant outside the United Kingdom.

KEYNOTE

A court may make a SHPO when it deals with a person in respect of an offence listed in sch. 3 or sch. 5 to the Sexual Offences Act 2003, or in the case of an offender lacking capacity, deals with that offender in respect of a finding relating to such an offence.

The order can include *any prohibition* the court considers necessary for this purpose, including the prevention of foreign travel to the country or countries specified in the order (or to all foreign countries, if that is what the order provides) (see para. 1.12.4.3).

Schedule 3 or 5 Offences

The offences listed in schs 3 and 5 are numerous and include a large number of the offences detailed in chapter 1.11 such as rape, assault by penetration, sexual touching, sexual offences against children, offences associated with an abuse of a position of trust and familial child sex offences. Offences listed in sch. 5 include offences of murder, manslaughter, kidnapping, false imprisonment and offences against the person under ss. 20 and 18 of the Offences Against the Person Act 1861.

For a full list of the offences, reference should be made to Schedules 3 and 5 of the Act.

The Public

This means the public in the United Kingdom.

Sexual Harm

The phrase 'sexual harm' from a person means physical or psychological harm caused:

(a) by the person committing one or more offences listed in sch. 3, or

(b) (in the context of harm outside the United Kingdom) by the person doing, outside the United Kingdom, anything which would constitute an offence listed in sch. 3 if done in any part of the United Kingdom.

1.12.4.1 Police/NCA Application for a SHPO

The Sexual Offences Act 2003, s. 103A states:

(3) This subsection applies to the defendant where—

    (a) an application under subsection (4) has been made in respect of the defendant and it is proved on the application that the defendant is a qualifying offender, and

    (b) the court is satisfied that the defendant's behaviour since the appropriate date makes it necessary to make a sexual harm prevention order, for the purpose of—

        (i) protecting the public or any particular members of the public from sexual harm from the defendant, or

        (ii) protecting children or vulnerable adults generally, or any particular children or vulnerable adults, from sexual harm from the defendant outside the United Kingdom.

(4) A chief officer of police or the Director General of the National Crime Agency ('the Director General') may by complaint to a magistrates' court apply for a sexual harm prevention order in respect of a person if it appears to the chief officer or the Director General that—

    (a) the person is a qualifying offender, and

    (b) the person has since the appropriate date acted in such a way as to give reasonable cause to believe that it is necessary for such an order to be made.

(5) A chief officer of police may make an application under subsection (4) only in respect of a person—

    (a) who resides in the chief officer's police area, or

    (b) who the chief officer believes is in that area or is intending to come to it.

(6) An application under subsection (4) may be made to any magistrates' court acting for a local justice area that includes—

    (a) any part of a relevant police area, or

    (b) any place where it is alleged that the person acted in a way mentioned in subsection (4)(b).

KEYNOTE

A magistrates' court (or youth court, where the defendant is under 18) may make a SHPO when an application for such an order is made to it by the chief officer of police or the Director General of the NCA in respect of a person. The court must be satisfied that the person concerned is a 'qualifying offender'.

Qualifying Offender

A qualifying offender is a person who has been dealt with by a court in respect of an offence listed in sch. 3 (other than at para. 60) or sch. 5 to the Sexual Offences Act or has been dealt with by a court abroad in respect of an act which was an offence under the law of that territory and which would, if committed in any part of the United Kingdom, have constituted an offence listed in sch. 3 (other than at para. 60) or sch. 5.

Appropriate Date

The 'appropriate date', in relation to a qualifying offender, means the date or (as the case may be) the first date on which the offender was convicted, found or cautioned as mentioned in the above paragraph (Qualifying Offender).

In addition to being satisfied that the person is a qualifying offender, the court must be satisfied that the person's behaviour, since the date on which they were first dealt with in this way, means it is necessary to make the order for the purpose of:

- protecting the public or any particular members of the public from sexual harm from the defendant; or
- protecting children or vulnerable adults generally, or any particular children or vulnerable adults, from sexual harm from the defendant outside the United Kingdom.

The Director General must as soon as practicable notify the chief officer of police for a relevant police area of any application that the Director has made under subs. (4) (s. 103(7)).

Where the defendant is a child, a reference in this section to a magistrates' court is to be taken as referring to a youth court (subject to any rules of court made under s. 103K(1)) (s. 103(8)).

'Relevant police area' means:

(a) where the applicant is a chief officer of police, the officer's police area;
(b) where the applicant is the Director General—
  (i) the police area where the person in question resides, or
  (ii) a police area which the Director General believes the person is in or is intending to come to. s. 103(9).

1.12.4.2 Effect of a SHPO

The Sexual Offences Act 2003, s 103C states:

(1) A sexual harm prevention order prohibits the defendant from doing anything described in the order.
(2) Subject to section 103D(1), a prohibition contained in a sexual harm prevention order has effect—
  (a) for a fixed period, specified in the order, of at least 5 years, or
  (b) until further order.
(3) A sexual harm prevention order—
  (a) may specify that some of its prohibitions have effect until further order and some for a fixed period;
  (b) may specify different periods for different prohibitions.

KEYNOTE

An order will last a *minimum of five years* and has *no maximum period* (with the exception of any foreign travel restriction which, if applicable, has a *maximum duration of five years* but may be renewed).

Section 103C(4) states that the only prohibitions that may be included in a SHPO are those necessary for the purpose of:

(a) protecting the public or any particular members of the public from sexual harm from the defendant, or
(b) protecting children or vulnerable adults generally, or any particular children or vulnerable adults, from sexual harm from the defendant outside the United Kingdom.

Where a court makes a SHPO in relation to a person who is already subject to such an order (whether made by that court or another), the earlier order ceases to have effect (s. 103C(6)).

1.12.4.3 SHPOs—Prohibitions on Foreign Travel

Section 103D details the provisions in relation to prohibitions on foreign travel. Such a prohibition must be for a fixed period of not more than five years (s. 103D(1)). The prohibition can be extended for a further period (of no more than five years each time) under s. 103E.

Under s. 103D(2) the prohibition can prohibit travelling to:

- any country outside the United Kingdom named or described in the order,
- any country outside the United Kingdom other than a country named or described in the order, or
- any country outside the United Kingdom.

Any SHPO that contains a prohibition on travel must require the defendant to surrender all of his/her passports at a police station specified in the order on or before the date when the prohibition takes place or within a period specified in the order (s. 103D(4)). Unless the person is subject to an equivalent prohibition under another order, all passports surrendered must be returned as soon as is reasonably practicable after he/she ceases to be subject to a SHPO containing the prohibition on foreign travel (s. 103D(5)). This does not apply in relation to a passport issued by or on behalf of the authorities of a country outside the United Kingdom if the passport has been returned to those authorities, or to a passport issued by or on behalf of an international organisation if the passport has been returned to that organisation (s. 103D(6)).

In this section 'passport' means:

- a United Kingdom passport within the meaning of the Immigration Act 1971;
- a passport issued by or on behalf of the authorities of a country outside the United Kingdom, or by or on behalf of an international organisation;
- a document that can be used (in some or all circumstances) instead of a passport.

1.12.4.4 SHPOs—Variations, Renewals and Discharges

Section 103E states that an application to vary, renew or discharge a SHPO may be made by:

- the defendant;
- the chief officer of police for the area in which the defendant resides;
- a chief officer of police who believes that the defendant is in, or is intending to come to that officer's police area; or
- where the order was made on an application by a chief officer of police under s. 103A(4), that officer.

After hearing the application the court may make any order, varying, renewing or discharging the sexual harm prevention order, that the court considers appropriate (s. 103E(4)). Such an order may be renewed, or varied so as to impose additional prohibitions on the defendant, only if it is necessary to do so for the purpose of—

(a) protecting the public or any particular members of the public from sexual harm from the defendant, or
(b) protecting children or vulnerable adults generally, or any particular children or vulnerable adults, from sexual harm from the defendant outside the United Kingdom.

Any renewed or varied order may contain only such prohibitions as are necessary for this purpose (s. 103E(5)).

KEYNOTE

Section 103E(7) states that the court *must not* discharge an order before the end of five years beginning with the day on which the order was made, without the consent of the defendant and:

(a) where the application is made by a chief officer of police, that chief officer, or
(b) in any other case, the chief officer of police for the area in which the defendant resides.

Subsection (7) does not apply to an order containing a prohibition on foreign travel and no other prohibitions (s. 103E(8)).

1.12.4.5 Interim SHPOs

Where an application under s. 103A(4) ('the main application') has not been determined, an application for an order under this section ('an interim sexual harm prevention order') may be made by the complaint by which the main application is made, or if the main application has been made, may be made by the person who has made that application, by complaint to the court to which that application has been made.

In appropriate cases, this enables the court to place prohibitions on the person (and results in their becoming subject to the notification requirements) pending the full application for the order being determined (s. 103F).

1.12.4.6 SHPOs and Interim SHPOs—Notification Requirements

Where a SHPO is made in respect of a defendant who was a relevant offender immediately before the making of the order, and the defendant would (apart from this subsection) cease to be subject to the notification requirements of this part while the order (as renewed from time to time) has effect, the defendant remains subject to the notification requirements (s. 103G(1)).

Where a SHPO is made in respect of a defendant who was not a relevant offender immediately before the making of the order, the order causes the defendant to become subject to the notification requirements from the making of the order until the order (as renewed from time to time) ceases to have effect. This applies to the defendant from the date of service of the order (s. 103G (2) and (3)).

These notification requirements apply equally to an interim SHPO (s. 103G(4)).

On an application for a SHPO made by a chief officer of police, the court must make a notification order in respect of the defendant (either in addition to or instead of a SHPO) if the applicant invites the court to do so, and it is proved that the conditions in s. 97(2)–(4) are met (**see para. 1.12.2.7**) (s. 103G(6)).

On an application for an interim SHPO made by a chief officer of police, the court may, if it considers it just to do so, make an interim notification order (either in addition to or instead of an interim SHPO) (s. 103G(7)).

1.12.4.7 SHPOs and Interim SHPOs—Appeals

There is a system by which the defendant can appeal against the making of a SHPO (including an interim order)—this is set out in s. 103H. There is no equivalent section allowing the police to appeal against a decision.

1.12.4.8 Breach of a SHPO or Interim SHPO

OFFENCE: **Breach of SHPO or Interim SHPO—*Sexual Offences Act 2003, s. 103I***
- Triable either way • Five years' imprisonment on indictment • Six months' imprisonment and/or a fine summarily

The Sexual Offences Act 2003, s. 103I states:

(1) A person who, without reasonable excuse, does anything that the person is prohibited from doing by—
   (a) a sexual harm prevention order,
   (b) an interim sexual harm prevention order,
   (c) a sexual offences prevention order,
   (d) an interim sexual offences prevention order, or
   (e) a foreign travel order,
   commits an offence.
(2) A person commits an offence if, without reasonable excuse, the person fails to comply with a requirement imposed under section 103D(4).

KEYNOTE

Where a person is convicted of an offence under this section, it is not open to the court to make, in respect of the offence, an order for conditional discharge (s. 103I(4)).

The requirement under s. 103D(4) is to surrender passports at a police station (**see para. 1.12.4.3**).

1.12.5 Sexual Risk Orders (SRO)

The SRO is a civil preventative order designed to protect the public from sexual harm which replaces the Risk of Sexual Harm Order (RoSHO). The person concerned ('the defendant') *may or may not* have a conviction for a sexual (or any other) offence.

1.12.5.1 SROs—Applications, Grounds and Effects

The Sexual Offences Act 2003, s. 122A states:

(1) A chief officer of police or the Director General of the National Crime Agency ('the Director General') may by complaint to a magistrates' court apply for an order under this section (a 'sexual risk order') in respect of a person ('the defendant') if it appears to the chief officer or the Director General that the following condition is met.

(2) The condition is that the defendant has, whether before or after the commencement of this Part, done an act of a sexual nature as a result of which there is reasonable cause to believe that it is necessary for a sexual risk order to be made.

(3) A chief officer of police may make an application under subsection (1) only in respect of a person—

    (a) who resides in the chief officer's police area, or

    (b) who the chief officer believes is in that area or is intending to come to it.

(4) An application under subsection (1) may be made to any magistrates' court acting for a local justice area that includes—

    (a) any part of a relevant police area, or

    (b) any place where it is alleged that the person acted in a way mentioned in subsection (2).

KEYNOTE

Where the defendant is a child, a reference in that section to a magistrates' court is to be taken as referring to a youth court (subject to any rules of court made under s. 122K(1) (s. 122B(2)).

The Director General must, as soon as practicable, notify the chief police officer for a relevant police area of any application that the Director has made under subs. (1) (s. 122A(5)). For 'relevant police area' see para. 1.12.4.1).

Under s. 122A(6), the SRO will be available to the police and the NCA on application to a magistrates' court in relation to a defendant who has done an act of a sexual nature and, as a result, the police or NCA have reasonable grounds to believe that an order is necessary to:

- protect the public or any particular members of the public from harm from the defendant or
- protect children or vulnerable adults generally, or any particular children or vulnerable adults, from harm from the defendant outside the United Kingdom.

'Harm' from the defendant means physical or psychological harm caused by the defendant doing an act of a sexual nature.

For the meaning of 'the public', 'child' and 'vulnerable adults' see para. 1.12.4.

The court may make an order if it is satisfied that the defendant has done an act of a sexual nature as a result of which it is necessary to make the order for one or both of those purposes.

The SRO differs from the previous RoSHO in that it can be made after the defendant has committed *one such act*, whereas the RoSHO could only be made following two acts.

The order can include any prohibition the court considers necessary for this purpose, including the prevention of foreign travel to the country or countries specified. The order may specify different periods for different prohibitions (s. 122A(8)).

The order will last a *minimum of two years* and has *no maximum period* (with the exception of any foreign travel restriction which expires after *a maximum of five years*, unless renewed) (s. 122A(7)).

Where a court makes a SRO in relation to a person who is already subject to such an order (whether made by that court or another), the earlier order ceases to have effect (s. 122A(10)).

1.12.5.2 SRO—Prohibitions on Foreign Travel

The law governing a prohibition on foreign travel in relation to a SRO (s. 122C) operates in exactly the same way as a prohibition on foreign travel does in relation to a SHPO (**see para. 1.12.4.3**).

1.12.5.3 SRO—Variations, Renewals and Discharges

Section 122D provides that a court can vary, renew or discharge a SRO upon the application of the defendant or the police. With some minor variations (see the Keynote below), such variations, renewals and discharges are regulated in the same way as those governing the variation, renewal and discharge of SHPOs (**see para. 1.12.4.4**).

KEYNOTE

Although the law in relation to the variation, renewal or discharge of SHPOs and SROs operates in the same way, it should be remembered that SHPOs relate to 'sexual harm' whereas SROs relate to 'harm'.

An SRO cannot be discharged before the end of two years from the date the order was made without the consent of the defendant and the police, with the exception of an order containing only foreign travel prohibitions (s. 122D(5)).

1.12.5.4 Interim SROs

Section 122E allows the police or the NCA to apply for an interim SRO where an application has been made for the full order. This enables a prohibition to be placed on the defendant's behaviour and to ensure that they will be subject to the notification requirements pending the full order being determined. The application process for an interim SRO follows that of an interim SHPO (**see para. 1.12.4.5**).

1.12.5.5 SROs and Interim SROs—Notification Requirements

The Sexual Offences Act 2003, s. 122F states:

(1) A person in respect of whom a court makes—
   (a) a sexual risk order (other than one that replaces an interim sexual risk order), or
   (b) an interim sexual risk order,
   must, within the period of 3 days beginning with the date of service of the order, notify to the police the information set out in subsection (2) (unless the person is subject to the notification requirements of this Part on that date).
(2) The information is—
   (a) the person's name and, where the person uses one or more other names, each of those names;
   (b) the person's home address.
(3) A person who—
   (a) is subject to a sexual risk order or an interim sexual risk order (but is not subject to the notification requirements of this Part), and
   (b) uses a name which has not been notified under this section (or under any other provision of this Part), or changes home address,
   must, within the period of 3 days beginning with the date on which that happens, notify to the police that name or (as the case may be) the new home address.
(4) Sections 87 (method of notification and related matters) and 91 (offences relating to notification) apply for the purposes of this section—
   (a) with references to section 83(1) being read as references to subsection (1) above,
   (b) with references to section 84(1) being read as references to subsection (3) above, and
   (c) with the omission of section 87(2)(b).

1.12.5.6 SROs and Interim SROs—Appeals

There is a system by which the defendant can appeal against the making of a SHPO (including an interim order)—this is set out in s. 122G. There is no equivalent section allowing the police to appeal against a decision.

1.12.5.7 Breach of SRO

OFFENCE: **Breach of SRO or Interim SRO—*Sexual Offences Act 2003, s. 122H***
> • Triable either way • Five years' imprisonment on indictment • Six months' imprisonment and/or a fine summarily

The Sexual Offences Act 2003, s. 122H states:

(1) A person who, without reasonable excuse, does anything that the person is prohibited from doing by—
   (a) a sexual risk order,
   (b) an interim sexual risk order,
   (c) a risk of sexual harm order,
   (d) an interim risk of sexual harm order,
   …
   commits an offence.
(2) A person commits an offence if, without reasonable excuse, the person fails to comply with a requirement imposed under section 122C(4).

KEYNOTE

The requirement under s. 122C(4) is to surrender passports at a police station (in the same way a SHPO requirement operates: see para. 1.12.4.3).

Where a person is convicted of an offence under this section, it is not open to the court to make, in respect of the offence, an order for conditional discharge (s. 122H(4)).

If a person is convicted of or cautioned for an offence under s. 122H (or found not guilty by reason of insanity or to have been under a disability), and the defendant was a relevant offender immediately before this section applied to the defendant and the defendant would (apart from this subsection) cease to be subject to the notification requirements of this part while the relevant order (as renewed from time to time) has effect, the defendant remains subject to the notification requirements (s. 122I(3)). Where the defendant was not a relevant offender immediately before this section applied to the defendant then he/she becomes subject to the relevant notification requirements until the relevant order ceases to have effect (s. 122I(4)).

The 'relevant date' here is the date on which this section first applied to the defendant.

In this section, 'relevant order' means:

• where the conviction, finding or caution is in respect of a breach of a sexual risk order or a risk of sexual harm order, that order;
• where the conviction, finding or caution is in respect of a breach of an interim sexual risk order or an interim sexual harm order, any sexual risk order or risk of sexual harm order made on the hearing of the application to which the interim order relates or, if no such order is made, the interim order.

(s. 122I(6).)

1.13 Child Protection

1.13.1 Introduction

The application of the law and the use of measures to protect children, particularly those relating to 'police protection', are among some of the most contentious issues that any police officer may be involved in.

1.13.2 Child Abduction

There are two offences of abducting children; the first applies to people 'connected with the child', the second to others 'not connected to the child'.

1.13.2.1 Person Connected with Child

> OFFENCE: **Child Abduction—Person Connected with Child—***Child Abduction Act 1984, s. 1*
> • Triable either way • Seven years' imprisonment on indictment • Six months' imprisonment and/or a fine summarily

The Child Abduction Act 1984, s. 1 states:

> (1) Subject to subsections (5) and (8) below, a person connected with a child under the age of 16 commits an offence if he takes or sends the child out of the United Kingdom without the appropriate consent.

'Connected with a Child'

The Child Abduction Act 1984, s. 1 states:

> (2) A person is connected with the child for the purposes of this section if—
> (a) he is a parent of the child; or
> (b) in the case of a child whose parents were not married to each other at the time of his birth, there are reasonable grounds for believing that he is the father of the child; or
> (c) he is a guardian of the child; or
> (ca) he is a special guardian of the child; or
> (d) he is a person in whose favour a residence order is in force with respect to the child; or
> (e) he has custody of the child.

'Appropriate Consent'

The Child Abduction Act 1984, s. 1 states:

> (3) In this section 'the appropriate consent' in relation to a child, means—
> (a) the consent of each of the following—
> (i) the child's mother;
> (ii) the child's father, if he has parental responsibility for him;
> (iii) any guardian of the child;
> (iiia) any special guardian of the child;
> (iv) any person in whose favour a residence order is in force with respect to the child;
> (v) any person who has custody of the child; or
> (b) the leave of the court granted under or by virtue of any provision of Part II of the Children Act 1989; or
> (c) if any person has custody of the child, the leave of the court which awarded custody to him.

1.13.2.2 Defence for Person Connected with a Child

The Child Abduction Act 1984, s. 1 states:

(4) A person does not commit an offence under this section by taking or sending a child out of the United Kingdom without obtaining the appropriate consent if—

  (a) he is a person in whose favour there is a residence order in force with respect to the child, and he takes or sends the child out of the United Kingdom for a period of less than one month; or

  (b) he is a special guardian of the child and he takes or sends the child out of the United Kingdom for a period of less than three months.

(4A) Subsection (4) above does not apply if the person taking or sending the child out of the United Kingdom does so in breach of an order under Part II of the Children Act 1989.

(5) A person does not commit an offence under this section by doing anything without the consent of another person whose consent is required under the foregoing provisions if—

  (a) he does it in the belief that the other person—

    (i) has consented; or

    (ii) would consent if he was aware of all the relevant circumstances; or

  (b) he has taken all reasonable steps to communicate with the other person but has been unable to communicate with him; or

  (c) the other person has unreasonably refused to consent.

1.13.2.3 Person Not Connected with Child

OFFENCE: **Child Abduction—Person Not Connected with Child—*Child Abduction Act 1984, s. 2***

  • Triable either way • Seven years' imprisonment on indictment • Six months' imprisonment and/or a fine summarily

The Child Abduction Act 1984, s. 2 states:

(1) Subject to subsection (3) below, a person other than one mentioned in subsection below, commits an offence if, without lawful authority or reasonable excuse, he takes or detains a child under the age of 16—
   (a) so as to remove him from the lawful control of any person having lawful control of the child: or
   (b) so as to keep him out of the lawful control of any person entitled to lawful control of the child.

(2) The persons are—
   (a) where the father and mother of the child in question were married to each other at the time of his birth, the child's father and mother;
   (b) where the father and mother of the child in question were not married to each other at the time of his birth, the child's mother; and
   (c) any other person mentioned in section 1(2)(c) to (e) above.

KEYNOTE

This offence will include keeping a child in the place where he/she is found and inducing the child to remain with the defendant or another person.

The consent of the victim is irrelevant.

The word 'remove' for the purpose of s. 2(1)(a) means effectively a substitution of authority by a defendant for that of the person lawfully having it and physical removal from a particular place is not required (*Foster* v *DPP* [2004] EWHC 2955 (Admin)).

Section 2(1)(a) requires the child *there and then* to be in the lawful control of someone entitled to it when he/she is taken or detained, whereas s. 2(1)(b) requires only that the child be kept out of the lawful control of someone entitled to it when taken or detained. Whether or not a person is under the lawful control of another is a question of fact (*R* v *Leather* [1993] Crim LR 516). A child can be removed from lawful control without necessarily being taken to another place. It may suffice if the child is deflected into some unauthorised activity induced by the defendant.

1.13.2.4 Defence for Person Not Connected with a Child

The Child Abduction Act 1984, s. 2 states:

(3) ...it shall be a defence for [the defendant] to prove—
   (a) where the father and mother of the child in question were not married to each other at the time of his birth—
      (i) that he is the child's father; or
      (ii) that, at the time of the alleged offence, he believed, on reasonable grounds, that he was the child's father; or
   (b) that, at the time of the alleged offence, he believed that the child had attained the age of 16.

KEYNOTE

The defence under s. 2(3)(a) of the Child Abduction Act 1984 will not apply where D mistakenly takes the wrong child from a nursery, thinking it to be his daughter, although it is just possible that D may, in such circumstances, be able to advance a defence of reasonable excuse under s. 2(1) (*R* v *Berry* [1996] 2 Cr App R 226).

1.13.3 Child Cruelty

OFFENCE: **Child Cruelty—*Children and Young Persons Act 1933, s. 1***
   • Triable either way • 10 years' imprisonment on indictment • Six months' imprisonment and/or a fine summarily

The Children and Young Persons Act 1933, s. 1 states:

(1) If any person who has attained the age of 16 years and has responsibility for any child or young person under that age, wilfully assaults, ill-treats (whether physically or otherwise), neglects, abandons, or exposes him, or causes or procures him to be assaulted, ill-treated (whether physically or otherwise), neglected, abandoned, or exposed, in a manner likely to cause him unnecessary suffering or injury to health (whether the suffering or injury is of a physical or a psychological nature), that person shall be guilty of a misdemeanour...

KEYNOTE

This offence may be considered to fall into two broad categories:

- instances of violent assault;
- cases of cruelty and neglect.

Instances of violent assault may be more appropriately dealt with by charging with assault offences.

To be convicted of the offence, D must be over 16 at the time of the offence and have 'responsibility' for the child. Responsibility for a child or young person can be shared and whether a person had such responsibility in each case will be a matter of both fact and law (*Liverpool Society for the Prevention of Cruelty to Children* v *Jones* [1914] 3 KB 813). Anyone having parental responsibility or any other legal liability to maintain a child or young person will be presumed to have responsibility for that child and that responsibility does not cease simply because the person ceases to have care of the child. Others such as babysitters may also have 'responsibility' for the child while in their care (see generally s. 17).

The Act makes provisions and presumptions in relation to issues of causation. So, for example, if a parent or other person legally liable to maintain the child or young person, or a guardian, has failed to provide adequate food, clothing, medical aid or lodging for the child or young person, he/she will be deemed to have neglected the child or young person for the above purposes (s. 1(2)).

Similarly, a person will be presumed to have neglected the child where it is proved that the child was an infant under three years old who died as a result of suffocation (other than by disease or blockage of the airways by an object) while in bed with someone of 16 years or over who was under the influence of drink or a prohibited drug when he/she went to bed or at any later time before the suffocation (s. 1(2)(b)).

The reference in s. 1(2)(b) to the infant being 'in bed' with another ('the adult') includes a reference to the infant lying next to the adult in or on any kind of furniture or surface being used by the adult for the purpose of sleeping (and the reference to the time when the adult 'went to bed' is to be read accordingly) (s. 1(2A)). A drug is a prohibited drug for the purpose of s. 1(2)(b) in relation to a person if the person's possession of the drug immediately before taking it constituted an offence under s. 5(2) of the Misuse of Drugs Act 1971.

A defendant may be charged with the above offence even where the child has died (s. 1(3)(b)).

Section 1 creates only one single offence, albeit one that can be committed in many different ways, by both positive acts (assault, ill-treatment, abandonment or exposure) and omission (neglect) (*R* v *Hayles* [1969] 1 QB 364). Although any aspect of neglect must be shown to have occurred in a manner likely to cause unnecessary suffering or injury to health, there is no need to show that any such suffering or injury actually came about.

1.13.4   Police Powers under the Children Act 1989

The police have specific statutory powers to deal with the threat of significant harm posed to children and these are set out below.

Section 46 of the Children Act 1989 states:

(1) Where a constable has reasonable cause to believe that a child would otherwise be likely to suffer significant harm, he may—
   (a) remove the child to suitable accommodation and keep him there; or
   (b) take such steps as are reasonable to ensure the child's removal from any hospital, or other place, in which he is then being accommodated is prevented.

(2) For the purposes of this Act, a child with respect to whom a constable has exercised his powers under this section is referred to as having been taken into police protection.

KEYNOTE

For most purposes of the 1989 Act, someone who is under 18 years old is a 'child' (s. 105).

The wording of s. 46(1) means that an officer may use the powers at s. 46(1)(a) and (b) if he/she has reasonable cause to believe that, if the powers are not used, a child is likely to suffer significant harm. The issues arising from similar wording in relation to powers of arrest have been considered by the courts on a number of occasions. Generally, tests of reasonableness impose an element of objectivity and the courts will consider whether, in the circumstances, a reasonable and sober person might have formed a similar view to that of the officer.

'Harm' is defined under s. 31(9). It covers all forms of ill treatment including sexual abuse and forms of ill treatment that are not physical. It also covers the impairment of health (physical or mental) and also physical, intellectual, emotional, social or behavioural development. The definition also extends to impairment suffered from seeing or hearing the ill-treatment *of any other person*.

When determining whether harm to a child's health or development is *'significant'*, the child's development will be compared with that which could reasonably be expected of a similar child (s. 31(10)).

The power under s. 46 is split into two parts:

- a power to *remove* a child to suitable accommodation and keep him/her there, and
- a power to take reasonable steps to *prevent* the child's removal from a hospital or other place.

The longest a child can spend in police protection is 72 hours (s. 46(6)). It should be remembered that this is the *maximum* time that a child can be kept in police protection, not the norm.

As soon as is reasonably practicable after using the powers under the Act, the 'Initiating Officer' (the officer who takes the child into police protection and undertakes the initial inquiries) must do a number of things as set out above. These include:

- telling the local authority within whose area the child was found what steps have been, and are proposed to be, taken and why. This aspect of communicating with the local authority is a critical part of the protective powers;
- giving details to the local authority within whose area the child is ordinarily resident of the place at which the child is being kept;
- telling the child (if he/she appears capable of understanding) of what steps have been taken and why, and what further steps may be taken;
- taking such steps as are reasonably practicable to discover the wishes and feelings of the child;
- making sure that the case is inquired into by a 'designated officer' (**see para. 1.13.4.1**);
- taking such steps as are reasonably practicable to inform:
  + the child's parents
  + every person who is not the child's parent but who has parental responsibility for the child and
  + any other person with whom the child was living immediately before being taken into police protection,
- of the steps that the officer has taken under this section, the reasons for taking them and the further steps that may be taken with respect to the child. This element of informing the child, parent and/or relevant carers of what is happening and why is also a vital part of the protective process.

Where the child was taken into police protection by being removed to accommodation which is not provided by or on behalf of a local authority or as a refuge (under s. 51), the officer must, as soon as is reasonably practicable after taking a child into police protection, make sure that the child is moved to accommodation provided by the local authority. Every local authority must receive and provide accommodation for children in police protection where such a request is made (s. 21).

The 'Initiating Officer' and the 'Designated Officer' must not carry out these two separate roles (Home Office Circular 17/2008). The Circular also states that a police station is not 'suitable accommodation' and children should not be brought to a police station except in exceptional circumstances, such as a lack of immediately available local authority accommodation, and then only for a short period. *On no account* should a child who has been taken into police protection be taken to the cell block area of a police station.

When considering action under s. 46, it is possible that the child may already be the subject of an Emergency Protection Order (EPO) applied for by a local authority or authorised body under s. 44.

In considering the proper approach under these circumstances the Court of Appeal has held that:

- There is no express provision in the Act prohibiting the police from invoking s. 46 where an EPO is in place and it is not desirable to imply a restriction which prohibits a constable from removing a child under s. 46 where the constable has reasonable cause to believe that the child would otherwise be likely to suffer significant harm.
- The s. 46 power to remove a child can therefore be exercised even where an EPO is in force in respect of the child.
- Where a police officer knows that an EPO is in force, he/she should not exercise the power of removing a child under s. 46, unless there are compelling reasons to do so.
- The statutory scheme accords primacy to the EPO procedure under s. 44 because removal under that section is sanctioned by the court and involves a more elaborate, sophisticated and complete process of removal than under s. 46.
- Consequently, the removal of children should usually be effected pursuant to an EPO, and s. 46 should only be invoked where it is not reasonably practicable to execute an EPO.
- In deciding whether it is practicable to execute an EPO, the police should always have regard to the paramount need to protect children from significant harm.
- Failure to follow the statutory procedure may amount to the police officer's removal of the child under s. 46 being declared unlawful.

(*Langley* v *Liverpool City Council and Chief Constable of Merseyside* [2005] EWCA Civ 1173.)

1.13.4.1 Designated Officer

The reference at s. 46(3)(e) of the Act to a 'designated officer' is a reference to the appropriate officer designated for that police station for the purposes of this legislation by the relevant chief officer of police. This is a key role in ensuring the effective use of the statutory framework set up for the protection of children in these circumstances. The responsibility for ensuring that the case is inquired into by the designated officer, together with the other responsibilities under s. 46(3) and the responsibility for taking steps to inform people under s. 46(4), clearly rest with the police officer exercising the power under s. 46.

The designated officer must inquire fully and thoroughly into the case; he/she must also do what is reasonable in all the circumstances for the purpose of safeguarding or promoting the child's welfare (having regard in particular to the length of the period during which the child will be so protected) (s. 46(9)(b)).

Where a child has been taken into police protection, the designated officer shall allow:

- the child's parents
- any person who is not a parent of the child but who has parental responsibility for the child
- any person with whom the child was living immediately before being taken into police protection
- any person in whose favour a contact order is in force with respect to the child
- any person who is allowed to have contact with the child by virtue of an order under s. 34 and
- any person acting on behalf of any of those persons,

to have such contact (if any) with the child as, in the opinion of the designated officer, is both reasonable and in the child's best interests (s. 46(10)).

The designated officer may apply for an 'emergency protection order' under s. 44 (s. 46(7)). Such an order allows the court to order the removal of the child to certain types of accommodation and to prevent the child's removal from any other place (including a hospital) where he/she was being accommodated immediately before the making of the order (s. 44(4)). An emergency protection order gives the applicant 'parental responsibility' for the child while it is in force. It also allows the court to make certain directions in relation to contact with the child and a medical or psychiatric assessment. Section 44A allows the court to make an order excluding certain people from a dwelling house where the child lives and to attach a power of arrest accordingly.

While the designated officer can apply for an emergency protection order without the local authority's knowledge or agreement (see s. 46(8)), there should be no reason why, given proper multi-agency co-operation and a well-planned child protection strategy, this situation would come about.

On completing the inquiry into the case, the designated officer must release the child from police protection *unless he/she considers that there is still reasonable cause for believing that the child would be likely to suffer significant harm if released* (s. 46(5)).

While a child is in police protection, neither the officer concerned nor the designated officer will have parental responsibility for the child (s. 46(9)(a)).

When a local authority is informed that a child is in police protection, they have a duty to make 'such enquiries as they consider necessary to enable them to decide whether they should take any action to safeguard' the child (s. 47(1)(b)). A court may issue a warrant for a constable to assist a relevant person to enter premises in order to enforce an emergency protection order.

1.13.4.2 Contravention of Protection Order or Police Protection

OFFENCE: **Acting in Contravention of Protection Order or Power Exercised under s. 46—*Children Act 1989, s. 49***

- Triable summarily • Six months' imprisonment

The Children Act 1989, s. 49 states:

(1) A person shall be guilty of an offence if, knowingly and without lawful authority or reasonable excuse, he—
  (a) takes a child to whom this section applies away from the responsible person;
  (b) keeps such a child away from the responsible person; or
  (c) induces, assists or incites such a child to run away or stay away from the responsible person.
(2) This section applies in relation to a child who is—
  (a) in care;
  (b) the subject of an emergency protection order; or
  (c) in police protection,
and in this section 'the responsible person' means any person who for the time being has care of him by virtue of the care order, the emergency protection order, or section 46, as the case may be.

KEYNOTE

Where a child is taken in contravention of s. 49, the court may issue a 'recovery order' under s. 50. The order, which is also available where a child is missing or has run away, requires certain people to produce the child to an authorised person (which includes a constable (s. 50(7)(b)) or to give certain information about the child's whereabouts to a constable or officer of the court (s. 50(3)). It can authorise a constable to enter any premises and search for the child.

Under s. 102 of the 1989 Act a court may issue a warrant to enter premises in connection with certain provisions of the Act which regulate children's homes, foster homes, child-minding premises and nursing homes for children. Section 102 allows for constables to assist any person in the exercise of their powers under those provisions. It makes allowances for a constable to be accompanied by a medical practitioner, nurse or health visitor (s. 102(3)).

1.13.4.3 Disclosure of Information Regarding Child

Where a child is reported missing problems can arise once the child is discovered to be safe and well but one of the parents wants the police to disclose the whereabouts of the child. This situation arose in *S v S (Chief Constable of West Yorkshire Police Intervening)* [1998] 1 WLR 1716 and the Court of Appeal provided some clarification of the issues. In that case the mother left home with her three-year-old child after a marriage breakdown. The father reported the child's absence to the police who found the child and her mother in a refuge. At the request of the mother, the police advised the father that both she and the child were safe but refused to disclose their whereabouts. The father applied 'without notice' (i.e. without telling the police) to the county court which then made an order under s. 33 of the Family Law Act 1986, requiring the police to disclose the information. The chief constable was granted leave to intervene and, following another order from the court to disclose the child's whereabouts, the chief constable appealed. The Court of Appeal held that it was only in exceptional circumstances that the police should be asked to divulge the whereabouts of a child under a s. 33 order. Their primary role in such cases should continue to be finding missing children and ensuring their safety.

However, the court went on to say that, in such cases:

- The police are *not* in a position to give 'categoric assurances' of confidentiality to those who provide information as to the whereabouts of a child. The most they could say is that, other than by removing the child, it would be *most unlikely* that they would have to disclose the information concerning the child's whereabouts.
- An order under s. 33 provides for the information to be disclosed to the court, not to the other party or his/her solicitor.
- An order under s. 33 should not normally be made in respect of the police without their being present (ex parte).

Note that the provision of information by police officers in relation to civil proceedings involving children is governed by regulations; specific advice should therefore be sought before disclosing any such information.

1.14 Theft and Related Offences

1.14.1 Introduction

Many offences contained in this chapter are very common and you will be aware of the physical, emotional and financial cost to victims of offences such as theft, burglary and robbery. The prevalence and impact that these offences have on society as a whole can leave no doubt as to their importance.

1.14.2 Theft

OFFENCE: **Theft—*Theft Act 1968, s. 1***

> • Triable either way • Seven years' imprisonment on indictment • Six months' imprisonment and/or a fine summarily

The Theft Act 1968, s. 1 states:

(1) A person is guilty of theft if he dishonestly appropriates property belonging to another with the intention of permanently depriving the other of it; and 'thief' and 'steal' shall be construed accordingly.

KEYNOTE

The final line of s. 1 is important and states that the words '"thief" and "steal" shall be construed accordingly'. This means that in any Theft Act 1968 offence where the words 'thief' and/or 'steal' are used (such as in the Theft Act 1968 offence of robbery (s. 8) or handling stolen goods (s. 22)), the 'thief' is the person who commits the theft offence and 'steal' means to commit theft. *All of the elements of the theft offence must be present to 'steal'.* The definition of robbery (s. 8) tells us that 'A person is guilty of robbery if he steals'. If an element of theft has not been satisfied then the defendant will not commit theft and will not 'steal'. No 'steal' = no robbery.

Where the property in question belonged to D's spouse or civil partner, a prosecution for theft may only be instituted against D by or with the consent of the DPP (s. 30(4)). This restriction must also apply to charges of robbery or of burglary by stealing, etc. but does not apply to other persons charged with committing the offence jointly with D; nor does it apply when the parties are separated by judicial decree or order or under no obligation to cohabit (s. 30(4)(a)). Theft from businesses (classed as 'theft from a shop') involving first-time offenders who are not substance mis-users and where the value of the goods stolen is less than £100 can be dealt with by way of fixed penalty notice (see *General Police Duties*, para. 4.5.14).

1.14.2.1 Low-value Shoplifting

Section 176 of the Anti-social Behaviour, Crime and Policing Act 2014 inserts a new section (s. 22A) into the Magistrates' Courts Act 1980, which provides that low-value shoplifting is a *summary offence*. This is subject to one exception: where a person accused of shoplifting is 18 or over, they are to be given the opportunity to elect Crown Court trial, and if the defendant so elects, the offence is no longer summary and will be sent to the Crown Court (s. 22A(2)).

Otherwise, the effect of s. 22A is that offences of low-value shoplifting cannot be sent to the Crown Court for trial or committed there for sentence; they will attract a maximum penalty of six months' custody; and they will be brought within the procedure in s. 12 of the Magistrates' Courts Act 1980 that enables defendants in summary cases to be given the opportunity to plead guilty by post.

Shoplifting is not a specific offence as such but constitutes theft under s. 1 of the Theft Act 1968; accordingly s. 22A(3) defines shoplifting for the purposes of this provision, which applies if the value of the stolen goods is £200 or less. For these purposes the value of the goods is to be determined by the price at which they were offered for sale rather than the intrinsic value, and also for the value involved in several shoplifting offences to be aggregated where they are charged at the same time (s.22A(4)). So, for example, where a person is charged with three counts of shoplifting, having allegedly taken £80 worth of goods from three separate shops (a total of £240), the procedure would not apply in that case as the aggregate sum exceeds the £200 threshold.

Low-value shoplifting will be tried summarily (as it must be unless the defendant elects); the maximum penalty is six months' imprisonment or a fine.

An offence of shoplifting includes secondary offences such as aiding and abetting.

Section 22A(5) amends s. 1 of the Criminal Attempts Act 1981 to provide that it is an offence to attempt to commit low-value shoplifting.

Section 22A(6) provides that certain powers conferred by the Police and Criminal Evidence Act 1984 on the police and others in respect of indictable offences remain available in respect of low-value shoplifting, notwithstanding that it is reclassified as summary only. The powers concerned include a power of arrest exercisable by a person other than a constable (for example, a store detective), powers enabling police officers to enter and search premises and vehicles in various circumstances for the purposes of searching for evidence in connection with an investigation or arresting individuals suspected of committing offences, and powers enabling a magistrate to authorise such entry and search.

1.14.2.2 Dishonestly

If a person cannot be shown to have acted 'dishonestly', he/she is not guilty of theft. The decision as to whether or not a defendant was dishonest is a question of fact for the jury or magistrate(s) to decide. Whilst there is no statutory definition of the term 'dishonestly', the 1968 Act does deal with the issue by setting out a number of specific circumstances where the relevant person will *not* be treated as dishonest and one circumstance where a person *may* be dishonest.

The Theft Act 1968, s. 2 states:

(1) A person's appropriation of property belonging to another is not to be regarded as dishonest—
    (a) if he appropriates the property in the belief that he has in law the right to deprive the other of it, on behalf of himself or of a third person; or
    (b) if he appropriates the property in the belief that he would have the other's consent if the other knew of the appropriation and the circumstances of it; or
    (c) (except where the property came to him as trustee or personal representative) if he appropriates the property in the belief that the person to whom the property belongs cannot be discovered by taking reasonable steps.

KEYNOTE

In all three instances it is the person's *belief* that is important.

Right in Law

- X is owed £100 by Y. Y tells X that he will not give him the money so X, *honestly believing that he has a right in law to do so*, takes property belonging to Y (to the value of £100) as payment for the debt. It does not matter that there is no actual right in law for X to behave in this way; the honestly held belief by X that he does have a right in law means that he is not dishonest. The belief need not even be reasonable, only honestly held, and could be based on a 'mistake'. This would also include the situation where the person acts on the basis of belief in the legal right of another. So if X, acting for the benefit of Y, took property from Z (wrongly but honestly believing that Y was entitled to it), X would not be dishonest.

Consent

- Under s. 2(1)(b) the person appropriating the property must believe both elements, i.e. that the other person would have *consented* had he/she known of the appropriation *and the circumstances of it*. For example, a person is about to run out of time on a street parking meter and needs £5 to park for the next hour or risk incurring a fine. Believing that a work colleague would consent in this situation, the person takes £5 belonging to the colleague from a change jar on the colleague's desk. If the person *honestly believes the work colleague would consent to the taking and the circumstances of it*, this would not be dishonest. If the person knew that the work colleague would not approve, this would be dishonest.

Lost

- Under s. 2(1)(c), the belief has to be in relation to the likelihood of *discovering* the 'owner' by taking reasonable steps. The nature and value of the property, together with the attendant circumstances, will be relevant. The chances of finding the owner of a valuable, monogrammed engagement ring found after a theatre performance would be considerably greater than those of discovering the owner of a can of beer found outside a football ground. Again, it is the defendant's *honest belief* at the time of the appropriation that is important here, not that the defendant went on to take reasonable steps to discover the person to whom the property belongs.
- Trustees or personal representatives cannot rely on s. 2(1)(c). This is because a trustee or personal representative can never be personally entitled to the property in question (unless the trust or will states that is the case) as if the beneficiary cannot be found, the person entitled to the property in question (now effectively 'ownerless goods') is the Crown.

The Theft Act 1968, s. 2 states:

(2) A person's appropriation of property belonging to another may be dishonest notwithstanding that he is willing to pay for the property.

KEYNOTE

If a person appropriates another's property, leaving money or details of where he/she can be contacted to make restitution, this will not of itself negate dishonesty (*Boggeln* v *Williams* [1978] 1 WLR 873). The wording of s. 2(2) gives latitude to a court where the defendant was willing to pay for the property. The subsection says that such an appropriation *may* be dishonest, not that it *will always* be dishonest.

....

EXAMPLE

X wants to buy a pint of milk and sees an unattended milk float displaying a sign, 'Milk—50p a pint'. X waits for several minutes but nobody in charge of the milk float appears so X leaves 50p on the float and takes a pint of milk. The fact that the milk is for sale and X left payment would be convincing evidence to suggest that X is not dishonest.

The conclusion may be different if Y wants to own a painting that is on display in a museum. Y has made several approaches to buy the painting but has been told that the painting is not for sale. Y knows the painting is worth £10,000 and decides to take the painting from the museum, leaving a cheque for £10,000 in its place. Just because Y is willing to pay the market value for the painting does not mean to say that he is not dishonest.

1.14.2.3 Dishonesty: The Ruling in *Ghosh*

Section 2 will not cater for every circumstance and indeed ss. 2–6 only affect the interpretation of the basic elements of theft as set out in s. 1 unless the Act says otherwise (s. 1(3)). Since the case of *R v Ghosh* [1982] QB 1053 there has been a requirement for juries to be given some form of direction where the issue of dishonesty is raised and s. 2 is of no assistance. As well as clarifying that the defendant's dishonesty is a matter for a jury to decide, the Court of Appeal in *Ghosh* also identified two aspects which the jury should consider when so deciding. If s. 2 is not applicable or helpful then a jury must ask two questions:

- Was what was done dishonest according to the ordinary standards of reasonable and honest people? If the answer to that question is 'no' then the defendant is not guilty of theft but if it is 'yes' then the second question is asked.
- Did the defendant realise that what was done was dishonest *by those standards*?

This test against the standards of reasonable and honest people means that defendants who have a purely *subjective* belief that they are doing what is morally right although they know it is legally wrong (e.g. an anti-vivisectionist taking animals from a laboratory) can still be 'dishonest'. Taking the animals from the laboratory is dishonest according to the ordinary standards of reasonable and honest people and the anti-vivisectionist knows that to be the case.

1.14.2.4 Appropriates

The Theft Act 1968, s. 3 states:

> Any assumption by a person of the rights of an owner amounts to an appropriation, and this includes, where he has come by the property (innocently or not) without stealing it, any later assumption of a right to it by keeping or dealing with it as owner.

KEYNOTE

The owner of property has many rights in relation to it—the right to sell it, to give it away or to destroy it are just *some* examples. 'Appropriation' does not envisage that a person assumes *all* of those rights, just *one* of them would suffice for 'appropriation' to occur.

While damaging or destroying property is clearly an act of 'appropriation' (*R v Graham* [1997] 1 Cr App R 302) it does not follow that an act of destruction of property is also thereby automatically theft of that property. *Dishonestly* causing the destruction of property can itself amount to an offence of theft (*R v Kohn* (1979) 69 Cr App R 395) but this does not make theft an appropriate charge where D merely smashes V's car window by throwing a brick through it. Criminal damage would be the appropriate charge on such facts as there is clearly no 'dishonesty' present in such an act.

It is important to note that there can be an 'appropriation' without any criminal liability and appropriation itself does not amount to an offence of theft; it simply describes one of the elements of the criminal conduct that must exist before a charge of theft can be made out. An appropriation requires no mental state on the part of the appropriator. It is an objective act.

Where an appropriation takes place and is accompanied by the other elements of the offence, there will be a theft.

Appropriation under s. 3(1) envisages a *physical* act (*Biggs v R* (2003) 12 December, unreported).

When and where the particular act amounting to an appropriation took place is of importance when bringing a charge of theft (and in other offences such as robbery and aggravated burglary).

The decision of the House of Lords in *R v Gomez* [1993] AC 442 significantly developed the meaning of 'appropriation'. Following an earlier case (*Lawrence v Metropolitan Police Commissioner* [1972] AC 626), Lord Keith disagreed with the argument (made in *Gomez*) that an act expressly or impliedly authorised by the owner of the property in question can never amount to an 'appropriation' and pointed out that the decision in *Lawrence* was a direct contradiction of that proposition. The House of Lords upheld the convictions for theft in *Gomez* and accepted that there are occasions where property can be 'appropriated' for the purposes of the Theft Act 1968, *even though the owner has given his/her consent or authority.*

A number of issues come from this decision:

- *Taking or depriving.* It is not necessary that the property be 'taken' in order for there to be an appropriation, neither need the owner be 'deprived' of the property. Similarly, there is no need for the defendant to 'gain' anything by an appropriation.
- *Consent.* It is irrelevant to the issue of appropriation whether or not the owner consented to that appropriation. This is well illustrated in *Lawrence*, the decision followed by the House of Lords in *Gomez*. In *Lawrence* a tourist gave his wallet full of unfamiliar English currency to a taxi driver for the latter to remove the correct fare. The driver in fact helped himself to ('appropriated') far more than the amount owed. It was held that the fact that the wallet and its contents were handed over freely (with consent) by the owner did not prevent the taxi driver's actions from amounting to an 'appropriation' of it.
- *Interfering with goods.* Simply swapping the price labels on items displayed for sale in a shop *will* amount to an 'appropriation'. This is because to do so, irrespective of any further intention, involves an assumption of one of the owner's rights in relation to the property (the right to put a price on property). If that appropriation were accompanied by the other elements of the offence, then theft is committed.
- *More than one appropriation.* There may be an appropriation of the same property on more than one occasion. However, once property has been *stolen* (as opposed to merely appropriated), that same property cannot be stolen again by the same thief (*R v Atakpu* [1994] QB 69). Appropriation can also be a continuing act, that is, it can include the whole episode of entering and ransacking a house and the subsequent removal of property (*R v Hale* (1979) 68 Cr App R 415).

In *R v Hinks* [2001] 2 AC 24, the House of Lords was asked to rule on whether a person could 'appropriate' property belonging to another where the other person made her an absolute gift of property, retaining no proprietary interest in the property or any right to resume or recover it. In that case the defendant had befriended a middle-aged man of limited intelligence who had given her £60,000 over a period of time. The defendant was charged with five counts of theft and, after conviction, eventually appealed to the House of Lords. Their lordships held that:

- in a prosecution for theft it was unnecessary to prove that the taking was without the owner's consent (as in *Lawrence*);
- it was immaterial whether the act of appropriation was done with the owner's consent or authority (as in *Gomez*); and
- *Gomez* therefore gave effect to s. 3(1) by treating 'appropriation' as a neutral word covering 'any assumption by a person of the rights of an owner'.

The essence of the decision by the House of Lords in *Hinks* is that even though a person obtains good title to property under civil law (the gift) they can still be convicted of theft as the circumstances of the gift-giving are dishonest.

If a person, having come by property, innocently or not, without stealing it, later assumes any rights to it by keeping it or treating it as his/her own, then he/she 'appropriates' that property (s. 3(1)).

KEYNOTE

A later assumption of the rights of an owner amounts to 'appropriation' and could lead to an offence of theft.

EXAMPLE

X is shopping in a large department store and has placed several items in his shopping basket. Thinking about other things, X absent-mindedly walks out of the store without paying for the goods. Once outside the store

> X realises what he has done but as the store alarm has not activated and nobody has noticed X leaving the store without paying, X decides to keep the goods and walks away from the store. X initially came by the goods innocently but his later assumption of the rights of an owner means he has now 'appropriated' the goods and in the circumstances commits theft.

An exception to these circumstances is provided by the Theft Act 1968, s. 3 which states:

> (2) Where property or a right or interest in property is or purports to be transferred for value to a person acting in good faith, no later assumption by him of rights which he believed himself to be acquiring shall, by reason of any defect in the transferor's title, amount to theft of the property.

KEYNOTE

If a person buys a car in good faith and gives value for it (i.e. a reasonable price) but then discovers it has been stolen, a refusal to return it to the original owner would not, without more, *attract liability for theft.* Without s. 3(2) the retention of the vehicle would be caught by s. 3(1). This narrow exemption does not mean however that the innocent purchaser gets good title to the car (*National Employers' Mutual Insurance Association Ltd* v *Jones* [1990] 1 AC 24), nor would it provide a defence if the stolen goods are a gift and the 'donee' (recipient) subsequently discovers that they had been stolen (the 'donee' will not have given 'value' for the property).

1.14.2.5 Property

The Theft Act 1968, s. 4 states:

> (1) 'Property' includes money and all other property, real or personal, including things in action and other intangible property.
> (2) A person cannot steal land, or things forming part of land and severed from it by him or by his directions, except in the following cases, that is to say—
>   (a) when he is a trustee or personal representative, or is authorised by power of attorney, or as liquidator of a company, or otherwise, to sell or dispose of land belonging to another, and he appropriates the land or anything forming part of it by dealing with it in breach of the confidence reposed in him; or
>   (b) when he is not in possession of the land and appropriates anything forming part of the land by severing it or causing it to be severed, or after it has been severed; or
>   (c) when, being in possession of the land under a tenancy, he appropriates the whole or part of any fixture or structure let to be used with the land.
>   For purposes of this subsection 'land' does not include incorporeal hereditaments; 'tenancy' means a tenancy for years or any less period and includes an agreement for such a tenancy, but a person who after the end of a tenancy remains in possession as statutory tenant or otherwise is to be treated as having possession under the tenancy, and 'let' shall be construed accordingly.
> (3) A person who picks mushrooms growing wild on any land, or who picks flowers, fruit or foliage from a plant growing wild on any land, does not (although not in possession of the land) steal what he picks unless he does it for reward or for sale or other commercial purpose. For purposes of this subsection 'mushroom' includes any fungus, and 'plant' includes any shrub or tree.
> (4) Wild creatures, tamed or untamed, shall be regarded as property; but a person cannot steal a wild creature not tamed nor ordinarily kept in captivity, or the carcase of any such creature, unless either it has been reduced into possession by or on behalf of another person and possession of it has not since been lost or abandoned, or another person is in course of reducing it into possession.

KEYNOTE

Money

Coins and banknotes are property (*R* v *Davis* (1989) 88 Cr App R 347). 'Money' does not include cheques or credit balances held in banks and building societies (but see below).

Cheques and Credit Balances

Cheques will be property as they are pieces of paper ('personal' property albeit of very little value). The contents of a bank or building society account, however, are also a 'thing in action' that can be stolen provided the account is in credit or within the limits of an agreed overdraft facility (*R* v *Kohn* (1979) 69 Cr App R 395). Reducing the credit balance in one account and transferring a like sum into your own account amounts to an 'appropriation' of property within the meaning of s. 1. This principle (set out in *Kohn*) was reaffirmed in *R* v *Williams (Roy)* [2001] 1 Cr App R 23 by the Court of Appeal.

Personal Property

Personal property includes tangible personal property which might be described as 'things in possession'. The TV in your house, the settee you sit on etc. are all examples of 'personal' property.

Things in Action and Other Intangible Property

Under s. 4(1) 'things in action' would include patents, company shares and trademarks and other things which can only be enforced by legal action as opposed to physical possession. Other intangible property would include software programs and perhaps credits accumulated on 'smart cards'. Confidential information, such as the contents of an examination paper, is not intangible property *per se* (*Oxford* v *Moss* (1979) 68 Cr App R 183). However, if those contents were written on a piece of paper, the paper itself would be 'real' property. It has been accepted by the Court of Appeal that contractual rights obtained by buying a ticket for the London Underground may amount to a 'thing in action' (*R* v *Marshall* [1998] 2 Cr App R 282).

An area of criminal activity causing concern (and cost) is that of so-called 'identity theft'. This is a misleading description as adopting another person's characteristics and using his/her administrative data (such as national insurance number) is not theft of the information as this 'confidential information' is not 'property' for the purposes of the Theft Act 1968 (**see para. 1.14.2.6**).

Land

Under s. 4(2) you cannot generally steal land even though it is 'property' for the purposes of criminal damage (**see chapter 1.16**). However, there are three exceptions to this general rule:

(1) Trustees or personal representatives or someone in a position of trust to dispose of land belonging to another, can be guilty of stealing it if, in such circumstances, they dishonestly dispose of it.

....

EXAMPLE

Two company employees are asked by the company directors to sell land belonging to the company. The value of the land is £10,000 an acre. The company employees sell the land to each other for £1,000 an acre. The company employees are in a position of trust and have 'breached the confidence reposed in them' and commit theft of the land.

....

(2) Persons not in possession of the land may commit theft in a variety of ways. This may be accomplished by severing fixtures, plants, topsoil, etc. from the land or by appropriating such property after it has been severed. If X decides to take an established and cultivated rose bush from the garden of his neighbour by ripping it out of the ground and then planting it in his own garden, this would be theft as the rose bush has been severed from the land (see below for wild plants). This would not include a person who dishonestly moves a boundary fence so as to appropriate some part of a neighbouring property as the land has not been 'severed'.

(3) Tenants can steal land but only fixtures and structures let to be used with the land. Examples of 'fixtures' would be a fireplace or the kitchen sink; a structure might be a greenhouse or a garden shed which is fixed to the land. A tenant cannot steal land such as topsoil or a rosebush growing in the garden of the rented premises as these things are not 'fixtures or structures'.

Things Growing Wild

Things growing wild on any land are 'property' and could be stolen by a person not in possession of the land if he/she severed and appropriated them. However, s. 4(3) of the Act tells us that a person who picks mushrooms, flowers, fruit and foliage growing wild on any land will not commit theft by so doing, unless the picking is done for reward, sale or other commercial purpose. Except in the case of a mushroom, if the whole plant is removed this is theft as it is not 'picking'. Likewise, sawing through the trunk of a tree growing wild is not picking and would be theft. It is arguable that, if the person does not have such a purpose at the time of the picking, any later intention to sell the fruit, etc. may not bring it within the provisions of s. 4(3). If the mushroom, flower etc. is cultivated it will be theft to pick it wherever it is growing.

Wild Creatures

Section 4(4) states all wild creatures are 'property' whether they are tamed (your dog or cat) or untamed but ordinarily kept in captivity (a lion in a zoo). Wild creatures that are not tamed or ordinarily kept in captivity are not classed as property unless they have been reduced into possession or in the process of being so reduced. For example, X shoots a rabbit on land belonging to Y (with Y's permission to be there and shoot). Z takes the rabbit from X—Z commits theft. If the rabbit is lost or abandoned after it has been reduced into possession or killed then it cannot be 'stolen'.

1.14.2.6   What is not Property?

Confidential information is not property, so a student who reads and makes a copy of their examination paper may not be convicted of stealing intangible property.

Human bodies (dead or alive) are not property ('there is no property in a corpse' *Doodeward v Spence* (1908) 6 CLR 406). However, a body or body parts are capable of being stolen if they have been subject to a special application of human skill (an Egyptian mummy would be the property of the museum it was kept in). This principle was upheld by the Court of Appeal in *R v Kelly* [1999] QB 621, after the conviction of two people involved in the theft of body parts from the Royal College of Surgeons. The court upheld the convictions for theft on the grounds that the process of *alteration* (amputation, dissection and preservation) which the body parts had undergone did make them 'property' for the purposes of the 1968 Act.

Fluids taken from a living body are property so a motorist has been convicted of stealing a specimen of his own urine provided by him for analysis (*R v Welsh* [1971] RTR 478). The same rule would clearly apply to a blood sample.

Electricity is not property and is the subject of a specific offence.

1.14.2.7   Belonging to Another

The Theft Act 1968, s. 5 states:

(1)   Property shall be regarded as belonging to any person having possession or control of it, or having in it any proprietary right or interest (not being an equitable interest arising only from an agreement to transfer or grant an interest).

(2)   Where property is subject to a trust, the persons to whom it belongs shall be regarded as including any person having a right to enforce the trust, and an intention to defeat the trust shall be regarded accordingly as an intention to deprive of the property any person having that right.

KEYNOTE

Property can be 'stolen' from any person who has possession, control or a proprietary right or interest in that property. In one case where the defendant recovered his own recently repaired car from a street outside the garage where the repairs had taken place, he was convicted of stealing the car which at the time 'belonged to' the garage proprietor who had possession of it (*R v Turner (No. 2)* [1971] 1 WLR 901). In determining whether or not a person had 'possession' of property for the purposes of s. 5(1), the period of possession can be finite (i.e. for a given number of hours, days, etc.) or infinite (*R v Kelly* [1999] QB 621).

It is not necessary to show who does own the property, only that it 'belongs to' someone other than the defendant. An example of how this principle operates can be seen in a case where the two defendants went diving in a lake on a golf course, recovering sacks of 'lost' balls which it was believed they were going to sell. This activity was carried out without the permission of the golf club who owned the course. Although the defendants argued that the balls had been abandoned by their owners, the Crown had shown that they were 'property belonging to another' (the golf club) and therefore the convictions were safe (*R* v *Rostron; R* v *Collinson* [2003] EWCA Crim 2206).

Where money is given to charity collectors it becomes the property of the relevant charitable trustees at the moment it goes into the collecting tin (*R* v *Dyke* [2001] EWCA Crim 2184). If s. 5(2) did not exist, those charitable trustees could take the donation to the charity and do what they wished with it, including placing the charitable funds in their own bank account. Charitable trusts are enforceable by the Attorney-General, and an appropriation of the trust property by a charitable trustee will amount to theft from the Attorney-General.

When a cheque is written it creates a 'thing in action'. That thing in action belongs only to the payee. Therefore a payee of a cheque cannot 'steal' the thing in action which it creates (*R* v *Davis* (1989) 88 Cr App R 347).

You must show that the property belonged to another *at the time of the appropriation*. This requirement has caused some difficulty where a defendant's decision not to pay for goods has been made *after* property passed to him/her. In such cases (e.g. people refusing to pay for meals after they have eaten or deciding to drive off having filled their car with petrol), the proper charge is found under the Fraud Act 2006 (**see chapter 1.15**) or by charging with the offence of making off without payment. The House of Lords' ruling in *Gomez* raises some questions over such cases (**see para. 1.14.2.4**). As the consent of the owner is irrelevant to the issue of 'appropriation', the key element in such cases is whether the property 'belonged to another' at the time of the act of appropriation. If ownership of the property had passed to the defendant *before* he/she appropriated it (e.g. by virtue of the Sale of Goods Act 1979; *Edwards* v *Ddin* [1976] 1 WLR 942) then this element of theft would not be made out and an alternative charge should be considered.

1.14.2.8 Obligations Regarding Another's Property

The Theft Act 1968, s. 5 states:

> (3) Where a person receives property from or on account of another, and is under an obligation to the other to retain and deal with that property or its proceeds in a particular way, the property or proceeds shall be regarded (as against him) as belonging to the other.

KEYNOTE

'Obligation' means a legal obligation, not a moral one (*R* v *Hall* [1973] QB 126). Whether or not such an obligation exists is a matter of law for a trial judge to decide (*R* v *Dubar* [1994] 1 WLR 1484).

Instances under s. 5(3) most commonly involve receiving money from others to retain and use in a certain way (e.g. travel agents taking deposits; solicitors holding funds for mortgagees; or pension fund managers collecting contributions (*R* v *Clowes (No. 2)* [1994] 2 All ER 316)). The Court of Appeal has held that one effect of s. 5(3) is that property can be regarded as belonging to another even where it does not 'belong' to that person on a strict interpretation of civil law (*R* v *Klineberg* [1999] 1 Cr App R 427). In that case the defendants collected money from customers in their timeshare business and told the customers that their deposits would be placed with an independent trustee. Instead, the defendants paid the sums into their company account, thereby breaching the 'obligation' under s. 5(3) to deal with the money in a particular way.

Section 5(3) would also include, say, the owner of a shopping centre who invites shoppers to throw coins into a fountain which will be donated to charity; if the owner did not deal with those coins in the way intended (e.g. keeping the money), the provisions of s. 5(3) may well apply.

1.14.2.9 Obligation to Restore Another's Property

The Theft Act 1968, s. 5 states:

> (4) Where a person gets property by another's mistake, and is under an obligation to make restoration (in whole or in part) of the property or its proceeds or of the value thereof, then to the extent of

that obligation the property or proceeds shall be regarded (as against him) as belonging to the person entitled to restoration, and an intention not to make restoration shall be regarded accordingly as an intention to deprive that person of the property or proceeds.

KEYNOTE

Where extra money is mistakenly credited into an employee's bank account, the employee will be liable for stealing the extra money if he/she dishonestly keeps it (see *Attorney-General's Reference (No. 1 of 1983)* [1985] QB 182 where a police officer's account was credited with money representing overtime which she had not actually worked).

Section 5(4) only applies where someone *other than the defendant* has made a mistake. Such a mistake can be a mistake as to a material fact; whether or not a mistake as to *law* would be covered is unclear.

The obligation to make restoration is a *legal* one and an unenforceable or moral obligation will not be covered by s. 5(4). For example, in *R* v *Gilks* [1972] 1 WLR 1341 a relief manager at a betting shop mistakenly paid out winnings against the wrong horse. The Court of Appeal held that the defendant did not owe a legal obligation to return the money because the bookmaker could not have sued on a gaming transaction and therefore s. 5(4) did not apply.

1.14.2.10 Intention of Permanently Depriving

If you cannot prove an intention permanently to deprive you cannot prove theft (*R* v *Warner* (1970) 55 Cr App R 93).

If there is such an intention at the time of the appropriation, giving the property back later will not alter the fact and the charge will be made out (*R* v *McHugh* (1993) 97 Cr App R 335).

In certain circumstances s. 6 may help in determining the presence or absence of such an intention.

The Theft Act 1968, s. 6 states:

(1) A person appropriating property belonging to another without meaning the other permanently to lose the thing itself is nevertheless to be regarded as having the intention of permanently depriving the other of it if his intention is to treat the thing as his own to dispose of regardless of the other's rights; and a borrowing or lending of it may amount to so treating it if, but only if, the borrowing or lending is for a period and in circumstances making it equivalent to an outright taking or disposal.

KEYNOTE

The key feature of s. 6(1) is the intention to treat 'the thing' as one's own to dispose of regardless of the other's rights. An example of such a case would be where property is 'held to ransom' (*R* v *Coffey* [1987] Crim LR 498). If X kidnaps a dog belonging to Y and tells Y that the dog will be returned in exchange for £500, the conclusion to be drawn is that if the ransom is not paid the dog will not be returned, i.e. there is an intention to permanently deprive.

The borrowing or lending of another's property is specifically caught within s. 6(1). If a person takes property from his/her employer (e.g. carpet tiles) and uses it in a way which makes restoration unlikely or impossible (e.g. by laying them in his/her living room), s. 6(1) will apply (*R* v *Velumyl* [1989] Crim LR 299).

If X is given a football season ticket by Y to use for one match but then X holds on to the season ticket for several matches knowing that this was not part of the arrangement and against the wishes of Y, s. 6(1) would help prove the required intention to permanently deprive because the circumstances of the borrowing make it equivalent to an outright taking.

In a case involving robbery, the defendants took the victim's personal stereo headphones from him and broke them in two, rendering them useless before returning them to him. The Administrative Court held that a person who took something and dealt with it for the purpose of rendering it useless in this way demonstrated the intention of treating that article as his/her own to dispose of. The court did not accept the argument that the property had to be totally exhausted before s. 6 applied and held that the magistrates had been wrong to accept the submission of no case to answer on this point (*DPP* v *J* [2002] EWHC 291 (Admin)). Therefore, the deliberate breaking of an item of property will amount to the 'intention to permanently deprive'; however, unless this action is accompanied by the other theft elements it will be criminal damage. Note that in this case the offence dealt with was robbery so that the other elements of theft were plainly satisfied when the defendant initially took the property.

The Theft Act 1968, s. 6 states:

(2) Without prejudice to the generality of subsection (1) above, where a person, having possession or control (lawfully or not) of property belonging to another, parts with the property under a condition as to its return which he may not be able to perform, this (if done for purposes of his own and without the other's authority) amounts to treating the property as his own to dispose of regardless of the other's rights.

KEYNOTE

Section 6(2) deals with occasions such as pawning another's property. In pawning the property the defendant parts with the property on the basis that he/she *might* be able to recover it (there could never be certainty of recovery). So, there is a possibility that the defendant may not be able to do so, i.e. that he/she will be unable to meet the conditions under which he/she parted with another person's property. In such a case, s. 6(2) would help in proving an intention permanently to deprive.

1.14.3 Burglary

The main offence of burglary is split into two—s. 9(1)(a) and s. 9(1)(b).

1.14.3.1 Section 9(1)(a)

OFFENCE: **Burglary—*Theft Act 1968, s. 9***
  • Triable on indictment if 'ulterior offence' is so triable, or if committed in dwelling and violence used; otherwise triable either way • 14 years' imprisonment if building/part of building is dwelling • Otherwise 10 years' imprisonment on indictment
  • Six months' imprisonment and/or a fine summarily

The Theft Act 1968, s. 9 states:

(1) A person is guilty of burglary if—
  (a) he enters any building or part of a building as a trespasser and with intent to commit any such offence as is mentioned in subsection (2) below; or ...
(2) The offences referred to in subsection (1)(a) above are offences of stealing anything in the building or part of a building in question, of inflicting on any person therein any grievous bodily harm and of doing unlawful damage to the building or anything therein.

KEYNOTE

Enters

The Theft Act 1968 does not define the term 'entry' and so we are left to resolve the meaning of this term by reference to case law and the decisions of the courts. The common law rule was that the insertion of any part of the body, *however small*, was sufficient to be considered an 'entry'. So where D pushed in a window pane and the forepart of his finger was observed in the building that was enough (*R* v *Davis* (1823) Russ & Ry 499). This approach was narrowed considerably in *R* v *Collins* [1973] QB 100, where it was said that entry needed to be 'effective and substantial'. The ruling in *Collins* was rejected by the Court of Appeal in *R* v *Brown* [1985] Crim LR 212, where it was stated that the 'substantial' element was surplus to requirements and that entry need only be 'effective'. Whether an entry was 'effective' or not was for the jury to decide. So the decision of the court in *Brown* appears to be the current accepted approach to defining the term; entry must therefore be 'effective'.

An 'effective' entry does not mean that the defendant has to enter a building or part of a building to such a degree that the ulterior offence, which he/she is entering with the intention to commit (the theft, GBH or criminal damage), can be committed (*R* v *Ryan* [1996] Crim LR 320). Nor does it mean that the defendant must get his/her whole body into the building. In *Brown*, the defendant had his feet on the ground outside the building with the upper half inside the building as he searched for goods to steal; this was held to be an entry. In *Ryan*, the defendant, who had become trapped by his neck with only his head and right arm inside the window, was held to have 'entered' the building. In *Brown*, the Court of Appeal stated that it would be astounding if a smash-and-grab raider, who inserted his hand through a shop window to grab goods, was not considered to have 'entered' the building.

At common law, the insertion of an instrument would constitute entry as long as the instrument was inserted to enable the ulterior offence to take place, e.g. a hook inserted into premises to steal property or the muzzle of a gun pushed through a letterbox with a view to cause GBH. Insertion of an instrument merely to facilitate entry, e.g. using a coat hanger to open a window lock, *would not* be entry. Although there is no recent authority on the issue, it is likely that this line of reasoning in relation to the use of instruments in burglary is still acceptable.

Entry must be deliberate and not accidental.

Ultimately, whether the defendant has entered a building or not will be a question of fact for the jury or magistrate(s).

Trespasser

To be guilty of the offence of burglary people must know that they are entering as a trespasser (i.e. they must know they are entering without a right by law or with express or implied permission to do so) or be reckless as to that fact. Sometimes a defendant may have a general permission to enter a building or part of a building for a legitimate purpose; however, the true intention of the defendant when entering is not for that legitimate purpose but in order to steal or commit grievous bodily harm or to cause criminal damage. As these intentions invariably form no part of the permission to enter the building or part of it, any entry in such circumstances means that the defendant becomes a trespasser the moment he/she enters the building or part of the building. In such circumstances the exceeding of the granted permission places the defendant in a position of being a trespasser from the outset. In *R* v *Jones and Smith* [1976] 1 WLR 672, the defendant was convicted of burglary when he took two televisions from his father's home. He had a key to the premises and was free to come and go as he liked but when he entered his father's house (using the key) accompanied by a friend at 3 am and stole the television sets, he committed burglary as it was his intention to steal as such an intent voids the general permission to enter.

1.14.3.2 **Building**

The Theft Act 1968 s. 9 states:

(4) References in subsections (1) and (2) above to a building, and the reference in subsection (3), above, to a building which is a dwelling, shall apply also to an inhabited vehicle or vessel, and shall apply to any such vehicle or vessel at times when the person having a habitation in it is not there as well as at times when he is.

KEYNOTE

Building

A building is generally considered to be a structure of a permanent nature (*Norfolk Constabulary* v *Seekings and Gould* [1986] Crim LR 167), although a substantial portable structure with most of the attributes of a building can be a 'building' for the purposes of burglary. For example, in *B & S* v *Leathley* [1979] Crim LR 314, a portable container measuring 25ft by 7ft by 7ft and weighing three tons, which had occupied the same position for three years, was connected to mains electricity, and which was due to remain in the same position for the foreseeable future, was considered to be a building for the purposes of burglary. An unfinished house can be a building for the purposes of burglary (*R* v *Manning* (1871) LR 1 CCR 338), although at what precise point a pile of building materials becomes an 'unfinished house' and therefore a building or part of a building would be a question of fact for the jury to decide. Tents and marquees are considered to fall outside the term, even if the tent is someone's home (the Criminal Law Revision Committee intended tents to be outside the protection of burglary).

The effect of s. 9(4) is to include *inhabited* vehicles and vessels (such as house boats or motor homes) within the term. A canal boat that is not inhabited is not a building as whilst it may be capable of habitation, it is not being lived in.

Part of a Building

People may commit burglary when, although they are in one part of a building with legitimate access, they enter another part of it as a trespasser.

- A tenant of a block of flats has a key that provides access to a communal foyer of the block of flats. He uses the key to enter the foyer (*entering a building and plainly not a trespasser at this stage*). Instead of entering his own flat he forces entry to a neighbour's flat by breaking down the neighbour's door that can be accessed via the communal foyer (*moving from one part of a building to another in the process and certainly a trespasser at this stage*).

The Court of Appeal decided that it is for the jury to decide whether an area physically marked out is sufficiently segregated to amount to 'part of a building'. In *R* v *Walkington* [1979] 1 WLR 1169, the defendant walked behind a moveable sales counter in a shop with the intention to steal and was found guilty of burglary as this was held to be 'part of a building'. A 'No Entry' sign or a rope could mark off one part of a building from another.

1.14.3.3 Intentions at the Time of Entry

The intentions at the time of entry (not before or after) must be as follows:

- Stealing. This means an intention to commit theft under s. 1 (and 'thief' and 'steal' will be construed accordingly). It will not include abstracting electricity because electricity is not 'property' for the purposes of theft (*Low* v *Blease* [1975] Crim LR 513), neither will it include taking a conveyance (no intention to permanently deprive). The property which the defendant intends to steal must be in a building or part of a building.
- Inflicting grievous bodily harm. If grievous bodily harm is inflicted (**see chapter 1.9**), then the second offence under s. 9(1)(b) would apply. In proving an intention to commit grievous bodily harm under s. 9(1)(a), it is not necessary to prove that a wounding/ grievous bodily harm offence was actually committed (*Metropolitan Police Commissioner* v *Wilson* [1984] AC 242). The offence in question in respect of a burglary under s. 9(1)(a) is of grievous bodily harm contrary to s. 18 of the Offences Against the Person Act 1861.
- Causing unlawful damage. This includes damage, not only to the building but to anything in it (**see chapter 1.16**).

1.14.3.4 Conditional Intent

Provided the required intention can be proved, it is immaterial whether or not there is anything 'worth stealing' within the building (*R* v *Walkington* [1979] 1 WLR 1169). The same will be true if the person whom the defendant intends to cause serious harm is not in the building or part of the building at the time (**see also para. 1.3.4**).

Section 9(1)(b)

OFFENCE: **Burglary—*Theft Act 1968, s. 9***

• Triable on indictment if 'ulterior offence' is so triable, or if committed in dwelling and violence used; otherwise triable either way • 14 years' imprisonment if building/part of building is a dwelling • Otherwise 10 years' imprisonment on indictment • Six months' imprisonment and/or a fine summarily

The Theft Act 1968, s. 9 states:

(1) A person is guilty of burglary if—

…

(b) having entered any building or part of a building as a trespasser he steals or attempts to steal anything in the building or that part of it or inflicts or attempts to inflict on any person therein any grievous bodily harm.

KEYNOTE

This type of burglary involves a defendant's behaviour *after* entering a building or part of a building as a trespasser.

The defendant must have entered the building or part of a building as a trespasser; it is not enough that the defendant subsequently became a trespasser by exceeding a condition of entry (e.g. hiding in the public area of a shop during open hours until the shop closes). However, where a person has entered a particular building (such as a shop) lawfully and without trespassing, if he/she later moves to *another part* of the building as a trespasser, this element of the offence will be made out.

....

EXAMPLE

D enters a public house near closing time with a friend who buys him a drink from the bar. D's entry onto that part of the premises has been authorised by the implied licence extended to members of the adult public by the publican and therefore D is not a trespasser. D then goes into the lavatories to use them as such. At this point he has entered another part of a building but again his entry is made under the implied licence to customers wishing to use the lavatories. While inside the lavatory area, D decides to hide until after closing time in order to avoid buying his friend a drink.

Once the publican has shut the pub for the night, D becomes a trespasser in the lavatory. This is because he is not supposed to be there, i.e. he has no express or implied permission or lawful right to be in the lavatory after the pub has closed. While D is a trespasser at this point in time, if he went on to steal from the lavatory he *would not* commit burglary because he did not enter the lavatory as a trespasser, he became one at a later stage by exceeding a condition of entry. It is essential, for an offence of burglary to occur, that the defendant *has entered the building or part of a building as a trespasser*. D then leaves the lavatory and walks into the lounge area. Now D has entered *a part of a building as a trespasser*. Having no particular intention at this point, however, D has still not committed an offence of burglary.

On seeing the gaming machines in the lounge, D decides to break into them and steal the money inside. At this point, although he has *two* of the required intentions for s. 9(1)(a) (an intention to steal and an intention to cause unlawful damage), those intentions were formed *after* his entry into the lounge. Therefore, D has not committed burglary under s. 9(1)(a). Because he has not stolen/attempted to steal or inflicted/attempted to inflict grievous bodily harm on any person therein, D has not committed burglary under s. 9(1)(b) either.

D then breaks open a gaming machine in order to steal the cash contents. At this point he commits burglary under s. 9(1)(b). This is because, having entered a part of a building (the lounge) as a trespasser (because the pub is closed and D knows that to be the case), he *attempts to steal*. If he simply caused criminal damage to the machine without an intention of stealing the contents, D would not commit this offence because causing unlawful damage is only relevant to the offence under s. 9(1)(a).

....

Unlike s. 9(1)(a), there are only two further elements to the offence under s. 9(1)(b): the subsequent theft/attempted theft of anything in the building or part of it, and the subsequent inflicting/attempted inflicting of grievous bodily harm to any person therein. The assault offences in question in respect of a burglary under s. 9(1)(b) are grievous bodily harm contrary to s. 18 or s. 20 of the Offences Against the Person Act 1861.

It has been suggested that if, having entered a building or part of a building as a trespasser, the defendant commits an offence of criminal damage, this will be an offence under s. 9(1)(b) of the Act as to damage or destroy something is also to steal it. *This is not the case.* If a person enters in such circumstances and causes criminal damage, there is little argument that such an activity would satisfy part of the offence of theft, i.e. appropriating property (see para. 1.14.2.4), but where is the 'dishonesty'? In addition, this would clearly be an unwarranted extension of the burglary offence under s. 9(1)(b) of the Theft Act 1968. If Parliament wanted such activity to be caught by the legislation, it would have included the offence of criminal damage within the definition of burglary under s. 9(1)(b).

1.14.4 Aggravated Burglary

OFFENCE: **Aggravated Burglary—*Theft Act 1968, s. 10***
- Triable on indictment • Life imprisonment

The Theft Act 1968, s. 10 states:

(1) A person is guilty of aggravated burglary if he commits any burglary and at the time has with him any firearm or imitation firearm, any weapon of offence, or any explosive; ...

KEYNOTE

An aggravated burglary is committed when a person commits an offence of burglary (either a s. 9(1)(a) or a s. 9(1)(b)) and at the time he/she has with him/her a **WIFE**.

W – Weapon of offence
I – Imitation firearm
F – Firearm
E – Explosive

At the time

These words require consideration of the type of burglary the defendant is charged with. The moment at which a burglary under s. 9(1)(a) is committed is at the point of entry, therefore it is essential that the defendant has the WIFE with him/her when entering a building or part of a building with the intention of committing one of the trigger offences under s. 9(1)(a). If that is the case, the defendant commits aggravated burglary. The moment at which a burglary under s. 9(1)(b) is committed is when the defendant steals, inflicts grievous bodily harm on any person or attempts to do either. If the defendant has the WIFE with him/her when committing or attempting to commit either offence, an aggravated burglary is committed.

EXAMPLE

A person (X) enters the kitchen of a house as a trespasser intending to steal property. At the point of entry X does not have any WIFE item with him, so at this point in time X has committed a s. 9(1)(a) burglary. While X is in the kitchen the occupier of the house enters the kitchen and disturbs him. X picks up a carving knife (not intending to steal it but to hurt the occupier with it if necessary) and threatens the occupier with it. At this point the carving knife becomes a weapon of offence (intended to cause injury and because of the concept of 'instant arming' (see below)) but this is not an aggravated burglary as X has not committed or attempted to commit theft or to inflict GBH. The occupier rushes towards X who stabs the occupier, inflicting GBH in the process. This is a s. 9(1)(b) burglary and at the time of its commission X has a WIFE item with him; as a result this becomes an aggravated burglary.

Has with him

'Has with him' is more restrictive than the term 'possession'. It will require the defendant to have some degree of *immediate control* of the item (*R* v *Pawlicki* [1992] 1 WLR 827) and will normally (but not exclusively) be the same as 'carrying' (*R* v *Klass* [1998] 1 Cr App R 453) although the defendant need not actually have the WIFE item *on his/her person* to be in *immediate control* of it. It is also essential that the individual has knowledge of the presence of the WIFE item. So if a burglary is committed by a single offender who knows he/she has a bayonet in his/her coat pocket when the offence is committed, the issue of aggravated burglary is clear. However, what of the situation where two offenders commit such a burglary? Liability depends on knowledge.

....

EXAMPLE

X and Y decide to commit a burglary together. X is concerned about being disturbed during the burglary and decides to take a knuckle-duster (a weapon of offence *per se* as it is made for causing injury) along with him when the burglary takes place; he does not tell Y about the knuckle-duster. When X and Y enter the building they intend to burgle, both commit a s. 9(1)(a) burglary. As X has a knuckle-duster with him at the time, X commits an aggravated burglary. However, Y does not commit the aggravated offence because he has no knowledge of the existence of the WIFE item. If X had told Y about the knuckle-duster then Y would have the required knowledge and would be deemed to have it with him so both would be guilty under s. 10 (*R* v *Jones* [1979] CLY 411).

....

Therefore, if the defendant has no knowledge of the WIFE item he/she does not commit the aggravated offence. If several people are charged with the offence of aggravated burglary, it must be shown that one of the defendants who actually entered the building or part of a building had the weapon with him/her (*R* v *Klass* [1998] 1 Cr App R 453).

It is important to note that the aggravated offence is committed due to the presence of the WIFE when the s. 9(1)(a) or s. 9(1)(b) burglary is carried out. It is irrelevant that the defendant had the item with him/her for some other purpose unconnected with the burglary offence.

Instant Arming

Ordinary items can, instantaneously, change into weapons of offence; it is the intention of the person to use an item in a particular way that allows this to take place. In *R* v *Kelly* (1993) 97 Cr App R 245, the defendant entered a building using a screwdriver to facilitate entry. When he was confronted he prodded the person confronting him in the stomach with the screwdriver. At that moment the screwdriver instantly became a weapon of offence and the defendant was later convicted of aggravated burglary.

1.14.4.1 Firearm/Weapon of Offence/Explosive

The Theft Act 1968, s. 10 goes on to state:

> (1) ... and for this purpose—
>   (a) 'firearm' includes an airgun or pistol, and 'imitation firearm' means anything which has the appearance of being a firearm, whether capable of being discharged or not, and
>   (b) 'weapon of offence' means any article made or adapted for use for causing injury to or incapacitating a person, or intended by the person having it with him for such use; and
>   (c) 'explosive' means any article manufactured for the purpose of producing a practical effect by explosion, or intended by the person having it with him for that purpose.

Weapon of Offence

This includes:

* Items *made* for causing injury, e.g. a bayonet or a knuckle-duster (**see para. 1.14.4**).
* Items *adapted* for causing injury, e.g. a screwdriver that has been sharpened at the tip.

- Items *intended* for causing injury, e.g. an ordinary cutlery knife. The cutlery knife is certainly inoffensive in everyday use but if the defendant *intends* to use it to injure, it will fall into this category.
- Items *made, adapted or intended* to incapacitate a person, e.g. handcuffs, rope, CS spray and chloroform.

The defendant must not only know of the presence of the weapon but also that it is a weapon of offence.

Note that the defences of lawful authority or reasonable excuse in relation to the possession of an offensive weapon appear not to apply to the offence of aggravated burglary.

Imitation Firearm

This includes anything which has the appearance of being a firearm, whether capable of being discharged or not (but note that this will not include the defendant's fingers pointed at someone under a coat to resemble a firearm (*R* v *Bentham* [2005] UKHL 18)).

Firearm

This does not relate to the definition under the Firearms Act 1968. Indeed, the term is not defined other than to include airguns and air pistols.

Explosive

This would cover explosives such as TNT and items such as grenades as they are both manufactured to produce a practical effect by explosion. It also covers an item intended by the person having it with him/her for such a purpose, potentially bringing home-made devices or substances into the equation. The issue in relation to fireworks has yet to be firmly resolved by the courts, although they may well be excluded from the definition as fireworks are, by and large, manufactured to produce a pyrotechnic rather than practical effect by explosion and have been described as 'things that are made for amusement' (*Bliss* v *Lilley* (1862) 32 LJMC 3)).

1.14.5 Taking a Conveyance without Consent

OFFENCE: **Taking a Conveyance without the Owner's Consent—*Theft Act 1968, s. 12***
- Triable summarily • Six months' imprisonment and/or a fine

The Theft Act 1968, s. 12 states:

Subject to subsections (5) and (6) below, a person shall be guilty of an offence if, without having the consent of the owner or other lawful authority, he takes any conveyance for his own or another's use or, knowing that any conveyance has been taken without such authority, drives it or allows himself to be carried in or on it.

KEYNOTE

Taking a conveyance without consent (usually referred to as TWOC) is a summary only offence and as such there can be no 'attempt' (Criminal Attempts Act 1981, s. 1(1) and (4)).

As a summary offence, s. 12(1) proceedings are ordinarily subject to the time limit of six months from the day when the offence was committed (s. 127 of the Magistrates' Courts Act 1980). However, this restriction has caused significant problems in cases where the analysis of forensic evidence has been needed. As a result, the Vehicles (Crime) Act 2001 extended the time limit for s. 12(1) offences. Where there is a certificate setting out the date on which sufficient evidence came to the knowledge of the person responsible for commencing the prosecution, proceedings should be commenced within six months of the date specified. This is subject to the proviso that such proceedings shall not be commenced after the end of the period of three years beginning with the day on which the offence was committed.

Once a conveyance has been 'taken' it cannot be 'taken' again by the same person before it has been recovered (*DPP* v *Spriggs* [1994] RTR 1). However, where the original taker abandons the conveyance, it may be 'taken' again by a further defendant and the original taker may be responsible for further offences arising out of its use before it is recovered.

The person taking the conveyance must do so intentionally, i.e. not simply by moving it accidentally (*Blayney* v *Knight* (1974) 60 Cr App R 269).

1.14.5.1 Consent of the Owner

Any 'consent' given must be true consent if the defendant is to avoid liability.

This area of the law has been subject to some rather unusual decision-making in the courts, one of which relates to consent. Consent, even if obtained by a deception, is still a valid consent. *This will be the case unless the deception is one where identity is an issue.*

....

EXAMPLE

John Smith (who does not possess a driving licence) is walking along the street when he finds a driving licence in the name of Paul Grey. Smith takes the driving licence and visits a car hire company and asks to hire a car for a day. The assistant at the reception of the car hire company asks Smith for a driving licence and Smith produces the licence he found in the street (in the name of Paul Grey). The assistant photocopies the licence and asks for the fee of £100 which Smith pays. The assistant hands over a set of car keys and Smith drives away in the car (intending to return it later that day).

....

The above scenario *would not* represent an offence of TWOC; this is because the assistant has handed over a set of keys to Smith and consented to Smith taking the car. The relevant deception here relates to the possession of the driving licence, *not to the name on the driving licence*. The assistant would have handed over the keys to the car if the name on the driving licence was 'Bugs Bunny'; identity is not an issue (*Whittaker* v *Campbell* [1984] QB 318).

Where consent is obtained by misrepresentation as to the purpose or destination of the journey, that misrepresentation has been held not to negate the consent given. So where D falsely represented to the owner of a car that he needed to drive it from Bedlington to Alnwick to sign a contract and was given the vehicle by the owner, he did not commit the offence when he drove it to Burnley instead. Once again, identity is not an issue when such consent is given (*R* v *Peart* [1970] 2 QB 672).

If, after a lawful purpose had been fulfilled, the defendant does not return the car but drove it off on his own business, the offence is committed as the defendant is going beyond the limits of the consent that had been given by the owner (*R* v *Phipps* (1970) 54 Cr App R 300).

Going beyond the express or implied permission of the owner may negate consent (*Phipps*). This is often encountered when employees deviate substantially from an agreed route in their employer's vehicle or take the vehicle for a purpose entirely different from that permitted.

....

EXAMPLE

X delivers bread on an established and precise route in his employer's van. X decides to visit his friend who lives 50 miles away and diverts from the established route to do so.

....

This would constitute TWOC. X (the employee) has custody of the vehicle (that custody is known as control). When he substantially diverts from the delivery route he radically alters the purpose for which he was given the vehicle and can no longer be said to be in control of the vehicle for his employer's purposes and he 'takes' the vehicle. A minor deviation, for example if X were to visit his favourite café (150 metres off the established route) and then return to his delivery round would not amount to an offence as the vehicle is still substantially being used for the employer's purpose.

1.14.5.2 Lawful Authority

A police officer removing a vehicle which is obstructing traffic after an accident, council workers removing a vehicle parked in contravention of parking restrictions or an agent of a finance company repossessing a vehicle would be examples of such lawful authority.

1.14.5.3 Takes

You must show that the conveyance was moved. It does not matter by how little the conveyance is moved but simply starting the engine is not enough (*R v Bogacki* [1973] QB 832) nor is hiding in a car or doing anything else in it while it is stationary. A conveyance is taken even if it is put onto another vehicle to do so (*R v Pearce* [1973] Crim LR 321, where a rubber dinghy was put on the roof rack of a car and taken away).

1.14.5.4 Conveyance

The Theft Act 1968, s. 12(7) states:

(a) 'conveyance' means any conveyance constructed or adapted for the carriage of a person or persons whether by land, water or air, except that it does not include a conveyance constructed or adapted for use only under the control of a person not carried in or on it, and 'drive' shall be construed accordingly...

KEYNOTE

This definition includes cars, motor cycles, boats or aircraft. Pedal cycles are expressly excluded by virtue of s. 12(5) of the Act. The definition does not extend to hand carts or animals used as conveyances as neither are constructed or adapted for the carriage of persons.

1.14.5.5 For His Own or Another's Use

The conveyance must be taken for the taker's or someone else's ultimate use *as a conveyance*. So standing at the rear of a conveyance and pushing it around a corner to hide it as a practical joke satisfies the first part ('taking') but not the second 'for his own or another's use as a conveyance' (*R v Stokes* [1983] RTR 59). This is because although the defendants may have 'taken' the conveyance it did not 'convey' them because they were in it or on it and further, they did not take it so someone could ultimately use it as such. If the practical joker pushed the car round a corner in order for a friend to then get into it and start it out of earshot and drive it to a further location, the offence would be committed at the time of pushing the car (it is being 'taken' to be used as a conveyance in the future).

When a person got into a Land Rover that was blocking his path and released the handbrake, allowing the vehicle to coast for several metres, it was held that his actions satisfied both elements (*R v Bow* (1977) 64 Cr App R 54). This is because getting into (or onto) a conveyance and moving it necessarily amounts to *taking it for use as a conveyance*, therefore the motives of the defendant in doing so are irrelevant. In the rubber dinghy example (**see para. 1.14.5.3**) the dinghy was ultimately going to be used as a conveyance by someone in the future.

1.14.5.6 Allow to be Carried

The person who commits this offence *must know* that the conveyance has been taken without the consent of the owner or other lawful authority; 'suspecting' the conveyance has been taken would not be enough. Further, the conveyance must *actually move* when the person drives it or allows him/herself to be carried in or on it (the same as the 'take' element of the offence).

1.14.5.7 Defences

The Theft Act 1968, s. 12(6) states:

> (6) A person does not commit an offence under this section by anything done in the belief that he has lawful authority to do it or that he would have had the owner's consent if the owner knew of his doing it and the circumstances of it.

It is essential that this belief exists at the time of the taking. It is not enough if the owner says, later, that he would have consented had he known (*R* v *Ambler* [1979] RTR 217).

1.14.6 Aggravated Vehicle-Taking

OFFENCE: **Aggravated Vehicle-taking—*Theft Act 1968, s. 12A***
- Triable either way • If the accident under s. 12A(2)(b) caused death 14 years' imprisonment, otherwise two years' imprisonment and/or a fine on indictment
- Six months' imprisonment and/or a fine summarily

The Theft Act 1968, s. 12A states:

> (1) Subject to subsection (3) below, a person is guilty of aggravated taking of a vehicle if—
>   (a) he commits an offence under section 12(1) above (in this section referred to as a 'basic offence') in relation to a mechanically propelled vehicle; and
>   (b) it is proved that, at any time after the vehicle was unlawfully taken (whether by him or another) and before it was recovered, the vehicle was driven, or injury or damage was caused, in one or more of the circumstances set out in paragraphs (a) to (d) of subsection (2) below.
> (2) The circumstances referred to in subsection (1)(b) above are—
>   (a) that the vehicle was driven dangerously on a road or other public place;
>   (b) that, owing to the driving of the vehicle, an accident occurred by which injury was caused to any person;
>   (c) that, owing to the driving of the vehicle, an accident occurred by which damage was caused to any property, other than the vehicle;
>   (d) that damage was caused to the vehicle.

KEYNOTE

In addition to the above sentences, where a person is convicted of aggravated vehicle-taking, disqualification from driving (for a minimum of 12 months) is obligatory, endorsement of licence is obligatory and the penalty points which may be imposed for the offence are 3 to 11. The fact that the person concerned did not drive the vehicle at any particular time or at all is not a special reason to avoid obligatory disqualification (Road Traffic Offenders Act 1988, s. 34).

Before this offence is made out there must first of all be an offence under s. 12(1) which includes an offence of 'being carried', and the conveyance involved must be a 'mechanically propelled vehicle' (see *Road Policing*, chapter 3.1).

You need only prove that *one* of the consequential factors occurred before the vehicle was recovered (*Dawes* v *DPP* [1995] 1 Cr App R 65) namely that, between the vehicle being taken and its being recovered:

- it was driven dangerously on a road/public place;
- owing to the driving of it, an accident occurred by which injury was caused to anyone or damage was caused to any other property; or
- damage was caused to it.

Damage to the vehicle does not include damage caused by breaking into it in order to commit the 'basic offence'. This is because damage caused at this point will be caused before the vehicle has been 'taken' and so at that stage, the 'basic offence' will not have been carried out.

If the person taking the car disposes of it in a way that amounts to an intention permanently to deprive the owner of it, he/she may commit an offence of theft.

'Dangerous driving' will require the same proof as the substantive offence (see *Road Policing*, chapter 3.3). There is no need to show any lack of care in the driving of the vehicle to prove s. 12A(2)(b), (c) or (d) (*R v Marsh* [1997] 1 Cr App R 67). A vehicle will be 'recovered' once it has been restored to its owner or other lawful possession or custody (s. 12A(8)). This would include occasions where a vehicle has come into the possession of the police.

The word 'accident' for the purposes of the offence of aggravated vehicle taking gets its meaning from the context of that legislation. As such, s. 12A is intended to have regard to *the consequences of what occurred* and is not particularly concerned about the way in which those consequences came about. Therefore where a vehicle had been in motion and thereby caused the victim's death, the word 'accident' applied (*R v Branchflower* [2004] EWCA Crim 2042).

1.14.6.1 Defence to Aggravated Vehicle Taking

The Theft Act 1968, s. 12A(3) states:

> A person is not guilty of an offence under this section if he proves that, as regards any such proven driving, injury or damage as is referred to in subsection (1)(b) above, either—
> (a) the driving, accident or damage referred to in subsection (2) above occurred before he committed the basic offence; or
> (b) he was neither in nor on nor in the immediate vicinity of the vehicle when that driving, accident or damage occurred.

KEYNOTE

'Immediate vicinity' is not defined but will be a question of fact for the jury/magistrate(s) to determine in each case.

1.14.7 Pedal Cycles

It is a separate summary offence (punishable with a fine) for a person, without having the consent of the owner or other lawful authority, to take a pedal cycle for his/her own or another's use, or to ride a pedal cycle knowing it to have been taken without such authority (Theft Act 1968, s. 12(5)). The defence under s. 12(6) also applies to pedal cycles.

1.14.8 Interfering with Vehicles

OFFENCE: **Interfering with Vehicles—*Criminal Attempts Act 1981, s. 9***
• Triable summarily • Three months' imprisonment and/or a fine

The Criminal Attempts Act 1981, s. 9 states:

> (1) A person is guilty of the offence of vehicle interference if he interferes with a motor vehicle or trailer or with anything carried in or on a motor vehicle or trailer with the intention that an offence specified in subsection (2) below shall be committed by himself or some other person.
> (2) The offences mentioned in subsection (1) above are—
> (a) theft of the motor vehicle or trailer or part of it;
> (b) theft of anything carried in or on the motor vehicle or trailer; and

(c) an offence under section 12(1) of the Theft Act 1968 (taking and driving away without consent);

and, if it is shown that a person accused of an offence under this section intended that one of those offences should be committed, it is immaterial that it cannot be shown which it was.

(3)–(4) …

(5) In this section 'motor vehicle' and 'trailer' have the meanings assigned to them by section 185(1) of the Road Traffic Act 1988.

KEYNOTE

The term 'interference' is not defined.

This offence is one of specific intent and you must prove that the defendant interfered with the vehicle, etc. with one of the intentions listed (note, however, that it is not necessary to show which *particular* intention).

For the definitions of motor vehicle and trailer, see *Road Policing*, chapter 3.1.

The above offence is a specified offence for the purposes of the Vehicles (Crime) Act 2001, s. 3(4)(b) (as to which, see *Road Policing*).

1.14.9 Going Equipped

OFFENCE: **Going Equipped for Stealing etc.—*Theft Act 1968, s. 25***

• Triable either way • Three years' imprisonment on indictment • Six months' imprisonment and/or a fine summarily

The Theft Act 1968, s. 25 states:

(1) A person shall be guilty of an offence if, when not at his place of abode, he has with him any article for use in the course of or in connection with any burglary or theft.

KEYNOTE

The power of search under s. 1 of the Police and Criminal Evidence Act 1984 applies to this offence (see *General Police Duties*, chapter 4.6).

A person's place of abode means where he/she resides; it does not include his/her place of business (unless, presumably, they are one and the same place) (*R v Bundy* [1977] 1 WLR 914). If a person lives in a vehicle then that vehicle will be regarded only as his/her 'place of abode' if it is parked at the place where the person 'abides' or intends to 'abide' (*Bundy*). Therefore, if a person is found in his/her vehicle away from such a site and at the time has with him/her articles as described under s. 25, this offence is committed.

'Has with him' is a narrower requirement than 'possession' and, as with aggravated burglary generally means that defendants must have the article within their immediate control. It would suffice if defendants had the article within their immediate control in their car or bag, at their workplace, or on their person.

You do not need to prove that persons having the article with them intended to use it themselves and it will be enough to show that they intended it to be used *by someone* for one of the purposes in s. 25(1) (*R v Ellames* [1974] 1 WLR 1391). Simply being a passenger in a car where such an article is found is not enough to prove the offence (*R v Lester* (1955) 39 Cr App R 157). The articles must be for some *future use*; it is not enough to show that the defendant had articles that *had been used* in the course of, or in connection with, one of the proscribed offences.

If you can prove that the article was made, adapted or intended for burglary or theft, that fact will be evidence that the person had it with him/her for that purpose (s. 25(3)).

The offence is directed against acts preparatory to the offences of burglary (contrary to s. 9 of the Theft Act 1968), theft (contrary to s. 1 of the Theft Act 1968) and taking a conveyance (contrary to s. 12 of the Theft Act 1968). 'Theft' includes theft with force which would amount to robbery.

'Article' can mean almost any physical object, such as a bunch of skeleton keys (*R v Metcalfe* [1971] Crim LR 112) or a torch and screwdriver (*R v Harrison* [1970] Crim LR 415). The indictment in *Ellames* referred to a 'sawn-off shotgun, a wig, three woollen hats, two masks, a pair of goggles, a boiler suit, a motor vehicle, two containers and a quantity of ammonia, gloves and shot-gun cartridges'. 'Article' would appear not to include *animate* objects, e.g. a trained monkey (*Daly* v *Cannon* [1954] 1 WLR 261).

1.14.10 Robbery

OFFENCE: **Robbery—*Theft Act 1968, s. 8***
- Triable on indictment • Life imprisonment

The Theft Act 1968, s. 8 states:

(1) A person is guilty of robbery if he steals, and immediately before or at the time of doing so, and in order to do so, he uses force on any person or puts or seeks to put any person in fear of being then and there subjected to force.

KEYNOTE

The Theft Element of the Offence

For there to be a robbery, there must be a theft; so if there is no theft, then there can be no robbery. The word 'steal' in the offence relates to the offence under s. 1 of the Theft Act 1968 and, therefore, if *any* element of theft cannot be proved the offence of robbery will not be made out. For example, in *R* v *Robinson* [1977] Crim LR 173, D, who was owed £7 by P's wife, approached P, brandishing a knife. A fight followed, during which P dropped a £5 note. D picked it up and demanded the remaining £2 owed to him. Allowing D's appeal against a conviction for robbery, the Court of Appeal held that the prosecution had to prove that D was guilty of theft, and that he would not be (under the Theft Act 1968, s. 2(1)(a)) if he believed that he had a right In law to deprive P of the money, even though he knew that he was not entitled to use the knife to get it, i.e. there was no dishonesty (but see para. 1.14.11 for blackmail).

The Robbery Time Frame

Section 8(1) requires that the force must be used or the threat made 'immediately before or at the time' of the theft. There is no guidance as to what 'immediately before' means. Clearly, if the force used or threatened is *after* the offence of theft has taken place, there will be no robbery; however theft can be a continuing offence. This was decided in *R* v *Hale* (1979) 68 Cr App Rep 415, where the Court of Appeal stated that appropriation is a continuing act and whether it has finished or not is a matter for the jury to decide. From the robbery perspective, *Hale* decides that where D had assumed ownership of goods in a house, the 'time' of stealing is a continuing process. It does not end as soon as the property is picked up by the defendant and can be a continuing act so long as he/she is in the course of removing it from the premises. So, if D uses or threatens force to get away with the property (while still in the house for example), a robbery is committed. This would not be the case if the defendant used force outside the house as there must come a time when the appropriation ends. The issue may be resolved by asking the question, 'Was D still on the job?' (*R* v *Atakpu* [1994] QB 69).

In Order to Do So

The use or threat of force must be 'in order' to carry out the theft. Force used in any other context means the offence is not committed, for example:

- Two men are fighting outside a pub. One man punches the other in the face and the force of the blow knocks the man out. As the injured man falls to the floor, his wallet drops out of his jacket pocket and onto the pavement. His opponent decides that he will steal the wallet. *No robbery is committed in these circumstances because the force is used for a purpose other than to steal.*

The question to ask in such circumstances is 'Why has the force been used and/or threatened?' If the answer is anything other than 'To enable the defendant to commit theft' then there is no offence of robbery.

Force

A small amount of force used in order to accomplish a theft may change that theft into a robbery. For example in *R* v *Dawson* (1977) 64 Cr App R 170, the defendant and two others surrounded their victim. One of the attackers 'nudged' the victim and while he was unbalanced another stole his wallet. In *Dawson*, the court declined to define 'force' any further than to say that juries would understand it readily enough. In line with general principles of *actus reus* (criminal conduct), the force used by the defendant must be used voluntarily. Therefore, the accidental use of force such as when a pickpocket, in the process of stealing a wallet from his victim on a train, is pushed into his victim by the train jolting on the railway line would not be a robbery.

On Any Person

The force used to accomplish a robbery need not be used against the owner or possessor of the property. For example, a gang of armed criminals use force against a security guard in order to overpower him and steal cash from the bank he is standing outside and guarding.

Use of Force on Property

Force does not actually have to be used 'on' the *person,* i.e. on the actual body of the victim. It may be used indirectly, for example on something that the victim is carrying and thereby transferring the force to the person. This was the case in *R* v *Clouden* [1987] Crim LR 65, where the Court of Appeal dismissed an appeal against a conviction for robbery when the defendant had wrenched the victim's shopping basket from her hand and ran off with it. However, in *P* v *DPP* [2012] EWHC 1657 (Admin), it was held that snatching a cigarette from the hand of the victim was incapable of amounting to robbery. Mitting J stated 'It cannot be said that the minimum use of force required to remove a cigarette from between the fingers suffices to amount to the use of force against that person'. In this case there was no evidence of direct physical contact between the victim and the thief.

The Fear of Force

Where only the *threat* of force is involved the intention must be to put a person in fear for *him/herself,* an intention to put someone in fear for *another* is not enough (*R* v *Taylor* [1996] 10 Archbold News 2). This may seem at odds with the approach to the actual *use* of force in the offence of robbery (in that force *can* be used against a third party who is unconnected with the property subject to the theft). For example:

- A man enters a betting shop and approaches the cashier. Without saying a word he passes a note to the cashier that simply says, 'Look to your left'. The cashier looks and sees the man's accomplice standing several feet away and pointing a knife at the back of one of the shop customers. The customer is oblivious to the actions of the man's accomplice. The man passes a second note to the cashier that says, 'Give me the money in the till or else he gets it!' The cashier, fearing for the customer, hands over the contents of the betting shop till. *This is not robbery as the cashier cannot fear force for the betting shop customer. However, whilst there is no robbery there would be an offence of blackmail* (Theft Act 1968, s. 21). Let us say that instead of handing the contents of the betting shop till over to the offender, the cashier shakes her head and refuses to hand over any money. At this point, the man signals to his accomplice who pulls the customer's head backwards and drags the knife across the side of the customer's throat causing a small cut. The customer screams in terror and at this point the cashier concedes to the man's demand and hands over the till contents. *At this point in time a robbery is committed as force is actually being used (albeit on a third party).*

General Points

Any threats to use force at some time in the future (even by a matter of minutes) would constitute an offence of blackmail. Threats to use force at some place other than the location of the offence fall into the same category. This effectively excludes threats made via the telephone in all but the most improbable of situations.

1.14.11   Blackmail

OFFENCE: **Blackmail—*Theft Act 1968, s. 21***

- Triable on indictment
- 14 years' imprisonment

The Theft Act 1968, s. 21 states:

(1) A person is guilty of blackmail if, with a view to gain for himself or another or with intent to cause loss to another, he makes any unwarranted demand with menaces; and for this purpose a demand with menaces is unwarranted unless the person making it does so in the belief—

  (a) that he has reasonable grounds for making the demand; and

  (b) that the use of the menaces is a proper means of reinforcing the demand.

(2) The nature of the act or omission demanded is immaterial, and it is also immaterial whether the menaces relate to action to be taken by the person making the demand.

KEYNOTE

The phrase 'with a view to' has been held (albeit under a different criminal statute) by the Court of Appeal to be less than 'with intent to' (*R* v *Zaman* [2002] EWCA Crim 1862). In *Zaman*, the court accepted that 'with a view to' simply that the defendant had something in his contemplation as *something that realistically might occur*, not that he necessarily intended or even wanted it to happen. Clearly this is a very different test from 'intent'. In the above offence then, it appears that the state of mind needed to prove the first element is that the defendant contemplated some gain for himself or for another as being realistically likely to flow from his actions. The alternative is an 'intent' to cause loss.

There is no requirement for dishonesty or theft and the offence is aimed at the making of the demands rather than the consequences of them.

1.14.11.1   Meaning of Gain and Loss

Section 34 of the 1968 Act states:

(2) For the purposes of this Act—

  (a) 'gain' and 'loss' are to be construed as extending only to gain or loss in money or other property, but as extending to any such gain or loss whether temporary or permanent; and—

   (i) 'gain' includes a gain by keeping what one has, as well as a gain by getting what one has not; and

   (ii) 'loss' includes a loss by not getting what one might get, as well as a loss by parting with what one has; . . .

KEYNOTE

Keeping what you already have can amount to a 'gain'. Similarly, not getting something that you might expect to get can be a 'loss'.

For example, a person makes unwarranted demands with menaces with a view to getting a sports fixture cancelled and avoid losing money that he/she has bet on the outcome of that fixture. Here the intention of keeping what the defendant already had (the money at risk on the bet) amounts to 'gain' as defined under s. 34(2). Similarly, the intention of preventing others getting what they might have got (their winnings or the club's earnings) could amount to a 'loss'.

A blackmailer need not be seeking any kind of material profit. In *R* v *Bevans* (1988) 87 Cr App R 64, D used menaces in order to obtain a pain-killing injection from a doctor; this was held to be blackmail as the drug involved was a form of property.

Note that a demand for sexual favours would not constitute an offence of blackmail as those sexual favours are not 'money or other property'.

1.14.11.2 Criminal Conduct

The offence of blackmail is complete when the demand with menaces is made. As a result it is extremely difficult, if not impossible, to have an offence of attempted blackmail as the defendant will either be preparing to make the demand or will have made it. It does not matter whether the demands bring about the desired consequences or not. If a demand is made by letter, the act of making it is complete when the letter is posted. The letter does not have to be received (*Treacy* v *DPP* [1971] AC 537).

The Court of Appeal has held that words or conduct which would not intimidate or influence anyone to respond to the demand would not be 'menaces'. As such, the term requires threats and conduct of such a nature and extent that a person of normal stability and courage might be influenced or made apprehensive so as to give in to the demands (*R* v *Clear* [1968] 1 QB 670).

Menaces will therefore include threats but these must be significant *to the victim*. If a threat bears a particular significance for a victim (such as being locked in the boot of a car to someone who is claustrophobic) that will be enough, provided the defendant was aware of that fact. If a victim is particularly timid and the defendant knows it, that timidity may be taken into account when assessing whether or not the defendant's conduct was 'menacing' (*R* v *Garwood* [1987] 1 WLR 319).

In the converse situation, where an apparently serious threat fails to intimidate the victim at all, the offence is still committed. For example, if X approaches Y and threatens to break Y's legs unless Y gives X £50 but Y is unconcerned by the threat, this would still constitute blackmail as a threat to break someone's legs would influence a person of normal stability and courage.

1.14.11.3 Unwarranted?

If a defendant raises the issue that his/her demand was reasonable and proper, you will have to prove that he/she did not genuinely believe:

- that he/she had reasonable grounds for making the demand; and
- that the use of the particular menaces employed was not a proper means of reinforcing it.

The defendant's *belief* will be subjective and therefore could be entirely unreasonable. However, if the threatened action would itself be unlawful (such as a threat to rape the victim) then it is unlikely that the courts would accept any claim by a defendant that he/she believed such a demand to be 'proper' (*R* v *Harvey* (1981) 72 Cr App R 139).

1.14.12 Abstracting Electricity

OFFENCE: **Abstracting Electricity—*Theft Act 1968, s. 13***
- Triable either way • Five years' imprisonment on indictment • Six months' imprisonment and/or a fine summarily

The Theft Act 1968, s. 13 states:

A person who dishonestly uses without due authority, or dishonestly causes to be wasted or diverted, any electricity shall be guilty of an offence.

KEYNOTE

As electricity is not 'property' (for the purpose of theft), this offence was created to deal with its dishonest use, waste or diversion. As electricity cannot be 'stolen', its dishonest use or wastage cannot form an element of burglary. Diverting a domestic electrical supply so as to bypass the meter, using another's telephone without authority (*Low* v *Blease* [1975] Crim LR 513) or unauthorised surfing on the Internet by an employee at work are examples of the offence (provided in each case that dishonesty was present).

1.14.13 Advertising Rewards

OFFENCE: **Advertising a Reward—*Theft Act 1968, s. 23***
> • Triable summarily • Fine

The Theft Act 1968, s. 23 states:

> Where any public advertisement of a reward for the return of any goods which have been stolen or lost uses any words to the effect that no questions will be asked, or that the person producing the goods will be safe from apprehension or inquiry, or that any money paid for the purchase of the goods or advanced by way of loan on them will be repaid, the person advertising the reward and any person who prints or publishes the advertisement shall [commit an offence].

KEYNOTE

This offence applies to the person advertising such a reward and the person/company who prints/publishes that advertisement. This second aspect attracts 'strict liability', in that there is no need to demonstrate any particular *mens rea* on the part of the printer/publisher (*Denham* v *Scott* (1983) 77 Cr App R 210). The important features are the fact that no questions will be asked or that the person will be given some form of 'immunity' from arrest or investigation. There is no mention of any promise of immunity from prosecution or civil claim.

So advertising a reward in a newspaper for a lost cat taking the form '£50 reward for finding "Mr Tibbs" lost in Smith Street' is not an offence. The same advert including a phrase 'No questions asked on return' *would be* an offence. It is not an offence to advertise a reward but it is *in combination with* the addition to the advert that any person returning the goods will be safe from apprehension etc.

1.14.14 Making Off without Payment

OFFENCE: **Making Off without Payment—*Theft Act 1978, s. 3***
> • Triable either way • Two years' imprisonment on indictment • Six months' imprisonment and/or a fine summarily

The Theft Act 1978, s. 3 states:

> (1) Subject to subsection (3) below, a person who, knowing that payment on the spot for any goods supplied or service done is required or expected from him, dishonestly makes off without having paid as required or expected and with intent to avoid payment of the amount due shall be guilty of an offence.
> (2) For purposes of this section 'payment on the spot' includes payment at the time of collecting goods on which work has been done or in respect of which service has been provided.
> (3) Subsection (1) above shall not apply where the supply of the goods or the doing of the service is contrary to law, or where the service done is such that payment is not legally enforceable.

KEYNOTE

This offence is often committed by motorists who drive off without paying for petrol, diners who run off after a meal and 'punters' who jump out of taxi cabs (*DPP* v *Ray* [1974] AC 370; *Edwards* v *Ddin* [1976] 1 WLR 942; *R* v *Brooks* (1983) 76 Cr App R 66). Some problems can arise in cases of alleged theft where the ownership in the property has passed to the defendant before the act of appropriation; this offence offers a solution to some such cases.

Occasions where the supply of goods or services is contrary to law or is not legally enforceable, e.g. prostitution, are excluded (s. 3(3)). Making off without payment after the provision of an unlawful service, or one for which payment is not legally enforceable would not then be caught by s. 3. If there is doubt as to whether the defendant has actually 'made off' from the spot then he/she can be charged with attempting the offence.

There must be an intention to *avoid* payment; delaying payment due or making someone wait for payment is not enough. In *R* v *Vincent* [2001] 1172 EWCA Crim 295, the Court of Appeal acknowledged a 'loophole' in s. 3. This loophole might be illustrated as follows:

- A person checks into an hotel and runs up a bill.
- The person deceives the proprietor into agreeing that the bill will be settled at some later date (as opposed to on departure).
- Having gained that agreement, the person checks out of the hotel and never makes any payment.

In such a situation, there was no longer an expectation of payment at the time when the person checked out of the hotel. This expectation had been removed by the agreement; the fact that the agreement had been obtained dishonestly did not reinstate the expectation of payment on departure. The offence under s. 3 is a simple and straightforward one which applies to a limited set of circumstances only (which were not covered by the above facts). The limited scope of this offence would suggest that alternative charges of theft and/or fraud should be considered.

If the person driving or running away from the garage, restaurant, taxi cab, etc. does so because he/she feels aggrieved at the service received or is in dispute with the supplier, then the question of fraud should be considered against the standards of ordinary, honest people (per *R* v *Ghosh* [1982] QB 1053).

1.14.15 Retaining a Wrongful Credit

OFFENCE: **Dishonestly Retaining a Wrongful Credit—*Theft Act 1968, s. 24A***
- Triable either way • 10 years' imprisonment on indictment • Six months' imprisonment and/or a fine summarily

The Theft Act 1968, s. 24A states:

(1) A person is guilty of an offence if—
    (a) a wrongful credit has been made to an account kept by him or in respect of which he has any right or interest;
    (b) he knows or believes that the credit is wrongful; and
    (c) he dishonestly fails to take such steps as are reasonable in the circumstances to secure that the credit is cancelled.
(2) References to a credit are to a credit of an amount of money.
(2A) A credit to an account is wrongful to the extent that it derives from—
    (a) theft;
    (b) blackmail;
    (c) fraud (contrary to section 1 of the Fraud Act 2006); or
    (d) stolen goods.
    (subsections (3) and (4) repealed by the Fraud Act 2006)
    ...
(5) In determining whether a credit to an account is wrongful, it is immaterial (in particular) whether the account is overdrawn before or after the credit is made.
(6) ...
(7) Subsection (8) below applies for purposes of provisions of this Act relating to stolen goods (including subsection (2A) above).
(8) References to stolen goods include money which is dishonestly withdrawn from an account to which a wrongful credit has been made, but only to the extent that the money derives from the credit.

(9) 'Account' means an account kept with—

(a) a bank;

(b) a person carrying on a business which falls within subsection (10) below; or

(c) a person falling within any of paragraphs (a) to (j) of the definition of 'electronic money issuer' in regulation 2(1) of the Electric Money Regulations 2011.

(10) A business falls within this subsection if—

(a) in the course of the business money received by way of deposit is lent to others; or

(b) any other activity of the business is financed, wholly or to any material extent, out of the capital of or the interest on any money received by way of deposit.

(11) References in subsection (10) above to a deposit must be read with—

(a) section 22 of the Financial Services and Markets Act 2000;

(b) any relevant order under that section; and

(c) Schedule 2 of that Act;

but any restriction on the meaning of deposit which arises from the identity of the person making it, is to be disregarded.

(12) For the purposes of subsection (10) above—

(a) all the activities which a person carries on by way of business shall be regarded as a single business carried on by him; and

(b) 'money' includes money expressed in a currency other than sterling.

KEYNOTE

The wrongful credit to an account can occur in two ways: it may come from the circumstances outlined under s. 1 of the Fraud Act 2006 or it may come from one of the dishonest sources set out in s. 24A(2A).

These offences will generally be restricted to transactions involving the crediting of accounts held with financial institutions.

There is a requirement for dishonesty (in the *Ghosh* sense, **see para. 1.14.2.3**). However, there is no requirement for any *deception*.

The effects of s. 24A(8) are that *money* derived from credit received under s. 24A of the Theft Act 1968 may amount to stolen goods.

- -

EXAMPLE

- If the proceeds of a theft by A are paid into his/her bank account they are stolen goods because they represent the stolen goods in the hands of the thief (s. 24(4)).

- If they are then transferred into B's bank account, they cease to be stolen goods. This is because the 'thing in action' (the credit balance) created by the transfer in B's name is a different 'thing in action' from the one originally created by A (*R* v *Preddy* [1996] AC 815).

- As such, the credit balance in B's name has never represented the proceeds of the theft *in the hands of the thief*.

- But if B retains the wrongful credit made to his/her account then he/she commits the s. 24A offence if he/she dishonestly retains it, knowing or believing it to be derived from one or other of those offences.

- If B withdraws money from the credited account, that money then, by virtue of s. 24A(8), becomes stolen goods once more.

- -

This offence is also unusual in that the *actus reus* not only *can be* satisfied by an 'omission', but necessarily *involves* an omission or a failure to act (i.e. retaining something does not involve a positive act).

1.14.16 Re-programming Mobile Phones

OFFENCE: **Re-programming Mobile Phones—*Mobile Telephones (Re-programming) Act 2002, s. 1***

- Triable either way • Five years' imprisonment on indictment • Six months' imprisonment and/or a fine summarily

The Mobile Telephones (Re-programming) Act 2002, s. 1 states:

(1) A person commits an offence if—
  (a) he changes a unique device identifier,
  (b) he interferes with the operation of a unique device identifier,
  (c) he offers or agrees to change, or interfere with the operation of, a unique device identifier, or
  (d) he offers or agrees to arrange for another person to change, or interfere with the operation of, a unique device identifier.
(2) A unique device identifier is an electronic equipment identifier which is unique to a mobile wireless communications device.
(3) But a person does not commit an offence under this section if—
  (a) he is the manufacturer of the device, or
  (b) he does the act mentioned in subsection (1) with the written consent of the manufacturer of the device.

KEYNOTE

The unique device identifier is currently the International Mobile Equipment Identity (IMEI) number which identifies the handset of a mobile phone. It can be found on most mobile phones either behind the battery or by keying in the number *#06#. The wording of the section allows for future development of mobile phones which may use different equipment identifiers. Changing the unique identifier, adding a chip or otherwise interfering with that identifier is an offence.

It is the view of the Home Office that the international Global System for Mobiles (GSM) standards make it unnecessary for anyone other than a manufacturer or its agent to alter an IMEI number. For that reason, s. 1(3) creates a statutory defence for manufacturers or people with the *written* consent of the manufacturer.

1.14.16.1   Having or Supplying Anything to Facilitate Re-programming

OFFENCE: **Having or Supplying Anything for Re-programming Mobile Phones—**
Mobile Telephones (Re-programming) Act 2002, s. 2
  • Triable either way • Five years' imprisonment on indictment • Six months' imprisonment and/or a fine summarily

The Mobile Telephones (Re-programming) Act 2002, s. 2 states:

(1) A person commits an offence if—
  (a) he has in his custody or under his control anything which may be used for the purpose of changing or interfering with the operation of a unique device identifier, and
  (b) he intends to use the thing unlawfully for that purpose or to allow it to be used unlawfully for that purpose.
(2) A person commits an offence if—
  (a) he supplies anything which may be used for the purpose of changing or interfering with the operation of a unique device identifier, and
  (b) he knows or believes that the person to whom the thing is supplied intends to use it unlawfully for that purpose or to allow it to be used unlawfully for that purpose.
(3) A person commits an offence if—
  (a) he offers to supply anything which may be used for the purpose of changing or interfering with the operation of a unique device identifier, and
  (b) he knows or believes that the person to whom the thing is offered intends if it is supplied to him to use it unlawfully for that purpose or to allow it to be used unlawfully for that purpose.

1.14.17 Handling Stolen Goods

OFFENCE: **Handling Stolen Goods—*Theft Act 1968, s. 22***

> • Triable either way • 14 years' imprisonment on indictment • Six months' imprisonment and/or a fine summarily

The Theft Act 1968, s. 22 states:

(1) A person handles stolen goods if (otherwise than in the course of the stealing) knowing or believing them to be stolen goods he dishonestly receives the goods, or dishonestly undertakes or assists in their retention, removal, disposal or realisation by or for the benefit of another person, or if he arranges to do so.

1.14.17.1 'Goods' and 'Stolen Goods'

Goods

The Theft Act 1968, s. 34(2)(b) states:

> 'Goods', except insofar as the context otherwise requires, includes money and every other description of property except land, and includes things severed from the land by stealing.

Stolen Goods

The Theft Act 1968, s. 24 states:

(1) The provisions of this Act relating to goods which have been stolen shall apply whether the stealing occurred in England or Wales or elsewhere, and whether it occurred before or after the commencement of this Act, provided that the stealing (if not an offence under this Act) amounted to an offence where and at the time when the goods were stolen; and references to stolen goods shall be construed accordingly.

(2) For purposes of those provisions references to stolen goods shall include, in addition to the goods originally stolen and parts of them (whether in their original state or not),—

(a) any other goods which directly or indirectly represent or have at any time represented the stolen goods in the hands of the thief as being the proceeds of any disposal or realisation of the whole or part of the goods stolen or of goods representing the stolen goods; and

(b) any other goods which directly or indirectly represent or have at any time represented the stolen goods in the hands of a handler of the stolen goods or any part of them as being the proceeds of any disposal or realisation of the whole or part of the stolen goods handled by him or of goods so representing them.

(3) But no goods shall be regarded as having continued to be stolen goods after they have been restored to the person from whom they were stolen or to other lawful possession or custody, or after that person and any other person claiming through him have otherwise ceased as regards those goods to have any right to restitution in respect of the theft.

(4) For purposes of the provisions of this Act relating to goods which have been stolen (including subsections (1) to (3) above) goods obtained in England or Wales or elsewhere either by blackmail or subject to subsection (5) below, by fraud (within the meaning of the Fraud Act 2006) shall be regarded as stolen; and 'steal', 'theft' and 'thief' shall be construed accordingly.

(5) Subsection (1) above applies in relation to goods obtained by fraud as if—

(a) the reference to the commencement of this Act were a reference to the commencement of the Fraud Act 2006, and

(b) the reference to an offence under this Act were a reference to an offence under section 1 of that Act.

The Theft Act 1968, s. 24A states:

(7) Subsection (8) below applies for purposes of provisions of this Act relating to stolen goods (including subsection (4) above).

(8) References to stolen goods include money which is dishonestly withdrawn from an account to which a wrongful credit has been made, but only to the extent that the money derives from the credit.

KEYNOTE

If goods are not stolen there is no handling. Whether they are so stolen is a question of fact for a jury or magistrate(s).

If the property in question appears to represent the proceeds of an offence that falls outside the scope of s. 24 or s. 24A(8), it may be possible to consider charges under the 'money laundering' provisions (see para. 1.14.19).

Goods obtained by fraud and blackmail are included in the definition of 'stolen goods' under s. 24(4) and (5). The references to fraud are to the general offence of fraud under s. 1 of the Fraud Act 2006. Goods gained through robbery or burglary will be 'stolen' as theft is an intrinsic element of both offences.

'Wrongful credits' are included within the meaning of stolen goods under certain circumstances and were dealt with earlier in this chapter (see para. 1.14.15).

1.14.17.2 Section 24 Explained

Under s. 24(1) a person can still be convicted of handling if the goods were stolen outside England and Wales but only if the goods were taken under circumstances which amounted to an offence in the other country.

Under s. 24(2), goods will be classed as stolen only if they are the property which was originally stolen or if they have at some time represented the *proceeds* of that property in the hands of the thief or a 'handler'.

Therefore if an iPhone is stolen, and sold to an unsuspecting party who then part-exchanges it for a new one at a high street retailer, the first iPhone will be 'stolen' goods, the new one will not. If the first person buying the original iPhone *knew* or *believed* that it was stolen, the new iPhone will be treated as stolen goods.

Under s. 24(3), once goods have been restored to lawful possession they cease to be stolen. This situation does not cause problems when police officers recover stolen property and then wait for it to be collected by a handler (*Houghton* v *Smith* [1975] AC 476) as the Criminal Attempts Act 1981 and the common-law rulings on 'impossibility' **(see chapter 1.3)** mean that a defendant could be dealt with in a variety of ways:

- Theft—collecting the property will be an 'appropriation'.
- Handling—an *arrangement* to come and collect stolen goods will probably have been made while they were still 'stolen'.
- Criminal attempt—the person collecting the goods has gone beyond merely preparing to handle them.

1.14.17.3 Proof that Goods were Stolen

The Theft Act 1968, s. 27 states:

(4) In any proceedings for the theft of anything in the course of transmission (whether by post or otherwise), or for handling stolen goods from such a theft, a statutory declaration made by any person that he dispatched or received or failed to receive any goods or postal packet, or that any goods or postal packet when dispatched or received by him were in a particular state or condition, shall be admissible as evidence of the facts stated in the declaration, subject to the following conditions:—

    (a) a statutory declaration shall only be admissible where and to the extent to which oral evidence to the like effect would have been admissible in the proceedings; and

    (b) a statutory declaration shall only be admissible if at least seven days before the hearing or trial a copy of it has been given to the person charged, and he has not, at least three days before the hearing or trial or within such further time as the court may in special circumstances allow, given the prosecutor written notice requiring the attendance at the hearing or trial of the person making the declaration.

KEYNOTE

Section 27(4) allows for evidence to be admitted proving that goods 'in the course of transmission' have been stolen. They allow for a statutory declaration by the person dispatching or receiving goods or postal packets as to when and where they were dispatched and when or if they arrived and, in each case, their state or condition (e.g. if they had been opened or interfered with). The declaration will only be admissible in circumstances where an oral statement would have been admissible *and* if a copy has been served on the defendant at least seven days before the hearing and he/she has not, within three days of the hearing, served written notice on the prosecutor requiring the attendance of the person making the declaration.

This section is to be construed in accordance with s. 24 generally (s. 27(5)).

1.14.17.4 Handling

The offence of handling stolen goods is made up of many facets. Therefore to charge a defendant without specifying a particular form of handling is not bad for duplicity (*R* v *Nicklin* [1977] 1 WLR 403). However, the offence can be divided for practical purposes into two parts:

- *receiving/arranging to receive* stolen goods, in which case the defendant acts for his/her own benefit, and
- *assisting/acting for the benefit of another* person, in which case that assistance to another or benefit of another must be proved.

1.14.17.5 Receiving

Receiving does not require the physical reception of goods and can extend to exercising control over them. Things in action, such as bank credits from a stolen cheque, can be 'received'.

'Arranging to receive' would cover circumstances which do not go far enough to constitute an attempt, that is, actions which *are* merely preparatory to the receiving of stolen goods may satisfy the elements under s. 22 even though they would not meet the criteria under the Criminal Attempts Act 1981.

1.14.17.6 Assisting/Acting for Another's Benefit

Assisting or acting for the benefit of another can be committed by misleading police officers during a search (*R* v *Kanwar* [1982] 1 WLR 845).

Disposing of the stolen goods or assisting in their disposal or realisation usually involves physically moving them or converting them into a different form (*R* v *Forsyth* [1997] 2 Cr App R 299).

If the only person 'benefiting' from the defendant's actions is the defendant, this element of the offence will not be made out (*R* v *Bloxham* [1983] 1 AC 109). Similarly, if the only 'other' person to benefit is a co-accused on the same charge, the offence will not be made out (*R* v *Gingell* [2000] 1 Cr App R 88).

1.14.17.7 Power to Search for Stolen Goods

The Theft Act 1968, s. 26 states:

(1) If it is made to appear by information on oath before a justice of the peace that there is reasonable cause to believe that any person has in his custody or possession or on his premises any stolen goods, the justice may grant a warrant to search for and seize the same; but no warrant to search for stolen goods shall be addressed to a person other than a constable except under the authority of an enactment expressly so providing.

(2) ...

(3) Where under this section a person is authorised to search premises for stolen goods, he may enter and search the premises accordingly, and may seize any goods he believes to be stolen goods.

(4) ...

(5) This section is to be construed in accordance with section 24 of this Act; and in subsection (2) above the references to handling stolen goods shall include any corresponding offence committed before the commencement of this Act.

> **KEYNOTE**
>
> Section 26 provides a general power to search for and seize stolen goods, whether identified in the search warrant or not and magistrates are entitled to act on material provided by the police that gives rise to a reasonable belief that stolen goods will be found (*R Cruickshank Ltd* v *Chief Constable of Kent Constabulary* [2002] EWCA Civ 1840).

1.14.17.8 Guilty Knowledge in Cases of Handling and Theft

Section 27 of the Theft Act 1968 allows for the admissibility of previous misconduct and states:

(3) Where a person is being proceeded against for handling stolen goods (but not for any offence other than handling stolen goods), then at any stage of the proceedings, if evidence has been given of his having or arranging to have in his possession the goods the subject of the charge, or of his undertaking or assisting in, or arranging to undertake or assist in, their retention, removal, disposal or realisation, the following evidence shall be admissible for the purpose of proving that he knew or believed the goods to be stolen goods—

    (a) evidence that he has had in his possession, or has undertaken or assisted in the retention, removal, disposal or realisation of, stolen goods from any theft taking place not earlier than 12 months before the offence charged; and

    (b) (provided that seven days' notice in writing has been given to him of the intention to prove the conviction) evidence that he has within the five years preceding the date of the offence charged been convicted of theft or of handling stolen goods.

KEYNOTE

This provision applies to all forms of handling (*R* v *Ball* [1983] 1 WLR 801) but it can only be used where handling is the *only offence* involved in the proceedings.

What constitutes recent possession is a matter of fact and degree dependent on the circumstances of each case. This presumption can be rebutted by the person offering a true explanation for the possession (*R* v *Schama* (1914) 84 LJ KB 396, *R* v *Garth* [1949] 1 All ER 773, *R* v *Aves* [1950] 2 All ER 330 and *R* v *Williams* [1962] Crim LR 54).

'Recent possession' is not defined and so is a question of fact in each case. In *R* v *Smythe* (1981) 72 Cr App R 8, the Court of Appeal held that property found in the possession of an accused, stolen two or three months earlier during some robberies and burglaries, did not amount to recent possession for the offence of handling stolen goods generally.

1.14.18   Buying Scrap Metal for Cash

1.14.18.1   Offence of Buying Scrap Metal for Cash

Metal theft has a significant and sometimes disproportionate impact on industry and the wider community. The impact for the railway network can be particularly severe and is a major concern for Network Rail and the British Transport Police (BTP).

Dealing in stolen metal can of course be dealt with as handling stolen goods or via the Proceeds of Crime Act although the framework that regulates scrap metal dealers' operations contains an offence of buying scrap metal for cash.

OFFENCE: **Buying Scrap Metal for Cash—*Scrap Metal Dealers Act 2013***
      • Summary only • Fine

The Scrap Metal Dealers Act 2013, s. 12 states:

    (1) A scrap metal dealer must not pay for scrap metal except—

      (a) by a cheque which under section 81A of the Bills of Exchange Act 1882 is not transferable, or

      (b) by an electronic transfer of funds (authorised by credit or debit card or otherwise).

KEYNOTE

The Secretary of State may by order amend s.12(1) to permit other methods of payment (s. 12(2)).

'Paying' includes paying in kind (with goods or services) (s. 12(3)).

Section 12(4) states that if a scrap metal dealer pays for scrap metal in breach of subs. (1), each of the following is guilty of an offence:

    (a) the scrap metal dealer;

    (b) if the payment is made at a site, the site manager;

    (c) any person who makes the payment acting for the dealer.

Under s.12(5) it is a defence for a person within subs. (4)(a) or (b) who is charged with an offence under this section to prove that the person:

(a) made arrangements to ensure that the payment was not made in breach of subsection (1), and

(b) took all reasonable steps to ensure that those arrangements were complied with.

1.14.19 Proceeds of Crime

1.14.19.1 Proceeds of Crime Act 2002

The offences and powers under the Proceeds of Crime Act 2002 are connected with day to day criminality and are relevant to all police officers. This section provides an overview of the three principal offences relating to 'Money Laundering' created by s. 327 (concealing criminal property), s. 328 (arrangements in relation to criminal property) and s. 329 (acquisition, use and possession of criminal property) of the Act. To begin with we examine the concepts of 'criminal conduct' and 'criminal property'.

1.14.19.2 Criminal Conduct

The Proceeds of Crime Act 2002, s. 340 states:

(2) Criminal conduct is conduct which—
   (a) constitutes an offence in any part of the United Kingdom, or
   (b) would constitute an offence in any part of the United Kingdom if it occurred there.

Section 340(4) states that it is immaterial:

- who carried out the criminal conduct
- who benefited from it
- whether the conduct occurred before or after the passing of the Act.

So criminal conduct not only includes the behaviour of the defendant but also of any other person. Effectively this states that *any offence*, committed by *any person, anywhere* at all and at *any time* is 'criminal conduct'. As a consequence of s. 340, a conviction can be obtained under the Proceeds of Crime Act even if the prosecution cannot specify the offence or offences that gave rise to the proceeds or identify the person(s) responsible for the offence(s).

1.14.19.3 Criminal Property

The Proceeds of Crime Act 2002, s. 340 states:

(3) Property is criminal property if—
   (a) it constitutes a person's benefit from criminal conduct or it represents such a benefit (in whole or in part and whether directly or indirectly) and,
   (b) the alleged offender knows or suspects that it constitutes or represents such a benefit.

KEYNOTE

The offences under ss. 327, 328 and 329 are often referred to as 'money laundering'. Note that the definition of 'property' *does not just relate to money*. Section 340(9) of the Act defines property as *all* property *wherever* situated and includes:

- money
- all forms of property, real or personal, heritable or movable, and
- things in action and other intangible or incorporeal property.

(Incorporeal property relates to property or an asset that does not have value in material form, such as a right or a patent.)

The *mens rea* relating to criminal property and therefore to all three offences is knowing or *suspecting*. Dishonesty is not required. In *R* v *Da Silva* [2006] EWCA Crim 1654, it was said that:

to suspect something, you have to have a state of mind well short of knowing that the matter you suspect is true. It is an ordinary English word…the dictionary definition of 'suspicion' [is] an act of suspecting, the imagining of something without evidence or on slender evidence, inkling, mistrust.

The Court of Appeal upheld the conviction, concluding that the word 'suspect' meant that the defendant had to think that there was a possibility, which was more than fanciful, that the relevant facts existed. A vague feeling of unease would not suffice. The fact the suspicion alone will suffice means that proving such offences is remarkably less burdensome for the prosecution than the potential alternative to such offences, a charge of handling stolen goods where the defendant must be proved to know or believe that goods are stolen goods.

1.14.19.4 Concealing Criminal Property

OFFENCE: **Concealing Criminal Property—*Proceeds of Crime Act 2002, s. 327***
- Triable either way • 14 years' imprisonment on indictment and/or a fine
- Six months' imprisonment and/or a fine summarily

The Proceeds of Crime Act 2002, s. 327 states:

(1) A person commits an offence if he—
  (a) conceals criminal property;
  (b) disguises criminal property;
  (c) converts criminal property;
  (d) transfers criminal property;
  (e) removes criminal property from England and Wales and Scotland or from Northern Ireland.
(2) But a person does not commit such an offence if—
  (a) he makes an authorised disclosure under section 338 and (if the disclosure is made before he does the act mentioned in subsection (1)) he has the appropriate consent;
  (b) he intended to make such a disclosure but had a reasonable excuse for not doing so;
  (c) the act he does is done in carrying out a function he has relating to the enforcement of any provision of this Act or of any other enactment relating to criminal conduct or benefit from criminal conduct.
(3) Concealing or disguising criminal property includes concealing or disguising its nature, source, location, disposition, movement or ownership or any rights with respect to it.

KEYNOTE

There is an overlap between offences of concealing criminal property and handling stolen goods. However, whereas handling only occurs 'otherwise than in the course of stealing' and 'by or for the benefit of another', the offence under s. 327 can potentially be committed *during the commission of an offence* and *for the benefit of the thief*. On a literal reading of s. 327, a thief who conceals, disguises or sells property that he has just stolen may thereby commit offences under that section because the definition of criminal property applies to the laundering of an offender's own proceeds of crime as well as those of someone else.

The offence can be committed in a variety of ways. In *R* v *Fazal* [2010] 1 WLR 694, D allowed his bank account to be used by a friend to launder money, and it was held that he was guilty of converting criminal property (contrary to s. 327(1)(c)) whenever such monies were deposited in, retained in, or withdrawn from the account.

In *R* v *Pace* [2014] EWCA Crim 186 the Court of Appeal rejected the argument that, on a charge of attempting to commit the offence under s. 327(1)(c), it would be sufficient for the prosecution to prove that D merely suspected the property in question to be criminal property. Suspicion of this kind suffices for the substantive offence (as it does for all such offences under ss. 327 to 329) but it cannot, said the Court, suffice for an attempt.

Section 327(2) creates several defences to charges under s. 327.

1.14.19.5 Arrangements in relation to Criminal Property

OFFENCE: **Arrangements in relation to Criminal Property—*Proceeds of Crime Act 2002, s. 328***

- Triable either way • 14 years' imprisonment on indictment and/or a fine
- Six months' imprisonment and/or a fine summarily

The Proceeds of Crime Act 2002, s. 328 states:

(1) A person commits an offence if he enters into or becomes concerned in an arrangement which he knows or suspects facilitates (by whatever means) the acquisition, retention, use or control of criminal property by or on behalf of another person.

KEYNOTE

This offence will often be apt for the prosecution of those who launder on behalf of others. This could catch persons who work in financial or credit institutions, accountants etc., who in the course of their work facilitate money laundering by or on behalf of other persons and also family members (husband/wife, partner etc.). The natural and ordinary meaning of s. 328(1) was that the arrangement to which it referred must be one which related to property which was criminal property at the time when the arrangement began to operate on it. To say that it extended to property which was originally legitimate but became criminal only as a result of carrying out the arrangement was to stretch the language of the section beyond its proper limits (*R* v *Geary* (*Michael*) [2010] EWCA Crim 1925).

Section 328 includes the same defences against committing the offence, as are included in s. 327(2).

1.14.19.6 Acquisition, Use and Possession of Criminal Property

OFFENCE: **Acquisition, Use and Possession of Criminal Property—*Proceeds of Crime Act 2002, s. 329***

- Triable either way • 14 years' imprisonment on indictment and/or a fine
- Six months' imprisonment and/or a fine summarily

The Proceeds of Crime Act 2002, s. 329 states:

(1) A person commits an offence if he—
  (a) acquires criminal property;
  (b) uses criminal property;
  (c) has possession of criminal property.

KEYNOTE

A thief who uses or retains possession of property that he has just stolen (this being criminal property as defined in s. 340) must therefore be guilty of an offence under s. 329(1)(b) or (c), the maximum penalty for which is twice that for basic theft. It does not follow that such a charge would be appropriate.

This offence is committed where a person knows or suspects that the property which is acquired etc, constitutes or represents his own or another's benefit from criminal conduct; the same defences against committing the offence apply as in s. 327.

An additional defence exists under s. 329(2)(c) which states that a person will not commit the offence if he acquired or used or had possession of the property for adequate consideration (e.g. being paid a proper market price of £3,000 to fix a roof). The effect of the defence in s. 329(2)(c) is that persons, such as tradesmen, who are paid for ordinary consumable goods and services in money that comes from crime are not under any obligation to question the source of the money. However, the defence is not available to a defendant who provides goods or services knowing or suspecting that those goods or services will help a person *to actually carry out criminal conduct*.

The coincidence between an offence of handling stolen goods and those described from the Proceeds of Crime Act 2002 might provide a dilemma as to which offence to charge. In such a situation, CPS guidance states that if it is possible to charge money laundering or handling stolen goods then money laundering may be more appropriate if 'either a defendant has possessed criminal proceeds in large amounts or in lesser amounts, but repeatedly and where assets are laundered for profit'. However, a money laundering charge should only be considered where proceeds are more than *de minimis* (about minimal things) in any circumstances where the defendant who is charged with the underlying offence has done more than simply consume the proceeds of crime.

1.15 Fraud

1.15.1 Introduction

The Fraud Act 2006 provides a general offence of fraud which can be committed in three ways (by false representation, by failing to disclose information, and by abuse of position). It also deals with offences of obtaining services dishonestly, and possessing, making, and supplying articles for use in fraud. In addition to the offence of fraud, there is a series of closely-related offences which deal with falsification of documents or other 'instruments'.

1.15.2 Fraud

OFFENCE: **Fraud—Fraud Act 2006, s. 1**
- • Triable either way • 10 years' imprisonment and/or a fine on indictment
- • 12 months' imprisonment and/or a fine summarily

The Fraud Act 2006, s. 1 states:

(1) A person is guilty of fraud if he is in breach of any of the sections listed in subsection (2) (which provide for different ways of committing the offence).
(2) The sections are—
    (a) section 2 (fraud by false representation),
    (b) section 3 (fraud by failing to disclose information), and
    (c) section 4 (fraud by abuse of position).

KEYNOTE

The essence of these fraud offences is in the *conduct and ulterior intent* of the defendant. This means that a defendant's unsuccessful 'attempt' to commit the offence of fraud may amount to the commission of the substantive offence, effectively excluding the possibility of an offence under the Criminal Attempts Act 1981.

1.15.3 Gain and Loss

Fraud offences under ss. 2, 3 and 4 are all committed when the defendant carries out the *actus reus* of the offence intending to 'make a gain for himself or another' and/or 'to cause loss to another'. As the 'gain' and 'loss' elements are essential to these offences it is useful to examine their meaning before looking at the specific offences.

The Fraud Act 2006, s. 5 states:

(1) The references to gain and loss in sections 2 to 4 are to be read in accordance with this section.
(2) 'Gain' and 'loss'—
    (a) extend only to gain and loss in money or other property;
    (b) include any such gain or loss whether temporary or permanent;
    and 'property' means any property whether real or personal (including things in action and other intangible property).
(3) 'Gain' includes a gain by keeping what one has, as well as getting what one does not have.
(4) 'Loss' includes a loss by not getting what one might get, as well as a loss by parting with what one has.

1.15.4 Fraud by False Representation

The Fraud Act 2006, s. 2 states:

(1) A person is in breach of this section if he—
   (a) dishonestly makes a false representation, and
   (b) intends, by making the representation—
      (i) to make a gain for himself or another, or
      (ii) to cause loss to another or to expose another to the risk of loss.
(2) A representation is false if—
   (a) it is untrue or misleading, and
   (b) the person making it knows that it is, or might be, untrue or misleading.
(3) 'Representation' means any representation as to fact or law, including a representation as to the state of mind of—
   (a) the person making the representation, or
   (b) any other person.
(4) A representation may be express or implied.
(5) For the purposes of this section a representation may be regarded as made if it (or anything implying it) is submitted in any form to any system or device designed to receive, convey or respond to communications (with or without human intervention).

KEYNOTE

Dishonestly

'Dishonestly' in s. 2(1)(a) refers to the test of dishonesty established in *R* v *Ghosh* [1982] QB 1053 (**see chapter 1.14**). The same test applies to ss. 3 and 4 of the Act.

Representation

A representation is false if it is untrue or misleading *and* the person making it knows this is or knows this might be the case; an untrue statement made in the honest belief that it is in fact true, would not suffice. The words 'or might be' involve a subjective belief of the person making the representation. Where a defendant makes a false representation knowing that it is false or might be, the offence of fraud is complete.

The representation may be express or implied and can be communicated in words or conduct. There is no limitation on the way in which the representation must be expressed, so it could be written, spoken or posted on a website.

A representation may be implied by conduct. For example, a person dishonestly misusing a credit card to pay for items hands the card to a cashier without saying a word. By handing the card to the cashier the person is falsely representing that he has the authority to use it for that transaction. It is immaterial whether the cashier accepting the card for payment is deceived by the representation as the cashier's state of mind plays no part in the commission of the offence.

Any representation made must be one as to fact or law, so a broken promise is not in itself a false representation. However, a statement may be false if it misrepresents the current intentions or state of mind of the person making it or anyone else. For example, D visits V's house and tells V that he needs emergency work carried out on his roof. D states that he is in a position to do the work immediately but only if V pays him £1,000 there and then. V gives D the money and D then leaves without carrying out the work; the truth of the matter was that D had never intended to carry out the work. Such a 'promise' by D would amount to an offence as it involved a false representation, i.e. he never intended to keep the promise.

A representation may be *proved* by inference. Where an elderly person has paid D vastly more for a job or product (such as gardening work) than it was worth, it may be open to a court or jury to *infer* that D must dishonestly have misrepresented the value of that job or product, even if there is no direct evidence of any such misrepresentation (*R* v *Greig* [2010] EWCA Crim 1183). When an unidentified imposter presented himself to take a driving test in D's name, it could be inferred that D was complicit in any false representations made by that person with a view to gaining a pass certificate in his name (*Idrees* v *DPP* [2011] EWHC 624 (Admin)).

The offence is complete the moment the false representation is made. The representation need never be heard nor communicated to the recipient and if carried out by post, would be complete when the letter is posted (*Treacy* v *DPP* [1971] AC 537).

Phishing

The offence is committed by someone who engages in 'phishing'. This is the practice of sending out e-mails in bulk, usually purporting to represent a well-known brand in the hope of sending victims to a bogus website that tricks them into disclosing bank account details.

Machines

The offence of fraud applies to cases where the representation is made to a machine (for example where a person enters a number into a 'Chip and PIN' machine) (s. 2(5)).

1.15.5   Fraud by Failing to Disclose

The Fraud Act 2006, s. 3 states:

A person is in breach of this section if he—
(a) dishonestly fails to disclose to another person information which he is under a legal duty to disclose, and
(b) intends, by failing to disclose the information—
    (i) to make a gain for himself or another, or
    (ii) to cause loss to another or to expose another to a risk of loss.

KEYNOTE

Section 3 creates an offence of dishonestly failing to disclose information where there is a *legal duty* to do so. The term 'legal duty' has not been defined but will include duties under oral contracts as well as written contracts. The Law Commission's *Report on Fraud* dealt with the concept of legal duty and stated that duties might arise:

- from statute
- where the transaction is one of the utmost good faith
- from the express or implied terms of a contract
- from the custom of a particular trade or market, or
- from the existence of a fiduciary relationship between parties.

The legal duty to disclose information will exist if:

- the defendant's actions give the victim a cause in action for damages, or
- if the law gives the victim the right to set aside any change in his/her legal position to which he or she may have consented as a result of the non-disclosure.

A fiduciary relationship is one relating to the responsibility of looking after someone else's money in a correct way. Examples of such behaviour would include solicitors failing to share vital information with a client in the context of their work relationship, in order to carry out a fraud upon that client, or if a person intentionally failed to disclose information relating to a heart condition when making an application for life insurance. Where recipients of benefits dishonestly fail to disclose income etc. that they are legally required to disclose, fraud by failing to disclose is an appropriate charge (*R* v *El-Mashta* [2010] EWCA Crim 2595).

1.15.6 Fraud by Abuse of Position

The Fraud Act 2006, s. 4 states:

> (1) A person is in breach of this section if he—
>   (a) occupies a position in which he is expected to safeguard, or not to act against, the financial interests of another person,
>   (b) dishonestly abuses that position, and
>   (c) intends, by means of the abuse of that position—
>   (i) to make a gain for himself or another, or
>   (ii) to cause loss to another or to expose another to a risk of loss.
> (2) A person may be regarded as having abused his position even though his conduct consisted of an omission rather than an act.

KEYNOTE

An offence under s. 4 may be committed in a variety of ways as the 'position' that the defendant occupies may be the result of an assortment of relationships. The Law Commission explained the meaning of 'position' at para. 7.38:

> The necessary relationship will be present between trustee and beneficiary, director and company, professional person and client, agent and principle, employee and employer, or between partners. It may arise otherwise, for example within a family, or in the context of voluntary work, or in any context where the parties are not at arm's length.

The term 'abuse' is not defined by the Act.

Liability for the offence could develop from a wide range of conduct, for example:

- An employee of a software company uses his position to clone software products with the intention of selling the products on.
- An estate agent values a house belonging to an elderly person at an artificially low price and then arranges for the agent's brother to purchase the house.
- A person who is employed to care for a disabled person and has access to that person's bank account, abuses that position by transferring funds to invest in a high-risk business venture of his own.

The offence can also be committed by omission, for example:

- An employee fails to take up the chance of a crucial contract in order that an associate or rival company can take it up instead of and at the expense of the employer.

1.15.7 Possession or Control of Articles for Use in Frauds

OFFENCE: **Possession or Control of Articles for Use in Frauds—*Fraud Act 2006, s. 6***
- Triable either way • Five years' imprisonment and/or a fine on indictment
- 12 months' imprisonment and/or a fine summarily

The Fraud Act 2006, s. 6 states:

> (1) A person is guilty of an offence if he has in his possession or under his control any article for use in the course of or in connection with any fraud.

1.15.8 Making or Supplying Articles for Use in Frauds

OFFENCE: **Making or Supplying Articles for Use in Frauds—*Fraud Act 2006, s. 7***
  • Triable either way • 10 years' imprisonment on indictment and/or a fine
  • 12 months' imprisonment and/or a fine summarily

The Fraud Act 2006, s. 7 states:

(1) A person is guilty of an offence if he makes, adapts, supplies or offers to supply any article—
  (a) knowing that it is designed or adapted for use in the course of or in connection with fraud, or
  (b) intending it to be used to commit, or assist in the commission of, fraud.

1.15.9 Obtaining Services Dishonestly

OFFENCE: **Obtaining Services Dishonestly—*Fraud Act 2006, s. 11***

- Triable either way • Five years' imprisonment and/or a fine on indictment
- 12 months' imprisonment and/or a fine summarily

The Fraud Act 2006, s. 11 states:

(1) A person is guilty of an offence under this section if he obtains services for himself or another—
  (a) by a dishonest act, and
  (b) in breach of subsection (2).

(2) A person obtains services in breach of this subsection if—
  (a) they are made available on the basis that payment has been, is being or will be made for or in respect of them,
  (b) he obtains them without any payment having been made for or in respect of them or without payment having been made in full, and
  (c) when he obtains them, he knows—
    (i) that they are being made available on the basis described in paragraph (a), or
    (ii) that they might be,
  but intends that payment will not be made, or will not be made in full.

KEYNOTE

Unlike the other Fraud Act 2006 offences, the offence under s. 11 is not a conduct crime; it is a *result crime* and requires the *actual obtaining* of the service. However, the offence does not require a fraudulent representation or deception. Someone would commit this offence if, intending to avoid payment, he/she slipped into a concert hall to watch a concert without paying for the privilege. The offence can be committed where the defendant intends to avoid payment or payment in full but the defendant must know that the services are made available on the basis that they are chargeable, i.e. services provided for free are not covered by the offence.

If D sneaks aboard a lorry or a freight train, and obtains a free ride, D would commit no offence under s. 11, because the haulage company or freight train operator does not provide such rides, even for payment.

The terms 'service' and 'obtaining' are not defined by the Act. The fact that 'service' is not defined means that in the situation where a person obtains the 'services' of a prostitute without intending to pay him/her, that person cannot be guilty of either rape (see para. 1.11.2) or making off without payment (see para. 1.14.14) but under the Fraud Act 2006 the s. 11 offence can be committed.

1.15.10 False Accounting

OFFENCE: **False Accounting—*Theft Act 1968, s. 17***

- Triable either way • Seven years' imprisonment on indictment • Six months' imprisonment and/or a fine summarily

The Theft Act 1968, s. 17 states:

(1) Where a person dishonestly, with a view to gain for himself or another or with intent to cause loss to another,—
  (a) destroys, defaces, conceals or falsifies any account or any record or document made or required for any accounting purpose; or
  (b) in furnishing information for any purpose produces or makes use of any account, or any such record or document as aforesaid, which to his knowledge is or may be misleading, false or deceptive in a material particular;
  he shall [commit an offence].

(2) For purposes of this section a person who makes or concurs in making in an account or other document an entry which is or may be misleading, false or deceptive in a material particular, or who omits or concurs in omitting a material particular from an account or other document, is to be treated as falsifying the account or document.

This section creates two offences: destroying, defacing, etc. accounts and documents; and using false or misleading accounts or documents in furnishing information. A record or account need not necessarily be a document. In *Edwards* v *Toombs* [1983] Crim LR 43 it was held that a turnstile meter at a soccer stadium was a record and thus within the scope of the section.

An offence under s. 17 can be committed by omission as well as by an act. Failing to make an entry in an accounts book, altering a till receipt or supplying an auditor with records that are incomplete may, if accompanied by the other ingredients, amount to an offence.

There is no requirement to prove an intention permanently to deprive but there is a need to show dishonesty in a *Ghosh* sense (as to both points, **see chapter 1.14**). The requirement as to gain and loss is the same as for blackmail (**see para. 1.14.11**).

The misleading, false or deceptive nature of the information furnished under s. 17(1)(b) must be 'material' to the defendant's overall purpose, i.e. the ultimate gaining or causing of loss. Such an interpretation means that the defendant's furnishing of information need not relate directly to an accounting process and could be satisfied by lying about the status of a potential finance customer (*R* v *Mallett* [1978] 1 WLR 820).

Where the documents falsified are not intrinsically 'accounting' forms, such as insurance claim forms filled out by policyholders, you must show that those forms are treated for accounting purposes by the victim (*R* v *Sundhers* [1998] Crim LR 497). An application for a mortgage or a loan to a commercial institution is a document required for an accounting purpose, the rationale being that applications for a mortgage or a loan to commercial institutions will, if successful, lead to the opening of an account which will show as credits in favour of the borrower, funds received from the borrower and as debits paid out by the lender to, or on behalf of, the borrower (*R* v *O and H* [2010] EWCA Crim 2233).

1.15.11 Forgery Offences

The offences dealt with under ss. 1, 2, 3, 4 and 5 of the Forgery and Counterfeiting Act 1981 have several common themes running through them:

- they deal with instruments
- that are false
- which are either made, used or copied in order to induce a person to do or not to do some act to his own or any other person's prejudice.

Before examining the specific offences under the Act, it is useful to explore what these terms actually mean.

1.15.11.1 'Instrument'

The Forgery and Counterfeiting Act 1981, s. 8 states:

(1) Subject to subsection (2) below, in this Part of this Act 'instrument' means—
    (a) any document, whether of a formal or informal character;
    (b) any stamp issued or sold by a postal operator;
    (c) any Inland Revenue stamp; and
    (d) any disc, tape, sound track or other device on or in which information is recorded or stored by mechanical, electronic or other means.
(2) A currency note within the meaning of Part II of this Act is not an instrument for the purposes of this Part of this Act.
(3) A mark denoting payment of postage which a postal operator authorises to be used instead of an adhesive stamp is to be treated for the purposes of this Part of this Act as if it were a stamp issued by the postal operator concerned.
(3A) In this section, 'postal operator' has the same meaning as in the Postal Services Act 2000.
(4) In this Part of this Act 'Inland Revenue stamp' means a stamp as defined in section 27 of the Stamp Duties Management Act 1891.

1.15.11.2 'False'

The Forgery and Counterfeiting Act 1981, s. 9 states:

(1) An instrument is false for the purposes of this Part of this Act—

   (a) if it purports to have been made in the form in which it is made by a person who did not in fact make it in that form; or

   (b) if it purports to have been made in the form in which it is made on the authority of a person who did not in fact authorise its making in that form; or

   (c) if it purports to have been made in the terms in which it is made by a person who did not in fact make it in those terms; or

   (d) if it purports to have been made in the terms in which it is made on the authority of a person who did not in fact authorise its making in those terms; or

   (e) if it purports to have been altered in any respect by a person who did not in fact alter it in that respect; or

   (f) if it purports to have been altered in any respect on the authority of a person who did not in fact authorise the alteration in that respect; or

   (g) if it purports to have been made or altered on a date on which, or at a place at which, or otherwise in circumstances in which, it was not in fact made or altered; or

   (h) if it purports to have been made or altered by an existing person but he did not in fact exist.

1.15.11.3 'Prejudice' and 'Induce'

The Forgery and Counterfeiting Act 1981, s. 10 states:

(1) Subject to subsections (2) and (4) below, for the purposes of this Part of this Act an act or omission intended to be induced is to a person's prejudice if, and only if, it is one which, if it occurs—

   (a) will result—

     (i) in his temporary or permanent loss of property; or

     (ii) in his being deprived of an opportunity to earn remuneration or greater remuneration; or

     (iii) in his being deprived of an opportunity to gain a financial advantage otherwise than by way of remuneration; or

   (b) will result in somebody being given an opportunity—

     (i) to earn remuneration or greater remuneration from him; or

     (ii) to gain a financial advantage from him otherwise than by way of remuneration; or

(c) will be the result of his having accepted a false instrument as genuine, or a copy of a false instrument as a copy of a genuine one, in connection with his performance of any duty.

(2) An act which a person has an enforceable duty to do and an omission to do an act which a person is not entitled to do shall be disregarded for the purposes of this Part of this Act.

(3) In this Part of this Act references to inducing somebody to accept a false instrument as genuine, or a copy of a false instrument as a copy of a genuine one, include references to inducing a machine to respond to the instrument or copy as if it were a genuine instrument or, as the case may be, a copy of a genuine one.

KEYNOTE

Section 10 provides an exhaustive definition of the concept of 'prejudice'. 'Inducing' is only defined to the extent that it applies to machines. The extension is limited to offences under part I of the 1981 Act and therefore does not apply to offences contained elsewhere such as counterfeiting (as to which, see para. 1.15.12).

1.15.11.4 Forgery Offences

OFFENCE: **Making a False Instrument with Intent—*Forgery and Counterfeiting Act 1981, s. 1***

• Triable either way • 10 years' imprisonment on indictment • Six months' imprisonment and/or a fine summarily

The Forgery and Counterfeiting Act 1981, s. 1 states:

A person is guilty of forgery if he makes a false instrument, with the intention that he or another shall use it to induce somebody to accept it as genuine, and by reason of so accepting it to do or not to do some act to his own or any other person's prejudice.

KEYNOTE

Making

The Forgery and Counterfeiting Act 1981, s. 9 states:

(2) A person is to be treated for the purposes of this part of this Act as making a false instrument if he alters an instrument so as to make it false in any respect (whether or not it is false in some other respect apart from that alteration).

This offence is committed by 'making' the false instrument; it does not matter that it is never used.

Convictions for offences under s. 1 have involved all types of false instruments. In *R* v *Mussa* [2012] EWCA Crim 693, the Court of Appeal dealt with a case in which the offenders admitted producing forged French identity documents. The documents were of high quality and would have enabled false bank accounts to be set up, driving penalties to be avoided and facilitate entry and residence in the United Kingdom. In *R* v *Lincoln* (1994) 15 Cr App R (S) 333, the offender was convicted of the offence for forging the signature of his estranged wife on a contract for sale of a house and a Land Registry transfer.

OFFENCE: **Copying a False Instrument with Intent—*Forgery and Counterfeiting Act 1981, s. 2***

• Triable either way • 10 years' imprisonment on indictment • Six months' imprisonment and/or a fine summarily

The Forgery and Counterfeiting Act 1981, s. 2 states:

It is an offence for a person to make a copy of an instrument which is, and which he knows or believes to be, a false instrument, with the intention that he or another shall use it to induce somebody to accept it as a copy of a genuine instrument, and by reason of so accepting it to do or not to do some act to his own or any other person's prejudice.

OFFENCE: **Using a False Instrument with Intent—** *Forgery and Counterfeiting Act 1981, s. 3*

- Triable either way • 10 years' imprisonment on indictment • Six months' imprisonment and/or a fine summarily

The Forgery and Counterfeiting Act 1981, s. 3 states:

It is an offence for a person to use an instrument which is, and which he knows or believes to be, false, with the intention of inducing somebody to accept it as genuine, and by reason of so accepting it to do or not to do some act to his own or any other person's prejudice.

OFFENCE: **Using a Copy of a False Instrument with Intent—***Forgery and Counterfeiting Act 1981, s. 4*

- Triable either way • 10 years' imprisonment on indictment • Six months' imprisonment and/or a fine summarily

The Forgery and Counterfeiting Act 1981, s. 4 states:

It is an offence for a person to use a copy of an instrument which is, and which he knows or believes to be, a false instrument, with the intention of inducing somebody to accept it as a copy of a genuine instrument, and by reason of so accepting it to do or not to do some act to his own or any other person's prejudice.

1.15.11.5 Forgery Offences in Relation to Specific Instruments

It is not generally an offence merely to have custody or control of false instruments, or materials etc. for making them, even if the instruments or materials are intended for some unlawful purpose. The instruments listed in s. 5(5) of the Forgery and Counterfeiting Act 1981 have been singled out for protection.

The Forgery and Counterfeiting Act 1981, s. 5 states:

(5) The instruments to which this section applies are—
- (a) money orders;
- (b) postal orders;
- (c) United Kingdom postage stamps;
- (d) Inland Revenue stamps;
- (e) share certificates;
- (f) ...
- (fa) ......

(g)　cheques and other bills of exchange;

(h)　travellers' cheques;

(ha)　bankers' drafts;

(hb)　promissory notes;

(j)　cheque cards;

(ja)　debit cards;

(k)　credit cards;

(l)　certified copies relating to an entry in a register of births, adoptions, marriages, civil partnerships or deaths and issued by the Registrar General, the Registrar General for Northern Ireland, a registration officer or a person lawfully authorised to issue certified copies relating to such entries; and

(m)　certificates relating to entries in such registers.

(6) In subsection (5)(e) above 'share certificate' means an instrument entitling or evidencing the title of a person to a share or interest—

(a) in any public stock, annuity, fund or debt of any government or state, including a state which forms part of another state; or

(b) in any stock, fund or debt of a body (whether corporate or unincorporated) established in the United Kingdom or elsewhere.

(7) An instrument is also an instrument to which this section applies if it is a monetary instrument specified for the purposes of this section by an order made by the Secretary of State.

KEYNOTE

'Immigration document' essentially means a card, adhesive label or other instrument given under the Immigration Acts to someone to confirm their right of entry to or residence in the United Kingdom. The expression extends to cards, labels and other instruments which carry information (including information wholly or partly stored electronically) about the leave granted to that person.

OFFENCE: **Having Custody or Control of Specific Instruments and Materials with Intent—** *Forgery and Counterfeiting Act 1981, s. 5(1) and (3)*
　　　　　• Triable either way • 10 years' imprisonment on indictment • Six months' imprisonment and/or a fine summarily

In addition to the above offences which apply to any instrument, there are several specific offences which apply to specific types of 'formal' instrument.

The Forgery and Counterfeiting Act 1981, s. 5 states:

(1) It is an offence for a person to have in his custody or under his control an instrument to which this section applies which is, and which he knows or believes to be, false, with the intention that he or another shall use it to induce somebody to accept it as genuine, and by reason of so accepting it to do or not to do some act to his own or any other person's prejudice.

(2) ...

(3) It is an offence for a person to make or to have in his custody or under his control a machine or implement, or paper or any other material, which to his knowledge is or has been specially designed or adapted for the making of an instrument to which this section applies, with the intention that he or another shall make an instrument to which this section applies which is false and that he or another shall use the instrument to induce somebody to accept it as genuine, and by reason of so accepting it to do or not to do some act to his own or any other person's prejudice.

OFFENCE: **Having Custody or Control of Specific Instruments and Materials—** *Forgery and Counterfeiting Act 1981, s. 5(2) and (4)*
　　　　　• Triable either way • Two years' imprisonment on indictment • Six months' imprisonment and/or a fine summarily

The Forgery and Counterfeiting Act 1981, s. 5 states:

(2) It is an offence for a person to have in his custody or under his control, without lawful authority or excuse, an instrument to which this section applies which is, and which he knows or believes to be, false.

(3) …

(4) It is an offence for a person to make or to have in his custody or under his control any such machine, implement, paper or material, without lawful authority or excuse.

KEYNOTE

These offences are not limited to a person having the offending item(s) on their person, or even 'with' them. It will suffice if a person keeps the items in their home, garage, car or workplace.

1.15.11.6 Powers of Search

The Forgery and Counterfeiting Act 1981, s. 7 states:

(1) If it appears to a justice of the peace, from information given him on oath, that there is reasonable cause to believe that a person has in his custody or under his control—

    (a) any thing which he or another has used, whether before or after the coming into force of this Act, or intends to use, for the making of any false instrument or copy of a false instrument, in contravention of section 1 or 2 above; or

    (b) any false instrument or copy of a false instrument which he or another has used, whether before or after the coming into force of this Act, or intends to use, in contravention of section 3 or 4 above; or

    (c) any thing custody or control of which without lawful authority or excuse is an offence under section 5 above,

the justice may issue a warrant authorising a constable to search for and seize the object in question, and for that purpose to enter any premises specified in the warrant.

1.15.12 Counterfeiting with Intent to Pass or Tender as Genuine

The counterfeiting of currency notes and 'protected coins' is dealt with in part II of the Forgery and Counterfeiting Act 1981.

1.15.12.1 Meaning of 'Currency Note' and 'Protected Coin'

The Forgery and Counterfeiting Act 1981, s. 27 states:

(1) In this Part of this Act—
'currency note' means—

    (a) any note which—

        (i) has been lawfully issued in England and Wales, Scotland, Northern Ireland, any of the Channel Islands, the Isle of Man or the Republic of Ireland; and

        (ii) is or has been customarily used as money in the country where it was issued; and

        (iii) is payable on demand; or

    (b) any note which—

        (i) has been lawfully issued in some country other than those mentioned in paragraph (a)(i) above; and

        (ii) is customarily used as money in that country; and

'protected coin' means any coin which—

    (a) is customarily used as money in any country; or

    (b) is specified in an order made by the Treasury for the purposes of this Part of this Act.

KEYNOTE

British or Irish notes come within the Act even if no longer customarily used as money (s. 27(1)(a)) but foreign or Commonwealth notes must be in current use (s. 27(1)(b)). Neither kind ever needs to have been legal tender; Scottish notes, for example, are not legal tender even in Scotland.

Coins must either be in current use or be specified by the Treasury for the purpose of the Act. Examples of coins that have been so specified include sovereigns, half-sovereigns and krugerrands.

1.15.12.2   Meaning of 'Counterfeit'

The Forgery and Counterfeiting Act 1981, s. 28 states:

(1) For the purposes of this Part of this Act a thing is a counterfeit of a currency note or of a protected coin—

    (a) if it is not a currency note or a protected coin but resembles a currency note or protected coin (whether on one side only or on both) to such an extent that it is reasonably capable of passing for a currency note or protected coin of that description; or

    (b) if it is a currency note or protected coin which has been so altered that it is reasonably capable of passing for a currency note or protected coin of some other description.

(2) For the purpose of this Part of this Act—

    (a) a thing consisting of one side only of a currency note, with or without the addition of other material is a counterfeit of such a note;

    (b) a thing consisting—

        (i) of parts of two or more currency notes; or

        (ii) of parts of a currency note, or of parts of two or more currency notes, with the addition of other material,

    is capable of being a counterfeit of a currency note.

(3) References in this Part of this Act to passing or tendering a counterfeit of a currency note or a protected coin are not to be construed as confined to passing or tendering it as legal tender.

KEYNOTE

It is not possible to argue that a one-sided note or coin is incapable of passing for a genuine one, but in other respects the question of what kind of imitation can amount to a counterfeit is one of fact.

1.15.12.3   Offences

OFFENCE: **Making Counterfeit Note or Coin with Intent—** *Forgery and Counterfeiting Act 1981, s. 14(1)*

Section 14(1)

• Triable either way • 10 years' imprisonment on indictment • Six months' imprisonment and/or a fine summarily

Section 15(2)

• Triable either way • Two years imprisonment and/or fine on indictment

• Six months imprisonment and/or a fine summarily

The Forgery and Counterfeiting Act 1981, s. 14 states:

(1) It is an offence for a person to make a counterfeit of a currency note or of a protected coin, intending that he or another shall pass or tender it as genuine.

(2) it is an offence for a person to make a counterfeit of a currency note or a protected coin without lawful authority or excuse.

KEYNOTE

Although there is a requirement to prove an intent in the offence under s. 14(1), there is no need to show that the defendant intended to induce someone to do something to his/her own prejudice or that anyone would actually believe the currency note or coin was genuine.

The offence under s. 14(2) means that counterfeiting is an offence (albeit a less serious one), unless the maker has lawful authority or reasonable excuse.

OFFENCE: **Passing Counterfeit Notes or Coins with Intent—*Forgery and Counterfeiting Act 1981, s. 15(1)(a) and (b)***

Section 15(1)(a) and (b)

- Triable either way • 10 years' imprisonment and/or a fine on indictment
- Six months' imprisonment and/or a fine summarily

Section 15(2)

- Triable either way • Two years' imprisonment and/or a fine on indictment
- Six months' imprisonment and/or a fine summarily

The Forgery and Counterfeiting Act 1981, s. 15 states:

(1) It is an offence for a person—
   (a) to pass or tender as genuine any thing which is, and which he knows or believes to be, a counterfeit of a currency note or of a protected coin; or
   (b) to deliver to another any thing which is, and which he knows or believes to be, such a counterfeit, intending that the person to whom it is delivered or another shall pass or tender it as genuine.

(2) It is an offence for a person to deliver to another, without lawful authority or excuse, anything which is, and which he knows or believes to be, a counterfeit of a currency note or of a protected coin.

KEYNOTE

'Passing' suggests acceptance by the person to whom the thing is given, but a counterfeit may be *tendered* as genuine, even if it is at once rejected, and the offence may be committed even where the item in question is not passed or tendered as legal tender (s. 28(3)).

It would not be an offence under s. 15 to pass or tender a note etc. which one suspects *may* be counterfeit, even if the suspicion is a strong one.

'Delivering' need not involve any intent to deceive as to the nature of the thing delivered, but the offence under s. 15(1)(b) may be committed if it is intended that the counterfeits should eventually be tendered as genuine by the recipient or some other person.

OFFENCE: **Having Custody or Control of Counterfeit Note or Coin with Intent—*Forgery and Counterfeiting Act 1981, s. 16(1)***

- Triable either way • 10 years' imprisonment on indictment • Six months' imprisonment and/or a fine summarily

The Forgery and Counterfeiting Act 1981, s. 16 states:

(1) It is an offence for a person to have in his custody or under his control anything which is, and which he knows or believes to be, a counterfeit of a currency note or of a protected coin, intending either to pass or tender it as genuine or to deliver it to another with the intention that he or another shall pass or tender it as genuine.

1.16 Criminal Damage

1.16.1 Introduction

The prevalence of offences of criminal damage is well documented and damage in all forms has a harmful effect on the environment, the community and the economy.

1.16.2 Simple Damage

OFFENCE: **Simple Damage—*Criminal Damage Act 1971, s. 1(1)***
- Triable either way • 10 years' imprisonment on indictment • Six months' imprisonment and/or a fine summarily

OFFENCE: **Racially or Religiously Aggravated—*Crime and Disorder Act 1998, s. 30(1)***
- Triable either way • 14 years' imprisonment and/or a fine on indictment
- Six months' imprisonment and/or a fine summarily

The Criminal Damage Act 1971, s. 1 states:

(1) A person who without lawful excuse destroys or damages any property belonging to another intending to destroy or damage any such property or being reckless as to whether any such property would be destroyed or damaged shall be guilty of an offence.

KEYNOTE

Although triable either way, if the value of the property destroyed or the damage done is less than £5,000, the offence is to be tried summarily (Magistrates' Courts Act 1980, s. 22). If the damage in such a case was caused by fire (arson), this rule will not apply.

The fact that the substantive offence is, by virtue of the value of the damage caused, triable only summarily does not make simple damage a 'summary offence' for all other purposes. If it did, you could only be found guilty of attempting to commit criminal damage if the value of the intended damage was more than £5,000 (because the Criminal Attempts Act 1981 does not extend to summary offences) (see chapter 1.3). Therefore, where a defendant tried to damage a bus shelter in a way that would have cost far less than £5,000 to repair, his argument that he had only attempted what was in fact a 'summary offence' was dismissed by the Divisional Court (*R* v *Bristol Magistrates' Court, ex parte E* [1999] 1 WLR 390). Where the damage caused is less than £300, the offence can be dealt with by way of fixed penalty notice (see *General Police Duties*, para. 4.5.14).

If the offence involves only the painting or writing on, or the soiling, marking or other defacing of, any property by whatever means, the power to issue a graffiti notice may apply (as to which see para. 1.16.7).

The racially or religiously aggravated form of this offence is triable either way irrespective of the cost of the damage.

'Simple' criminal damage is the *only* criminal damage offence that can be racially or religiously aggravated.

1.16.2.1 Destroy or Damage

The terms 'destroy' or 'damage' are not defined. 'Destroying' property suggests that it has been rendered useless but there is no need to prove that 'damage' to property is in any way permanent or irreparable.

Whether an article has been damaged will be a question of fact for each court to determine on the evidence before it. Defacing of a pavement by an artist using only water-soluble paint (*Hardman* v *Chief Constable of Avon and Somerset* [1986] Crim LR 330) and graffiti smeared in mud can amount to damage, even though it is easily washed off (*Roe* v *Kingerlee* [1986] Crim LR 735). In *R* v *Fiak* [2005] EWCA Crim 2381, the defendant had been arrested and placed in a police cell which he flooded by stuffing a blanket down the cell lavatory and repeatedly flushing. The defendant argued that there was no evidence that the blanket or the cell had been 'damaged'; the water had been clean and both the blanket and the cell could be used again when dry. The Court of Appeal disagreed and held that, while the effect of the defendant's actions in relation to the blanket and the cell was remediable, the reality was that the blanket could not be used until it had been dried and the flooded cell was out of action until the water had been cleared. Therefore both had sustained damage for the purposes of the Act. This case illustrates that putting property temporarily out of use, even for a short time and in circumstances where it will revert to its former state of its own accord, may fall within the definition of 'damage'.

1.16.2.2 Property

Property is defined in the 1971 Act by s. 10 which states:

(1) In this Act 'property' means property of a tangible nature, whether real or personal, including money and—
    (a) including wild creatures which have been tamed or are ordinarily kept in captivity and any other wild creatures or their carcasses if, but only if, they have been reduced into possession . . . or are in the course of being reduced into possession; but
    (b) not including mushrooms growing wild on any land or flowers, fruit or foliage of a plant growing wild on any land.
    . . .

> **KEYNOTE**
>
> This definition is similar to the definition of 'property' for the purposes of theft (see chapter 1.14) but there are some differences, e.g. 'real' property (i.e. land and things attached to it) *can be* damaged even though it cannot be stolen whereas intangible property (such as copyright) can be stolen but cannot be damaged. Trampling flower beds, digging up cricket pitches, chopping down trees in a private garden and pulling up genetically-modified crops could potentially amount to criminal damage.
>
> Pets or farm animals are property for the purposes of this Act. Cases of horses being mutilated would, in addition to the offence of 'cruelty' itself, amount to criminal damage.

1.16.2.3 Belonging to Another

Section 10 states:

(2) Property shall be treated for the purposes of this Act as belonging to any person—
    (a) having the custody or control of it;
    (b) having in it any proprietary right or interest (not being an equitable interest arising only from an agreement to transfer or grant an interest); or
    (c) having a charge on it.

1.16.2.4 Lawful Excuse

Section 5 of the Criminal Damage Act 1971 provides for two occasions where a defendant may have a 'lawful excuse'. These can be remembered as 'permission' (s. 5(2)(a)) and 'protection' (s. 5(2)(b)). Both involve the belief of the defendant.

1.16.2.5 Permission

A person shall be treated as having lawful excuse under s. 5(2):

(a) if at the time of the act or acts alleged to constitute the offence he believed that the person or persons whom he believed to be entitled to consent to the destruction of or damage to the property in question had so consented, or would have so consented to it if he or they had known of the destruction or damage and its circumstances...

EXAMPLE

An elderly motorist asks you to help him get his keys out of his partner's car as he had locked them inside. You tell the motorist that the car may be damaged as a result of your efforts but the motorist tells you that is alright and to go ahead. Section 5(2)(a) would provide a statutory defence to any later charge of criminal damage by the owner. The key element here would be that you believed you had the *consent* of the motorist (who is someone you believed to be *entitled to consent* to that damage) to damage the vehicle in these circumstances.

1.16.2.6 Protection

A person shall be treated as having lawful excuse under s. 5(2):

(b) if he destroyed or damaged or threatened to destroy or damage the property in question or, in the case of a charge of an offence under section 3 above, intended to use or cause or permit the use of something to destroy or damage it, in order to protect property belonging to himself or another or a right or interest in property which was or which he believed to be vested in himself or another, and at the time of the act or acts alleged to constitute the offence he believed—

  (i) that the property, right or interest was in immediate need of protection; and

  (ii) that the means of protection adopted or proposed to be adopted were or would be reasonable having regard to all the circumstances.

Belief

It is immaterial whether a 'belief' was justified as long as it was honestly held (s. 5(3)). Although this test is supposed to be an *objective* one, the evidence will be based largely on what was going through a defendant's mind at the time. In *Jaggard* v *Dickinson* [1981] QB 527 the defendant had broken a window to get into a house. Being drunk at the time, she had got the wrong house but the court accepted that her belief (that it was the right house and that the owner would have consented) had been honestly held, and that it did not matter whether that belief was brought about by intoxication, stupidity, forgetfulness or inattention. That is not to say, however, that *any* honestly held belief will suffice. An example of someone claiming, unsuccessfully, a defence under both s. 5(2)(a) and (b) can be seen in *Blake* v *DPP* [1993] Crim LR 586. There the defendant was a vicar who wished to protest against Great Britain's involvement in the Gulf War. In order to mark his disapproval, the defendant wrote a quotation from the Bible in ink on a pillar in front of the Houses of Parliament. He claimed:

- he was carrying out God's instructions and had a lawful excuse based on his belief that God was the person entitled to consent to such damage and that God had in fact consented or would have done so (s. 5(2)(a)); and
- he had damaged the property as a reasonable means of protecting other property located in the Gulf from being damaged by warfare (s. 5(2)(b)).

The Divisional Court did not accept either proposition holding that, in the first case a belief in God's consent was not a 'lawful excuse' and, in the second, that the defendant's conduct was too remote from any immediate need to protect property in the Gulf States. The test in relation to the defendant's belief appears then to be largely subjective (i.e. what was/was not going on in the defendant's head at the time) but with an objective element in that the judge/magistrate(s) must decide whether, on the facts as believed by the defendant, his/her acts were capable of protecting property.

Taking a different tack, peace campaigners in *R* v *Jones (Margaret)* [2004] EWCA Crim 1981 argued that their fear of the consequences of war in Iraq, which they claimed to be illegal, prompted them to conspire to cause damage at an airbase and that such fear amounted both to duress (as to which **see para. 1.4.7**) and lawful excuse under s. 5(2)(b). The Court of Appeal held that a jury would be entitled to consider some of the subjective beliefs of the defendants in determining the reasonableness of their actions.

In *R* v *Kelleher* [2003] EWCA Crim 2846, a demonstrator at the Guildhall Gallery knocked the head off a statue of Baroness Thatcher claiming he acted in fear for his son's future which had been placed in jeopardy by the joint actions of the US and UK governments, and for which Baroness Thatcher was partly responsible. His appeal against conviction brought under s. 5(2)(b) failed.

Section 5(5) allows for other general defences (**see chapter 1.4**) at criminal law to apply in addition to those listed under s. 5.

It is not an offence to damage your own property unless there are aggravating circumstances. This is the case even if the intention in doing so is to carry out some further offence such as a fraudulent insurance claim (*R* v *Denton* [1981] 1 WLR 1446).

1.16.2.7 Recklessness

An offence of criminal damage under s. 1(1) can be proved by showing that the defendant was 'reckless'. In *R* v *G and R* [2003] UKHL 50, the House of Lords held that a person acts recklessly for the purposes of s. 1(1) of the Act:

- with respect to a circumstance when he/she is aware of a risk that existed or would exist;
- with respect to a result or consequence when he/she is aware of a risk that it would occur and it is, in the circumstances known to him/her, unreasonable to take the risk.

In *R* v *G and R*, two children (aged 11 and 12) set fire to some newspapers in the rear yard of a shop premises while camping out. The children put the burning papers under a wheelie bin and left them, expecting the small fire to burn itself out on the concrete floor of the yard. In fact the fire spread causing around £1,000,000 of damage. Under the former law ('objective' recklessness), the children were convicted on the basis that the risk of the fire would have been obvious to any reasonable bystander. However, their convictions were quashed by the House of Lords who reinstated the general subjective element described above.

1.16.3 Aggravated Damage

OFFENCE: **Aggravated Damage—*Criminal Damage Act 1971, s. 1(2)***
• Triable on indictment • Life imprisonment

The Criminal Damage Act 1971, s. 1 states:

(2) A person who without lawful excuse destroys or damages any property, whether belonging to himself or another—
   (a) intending to destroy or damage any property or being reckless as to whether any property would be destroyed or damaged; and
   (b) intending by the destruction or damage to endanger the life of another or being reckless as to whether the life of another would be thereby endangered;
   shall be guilty of an offence.

KEYNOTE

The aggravating factor in this offence is the intention of endangering life or recklessness as to whether life is endangered.

The reference to 'without lawful excuse' *does not* refer to the statutory defences under s. 5 which are not applicable here, but to general excuses such as self-defence or the prevention of crime.

For the relevant test of recklessness **see para. 1.16.2.7.**

You must show that the defendant either intended or was reckless as to the following consequences:

• the damage being caused, and
• the risk of endangering the life of another.

Where a defendant fired a gun through a window pane he was clearly reckless as to the damage his actions would cause. However, the court felt that, even though two people were standing behind the window and they were obviously put in some danger, it was the *missile* which endangered their lives and not the *result of the damage.* Therefore the court held that the defendant was not guilty of this particular offence (*R* v *Steer* [1988] AC 111). In *R* v *Webster and Warwick* [1995] 2 All ER 168, damaging the windscreen of a car or ramming a car was held to be capable of endangering life as a result of the damage.

It is the damage which the defendant intended or was reckless about which is relevant, rather than the actual damage that happens to be caused (this could turn out to be minor damage). In *R* v *Dudley* [1989] Crim LR 57, trivial damage was caused but the conviction was upheld since the defendant created a risk of much more serious damage which was capable of endangering life.

1.16.4 Arson

OFFENCE: **Arson—*Criminal Damage Act 1971, s. 1(3)***
• Triable either way • Life imprisonment on indictment • Where life is not endangered six months' imprisonment and/or a fine summarily

The Criminal Damage Act 1971, s. 1 states:

> (3) An offence committed under this section by destroying or damaging property by fire shall be charged as arson.

KEYNOTE

When 'simple' or 'aggravated' damage is caused and the destruction or damage is caused by fire, the offence will be charged as 'arson'. The restrictions on the mode of trial for simple damage under s. 1(1) do not apply to cases of arson. *Aggravated damage* caused by arson is triable only on indictment and carries a maximum penalty of life imprisonment.

Criminal liability for either gross negligence or unlawful act manslaughter may arise from an offence of arson. In *R* v *Willoughby* [2004] EWCA Crim 3365, the defendant enlisted the help of another man in burning down a public house on which the defendant owed money. Having poured petrol around the inside of the building, the defendant set fire to it, killing the other person and injuring himself in the process. The defendant was convicted of both arson and manslaughter. The Court of Appeal held that by convicting the defendant of arson, the jury had showed that they were sure that he (on his own or jointly) had deliberately spread petrol by being reckless or with the intention that the premises would be destroyed. Provided that such conduct had been the cause of the death, the jury were therefore also bound to convict the defendant of manslaughter.

1.16.5   Threats to Destroy or Damage Property

OFFENCE: **Threats to Destroy or Damage Property—*Criminal Damage Act 1971, s. 2***

 • Triable either way • 10 years' imprisonment on indictment • Six months' imprisonment and/or a fine summarily

The Criminal Damage Act 1971, s. 2 states:

> A person who without lawful excuse makes to another a threat, intending that that other would fear it would be carried out,—
>
> (a) to destroy or damage any property belonging to that other or a third person; or
> (b) to destroy or damage his own property in a way which he knows is likely to endanger the life of that other or a third person;
>
> shall be guilty of an offence.

KEYNOTE

The key element is the defendant's *intention* that the person receiving the threat fears it would be carried out. So there is no need to show that the other person actually feared or believed that the threat would be carried out or that the defendant intended to carry it out; nor does it matter whether the threat was even capable of being carried out.

EXAMPLE

If a person, enraged by a neighbour's inconsiderate parking, shouts over the garden wall, '*When you've gone to bed I'm going to pour paint stripper over your car!*', the offence will be complete, provided you can show that the person making the threat intended the neighbour to fear it would be carried out.

Where a group of protestors staged a protest in the pods of the London Eye and threatened to set fire to themselves, their conduct was held to be capable of amounting to a threat to damage the property of another (as a consequence of setting themselves on fire) contrary to s. 2(a) (*R* v *Cakmak* [2002] EWCA Crim 500).

In *Cakmak* the court held that the gist of the offence under s. 2(a) was the making of a threat and that any such threat had to be considered objectively.

Whether:

- there has been such a threat to another
- the threat amounted to 'a threat to damage or destroy property'
- the defendant had the necessary state of mind at the time

are all questions of fact for the jury to decide (per *Cakmak*).

While not usually enough to amount to the substantive offence under s. 2, a person's *conduct* which represents a threat to damage property may be relevant in triggering police action. In *Clements* v *DPP* [2005] EWHC 1279 (Admin) several protestors left a public highway, crossed a ditch and approached the perimeter fence of an RAF base. The defendant ignored a police warning to return to the road and the police attempted to restrain the protestors in order to prevent criminal damage to the fence. After a scuffle the defendant was subsequently convicted of assaulting a police constable in the execution of his duty (as to which **see para. 1.9.8.2**). The key issues at trial were whether the police officer had acted in the course of his duty and the extent to which the officer had reasonable grounds to believe that the defendant would cause criminal damage. The Divisional Court held that the officer had to consider the whole event in context and at the relevant time a political protest was ensuing; the defendant had deliberately left the public highway and refused to return to it; he had no legitimate reason to approach the fence; and it was plainly reasonable for the police officer to believe that he could cause criminal damage to the fence.

The defence to criminal damage under s. 5(2) ('permission'—**see para. 1.16.2.5**) does not apply where the accused knows that the threatened damage is likely to endanger life.

1.16.6 Having Articles with Intent to Destroy or Damage Property

OFFENCE: **Having Articles with Intent to Destroy or Damage Property—*Criminal Damage Act 1971, s. 3***

- Triable either way • 10 years' imprisonment on indictment • Six months' imprisonment and/or a fine summarily

The Criminal Damage Act 1971, s. 3 states:

A person who has anything in his custody or under his control intending without lawful excuse to use it or cause or permit another to use it—
(a) to destroy or damage any property belonging to some other person; or
(b) to destroy or damage his own or the user's property in a way which he knows is likely to endanger the life of some other person;
shall be guilty of an offence.

KEYNOTE

This offence covers *anything* which a defendant has '*in his custody or under his control*', a broader term than 'possession'.

This offence applies to graffiti 'artists' carrying aerosols and advertisers with adhesives for sticking illicit posters. The key element is *intention*. This time the required intention is that the 'thing' be used to cause criminal damage to another's property or to the defendant's own property in a way which the defendant knows is likely to endanger the life of another. Such articles are 'prohibited' articles for the purposes of the power of stop and search under s. 1 of the Police and Criminal Evidence Act 1984 (see *General Police Duties*, chapter 4.6).

A conditional intent (an intent to use something to cause criminal damage if the need arises) will be enough (*R* v *Buckingham* (1976) 63 Cr App R 159).

> Just as it is not an offence to damage your own property in a way which endangers no one else, neither is it an offence to have something which you intend to use to cause damage under those circumstances.

....

EXAMPLE

If the owner of a 10 metre high conifer decides to trim the top with a chainsaw and a ladder, putting himself, but no one else, at considerable risk, he commits no offence, either by causing the damage or by having the chainsaw. If he intends to fell the tree in a way which he realises will endanger the life of his neighbours or passers by, then he may commit the offence under s. 3(b).

Police Powers

There is a statutory power to apply to a magistrate for a search warrant under s. 6 of the Criminal Damage Act 1971 for anything that could be used or is intended to be used to destroy or damage property.

1.16.7 Penalty and Removal Notices for Graffiti

Where authorised officers of a local authority have reason to believe that a person has committed a relevant offence in the area of that authority, they may give that person a penalty notice under s. 43 of the Anti-social Behaviour Act 2003 (unless the offence amounts to a racially or religiously aggravated damage offence).

Examples of a 'relevant offence' include:

- s. 1(1) of the Criminal Damage Act 1971 which involves only the painting or writing on, or the soiling, marking or other defacing of, any property by whatever means
- s. 132(1) of the Highways Act 1980 (painting or affixing things on structures on the highway etc.)
- para. 10 of s. 54 of the Metropolitan Police Act 1839 (affixing posters etc.)
- s. 20(1) of the London County Council (General Powers) Act 1954 (defacement of streets with slogans etc.)
- s. 131(2) of the Highways Act 1980 (including that provision as applied by s. 27(6) of the Countryside Act 1968) which involves only an act of obliteration
- s. 224(3) of the Town and Country Planning Act 1990 (displaying advertisement in contravention of regulations) (s. 44).

Police community support officers and accredited employees under schs 4 and 5 to the Police Reform Act 2002 can be given the power to issue these penalty notices.

In addition, where a local authority is satisfied that a relevant surface in an area has been defaced by graffiti and the defacement is detrimental to the amenity of the area or is offensive, the authority may serve a defacement removal notice upon any person who is responsible (s. 48). A 'relevant surface' means broadly the surface of any street or of any building, structure or other object in or on any street, or the surface of any land owned, occupied or controlled by an educational institution or any building, structure etc. on any such land (see s. 48(9)).

OFFENCE: **Sale of Aerosol Paint to Children—*Anti-social Behaviour Act 2003, s. 54***

   • Triable summarily • Fine

The Anti-social Behaviour Act 2003, s. 54 states:

(1) A person commits an offence if he sells an aerosol paint container to a person under the age of sixteen.

(2) ...

(3) ...

(4) It is a defence for a person charged with an offence under this section in respect of a sale to prove that—

    (a) he took all reasonable steps to determine the purchaser's age, and

    (b) he reasonably believed that the purchaser was not under the age of sixteen.

(5) It is a defence for a person charged with an offence under this section in respect of a sale effected by another person to prove that he (the defendant) took all reasonable steps to avoid the commission of an offence under this section.

KEYNOTE

An 'aerosol paint container' means a device which contains paint stored under pressure, and is designed to permit the release of the paint as a spray (s. 54(2)).

Once the elements in relation to the selling and the age of the buyer are proved, the offence is complete. There is no need to show that the person buying the aerosol intended to use it for causing damage (though if this can be shown, the offence under s. 3 of the Criminal Damage Act 1971 should be considered—**see para. 1.16.6**).

1.16.8 Contamination or Interference with Goods

OFFENCE: **Contamination or Interference with Goods—*Public Order Act 1986, s. 38(1)***

- Triable either way • 10 years' imprisonment and/or a fine on indictment
- Six months' imprisonment and/or a fine summarily

The Public Order Act 1986, s. 38 states:

(1) It is an offence for a person, with the intention—

    (a) of causing public alarm or anxiety, or

    (b) of causing injury to members of the public consuming or using the goods, or

    (c) of causing economic loss to any person by reason of the goods being shunned by members of the public, or

    (d) of causing economic loss to any person by reason of steps taken to avoid any such alarm or anxiety, injury or loss,

to contaminate or interfere with goods, or make it appear that goods have been contaminated or interfered with, or to place goods which have been contaminated or interfered with, or which appear to have been contaminated or interfered with in a place where goods of that description are consumed, used, sold or otherwise supplied.

(2) It is also an offence for a person, with any such intention as is mentioned in paragraph (a), (c) or (d) of subsection (1), to threaten that he or another will do, or to claim that he or another has done, any of the acts mentioned in that subsection.

(3) It is an offence for a person to be in possession of any of the following articles with a view to the commission of an offence under subsection (1)—

    (a) materials to be used for contaminating or interfering with goods or making it appear that goods have been contaminated or interfered with, or

    (b) goods which have been contaminated or interfered with, or which appear to have been contaminated or interfered with.

(4) ...

(5) In this section 'goods' includes substances whether natural or manufactured and whether or not incorporated in or mixed with other goods.

(6) The reference in subsection (2) to a person claiming that certain acts have been committed does not include a person who in good faith reports or warns that such acts have been, or appear to have been, committed.

'Goods' includes 'natural' goods (e.g. fruit and vegetables) or 'manufactured' goods (e.g. shampoo or disinfectant).

Section 38 creates two offences. The first involves the contamination of, interference with or placing of goods with the intentions set out at s. 38(1)(a)–(d). An example of this offence is the case of *R* v *Cruikshank* [2001] EWCA Crim 98, where the offender pleaded guilty to contaminating food in a supermarket by inserting pins, needles and nails into various items. He persisted in this behaviour for three months, and some minor injuries were incurred by customers who bought the contaminated products.

Section 38(2) involves the making of threats to do, or the claiming to have done any of the acts in s. 38(1), with any of the intentions set out at s. 38(1)(a), (c) or (d). It is difficult to see how a threat or claim made with the intention of causing injury to the public (s. 38(1)(b)) would not also amount to an intention to cause them alarm or anxiety but the legislation clearly excludes it.

Section 38(6) allows for people to communicate warnings in good faith where such acts appear to have been committed.

Where threats to contaminate goods are made there may also be grounds for charging blackmail. A good example of threats to commit this offence and the overlap with blackmail is the case of *R* v *Witchelo* (1992) 13 Cr App R (S) 371 where the defendant, a police officer, was sentenced to 13 years' imprisonment after obtaining £32,000 from food producers to whom he had sent threatening letters.

1.17 | Offences Against the Administration of Justice and Public Interest

1.17.1 Introduction

This chapter deals with a wide range of offences against the administration of justice and also the public interest. The first group of offences involve some form of interference with the machinery of justice such as perjury and witness intimidation, while others have an indirect effect on the process.

1.17.2 Perjury

OFFENCE: **Perjury—*Perjury Act 1911, s. 1***

> • Triable on indictment • Seven years' imprisonment

The Perjury Act 1911, s. 1 states:

(1) If any person lawfully sworn as a witness or as an interpreter in a judicial proceeding wilfully makes a statement material in that proceeding, which he knows to be false or does not believe to be true, he shall be guilty of perjury...

(2) The expression 'judicial proceeding' includes a proceeding before any court, tribunal, or person having by law power to hear, receive, and examine evidence on oath.

(3) Where a statement made for the purposes of a judicial proceeding is not made before the tribunal itself, but is made on oath before a person authorised by law to administer an oath to the person who makes the statement, and to record or authenticate the statement, it shall, for the purposes of this section, be treated as having been made in a judicial proceeding.

KEYNOTE

To commit this offence a defendant must have been *lawfully sworn*; this will include a person who makes a solemn affirmation in place of an oath (Evidence Act 1851, s. 16). The statement made in a 'judicial proceeding' can be one given orally before the court or tribunal, or in the form of an affidavit (sworn statement). If a witness tenders a false statement used under s. 89 of the Criminal Justice Act 1967, he/she commits a separate, lesser offence (see para. 1.17.3).

'Wilful' means deliberate or intentional and it must be proved that any alleged perjury was not the result of a misunderstanding or an accidental slip of the tongue (*R v Millward* [1985] QB 519).

A 'statement material in that proceeding' means that the content of the evidence tendered in that case, although perhaps not crucial to the case, must have some importance to it and not just be of passing relevance. Whether something is material to a case is a question of law for a judge to decide. Whether a motorist had taken a drink between the time of having a road traffic accident and being breathalysed would be such a material issue, and to get a witness to provide false evidence about that matter would be a 'statement material in that proceeding' (*R v Lewins* (1979) 1 Cr App R (S) 246).

To prove perjury you must also show that the defendant *knew* the statement to be false or *did not believe it to be true*.

Evidence of an opinion provided by a witness who does not genuinely hold such an opinion may also be perjury.

Perjury may be proved by using a court transcript or the evidence of others who were present at the proceeding in question (Perjury Act 1911, s. 14).

Corroboration is required in cases of perjury (Perjury Act 1911, s. 13), solely in relation to the *falsity* of the defendant's statement. There is no requirement under s. 13 for corroboration of the fact that the defendant *actually made* the alleged statement, nor that he/she knew or believed it to be untrue. However, as that corroboration can be documentary and may even come from the defendant's earlier conduct (*R* v *Threlfall* (1914) 10 Cr App R 112) this requirement does not appear to present much of a hurdle to the prosecution.

Evidence given by live TV link under the provisions of the Criminal Justice Act 1988, s. 32 is also subject to the offence of perjury.

1.17.2.1 Aiding and Abetting

OFFENCE: **Aiding and Abetting Perjury—*Perjury Act 1911, s. 7***
- If principal offence is contrary to s.1 triable on indictment • Seven years' imprisonment • Otherwise either way • Two years' imprisonment on indictment
- Six months' imprisonment and/or a fine summarily

The Perjury Act 1911, s. 7 states:

(1) Every person who aids, abets, counsels, procures, or suborns another person to commit an offence against this Act shall be liable to be proceeded against, indicted, tried and punished as if he were a principal offender.

(2) Every person who incites...another person to commit an offence against this Act shall be guilty of a misdemeanour.

KEYNOTE

'Subornation' is the same as procuring.

1.17.3 Offences Similar to Perjury

OFFENCE: **False Statements in Criminal Proceedings—*Criminal Justice Act 1967, s. 89***
- Triable either way • Two years' imprisonment and/or a fine on indictment
- Six months' imprisonment and/or a fine summarily

The Criminal Justice Act 1967, s. 89 states:

(1) If any person in a written statement tendered in evidence in criminal proceedings by virtue of section 9 of this Act, or in proceedings before a court-martial...wilfully makes a statement material in those proceedings which he knows to be false or does not believe to be true, he shall be liable...

(2) The Perjury Act 1911 shall have effect as if this section were contained in that Act.

OFFENCE: **False Statements on Oath—*Perjury Act 1911, s. 2***
- Triable either way • Seven years' imprisonment and/or a fine on indictment
- Six months' imprisonment and/or a fine summarily

The Perjury Act 1911, s. 2 states:

If any person—
(1) being required or authorised by law to make any statement on oath for any purpose, and being lawfully sworn (otherwise than in a judicial proceeding) wilfully makes a statement which is material for that purpose and which he knows to be false or does not believe to be true;...
he shall be [guilty of an offence].

1.17.4 Perverting the Course of Justice

OFFENCE: **Perverting the Course of Justice—*Common Law***
- Triable on indictment • Life imprisonment and/or a fine

It is an offence at common law to do an act tending and intended to pervert the course of public justice.

1.17.5 Considerations Affecting Witnesses, Jurors and Others

There are several areas of law to consider in relation to offences involving witnesses. The main legislative provisions are set out below.

The Serious Organised Crime and Police Act 2005 sets out provisions relating to witness protection arrangements. These arrangements stretch beyond witnesses and extend to a series of people involved in the criminal justice process, including people who are *or have been*:

* constables
* employees accredited under the Police Reform Act 2002
* jurors
* magistrates (or their equivalent outside the United Kingdom)
* holders of judicial office (whether in the United Kingdom or elsewhere)
* the DPP, criminal prosecutors and staff of the Crown Prosecution Service

(see the Serious Organised Crime and Police Act 2005, sch. 5).

Chapter 4 of the Act allows for the making of arrangements to protect these and other relevant people ordinarily resident in the United Kingdom where the 'protection provider' (usually the Chief Officer of Police or the Director General of the National Crime Agency) considers that the person's safety is at risk by virtue of being a witness, constable, juror etc. (s. 82(1)). A protection provider may vary or cancel any arrangements made by him/her under subs. (1) if the provider considers it appropriate to do so. Joint arrangements (e.g. between police forces) can be made where appropriate, and public authorities (other than courts and tribunals or parliament) are under a duty to take reasonable steps to assist protection providers where requested to do so (ss. 83 and 85).

1.17.5.1 Witnesses or Jurors in Investigation or Proceedings for an Offence

OFFENCE: **Intimidating Witnesses and Jurors—***Criminal Justice and Public Order Act 1994, s. 51*
  * Triable either way • Five years' imprisonment and/or a fine on indictment
  * Six months' imprisonment and/or a fine summarily

The Criminal Justice and Public Order Act 1994, s. 51 states:

(1) A person commits an offence if—
  (a) he does an act which intimidates, and is intended to intimidate, another person ('the victim'),
  (b) he does the act knowing or believing that the victim is assisting in the investigation of an offence or is a witness or potential witness or a juror or potential juror in proceedings for an offence, and
  (c) he does it intending thereby to cause the investigation or the course of justice to be obstructed, perverted or interfered with.
(2) A person commits an offence if—
  (a) he does an act which harms, and is intended to harm, another person or, intending to cause another person to fear harm, he threatens to do an act which would harm that other person,
  (b) he does or threatens to do the act knowing or believing that the person harmed or threatened to be harmed ('the victim'), or some other person, has assisted in an investigation into an offence or has given evidence or particular evidence in proceedings for an offence, or has acted as a juror or concurred in a particular verdict in proceedings for an offence, and
  (c) he does or threatens to do it because of that knowledge or belief.
(3) For the purposes of subsections (1) and (2) it is immaterial that the act is or would be done, or that the threat is made—
  (a) otherwise than in the presence of the victim, or
  (b) to a person other than the victim.

(4) The harm that may be done or threatened may be financial as well as physical (whether to the person or a person's property) and similarly as respects an intimidatory act which consists of threats.

(5) The intention required by subsection (1)(c) and the motive required by subsection (2)(c) above need not be the only or the predominating intention or motive with which the act is done or, in the case of subsection (2), threatened.

KEYNOTE

These offences are designed to exist alongside the common-law offence of perverting the course of justice, and there will be circumstances which may fall under both the statutory and the common-law offences.

This is an offence of 'specific intent' as it must be shown that the act was done with the intentions set out in s. 51(1)(a) and (c). It must also be shown that the defendant knew or believed the other person to be assisting in the investigation of an offence or that the person was going to testify/appear on the jury in proceedings for an offence.

In a decision which appears to contradict the specific wording of the statute (s. 51(1)(a), 'he does an act which intimidates, and is intended to intimidate, another person') the Court of Appeal has confirmed that 'an act which intimidates' does not have to result in the victim *actually* being intimidated; so no intimidation 'result' from the defendant's actions is required even though the statute appears to require one. Therefore if a defendant seeks to deter a witness from giving evidence by means of intimidation, the offence could be made out even if the victim was not actually in fear.

In *R* v *Patrascu* [2004] EWCA Crim 2417, the court provided further detail with regard to interpretation of the term 'intimidation'. The court held that a person did an act which intimidated another within the meaning of s. 51(1) if he/she put that other person in fear, or sought by threat or violence to deter that person from some relevant action such as giving evidence. However, mere pressure which did not put the victim in fear or contained no element of threat or violence was insufficient. In other words, while not requiring an intimidation 'result', the defendant must do something more than just pressurising a victim to be guilty of the offence.

'Harm' for the purposes of s. 51(2) means physical harm and not simply an assault or battery. Therefore spitting at a person does not amount to 'harm' for these purposes (*R* v *Normanton* [1998] Crim LR 220).

Section 51(2) provides a similar offence for acts done or threatened in the knowledge or belief that the person, *or another person*, has so assisted or taken part in proceedings. Doing acts to third parties in order to intimidate or harm the relevant person is also covered by this offence (s. 51(3)). Making threats by telephone will amount to 'doing an act to another' (*DPP* v *Mills* [1997] QB 300).

Section 51(8) creates a statutory presumption under certain circumstances that the defendant had the required motive at the time of the actions or threats.

Making a *threat* via a third person knowing it will be passed on and that the ultimate recipient would be intimidated by it amounts to an offence under s. 51(1) (*Attorney-General's Reference (No. 1 of 1999)* [2000] QB 365).

The intention to obstruct, pervert or interfere with the course of justice need not be the only or even the main intention (s. 51(5)).

1.17.5.2   Intimidation of Witnesses in Other Proceedings

OFFENCE: **Intimidation of Witnesses—*Criminal Justice and Police Act 2001, s. 39***
- Triable either way • Five years' imprisonment on indictment
- Six months' imprisonment and/or a fine summarily

The Criminal Justice and Police Act 2001, s. 39 states:

(1) A person commits an offence if—
    (a) he does an act which intimidates, and is intended to intimidate, another person ('the victim');
    (b) he does the act—

(i) knowing or believing that the victim is or may be a witness in any relevant proceedings; and

(ii) intending, by his act, to cause the course of justice to be obstructed, perverted or interfered with;

and

(c) the act is done after the commencement of those proceedings.

KEYNOTE

References to doing an act include threats against people and/or their property and the making of any other statement (s. 39(6)). This offence is concerned with protecting people who are in some way connected with 'relevant proceedings' which are '*any proceedings in or before the Court of Appeal, the High Court, the Crown Court or any county or magistrates' court which are not proceedings for an offence*' (s. 41(1)). This means that the offence will be relevant if the proceedings involved are civil proceedings in the higher courts or the county court or if they are non-offence proceedings in the Crown Court or magistrates' court (e.g. a hearing to deal with a breach of a community order). You must show that the relevant proceedings had already commenced by the time of the offence.

Inquests or police conduct hearings are not be covered by the above offences.

The offence requires proof of intent in that, as well as showing the intimidatory act, it must also be shown that the elements set out at s. 39(1)(a)–(c) are present. However, if you can prove that the defendant:

- did any act that intimidated, and was intended to intimidate, another person, and
- that the defendant did that act knowing or believing that that other person was or might be a 'witness' in any relevant proceedings that had already commenced,

there will be a presumption that the defendant did the act with the intention of causing the course of justice to be obstructed, perverted or interfered with (s. 39(3)). This presumption is rebuttable. 'Witness' here extends to anyone who provides, or is able to provide, any information, document or other thing which might be used in evidence in those proceedings (see s. 39(5)).

In proving the offence it is immaterial whether the act:

- is done in the presence of the victim
- is done to the victim him/herself or to another person

or whether or not the intention to obstruct, pervert or interfere with the course of justice is the main intention of the person doing it (s. 39(2)).

This offence is intended to exist alongside the common law offence of perverting the course of justice.

1.17.6 Harming Witnesses

OFFENCE: **Harming Witnesses—*Criminal Justice and Police Act 2001, s. 40***

- Triable either way • Five years' imprisonment on indictment
- Six months' imprisonment and/or a fine summarily

The Criminal Justice and Police Act 2001, s. 40 states:

(1) A person commits an offence if in circumstances falling within subsection (2)—

(a) he does an act which harms, and is intended to harm, another person; or

(b) intending to cause another person to fear harm, he threatens to do an act which would harm that other person.

(2) The circumstances fall within this subsection if—

(a) the person doing or threatening to do the act does so knowing or believing that some person (whether or not the person harmed or threatened or the person against whom harm is threatened) has been a witness in relevant proceedings; and

(b) he does or threatens to do that act because of that knowledge or belief.

This offence refers to someone who *has been* (or is believed to have been) a witness in relevant proceedings. Again, 'witness' extends to anyone who has provided any information, document, etc. which was (or might have been) used in evidence in those proceedings (s. 40(7)). For 'relevant proceedings' see the s. 39 offence. This offence is aimed at the general protection of people who have been involved in relevant proceedings. Therefore there is no requirement here for any intention to pervert or interfere with the course of justice. The harm caused or threatened does not have to be directed towards the witness him/herself; the key element is the motivation of the defendant. In relation to that motivation, the Act creates a presumption that if you can prove that, between the start of the proceedings and one year after they are concluded, the defendant:

- did an act which harmed, and was intended to harm, another person, or
- threatened to do an act which would harm another person intending to cause that person to fear harm

with the knowledge or belief required by s. 40(2)(a), the defendant will be presumed to have acted because of that knowledge or belief (s. 40(3)). Again, this is rebuttable. It is immaterial whether the act or threat is made (or would be carried out) in the presence of the person who is or would be harmed, or of the person threatened or whether the motive mentioned in s. 40(2)(b) is the main motive. The harm done or threatened can be physical or financial and can be made to a person or property (s. 40(4)).

1.17.7   Assisting Offenders

OFFENCE: **Assisting Offenders—*Criminal Law Act 1967, s. 4***

- Triable on indictment; either way if original offence is either way • Where sentence for original offence is fixed by law, 10 years' imprisonment and/or a fine on indictment; six months' imprisonment and/or a fine summarily • Where sentence for original offence is 14 years' imprisonment, seven years' imprisonment and/or a fine on indictment; six months' imprisonment and/or a fine summarily • Where sentence for original offence is 10 years' imprisonment, five years' imprisonment and/or a fine on indictment; six months' imprisonment and/or a fine summarily • Otherwise three years' imprisonment and/or a fine on indictment; six months' imprisonment and/or a fine summarily

The Criminal Law Act 1967, s. 4 states:

(1)   Where a person has committed a relevant offence, any other person who, knowing or believing him to be guilty of the offence or of some other relevant offence, does without lawful authority or reasonable excuse any act with intent to impede his apprehension or prosecution shall be guilty of an offence.

(1A)   In this section and section 5 below, 'relevant offence' means—
(a)   an offence for which the sentence is fixed by law,
(b)   an offence for which a person of 18 years or over (not previously convicted) may be sentenced to imprisonment for a term of five years (or might be so sentenced but for the restrictions imposed by section 33 of the Magistrates' Courts Act 1980).

This offence must involve some positive act by the defendant; doing or saying nothing will not suffice.

Although there is no duty on people to assist the police in their investigations generally, this offence and the one below create a negative duty not to interfere with investigations after an offence has taken place.

For there to be an offence under ss. 4 or 5 there must first have been a relevant offence committed by someone. That relevant offence must, in the case of the above offence, have been committed by the 'assisted' person.

The defendant can commit the offence before the person assisted is convicted of committing the relevant offence.

It must be shown that the defendant knew or believed the person to be guilty of that, *or some other* relevant offence. Therefore, if the defendant believed that the 'assisted' person had committed a robbery when in fact he/she had committed a theft, that mistaken part of the defendant's belief will not prevent a conviction for this offence.

Mere *suspicion*, however strong, that the 'assisted' person had committed a relevant offence will not be enough.

This offence requires the consent of the DPP before a prosecution is brought (s. 4(4)).

This offence cannot be 'attempted' (Criminal Attempts Act 1981, s. 1(4)).

1.17.8 Concealing Relevant Offences

OFFENCE: **Concealing Relevant Offences—*Criminal Law Act 1967, s. 5***
- Triable on indictment; either way if original offence is triable either way
- Two years' imprisonment on indictment • Six months' imprisonment and/or a fine summarily

The Criminal Law Act 1967, s. 5 states:

(1) Where a person has committed a relevant offence, any other person who, knowing or believing that the offence or some other relevant offence has been committed, and that he has information which might be of material assistance in securing the prosecution or conviction of an offender for it, accepts or agrees to accept for not disclosing that information any consideration other than the making good of loss or injury caused by the offence, or the making of reasonable compensation for that loss or injury, shall be liable....

KEYNOTE

This offence requires the consent of the DPP before a prosecution can be brought (s. 5(3)) and cannot be attempted (Criminal Attempts Act 1981, s. 1(4)).

Again, someone must have committed a relevant offence before this particular offence can be committed. The main focus of this offence is:

- the acceptance of, or agreement to accept 'consideration' (i.e. anything of value)
- beyond reasonable compensation for loss/injury *caused by the relevant offence*
- in exchange for not disclosing material information.

'Disclosure' does not appear to be confined to information passed to the police. It would probably extend to other agencies with a duty to investigate offences but is perhaps even wider than that.

This offence requires proof, not only of the defendant's knowledge or belief that a relevant offence had been committed, but also that the defendant has information that might be of material assistance in securing the *prosecution or conviction* of *an offender* for it.

1.17.9 Miscellaneous Offences Relating to Offenders

OFFENCE: **Escaping—*Common Law***
- Triable on indictment • Unlimited punishment

It is an offence at common law to escape from legal custody.

The 'custody' from which a person escapes must be shown to have been lawful. The offence applies to police custody or police detention (see the Police and Criminal Evidence Act 1984, s. 118) or custody following conviction. D is not lawfully confined if he/she has been mistakenly kept in prison after his/her proper release date (*R* v *O'Connor* [2010] EWCA Crim 2842) but note that it is irrelevant if he/she is guilty of the crime for which he/she was imprisoned.

Whether a person was 'in custody' is a question of fact and the word 'custody' is to be given its ordinary and natural meaning (*E* v *DPP* [2002] EWHC 433 (Admin) and *Richards* v *DPP* [1988] QB 701). In proving that a person was in custody at a particular time it should be shown that his/her liberty was restricted in a way that meant that he/she was confined by another and that his/her freedom of movement was controlled; it is not necessary, however, to show that the person's actual ability to move around was physically impeded, e.g. in secure accommodation (*E* v *DPP*).

People may be in lawful custody even if not directly in the custody of a sworn police officer, for example those people who are being dealt with by an investigating officer or escort officers under sch. 4 to the Police Reform Act 2002.

People detained under the Mental Health Act 1983, s. 136, are also in lawful custody.

If a defendant uses force to *break out* of a prison or a police station, he/she commits an offence of prison breach, again at common law and attracting the same punishment and mode of trial as escaping.

Under the Prisoners (Return to Custody) Act 1995, s. 1, a person who has been temporarily released under the Prison Act 1952 commits a summary offence if he/she remains unlawfully at large or fails to respond to an order of recall to prison.

Escort officers designated under sch. 4 to the Police Reform Act 2002 have a duty to prevent the escape of people in their charge whom they are escorting in accordance with their statutory powers (Police Reform Act 2002, sch. 4, part 4, para. 35).

OFFENCE: **Assisting Escape—*Prison Act 1952, s. 39***

- Triable on indictment • 10 years' imprisonment

The Prison Act 1952, s. 39 states:

(1) Any person who
  (a) assists a prisoner in escaping or attempting to escape from a prison, or
  (b) intending to facilitate the escape of a prisoner—
    (i) brings, throws or otherwise conveys anything into prison,
    (ii) causes another person to bring, throw or otherwise convey anything into prison, or
    (iii) gives anything to a prisoner or leaves anything in any place (whether inside or outside a prison),
  is guilty of an offence.

Assisting escape can take many different forms. In *R* v *Williams* (1992) 13 Cr App R (S) 236, the offender committed the offence by changing places with a prisoner in an open prison for one night to allow the prisoner to spend the night at home. In *R* v *Walker* (1990–91) 12 Cr App R (S) 65 the offence was committed by an offender who aided a prisoner to escape by meeting him outside the prison and giving him a lift in his car.

OFFENCE: **Harbouring Offenders—*Criminal Justice Act 1961, s. 22(2)***

- Triable either way • 10 years' imprisonment and/or a fine on indictment
- Six months' imprisonment and/or a fine summarily

The Criminal Justice Act 1961, s. 22 states:

(2) If any person knowingly harbours a person who has escaped from a prison or other institution to which the said section thirty-nine applies, or who, having been sentenced in any part of the United Kingdom or in any of the Channel Islands or the Isle of Man to imprisonment or detention, is otherwise unlawfully at large, or gives to any such person any assistance with intent to prevent, hinder or interfere with his being taken into custody, he shall be liable…

KEYNOTE

The offences under s. 39 of the 1952 Act and s. 22 of the 1961 Act do not apply to a prisoner who escapes while in transit to or from prison (*R* v *Moss and Harte* (1986) 82 Cr App R 116).

1.17.10 Wasting Police Time

OFFENCE: **Wasting Police Time—*Criminal Law Act 1967, s. 5(2)***

• Triable summarily • Six months' imprisonment and/or a fine

The Criminal Law Act 1967, s. 5 states:

(2) Where a person causes any wasteful employment of the police by knowingly making to any person a false report tending to show that an offence has been committed, or to give rise to apprehension for the safety of any persons or property, or tending to show that he has information material to any police inquiry, he shall be liable…

KEYNOTE

It is widely thought that there is a minimum number of hours which must be wasted before a prosecution can be brought for this offence. There is no reliable authority on this point.

No proceedings for this offence may be instituted except by or with the consent of the DPP (s. 5(3)). Under the Penalties for Disorderly Behaviour (Amount of Penalty) Order 2002 (SI 2002/1837), the offence under s. 5(2) is a penalty offence and the amount payable is £90.

1.18 Offences Arising from Immigration, Asylum and People Exploitation

1.18.1 Introduction

Immigration, asylum and the criminal exploitation of people is a significant area of criminal activity in England and Wales. There are a number of serious criminal offences associated with this area of law.

1.18.2 Illegal Entry into the United Kingdom

The law regulating immigration extends far beyond the scope of this Manual. Immigration legislation was reinforced by additional measures contained in the Immigration and Asylum Act 1999 (addressing the issues arising from asylum seekers and also from those criminals who specialise in smuggling illegal entrants into the country). The Anti-terrorism, Crime and Security Act 2001 made several amendments in relation to immigration and asylum.

1.18.2.1 Nationality, Immigration and Asylum

While most of the relevant legislation is contained in the Immigration Act 1971, that Act has been amended in relation to offences and powers.

The whole framework for nationality and asylum was created by the Nationality, Immigration and Asylum Act 2002. The more important aspects of the Act can be found in part 7 which sets out several offences, the key aspects of which are set out in this chapter. The 2002 Act has been reinforced and extended by the Asylum and Immigration (Treatment of Claimants etc.) Act 2004.

In addition, the Home Office has published a Circular (HOC 70/2004) reminding police officers of the availability of deportation orders which are available on the recommendation of a court (s. 3(6) of the Immigration Act 1971). Before a court can make such a recommendation the person to be deported must have been served with a warning notice at least seven days before sentence is imposed. Responsibility for service of such notices will usually fall to the police, and the Home Office Immigration and Nationality Directorate advises that such a notice should normally be served where a person who appears to be eligible for deportation is charged with an offence punishable by imprisonment.

1.18.2.2 Illegal Entry

OFFENCE: **Illegal Entry—*Immigration Act 1971, s. 24***
- Triable summarily • Six months' imprisonment and/or a fine

The Immigration Act 1971, s. 24 states:

(1) A person who is not a British citizen shall be guilty of an offence . . . in any of the following cases—
  (a) if contrary to this Act he knowingly enters the United Kingdom in breach of a deportation order or without leave;
  (aa) . . .

(b) if, having only a limited leave to enter or remain in the United Kingdom, he knowingly either—
  (i) remains beyond the time limited by the leave; or
  (ii) fails to observe a condition of the leave;
(c) if, having lawfully entered the United Kingdom without leave by virtue of section 8(1) above, he remains without leave beyond the time allowed by section 8(1);
(d) if, without reasonable excuse, he fails to comply with any requirement imposed on him under Schedule 2 to this Act to report to a medical officer of health or to attend, or submit to a test or examination, as required by such an officer;
(e) if, without reasonable excuse, he fails to observe any restriction imposed on him under Schedule 2 or 3 to this Act as to residence, as to his employment or occupation or as to reporting to the police or to an immigration officer or to the Secretary of State;
(f) if he disembarks in the United Kingdom from a ship or aircraft after being placed on board under Schedule 2 or 3 to this Act with a view to his removal from the United Kingdom;
(g) if he leaves or seeks to leave the United Kingdom through the tunnel system in contravention of a restriction imposed by or under an Order in Council under section 3(7) of this Act.

KEYNOTE

Section 24 is concerned with *non-British citizens* who enter the United Kingdom illegally or who 'overstay' having been granted limited leave to be here; it also addresses occasions where such people disregard some other lawful requirements placed upon them. The offence requires actual entry and *will not* have been committed if entry has not occurred.

For the offence to be committed, a person must *knowingly* enter in breach of a deportation order or without leave. By contrast, a person is an illegal entrant (for removal purposes) simply if he/she unlawfully enters or seeks to enter in breach of a deportation order or of the immigration laws.

A person commits an offence under s. 24(1)(b)(i) on the day when he/she first knows that the time limited by his/her leave has expired and continues to commit it throughout any period during which he/she is in the United Kingdom thereafter, but that person shall not be prosecuted under the provision more than once in respect of the same limited leave.

The reference in s. 24(1)(c) to 'section 8(1)' refers to the special provisions made for seamen, aircrew, etc. landing lawfully in the United Kingdom.

Although the burden of proof is normally on the prosecution, an exception is made in relation to the offence under s. 24 if the case is brought within six months of the date of entry. In these cases the burden is on the accused to show on the balance of probabilities that he/she entered the United Kingdom legally (Immigration Act 1971, s. 24(4)(b)).

Section 28 of the Immigration Act 1971 provides that an extended time limit will apply to the prosecution of the offence under s. 24. An information relating to an offence under s. 24 may, in England and Wales, be tried by a magistrates' court if it is laid within six months of the commission of the offence *or* it is laid within three years of the commission of the offence and not more than two months after the date certified by a police officer *above* the rank of chief superintendent to be the date on which evidence sufficient to justify proceedings came to the notice of an officer of the police force to which he/she belongs. A person charged with such an offence may be tried where the offence was committed or at any place he/she may be.

1.18.2.3 Use of Deception to Enter or Remain

OFFENCE: **Use of Deception—*Immigration Act 1971, s. 24A***
  • Triable either way • Two years' imprisonment on indictment • Six months' imprisonment and/or a fine summarily

The Immigration Act 1971, s. 24A states:

A person who is not a British citizen is guilty of an offence if, by means which include deception by him—

(a) he obtains or seeks to obtain leave to enter or remain in the United Kingdom; or

(b) he secures or seeks to secure the avoidance, postponement or revocation of enforcement action against him.

KEYNOTE

This offence is aimed at the more calculated actions by *non-British citizens* to get (or try to get) leave to enter or stay in the United Kingdom, or to evade deportation.

'Deception' here has its ordinary meaning and is not specifically defined within the 1971 Act.

The offence can be committed by *seeking to enter* as well as *actually by entering*, and also embraces action taken to remain in the United Kingdom and to prevent and defer removal. It has been used against failed asylum seekers who have sought asylum again under a false identity (*R v Nagmadeen* [2003] EWCA Crim 2004). The deception must be material (but it does not have to be the sole means of obtaining entry etc.) and must be by the immigrant personally.

It is worth noting that the relevant criminal conduct by the defendant here can be *any means which include deception by him*. Therefore, although the entire course of conduct by the defendant need not amount to a deception, it will be necessary to show that the defendant him/herself carried out some act of deception (e.g. giving false details, providing misleading information, etc.). It will not be enough for this offence to show that someone else practised a deception in order to bring about the consequences at s. 24A(1)(a) and (b) for another person (but **see para. 1.18.3.1** for the further offence of assisting and harbouring).

'Enforcement action' means:

- the giving of removal directions;
- the making of a deportation order; or
- removal.

Section 31 of the Immigration and Asylum Act 1999 sets out defences, based on Article 31 of the Convention Relating to the Status of Refugees ('the Refugee Convention), to the offence under s. 24A. Section 31 of the Immigration and Asylum Act 1999 states that it is a defence to the above deception offence (s. 24A) for a refugee who has come to the United Kingdom directly from another country to show that he/she:

(a) presented him/herself to the UK authorities without delay,

(b) showed good cause for his/her illegal entry or presence in the United Kingdom, and

(c) made a claim for asylum as soon as was reasonably practicable after his/her arrival in the United Kingdom.

The statutory defence applies only to those persons ultimately recognised as refugees, *not* to the offence of illegal entry under s. 24 of the Immigration Act 1971.

1.18.3 People Trafficking and Exploitation

A very specific and prevalent form of offence involving unlawful immigration is that falling under the general heading of 'people trafficking'.

1.18.3.1 Assisting Unlawful Immigration and Asylum-seekers

OFFENCE: **Assisting Unlawful Immigration to Member State—*Immigration Act 1971, s. 25***

- Triable either way • 14 years' imprisonment on indictment • Six months' imprisonment and/or a fine summarily

The Immigration Act 1971, s. 25 states:

(1) A person commits an offence if he—
   (a) does an act which facilitates the commission of a breach of immigration law by an individual who is not a citizen of the European Union,
   (b) knows or has reasonable cause for believing that the act facilitates the commission of a breach of immigration law by the individual, and
   (c) knows or has reasonable cause for believing that the individual is not a citizen of the European Union.

KEYNOTE

The offence refers to an act which 'facilitates' a breach of 'immigration law'. Thus, the first element in the offence is complicit dishonesty on the part of the person whose entry or stay is facilitated (e.g. that the visa applicant knew that the documents with which he had been provided by the accused and on which he relied in making his visa application were false); proof of dishonesty on the part of the accused is not sufficient (*R* v *Kaile* [2009] EWCA Crim 2868).

'Immigration law' means a law in a Member State (which includes Norway and Iceland) and which controls, in respect of some or all people who are not nationals of the State, entitlement to enter, travel across or be in the State (s. 25(2)). This means that the offence covers acts of facilitating entry or stay in *other Member States*. In *R* v *Kapoor* [2012] EWCA Crim 435, the Court of Appeal held that for the purposes of s. 25(2) an immigration law is a law which determines whether a person is lawfully or unlawfully either entering the United Kingdom, or in transit or being in the United Kingdom. Thus if a person, with the necessary knowledge or reasonable cause to believe, facilitates the unlawful entry or unlawful presence in the United Kingdom of a person who is not a citizen of the European Union, he commits the offence.

The Secretary of State may make an order prescribing additional States which are to be regarded as 'Member States' for the purposes of the section if they consider it necessary for the purpose of complying with the United Kingdom's EU obligations (s. 25(7)).

A document issued by the relevant government of a Member State will be conclusive in certifying any matter of law in this regard (s. 25(3)).

The offence includes acts assisting non-EU citizens who entered the United Kingdom lawfully to remain unlawfully. In *R* v *Javaherifard* [2005] EWCA Crim 3231, it was held that it is possible to facilitate entry by acts close to but following actual entry (e.g. by making arrangements to get illegal entrants away quickly from the port of disembarkation).

This offence can be committed outside the United Kingdom by British citizens and others with relevant forms of British citizenship (s. 25(4)).

The accused cannot rely on the protection of Article 31 of the Refugee Convention (see para. 1.18.2.3) in relation to facilitating the entry into the United Kingdom of another (*Sternaj* v *DPP* [2011] EWHC 1094 (Admin)).

It is worth noting the Court of Appeal's observations that drivers and others involved in these types of offences are often of previous good character; in fact that is one of the criteria by which they are selected by the main organisers so as not to arouse suspicion of the authorities (*R* v *Akrout* (2003) EWCA Crim 491).

OFFENCE: **Helping Asylum-seeker to Enter United Kingdom—*Immigration Act 1971, s. 25A***

     • Triable either way • 14 years' imprisonment on indictment • Six months' imprisonment and/or a fine summarily

The Immigration Act 1971, s. 25A states:

(1) A person commits an offence if—
   (a) he knowingly and for gain facilitates the arrival in, or the entry into, the United Kingdom of an individual, and
   (b) he knows or has reasonable cause to believe that the individual is an asylum-seeker.

The whole essence of this offence is profiteering thus financial gain is an essential element of the offence.

'Asylum seeker' means a person who *intends* to claim that to remove them from, or require them to leave the United Kingdom would be contrary to the United Kingdom's obligations under the Refugee Convention or the Human Rights Convention (in each case as defined under s. 167(1) of the Immigration and Asylum Act 1999) (s. 25A(2)). This presumably means that a person could be guilty of this offence even though the immigrant did not make a claim under the Refugee Convention or the European Convention on Human Rights, provided it can be established that the immigrant intended to make such a claim.

Section 25A applies in the case of an asylum seeker who arrives in or enters the United Kingdom without any breach of immigration law being committed by the person gaining entry (*Sternaj* v *DPP* [2011] EWHC 1094 (Admin)).

The right to claim asylum is protected by the Universal Declaration of Human Rights so the act of assisting asylum seekers to arrive in the United Kingdom and claim asylum cannot therefore be unlawful *per se*, hence the above offence does not apply to anything done by a person acting on behalf of an organisation which aims to assist asylum seekers and *does not charge for its services* (s. 25A(3)).

A conspiracy to 'assist persons claiming asylum in the United Kingdom ' is not an offence known to law (*R* v *Hadi* [2001] EWCA Crim 2534).

OFFENCE: **Assisting Entry to United Kingdom in Breach of Deportation Order—**
Immigration Act 1971, s. 25B
- Triable either way • 14 years' imprisonment on indictment • Six months' imprisonment and/or a fine summarily

The Immigration Act 1971, s. 25B states:

(1) A person commits an offence if he—
  (a) does an act which facilitates a breach of a deportation order in force against an individual who is a citizen of the European Union, and
  (b) knows or has reasonable cause for believing that the act facilitates a breach of the deportation order.
(2) ...
(3) A person commits an offence if he—
  (a) does an act which assists the individual to arrive in, enter or remain in the United Kingdom,
  (b) knows or has reasonable cause for believing that the act assists the individual to arrive in, enter or remain in the United Kingdom, and
  (c) knows or has reasonable cause for believing that the Secretary of State has personally directed that the individual's exclusion from the United Kingdom is conducive to the public good.

This offence applies *only* where the person being assisted is a citizen of the European Union.

For the first offence, there must be a deportation order in force and this will need to be proved before someone can be convicted. Additionally, the defendant must have known or had reasonable cause for believing that his/her act facilitated a breach of that order (therefore the defendant must have known/had reasonable cause to believe that there was such an order in existence). This offence also applies where the Secretary of State personally directs that the exclusion from the United Kingdom of an individual who is a citizen of the European Union is conducive to the public good (an exclusion order) (s. 25B(2)).

The second offence applies to acts that assist the person to arrive in, enter or remain in the United Kingdom. Again, however, the relevant knowledge or cause for belief are crucial.

It is a defence that the accused did not know or have reason to believe that the person being assisted was the subject of a deportation or exclusion order.

The courts' powers to order forfeiture of vehicles, ships and aircraft under s. 25C apply to this offence (see para. 1.18.3.2).

1.18.3.2 Powers of Seizure and Forfeiture

Where a person has been arrested for an offence under ss. 25, 25A or 25B, police officers may detain any vehicle or certain smaller ships and aircraft where they have reasonable grounds for believing that:

- the vehicle, ship or aircraft has been used or was intended to be used in carrying out the arrangements in respect of the offence, and
- the person arrested is the owner, driver or, in the case of a ship or aircraft, the captain (see generally s. 25D).

Extensive powers for entry and search under warrant are made for immigration officers and the police under ss. 28A and 28B.

Following the conviction of a defendant for a relevant offence, a court may order the forfeiture of any vehicle used or intended to be used in connection with the offence if the person owned or was driving the vehicle at the time the offence was committed, or was a director, manager or secretary of a company that owned the vehicle at the time (s. 25C). This power will extend to ships and aircraft but there are minimum requirements in relation to the size of the vessel or aircraft and to the number of illegal entrants carried on board.

1.18.3.3 Trafficking People for Exploitation

OFFENCE: **Trafficking People for Exploitation—*Asylum and Immigration (Treatment of Claimants etc.) Act 2004, s. 4***
- Triable either way • On indictment 14 years' imprisonment and/or a fine
- 12 months, and/or a fine summarily (unless committed before the commencement of s. 154 of the Criminal Justice Act 2003, in which case the reference to 12 months is six months)

The Asylum and Immigration (Treatment of Claimants etc.) Act 2004, s. 4 states:

(1A) A person ('A') commits an offence if A intentionally arranges or facilitates—
    (a) the arrival in, or entry into, the United Kingdom or another country of another person ('B'),
    (b) the travel of B within the United Kingdom or another country, or
    (c) the departure of B from the United Kingdom or another country,
    with a view to the exploitation of B.
(1B) For the purposes of subsection (1A)(a) and (c) A's arranging or facilitating is with a view to the exploitation of B if (and only if)—
    (a) A intends to exploit B, after B's arrival, entry or (as the case may be) departure but in any part of the world, or
    (b) A believes that another person is likely to exploit B, after B's arrival, entry or (as the case may be) departure but in any part of the world.
(1C) For the purposes of subsection (1A)(b) A's arranging or facilitating is with a view to the exploitation of B if (and only if)—
    (a) A intends to exploit B, during or after the journey and in any part of the world, or
    (b) A believes that another person is likely to exploit B, during or after the journey and in any part of the world.

KEYNOTE

The above offence covers arranging or facilitating the arrival in, departure from or travel within the United Kingdom of a whole series of different vulnerable categories of person, in each case with the relevant intention or belief with regard to that person's exploitation. For the purposes of this section a person is exploited if:

- he/she is the victim of behaviour that contravenes Article 4 of the European Convention on Human Rights (slavery and forced labour);
- he/she is encouraged, required or expected to do anything as a result of which he/she (or another person) would commit an offence relating to the transplant of human organs;

- he/she is subjected to force, threats or deception designed to induce him/her to provide services, to provide another person with benefits or to enable another person to acquire benefits of any kind;
- he/she is requested or induced to undertake *any activity*, having been chosen on the grounds that he/she is mentally or physically ill or disabled, young or has a family relationship with a person and a person without the illness, disability, youth or family relationship would be likely to refuse the request or resist the inducement (s. 4(4)).

Where the offence is committed within the context of employment there are further considerations and offences and the advice of the Home Office Immigration and Nationality Directorate should be sought.

Sections 25C and 25D of the Immigration Act 1971 (forfeiture or detention of vehicle etc.) apply in relation to an offence under s. 4.

1.18.3.4 The Gangmasters (Licensing) Act 2004

The Gangmasters (Licensing) Act 2004 establishes a regulatory body (the Gangmasters Licensing Authority—GLA) whose remit includes the issuing and inspection of licences and the provision of information held by it to specified persons in accordance with the Act.

In summary, the definition of a gangmaster is a person who supplies a worker to do work to which the Act applies for another person (s. 4). The 'work' to which the Act applies is essentially agricultural work and gathering shellfish and includes processing or packaging any produce derived from agricultural work, shellfish, fish or products derived from shellfish or fish (s. 3). It does not matter whether the worker supplied in this way is supplied directly or indirectly or whether the work done is for the purposes of a business carried on by the recipient of the worker or in connection with services provided by him/her to another person. Similarly, it does not matter whether the gangmaster supplies the worker him/herself or procures that the worker is supplied, whether the worker works under a contract or whether the work is done under the control of the gangmaster, recipient or an intermediary (see generally s. 4(3)). A person will still be a 'worker' for the purposes of the Act even if he/she has no right to be, or to work, in the United Kingdom (s. 26).

The Gangmasters (Licensing) Act 2004, s. 12 states:

OFFENCE: **Acting as a Gangmaster without Licence etc.—*Gangmasters (Licensing) Act 2004, s. 12***
- Triable either way • 10 years' imprisonment and/or a fine on indictment
- 12 months' imprisonment and/or a fine summarily; if committed before the commencement of s. 154(1) of the Criminal Justice Act 2003, six months

(1) A person commits an offence if he acts as a gangmaster in contravention of section 6 (prohibition of unlicensed activities)...
(2) A person commits an offence if he has in his possession or under his control—
   (a) a relevant document that is false and that he knows or believes to be false,
   (b) a relevant document that was improperly obtained and that he knows or believes to have been improperly obtained, or
   (c) a relevant document that relates to someone else,
   with the intention of inducing another person to believe that he or another person acting as a gangmaster in contravention of section 6 is acting under the authority of a licence.

KEYNOTE

Section 6 of the Act provides for the issuing of licences as monitored by the GLA. A person acting as a gangmaster does not contravene s. 6 by reason only of the fact that he/she breaches a condition of the licence (s. 12(1)).

A relevant document is a licence or any document issued by the GLA in connection with a licence (s. 12(6)). The concept of 'false' documents is the same as that used in the wider legislation relating to forgery (see para. 1.15.11.2).

It is a further summary offence to enter into an arrangement with a gangmaster where, in supplying the workers or services, the gangmaster contravenes s. 6 (s. 13(1)).

The Act makes provision for the appointment of enforcement officers and extends certain powers of arrest and enforcement to those officers; it also allows for the appointment of compliance officers (s. 15). Intentional obstruction of these officers in the exercise of their functions is a summary offence, as is failure without reasonable cause to comply with their proper instructions (s. 18).

1.18.4 Registration Cards

OFFENCE: **Misuse etc. of Registration Card—*Immigration Act 1971, s. 26A***
- Triable either way • 10 years' imprisonment on indictment • Six months' imprisonment and/or a fine summarily

The Immigration Act 1971, s. 26A states:

(3) A person commits an offence if he—
- (a) makes a false registration card,
- (b) alters a registration card with intent to deceive or to enable another to deceive,
- (c) …
- (d) uses or attempts to use a false registration card for a purpose for which a registration card is issued,
- (e) uses or attempts to use an altered registration card with intent to deceive,
- (f) makes an article designed to be used in making a false registration card,
- (g) makes an article designed to be used in altering a registration card with intent to deceive or to enable another to deceive…
- (h) …

KEYNOTE

A registration card here is a document which:

- carries information about a person (whether or not wholly or partly electronically), and
- is issued by the Secretary of State to the person wholly or partly in connection with a claim for asylum (whether or not made by that person) (s. 26A(1)).

These offences require different degrees of intent and the wording of each needs to be considered carefully. 'False registration card' means a document which is designed to appear to be a registration card (s. 26A(4)).

OFFENCE: **Possession of Registration Card or Immigration Stamp—*Immigration Act 1971, s. 26A(3)(c) and (h) and s. 26B***
- Triable either way • Two years' imprisonment on indictment • Six months' imprisonment and/or a fine summarily

The Immigration Act 1971, s. 26A states:

(3) A person commits an offence if he—
…
- (c) has a false or altered registration card in his possession without reasonable excuse,
…
- (h) has an article within paragraph (f) or (g) in his possession without reasonable excuse.

The Immigration Act 1971, s. 26B states:

(1) A person commits an offence if he has an immigration stamp in his possession without reasonable excuse.

(2) A person commits an offence if he has a replica immigration stamp in his possession without reasonable excuse.

KEYNOTE

As with the other offences, 'false registration card' here means a document which is designed to appear to be a registration card (s. 26A(4)).

'Immigration stamp' means a device which is designed for the purpose of stamping documents in the exercise of an immigration function; 'replica immigration stamp' means a device which is designed for the purpose of stamping a document so that it appears to have been stamped in the exercise of an immigration function; and 'immigration function' means a function of an immigration officer or the Secretary of State under the Immigration Acts (s. 26B(3)).

Immigration officers may arrest without warrant a person who has committed, or who they have reasonable grounds for suspecting has committed an offence under ss. 26A or 26B (s. 28A(9A)).

1.18.5 Passport Offences

OFFENCE: **Making Untrue Statement to Procure Passport—*Criminal Justice Act 1925, s. 36***

• Triable either way • Two years' imprisonment on indictment • Six months' imprisonment and/or a fine summarily

The Criminal Justice Act 1925, s. 36 states:

(1) The making by any person of a statement which is to his knowledge untrue for the purpose of procuring a passport, whether for himself or any other person, shall be [an offence].

OFFENCE: **Entering United Kingdom without Passport etc.—*Asylum and Immigration (Treatment of Claimants etc.) Act 2004, s. 2***

• Triable either way • Two years' imprisonment on indictment • 12 months' imprisonment and/or a fine summarily if after the commencement of s. 154 of the Criminal Justice Act 2003, otherwise six months

The Asylum and Immigration (Treatment of Claimants etc.) Act 2004, s. 2 states:

(1) A person commits an offence if at a leave or asylum interview he does not have with him an immigration document which—
    (a) is in force, and
    (b) satisfactorily establishes his identity and nationality or citizenship.
(2) A person commits an offence if at a leave or asylum interview he does not have with him, in respect of any dependent child with whom he claims to be travelling or living, an immigration document which—
    (a) is in force, and
    (b) satisfactorily establishes the child's identity and nationality or citizenship.

KEYNOTE

'Immigration document' means a passport or a document which relates to a national of a State other than the United Kingdom and which is designed to serve the same purpose as a passport (s. 2(12)).

Section 2 creates two offences. Section 2(8) provides that a person shall be presumed for the purposes of this section not to have a document with him/her if he/she fails to produce it to an immigration officer or official of the Secretary of State on request. Therefore the first offence is effectively committed where a person is unable to produce a current passport or similar document at a 'leave' or 'asylum' interview. The second offence applies where the person at such an interview is unable to produce a current passport or similar document in respect of a dependent child with whom he/she claims to be living or travelling.

The person does not commit the offences if the interview takes place *after* the person has entered the United Kingdom and within the period of three days (beginning with the date of that interview) the person provides a passport or similar immigration document to an immigration officer or to the Secretary of State (s. 2(3)).

A document which purports to be, or is designed to look like, a passport or relevant immigration document, is a false immigration document. In addition, if a passport (or document) is used outside the period for which it is expressed to be valid, if it is used by or in respect of a person other than the person to or for whom it was issued or it is used contrary to any formal provisions for its use, it will be regarded as a false immigration document (s. 2(13)). There are several specific defences to these offences. In addition to the more obvious ones (e.g. having a reasonable excuse for not being in possession of a passport being a European Economic Area national exercising a right in respect of entry/residence in the United Kingdom) it is also a defence to some of the above offences for a person to produce a *false passport or immigration document* and to prove that he/she used it as an immigration document for all purposes in connection with his/her journey to the United Kingdom (s. 2(4)). This is both important and unusual in that the defence to the offence above is itself an offence (see para. 1.15.11.5).

The section makes other detailed provisos as to when this specific defence will apply and what will amount to a 'reasonable excuse' in relation to the more general defence.

1.18.6 Forced Marriage

Forced marriage has been described as 'little more than slavery' and an 'indefensible abuse of human rights'. A forced marriage is where one or both people do not (or in cases of people with learning disabilities, cannot) consent to the marriage and pressure or abuse is used. It is recognised in the United Kingdom as a form of violence against women and men, domestic/child abuse and a serious abuse of human rights. The pressure put on people to marry against their will can be physical (including threats, actual physical violence and sexual violence) or emotional and psychological (for example when someone is made to feel they are bringing shame on their family). Financial abuse (taking someone's wages or not giving them any money) can also be a factor.

1.18.6.1 Offence of Forced Marriage

OFFENCE: **Offence of Forced Marriage: England and Wales—*Anti-social Behaviour, Crime and Policing Act 2014, s. 121***
- Triable either way • Seven years' imprisonment on indictment • 12 months' imprisonment and/or a fine summarily

The Anti-social Behaviour, Crime and Policing Act 2014, s. 121 states:

(1) A person commits an offence under the law of England and Wales if he or she—
  (a) uses violence, threats or any other form of coercion for the purpose of causing another person to enter into a marriage, and
  (b) believes, or ought reasonably to believe, that the conduct may cause the other person to enter into the marriage without free and full consent.
(2) In relation to a victim who lacks capacity to consent to marriage, the offence under subsection (1) is capable of being committed by any conduct carried out for the purpose of causing the victim to enter into a marriage (whether or not the conduct amounts to violence, threats or any other form of coercion).
(3) A person commits an offence under the law of England and Wales if he or she—

(a) practises any form of deception with the intention of causing another person to leave the United Kingdom, and

(b) intends the other person to be subjected to conduct outside the United Kingdom that is an offence under subsection (1) or would be an offence under that subsection if the victim were in England or Wales.

KEYNOTE

The offence of forced marriage catches a person who intentionally forces a person to enter into marriage, believing the person does not consent (s.1), or a person who deceives someone into going abroad for the specific purpose of forcing them to marry (s. 3).

An offence is committed whether or not the forced marriage goes ahead meaning that the offence is a conduct crime rather than a result crime.

The term 'marriage' is to be widely interpreted. A 'marriage' means any religious or civil ceremony of marriage recognised by the customs of the parties to it, or the laws of any country in which it is carried out, as constituting a binding agreement, whether or not it would be legally binding according to the law of England and Wales (s. 121(4)).

It is irrelevant whether the conduct mentioned in s. 121(1)(a) is directed at the victim of the offence under that subsection or another person. So, for example, the offence could be committed by a father threatening his daughter that if she does not marry a certain person, he will injure one of her friends (s. 121(6)).

The meaning of 'lacks the capacity to consent' is connected to the Mental Capacity Act 2005. Simply put, the 'capacity test' (under the Mental Capacity Act 2005) is the question 'Does this person have the capacity to make this decision at this time?' If the decision is that the person lacks capacity, the offence under s. 1 would be committed by any conduct carried out for the purpose of causing the victim to marry, whether or not it amounts to violence, threats or any other form of coercion (s. 121(2)).

The word 'deception' in s. 121(3) is not defined. What s. 121(3) does is to capture as a criminal offence any form of deception practised with the intention both of causing another person to leave the United Kingdom to travel to another country and that the other person be subjected to conduct that is an offence under subs. (1) or would be an offence if the victim were in England and Wales.

It is important to note that s. 121(7) and (8) make provision to take extra-territorial jurisdiction over both the coercion and deception elements.

(7) A person commits an offence under subsection (1) or (3) only if, at the time of the conduct or deception—
    (a) the person or the victim or both of them are in England or Wales,
    (b) neither the person nor the victim is in England or Wales but at least one of them is habitually resident in England and Wales, or
    (c) neither the person nor the victim is in the United Kingdom but at least one of them is a UK national.

(8) 'UK national' means an individual who is—
    (a) a British citizen, a British overseas territories citizen, a British National (Overseas) or a British Overseas citizen;
    (b) a person who under the British Nationality Act 1981 is a British subject; or
    (c) a British protected person within the meaning of that Act.

Any of the prohibited acts in s.121(1) and (2) carried out outside the United Kingdom by a UK national or person habitually resident in England or Wales, or against a UK national or person habitually resident in England or Wales, will be an offence under domestic law and triable in the courts of England and Wales. It will also be an offence under domestic law if the prohibited acts in s. 121(1) or (2) are conducted by or against a person habitually resident in England and Wales, but take place in Scotland or Northern Ireland.

Section 122 of the Act creates an offence of forced marriage in Scotland. The provisions of this section broadly mirror those in s. 121.

1.18.6.2 Breaching a Forced Marriage Protection Order

Part 4A of the Family Law Act 1996 (amended by s. 120 of the Anti-social, Crime and Policing Act 2014) empowers a court to make an order for the purpose of protecting:

- a person from being forced into a marriage or from any attempt to be forced into a marriage; or
- a person who has been forced into a marriage.

A forced marriage protection order may contain such prohibitions, restrictions or requirements and any other such terms as the court considers appropriate for the purposes of the order. A breach of such an order would otherwise be punishable only as a contempt of court. Speedy enforcement depends on whether the court attaches a power of arrest to the order. If no power of arrest is attached, the victim has to go to the civil court to get an arrest warrant.

Index

U

Undercover officers *see* **Covert human intelligence sources**
Unlawful act manslaughter 1.5.4.1
Use of force
  battery 1.9.3
  burglary 1.14.3.5
  police officers 1.4.9
  robbery 1.14.10
  self defence 1.4.8.1
  towards prostitutes 1.11.12.3

V

Vicarious liability 1.2.9
Victims
  aggravated offences 1.8.3.4
  anonymity of sexual victims 1.11.1.2
Voluntary acts
  criminal conduct
    general requirement 1.2.2
    intoxication 1.4.3
  manslaughter
    diminished responsibility 1.5.3.1
    loss of control 1.5.3.2
    overview 1.5.3
    suicide pacts 1.5.3.3
Voyeurism
  indecent exposure 1.11.9.1
  statutory offence 1.11.9.2

W

Wasting police time 1.17.10
Wilfully
  see also specific offences
  general meaning 1.1.6
Witnesses
  perverting the course of justice
    general considerations 1.17.5
    harming witnesses 1.17.6
    intimidation in criminal
      proceedings 1.17.5.1
    intimidation in other
      proceedings 1.17.5.2
Wounding or grievous bodily harm
  1.9.7.3
Wounding with intent 1.9.7.4
Wrongful credits 1.14.15

Y

Year and a day rule 1.5.2.2